U.S. STAMP YEARBOOK 1988

A comprehensive record of technical data, design development and stories behind all of the stamps, stamped envelopes, postal cards, souvenir cards and maximum cards issued by the United States Postal Service and the Bureau of Engraving and Printing in 1988.

By
George Amick

Published by *Linn's Stamp News,* the world's largest and most informative weekly stamp newspaper, Post Office Box 29, Sidney, Ohio 45365. *Linn's* is a division of Amos Press, Inc., which also publishes the *Scott* catalogs and publications; *Coin World,* a weekly newspaper for the numismatic field; and *Cars & Parts,* a monthly magazine for auto enthusiasts.
Copyright 1989 by Amos Press Inc.

ISSN 0748-996X

ISBN 0-940403-11-0

With Gratitude ...

The assembling of facts and pictures in this Yearbook would have been impossible without the generous assistance of many people. What the folks listed here have in common is a deep interest in stamps and a relish for talking about them — and for answering questions, even the most trivial — at any time. My colleagues at *Linn's* and I extend to them our thanks.

United States Postal Service, Washington, D.C.
    Joe Brockert, program manager, Philatelic Design
    Pete Davidson, director, Office of Stamps and Philatelic Marketing
    Linda Foster, accountable paper control assistant
    Don McDowell, general manager, Stamps Division
    Hugh McGonigle, Stamp Information Branch
    Jeanne O'Neill, Public and Employee Communications Department
    Peter Papadopoulos, Stamp Information Branch
    Kim Parks, Stamp Information Branch
    Dickey Rustin, manager, Stamp Information Branch
    Frank Thomas, Stamp Information Branch
    Mike West, Stamp Information Branch
    Jack Williams, program manager, Philatelic Design

Bureau of Engraving and Printing
    Carl D'Alessandro, assistant director, operations
    Leonard Buckley, foreman, Design and Engraving Section
    Peter Daly, director
    Edward Felver, manager, Product Design and Engraving Division
    Ralph Payne, special assistant to assistant director, operations

Also, special thanks go to CSAC members and design coordinators John Foxworth, Derry Noyes, Mary Ann Owens, Howard Paine, Jack Rosenthal and Richard Sheaff; stamp designers John Dawson (and his wife Kathleen), Lou Nolan, Chuck Ripper, Richard Schlecht and Bob Timberlake; Norma Opgrand, duck stamp coordinator for the U.S. Fish and Wildlife Service; Mark Drucker, curator of the Federal Hall National Memorial; Charles D. Cretors, president of C. Cretors & Company; officials of the Francis Ouimet Caddie Scholarship Fund; Jaime Cripe of the Photo Department of University of Notre Dame; George Godin of the Bureau Issues Association; and the indefatigable Charles Yeager, *Linn's* Washington Correspondent.

George Amick

CONTENTS

Introduction _____ 6

Commemoratives _____ 7
22¢ Georgia Statehood, January 6 _____ 9
22¢ Connecticut Statehood, January 9 _____ 15
22¢ Winter Olympics, January 10 _____ 21
22¢ Australian Bicentennial, January 26 _____ 26
22¢ James Weldon Johnson, February 2 _____ 33
22¢ Cats (4), February 5 _____ 38
22¢ Massachusetts Statehood, February 6 _____ 45
22¢ Maryland Statehood, February 15 _____ 50
22¢ Knute Rockne, March 9 _____ 55
25¢ South Carolina Statehood, May 23 _____ 63
25¢ Francis Ouimet, June 13 _____ 67
25¢ New Hampshire Statehood, June 21 _____ 72
25¢ Virginia Statehood, June 25 _____ 77
25¢ New York Statehood, July 26 _____ 83
25¢ Summer Olympics, August 19 _____ 91
25¢ Classic Cars booklet (5), August 25 _____ 95
25¢ Antarctic Explorers (4), September 14 _____ 105
25¢ Carousel (4), October 1 _____ 113

Special Stamps _____ 119
25¢ Love, July 4 _____ 120
45¢ Love, August 8 _____ 124
25¢ Christmas Greeting, October 20 _____ 127
25¢ Christmas Madonna and Child, October 20 _____ 133
25¢ Special Occasions booklet (4), October 22 _____ 138

Definitives _____ 144
3¢ Conestoga Wagon, February 29 _____ 147
E (25¢) sheet stamp, March 22 _____ 152
E (25¢) coil, March 22 _____ 156
E (25¢) booklet, March 22 _____ 158
25¢ Pheasant booklet, April 29 _____ 160
25¢ Jack London booklet ($1.50 and $3), May 3 _____ 166
25¢ Jack London booklet ($5), May 3 _____ 168
25¢ Flag With Clouds sheet stamp, May 6 _____ 174
25¢ Flag With Clouds booklet, July 5 _____ 177
25¢ Flag Over Yosemite, May 20 _____ 179
25¢ Owl and Grosbeak booklet, May 28 _____ 183
15¢ Buffalo Bill Cody, June 6 _____ 188
45¢ Harvey Cushing, June 17 _____ 194
10.1¢ Oil Wagon (new precancel), June 27 _____ 198

16.7¢ Popcorn Wagon, July 7 — 202
15¢ Tugboat, July 12 — 206
13.2¢ Railroad Coal Car, July 19 — 209
8.4¢ Wheelchair, August 12 — 212
21¢ Railroad Mail Car, August 16 — 216
7.6¢ Carreta, August 30 — 221
25¢ Honeybee, September 2 — 224
5.3¢ Elevator, September 16 — 233
20.5¢ Fire Engine, September 28 — 238
21¢ Chester Carlson, October 21 — 242
24.1¢ Tandem, October 26 — 247
20¢ Cable Car, October 28 — 250
13¢ Patrol Wagon, October 29 — 254
23¢ Mary Cassatt, November 4 — 257
65¢ General Henry "Hap" Arnold, November 5 — 261

Revised Definitives — 265
30¢ Frank Laubach (perf variety), June — 269
20¢ Harry Truman (perf variety), August — 270

Airmail Stamps — 271
44¢ New Sweden, March 29 — 272
45¢ Samuel P. Langley, May 14 — 278
36¢ Igor Sikorsky, June 23 — 282

Express Mail — 287
$8.75 Express Mail, October 4 — 287

Officials — 292
E Official Mail, March 22 — 293
20¢ Official Mail, May 19 — 296
15¢ Official Mail, June 11 — 298
25¢ Official Mail, June 11 — 300

Migratory Bird Hunting — 302
$10 Snow Goose duck stamp, July 1 — 302
Migratory Waterfowl souvenir card, October — 306

Stamped Envelopes — 308
E Official Mail Savings Bond, March 22 — 309
25¢ Stars, March 26 — 312
25¢ Official Mail, April 11 — 316
25¢ Official Mail Savings Bond, April 11 — 318
8.4¢ Constellation Nonprofit, April 12 — 320
25¢ Stars Double Window, August 18 — 323
25¢ Snowflake, September 8 — 325
25¢ Official Mail Savings Bond, November 28 — 329

39¢ Graphic Design Aerogramme, May 9 — 331

Postal Cards — 333
15¢ America the Beautiful, March 28 — 334
15¢ Blair House, May 4 — 339
36¢ DC-3 airmail, May 14 — 343
15¢ Official Mail, June 10 — 347
28¢ Yorkshire, June 29 — 349
15¢ Iowa Territory, July 2 — 353
15¢ America the Beautiful double reply, July 11 — 356
15¢ Ohio/Northwest Territory, July 15 — 358
15¢ Hearst Castle, September 20 — 362
15¢ Federalist Papers, October 27 — 366

Souvenir Cards — 369
FINLANDIA 88, June 1 — 370
STAMPSHOW 88, August 25 — 372
MIDAPHIL 88, November 18 — 374
SYDPEX 88, July 30 — 376

Appendix — 378
New U.S. postage rates — 378
Plate numbers — 380
Items withdrawn from sale — 383

INTRODUCTION

In 1988, the flood of new issues from the United States Postal Service continued unabated.

Ninety-nine collectible varieties of stamps and stationery flowed from the presses of the Postal Service's suppliers — the Bureau of Engraving and Printing, the American Bank Note Company, the Government Printing Office and Westvaco-USEnvelope Division.

Throw in an additional variety of a booklet (Jack London), and the count reaches 100.

The total falls a few numbers short of the 110 items USPS had issued the year before. But that 1987 figure was achieved with the substantial help of the American Wildlife commemoratives, which consisted of 50 varieties on a single pane.

There was no such blockbuster in 1988. The 1988 list included only a few multiple issues. There were three booklets that contained five, four and two stamp varieties, respectively, and there were also three se-tenant commemorative blocks of four.

The remaining items came out the old-fashioned way — in singles.

One measure of the pace of 1988's activity could be found in the fact that USPS' busy Stamp Information Branch put together 57 first-day ceremonies, an average of more than one a week. That's 19 more than it staged the year before.

The main reason for the heavy 1988 program can be summed up in two words: rate change.

The top-to-bottom overhaul of postal rates that took effect April 3 created a need (or, in a few cases perhaps, an excuse) for a large number of new definitives, Official Mail items, airmails and postal stationery.

The 1988 count of 99 varieties consisted of 31 commemoratives, eight special stamps, 32 definitives, one Express Mail, three airmail, four Official Mail, eight envelopes (including four Officials), 10 postal cards (including one Official), one aerogramme and one postal card overprinted for a stamp exhibition.

As mentioned, the two new 25 Jack London stamp varieties were issued in three different booklet formats, which gave collectors of booklets a 100th variety.

The year's philatelic count can be raised by one more, to 101, by adding the $10 Migratory Waterfowl Hunting stamp — a revenue, not a postage item, but a highly popular collectible.

COMMEMORATIVES

Forty years ago, the philatelic world was astonished by a wholly unexpected flood of commemorative stamps.

The Republican 80th Congress and the Democratic President, Harry Truman, in a rare election-year conjunction of interests, combined to enact a series of laws requiring the United States Post Office Department to issue stamps to mark specified events and anniversaries. When 1948 had ended, 28 commemoratives and one commemorative airmail had poured forth from the Bureau of Engraving and Printing — far more single issues than had been seen in any previous year.

The unprecedented outpouring — and the political logrolling behind it — attracted a lot of comment in the press, much of it derisive. "Too many," *Time* said of the year's stamps. "Juvenile," the Adrian, Michigan, *Daily Telegram* called the subject matter and the hastily made designs. "Unworthy stickers," chimed in *The Washington Star*. In the end, Congress itself, shocked at what it had done, swore off any future dabbling in the process of selecting stamp subjects.

Today's collector, looking back on those innocent days, might marvel at the restraint shown by all concerned. Twenty-nine commemoratives in a year? From 1973 to 1982, USPS — without Congress' help — issued an average of 40 commemoratives annually. In one of those years, the bicentennial year of 1976, there were 88. From 1983 through 1987, the average rose to almost 50 a year. The tally for 1987 was 77 — strongly boosted, of course, by the American Wildlife issue with 50 varieties on a single pane.

In a sense, though, 1948 set the precedent for today's massive program. It showed that wherever the limit on the stamp collector's tolerance might lie, it was much higher than most people had suspected.

By modern-day standards, 1988's output of commemoratives had almost a 1948 restraint about it. The year was dominated, instead, by definitives, produced to meet the across-the-board rate changes of April 3. Only 31 commemoratives, plus one airmail commemorative, made their appearance in 1988. These included three se-tenant blocks of four and one booklet of five varieties — 19 separate issues in all. In terms of the calendar, 1988 was front-end loaded with commemoratives; 14 of the 19 issues came out in the first six months.

The subject matter broke no new ground. There were eight stamps in the Statehood Bicentennial series begun the year before, celebrating the 200th anniversary of the ratification of the Constitution by Georgia, Connecticut, Massachusetts, Maryland, South Carolina, New Hampshire, Virginia and New York. Two new entries in the American Sports series honored Knute Rockne and Francis Ouimet.

The annual Black Heritage stamp depicted James Weldon Johnson. As usual, the Winter and Summer Olympics were postally marked; what was unusual was that it was done with only one stamp each.

Following a familiar pattern, USPS produced two joint issues in cooperation with foreign postal services — Australia for one, Sweden and Finland in a first-ever three-way issue for the other. Topical collectors were accommodated with a booklet depicting classic American cars and a se-tenant block showing carousel animals.

Finally, USPS in effect dropped the other shoe with two se-tenant issues that had been made inevitable by earlier ones. A block of four Cat stamps was produced as a sequel to the Dog stamps of 1984. And another block, depicting Antarctic explorers, was the natural follow-up to the 1986 block honoring explorers of the Arctic.

22¢ GEORGIA STATEHOOD

Date of Issue: January 6, 1988

Catalog Numbers: Scott 2339   Minkus CM1298   USPS 4430

Colors: magenta, yellow, cyan, black

First-Day Cancel: Atlanta, Georgia (State Capitol)

FDCs Canceled: 467,804

Format: Panes of 50, vertical, 10 across, 5 down. Gravure printing cylinders of 200 subjects (10 across, 20 around) manufactured by Roto Cylinder (Palmyra, New Jersey).

Perf: 10.9 (L perforator)

Selvage Markings: ©United States Postal Service 1987, Use Correct ZIP Code®

Designer: Greg Harlan of Annapolis, Maryland

Art Director: James Dean (CSAC)

Project Manager: Jack Williams (USPS)

Typographer: Bradbury Thompson (CSAC)

Modeler: Richard Sennett (Sennett Enterprises) for American Bank Note Company.

Printing: Stamps printed and sheeted out by American Bank Note Company on a leased gravure press (J.W. Fergusson and Sons, Richmond, Virginia) under the supervision of Sennett Enterprises (Fairfax, Virginia). Perforated, processed and shipped by ABNC (Chicago, Illinois)

Quantity Ordered: 165,845,000
Quantity Distributed: 165,845,000

Cylinder Number Detail: One group of 4 cylinder numbers preceded by the letter "A" over/under corner stamps.

Cylinder Number Combination: A1111

Tagging: block over vignette

Printing Base Impressions: A1111 (957,000)

The Stamp

The first U.S. stamp of 1988 commemorated the 200th anniversary of statehood for Georgia. It was the fourth in a series, begun in 1987, marking the bicentennial of each of the 13 original states.

Statehood, for these charter members of the Union, was conferred when they ratified the Constitution that had been signed in Philadelphia in the summer of 1787.

The 22¢ Georgia stamp was issued January 6 in Atlanta. The actual ratification date was January 2, 1788, and it is this date that appears on the stamp.

The Georgia stamp — along with the other seven Statehood Bicentennial stamps issued in 1988 — was announced July 20, 1987, in the first U.S. Postal Service news release on the 1988 stamp and stationery program. The date of issue and other first-day information weren't released until December 22, 1987, only a few days before it occurred.

The fact that the statehood anniversary date of January 2 was missed by four days caused no concern. With the three previous Statehood Bicentennial stamps — Delaware, New Jersey and Pennsylvania — the actual dates of issue had varied from the anniversaries by much wider margins. It wouldn't be until the next stamp in the series, for Connecticut, that USPS began matching up anniversaries and issue dates exactly.

The Georgia stamp was also the seventh item in a larger series of stamps and postal stationery marking the bicentennial of the U.S. Constitution. Helping launch that series in 1987 were a postal card honoring the Convention, a five-variety booklet pane for the drafting of the Constitution and a single commemorative for its signing.

The American Bank Note Company produced the Georgia stamp for USPS under its five-year contract to provide six commemoratives annually for USPS.

Georgia is the largest state in area east of the Mississippi River. Of the 13 colonies that fought the Revolutionary War, it was the last to be founded. It was settled under a royal charter in 1733 by about 120 colonists from England headed by James Edward Oglethorpe, soldier, member of Parliament and philanthropist.

The bicentennial of that event, in 1933, was postally commemorated with a 3¢ violet stamp bearing Oglethorpe's portrait. Its 250th anniversary was marked by a 1983 multicolor postal card depicting Oglethorpe and his landing party greeting the friendly Chief Tomochichi of the Yamacraw Indians atop the bluff where Oglethorpe would found the city of Savannah.

When revolution began brewing in the colonies, Georgia, the youngest, most remote and most sparsely settled of the 13, went along with its larger and more militant neighbors. Its delegates to the Continental Congress, Button Gwinnett, Lyman Hall and George Walton, voted for and signed the Declaration of Independence.

Eleven years later, at the Constitutional Convention, Georgia's representatives, William Few and Abraham Baldwin, consistently supported measures designed to strengthen the central government and give small states parity with the large ones in its operation.

Few and Baldwin were the last to sign the completed Constitution (the signing was done by states, geographically, north to south). Afterward, Georgia ratified the document unanimously. Ratification had never been in doubt.

"If a weak state," Washington had written, "with the Indians on its back and the Spaniards on its flank does not see the necessity of a General Government, there must I think be wickedness or insanity in the way."

Georgia events or places that have been postally commemorated include the death of General Casimir Pulaski at Savannah, the first steam voyage across the Atlantic by the *S.S. Savannah* in 1819, the founding of the Girl Scouts in Savannah in 1912 and the dedication of the Stone Mountain Confederate Memorial in 1970.

Among the Georgians whose achievements have won them recognition on postage stamps are Crawford Long, Joel Chandler Harris, Sidney Lanier, Juliette Gordon Low, Senator Walter F. George, Senator Richard Russell, Moina Michael, Margaret Mitchell, Bobby Jones, Jackie Robinson and Dr. Martin Luther King.

A future stamp subject some day is a former president — Jimmy Carter of Plains.

The Design

A live oak was selected as the subject of the finished stamp — but not this one.

"Tara-ble!" was the punning reaction of one CSAC member to this Scarlett O'Hara-type belle.

Several essays were created for the Georgia Statehood stamp.

The basic design and typography for all the Statehood Bicentennial stamps was developed by Richard Sheaff of Needham, Massachusetts, a design coordinator for the Citizens' Stamp Advisory Committee.

Arranged vertically, the format featured a rectangular image area about 1⅛ inch deep and 13/16 inch wide. Beneath, on a white background, was the date of statehood in black on one line and, in larger red type below it, the state's name. The denomination and "USA" appeared either at the lower right or in the vignette box.

"We expected that over a period of time, with different states, there would be a variety of subjects and artwork in the rectangles, and that they would be reproduced on a variety of presses," Sheaff said. "Some would be straight engraving, some offset/intaglio, some gravure.

"The format would provide consistency for the series, even though the printing processes, and what was in the rectangles, would vary widely."

Originally, he said, CSAC's plan was to use the format for all future statehood anniversary stamps, and to distinguish the original 13 states with some design addition "such as a star or a '13' in gold."

Accordingly, Sheaff provided type overlays for all 50 states. For a few states with extra long names, such as Massachusetts and West Virginia, the idea was to move the "USA" and denomination up into the picture area. But normally these elements would be in the lower right corner. To make sure there would be plenty of room for the statehood dates, the committee decreed that all dates capable of abbreviation would be abbreviated. No periods would be used.

Later, however, the committee changed its collective mind and decided to use Sheaff's design format for the first 13 states only. Stamps for other states — for instance, 1989's planned centennial commemoratives for the Dakotas, Montana and Washington — would be individualistic in treatment, as all previous statehood stamps issued over the years had been.

The dates on the first three stamps in the Statehood Bicentennial series (Delaware, New Jersey and Pennsylvania, all issued in 1987) were abbreviated, as planned. Beginning with the Georgia stamp of 1988, however, this practice was dropped, and the date "January 2, 1778" was spelled out in full. There was ample room to do this, because the "22 USA" had been bumped up into the picture. "I wish they hadn't," was Sheaff's reaction. "Even though I don't like abbreviations, I wish they had been consistent."

For the Georgia picture block, several different ideas were considered. Since 1986, CSAC had made a practice of soliciting art visualizations, or "idea sketches," from at least two different designers for each commemorative issue, in order to give itself a wide range of choices in selecting final design approaches. (CSAC deviates from this practice if, for example, it decides that a specific artist is ideally suited for an assignment — as it did with Chuck Ripper for the 1987 Wildlife pane of 50.)

The sketches examined by CSAC included agricultural scenes, the sea oats of Georgia's "Golden Isles," a Greek revival column against a background of Georgia rose marble, and a Scarlett O'Hara-type belle standing in front of an antebellum mansion (a suggestion that one committee member punningly dismissed as "Tara-ble").

The design the committee chose, however, was one submitted by Georgia native Greg Harlin of Annapolis, Maryland. Harlin provided a watercolor of a live oak, the state tree of Georgia, its branches festooned with Spanish moss. The skyline of modern-day Atlanta is seen faintly in the background. It was Harlin's first stamp design.

Because CSAC announces only the name of the artist whose design is selected, the identities of the other artists submitting sketches weren't disclosed.

The live oak (*Quercus virginiana*) is a massive tree with widespreading limbs. Its hard, ready-shaped branches were much sought after in early days for use in the hulls of wooden ships.

One collector pointed out in a letter to *Linn's Stamp News* that artist Harlin had exploited his artistic license in the painting by combining one of these trees with a view of Atlanta. The live oak occurs only along the Atlantic and Gulf coastal plains, the collector said, which puts Atlanta well outside the natural range of the species.

First-Day Facts

Among the speakers at the January 6 ceremony in the rotunda of the state capitol at Atlanta were Georgia Governor Joe Frank Harris and William A. Campbell, Southern regional postmaster general.

Campbell, a Georgia native, told the audience that "tomorrow, when 160 million of these stamps go on sale across the country, the whole nation will be singing *Georgia on My Mind*."

22¢ CONNECTICUT STATEHOOD

Date of Issue: January 9, 1988

Catalog Numbers: Scott 2340   Minkus CM1299   USPS 4431

Colors: green, orange, tan, blue (offset); red, black (intaglio)

First-Day Cancel: Hartford, Connecticut (Old State House)

FDCs Canceled: 379,706

Format: Panes of 50, vertical, 10 across, 5 down. Offset printing plates of 200 subjects (10 across, 20 around); intaglio printing sleeve of 400 subjects (10 across, 40 around).

Perf: 11.1 (Eureka off-line perforator)

Selvage Markings: ©United States Postal Service 1987, Use Correct ZIP Code®

Designer: Chris Calle of Ridgefield, Connecticut

Project Manager: Joe Brockert (USPS)

Typographer: Bradbury Thompson (CSAC)

Engravers: Thomas Hipschen (BEP, vignette)
Michael Ryan (BEP, lettering and numerals)

Modeler: Ronald Sharpe (BEP)

Printing: 6-color offset, 3-color intaglio D press (902)

Quantity Ordered: 155,400,000
Quantity Distributed: 155,170,0000

Plate/Sleeve Number Detail: Left-side panes: one group of 4 offset plate numbers over/under corner stamps; one intaglio sleeve number over/under adjacent stamps. Right-side panes: offset/intaglio numbers in reverse positions.

Plate/Sleeve Number Combination: 1111-1, 1112-1, 1113-1, 1213-1, 2223-1, 2224-1, 2225-1, 2325-1, 2335-1, 2336-1, 2337-1, 2438-1

Tagging: block over vignette

Printing Base Impressions: Offset Orange: 3(299,000), 4(33,000)
Offset Tan: 3(253,000)
Offset Blue: 6(33,000), 8(33,000)

The Stamp

The 22¢ Connecticut stamp was the fifth in the Statehood Bicentennial series, and the first to be issued on the exact anniversary of the date on which the state ratified the Constitution. Its first-day sale was January 9, 1988, in Hartford, the capital.

At the 1788 Constitutional Convention, Connecticut was represented by Oliver Ellsworth, a judge; Roger Sherman, a signer of the Declaration of Independence, and William Samuel Johnson, soon to become president of Columbia College.

They made many useful contributions to the convention, but the most important was the Connecticut Plan, which formed the basis for the Great Compromise that saved the Constitution. Under the plan, representation in the lower house of Congress would be by population, pleasing the large states; in the upper house each state would have an equal number of representatives, pleasing the small ones.

After the Constitution was signed, Connecticut's ratifying convention met January 1, 1788, in Hartford's wooden State House. Soon, however, the delegates moved to warmer quarters in a nearby church.

Here Ellsworth argued eloquently that a strong central government meant protection, not oppression, for the individual states. Under the Articles of Confederation, he noted, a single state could veto the most important measures. This had happened: "A very small minority has governed us. So far is this from being consistent with republican principles, that it is in effect the worst species of monarchy."

On January 9 the delegates approved the Constitution, 128 to 40. Most of the dissenters were simply rural Yankees who were satisfied with their tight communities and didn't want to be drawn into a government that would reach from New Hampshire to Georgia.

The first U.S. postal recognition of Connecticut came in 1935 with a 3¢ stamp commemorating the 300th anniversary of the settlement of the Connecticut Valley by families from Massachusetts in 1635-1936. It depicted the Charter Oak, a tree where, tradition has it, the colony's royal charter of 1662 was once hidden to protect it from an unfriendly colonial administrator.

In 1986, a 14¢ postal card was issued to commemorate the 350th anniversary of Connecticut's settlement.

Connecticut sons and daughters who have appeared on stamps include Nathan Hale, Sybil Ludington, Manassah Cutler, Abraham Baldwin, Noah Webster and Senator Brien McMahon.

The Design

The Connecticut stamp is in the same size and design format of its four predecessors in the Statehood series. It was printed by a combination process on the Bureau of Engraving and Printing's three-color intaglio, six-color offset webfed 902 D press.

Designing the stamp was an all-Connecticut affair. Christopher Calle of Stamford prepared the vignette; his earlier design credits for USPS had included Great Americans Harry Truman, John James Audubon, Chester Nimitz, Paul Dudley White, Father Flanagan, Hugo Black and Belva Lockwood. Lettering and numerals were by another Connecticut resident, Bradbury Thompson, design coordinator for the Citizens' Stamp Advisory Committee, who is the typographer for virtually all current U.S. stamps.

Among several pencil sketches Calle submitted to CSAC were treatments of the Charter Oak, the state capitol at Hartford, and a robin — the state bird — shown with a nutmeg, the basis of Connecticut's "Nutmeg State" nickname. (The latter sketch rather closely resembled the Connecticut stamp in the 1982 State Birds and Flowers pane.)

Other subjects proposed by the artist were a statue of Thomas Hooker, a leader of the early colonists, and three portrayals of Nathan Hale, one of which showed him at the gallows delivering his famous speech: "I only regret that I have but one life to give for my country." However, the committee decided that to depict a person, no matter how distinguished, as representative of a state was a no-win proposition. Any choice would be a target for criticism.

In the end, CSAC chose a picture with a maritime theme. Occupying more than half of the stamp's vignette block is the fully-rigged whaling ship *Charles W. Morgan*, shown from the bow in its berth in the coastal city of Mystic. In the background, across a tan dock and a small patch of blue water, are shown two buildings and some green trees. An orange sun hangs low in the pale blue sky.

Though the scene is an artist's conception, the buildings shown are actual buildings, identified by a Mystic Seaport Museum official as the Schaefer Tavern and the Mystic Bank. Both are open to visitors.

The intaglio portions of the design are the ship, which is black, and the lettering and numerals, done in black and red.

Before the engraving and the offset color separations were made, some refinements were made on the computer scanner at BEP's electronic Design Center.

The $2.6 million Design Center, installed in January 1987, was manufactured by Hell Graphic Systems of West Germany. It's an electronic image processing system of a kind devised for the commer-

Connecticut's Revolutionary War martyr Nathan Hale is shown with a portion of the state seal.

cial printing industry and adapted by BEP to the unique requirements of designing stamps and other security documents. Among the things it can do is input artwork, make image alterations, store data and make negatives for offset and photogravure printing.

With Calle and art director Joe Brockert of USPS looking on, BEP's Peter Cocci, seated at the computer controls, added blue to what had been a colorless sky, worked with it until it was the shade desired and provided a suitable gradation from dark to light. A few other minor changes also were made at this point.

The *Morgan* is the only surviving wooden whaler. It was built in 1841 for a syndicate headed by Charles W. Morgan of New Bedford, Massachusetts, which was then the whaling capital of the United States, and plied the seas until 1920. It made 37 voyages and brought home a reported $1.4 million worth of whale oil and other products.

In 1921 it was bought by a corporation called Whaling Enshrined, and in 1925 was towed to the South Dartmouth, Massachusetts, estate of Colonel H.R. Green, famous millionaire, eccentric — and the dilettante stamp collector who once owned the original sheet of 100 "Jenny" inverts. The ship had once been owned by Green's grandfather, whose daughter (Green's mother), Hetty Howland Robinson Green, was famous in her own right as "the Witch of Wall Street."

If this design featuring the Charter Oak had been used for the Connecticut stamp, it would have been the historic tree's second appearance on a U.S. stamp.

Additional essays for the Connecticut Statehood stamp.

After Green's death in 1936 the *Morgan* fell into disrepair and was damaged by the great New England hurricane of 1938. In 1941 it became the property of the Marine Historical Association Inc. of Mystic, and was saved from the fate that befell hundreds of other wooden whalers that once sailed from New England ports.

The ship was renovated and is now the featured exhibit of the Mystic Seaport, the 17-acre "living nautical museum" that features some 300 other historic vessels, a working shipyard, exhibit galleries, a planetarium and a children's museum.

The Connecticut stamp marked the *Morgan's* second appearance on U.S. postage. It had earlier been depicted, in a port-side view, on one of the four 8¢ stamps in the Historic Preservation se-tenant block in 1971.

Some second-guessing followed the disclosure of the stamp's design. Despite Connecticut's role as the *Morgan's* savior, a few stamp collectors questioned the appropriateness of using as a symbol of Connecticut's maritime tradition a ship that had been associated all its useful life with Massachusetts.

First-Day Facts

A heavy snow had fallen the day before, but the weather was clear and cold for the first-day ceremony at the Old State House in Hartford. The building, designed by Charles Bulfinch, built on the site of the previous capitol and completed in 1796, served until 1878, when it was replaced by the present building a few blocks away. It is now a museum — and it was a busy place that Saturday.

While the stamp ceremonies were taking place in the small Senate chamber on the second floor, the larger first-floor House chamber was filled with teenagers in colonial costume debating whether Connecticut should ratify the Constitution. (They finally decided that their ancestors' decision, 200 years earlier, was the right one.)

The Senate chamber was crowded, and only invited guests were able to sit. Hartford Postmaster William J. Dowling was master of ceremonies, and William R. Cummings, Northeast regional postmaster general, was principal speaker. Governor William A. O'Neill accepted the postal tribute to Connecticut on behalf of its citizens, and received a framed enlargement of the stamp. A brief autograph session — with stamp designer Calle as well as the speakers — concluded the ceremony.

At the nearby Old State House postal substation, many collectors sought the "Statehood Station" postmark, which was only available on a handback basis. Bearing an outline map of Connecticut, it was similar in arrangement to that used in other states on the actual bicentennial dates. But this was the first time the postmark could be used on the actual first day of issue of a Statehood stamp.

22¢ WINTER OLYMPICS

Date of Issue: January 10, 1988

Catalog Numbers: Scott 2369   Minkus CM1300   USPS 4432

Colors: magenta, yellow, cyan, black

First-Day Cancel: Anchorage, Alaska (William A. Egan Civic and Convention Center)

FDCs Canceled: 395,198

Format: Panes of 50, vertical, 10 across, 5 down. Gravure printing cylinders of 200 subjects (10 across, 20 around) manufactured by Roto Cylinder (Palmyra, New Jersey).

Perf: 10.9 (L perforator)

Selvage Markings: ©United States Postal Service 1987, Use Correct ZIP Code®

Designer: Bart Forbes of Dallas, Texas

Art Director: Jack Williams (USPS)

Typographer: Bradbury Thompson (CSAC)

Modeler: Richard Sennett (Sennett Enterprises) for American Bank Note Company.

Printing: Stamps printed and sheeted out by American Bank Note Company on a leased gravure press (J.W. Fergusson and Sons, Richmond, Virginia) under the supervision of Sennett Enterprises (Fairfax, Virginia). Perforated, processed and shipped by ABNC (Chicago, Illinois).

Quantity Ordered: 161,500,000
Quantity Distributed: 158,870,000

Cylinder Number Detail: One group of 4 cylinder numbers preceded by the letter "A" over/under corner stamps

Cylinder Number Combination: A1111

Tagging: block over vignette

Printing Base Impressions: A1111 (929,084) plus 21,250 (test)

The Stamp

Collectors can be thankful that USPS didn't respond to the 1988 Olympic Games with the same enthusiasm with which it greeted the Games of 1984, or even of 1980. If it had, the total count of U.S. stamps and stationery items for the year would have soared into the triple digits.

Instead, mercifully, USPS limited itself to one commemorative each for the Winter Games in Calgary, Alberta, Canada, and the Summer Games in Seoul, Republic of Korea.

In both 1984 and 1980 the United States played host to one or the other of the Games, thus providing some justification for the heavy postal output.

In 1984, when the Winter Games were held in Sarajevo, Yugoslavia, and the Summer Games in Los Angeles, USPS celebrated with no fewer than 24 different commemorative and airmail stamps in se-tenant blocks, plus three postal cards and an aerogramme.

That beat 1980's impressive record, when the Winter Games in Lake Placid, New York, and the Summer Games in Moscow inspired 15 items — nine commemoratives, one airmail stamp, one envelope, one aerogramme, two postal cards and one airmail postal card.

(As events that year turned out, the United States boycotted the Summer Games to protest the Soviet invasion of Afghanistan, and the stamps were abruptly pulled from sale at post offices and the Philatelic Sales Division.)

The first U.S. Olympics stamps appeared in 1932, when both sets of Games were held in this country. A single 2¢ stamp celebrated the Winter Games in Lake Placid, and (after an intervening rate change) 3¢ and 5¢ stamps marked the Summer Games in Los Angeles.

In 1960, a single 4¢ stamp commemorated the return of the Winter Games to the United States. They were held that year in Squaw Valley, California.

The first overseas Games to be the subject of U.S. stamps were those of 1972, when three commemoratives and an airmail marked the Winter Games in Sapporo, Japan, and the Summer Games in Munich, Germany. For the 1976 Winter Games in Innsbruck, Austria, and Summer Games in Montreal, USPS issued four commemoratives in a se-tenant block.

To return to 1988:

The single Olympics stamps for the Winter and Summer Games were announced July 20, 1987, in the first USPS listing of the 1988 stamp and stationery program. Later, on November 25, it was announced that the 22¢ Winter Olympics commemorative would be issued January 10 in Anchorage, Alaska. Design details were released December 16.

The Winter Olympics commemorative was the second stamp of 1988 to be produced for USPS by the American Bank Note Company. As with all ABNC work for USPS, it was printed by the J.W. Fergusson Company of Richmond, Virginia, on a leased Champlain eight-color webfed gravure press.

The modern Olympic Games — inspired by the athletic festivals of ancient Greece — began in 1896 as the brainchild of Baron Pierre de Coubertin, a French educator. They have been held every four years (the interval is called an "Olympiad") since then, with the exception of the war years of 1916, 1940 and 1944.

In 1924, for the first time, the Games were divided into Winter and Summer components. The Winter Games consist of bobsledding, ice hockey, luge (a form of tobogganing), figure skating, speed skating, Alpine skiing (downhill and slalom), Nordic skiing (cross-country), ski jumping and the biathlon (cross-country skiing and shooting).

A Bart Forbes essay for the Winter Olympics issue showed a ski jumper.

This working sketch depicted a luge racer in the awkward supine position.

Baron de Coubertin was said to dislike the Winter Games because they lacked universality. In other words, many nations didn't possess the frosty climate needed to compete effectively.

The Calgary Games, the first Winter Games held in Canada, set a number of records. They were the longest ever (16 days), attracted nearly 1,800 athletes from 57 countries, and sold 1.5 million tickets.

Outstanding performers included Alberto Tomba of Italy, winner of two golds in Alpine skiing; Katarina Witt of East Germany, the first female figure skater to repeat as a gold medalist in more than 50 years; Matti Nykaenen of Finland, winner of three golds in ski jumping, and Yvonne van Gennip of the Netherlands, who won three golds in speed skating.

Although the so-called Olympic ideal prescribes that competition is among individuals, not nations, country-by-country medal counts are a prominent part of the news coverage. At Calgary, the Soviet Union led all teams with 29 medals, including 11 golds, followed by East Germany with 25 (nine golds) and Switzerland with 15 (five golds). The United States, with six medals, had to settle for a tie for eighth place with Sweden.

Only two U.S. competitors won their events: Brian Boitano in figure skating and Bonnie Blair in the 500-meter speed skating race. It was the fewest medals this country has won in the Winter Olympics since 1936, and the fewest golds since 1968.

The Design

CSAC requested travel-poster type designs as a new approach to Olympic stamp art, and the resulting essays showed the Calgary skyline, a grain elevator, mountains and Canada geese. In the end, CSAC decided the Olympic connection wasn't readily recognizable with this type of art.

Bart Forbes of Dallas, Texas, was chosen by CSAC to design both the Winter Games and Summer Games stamps.

A free-lance artist, Forbes had painted sports covers for *Time* (basketball's Larry Bird, hockey's Wayne Gretzky) and *Sports Illustrated*. He describes his style as "loose and realistic, very identifiable." For USPS, he had previously designed the 22¢ Abigail Adams commemorative of 1985.

Because most previous U.S. Olympics stamps had featured athletes, CSAC decided to take a different approach in 1988 and try for "travel poster" type stamps featuring the sites of the Games. However, after examining several sketches — including a Forbes design showing Calgary's space needle, a grain elevator and a mountain range — it decided to go back to athletes after all. The consensus was that it was too hard for the viewer to pick up the connection between the travel scenes and the Olympic Games.

Forbes' design, arranged vertically, shows an Alpine skier slashing down a mountain past a slalom gate in a spray of snow. It features strong diagonal lines, upper left to lower right, in the slope of the hill, the skis and ski poles and the angle of the skier's arms and legs.

Skiers had been shown on seven of the 14 previous U.S. Winter Olympics stamps. The very first — the 1932 stamp, picturing a ski jumper — evoked criticism from experts that the jumper's form was defective; among other things, he had apparently crossed his skis in mid-air. Since then, the designers' accuracy has improved.

First-Day Facts

Anchorage was chosen as the first-day site to give a publicity boost to the local committee seeking the 1994 Winter Games for that city. The effort later turned out to have been in vain, as the International Olympic Committee, meeting at the Summer Games in Seoul, eliminated Anchorage on the second ballot and chose Lillehammer, Norway, over Oestersund, Sweden, on the third ballot.

Anchorage also had unsuccessfully sought the 1992 Games, which were awarded to Albertville, France. The reason there was also a 1994 Games to be sited was the IOC's decision to end the practice of holding both the Winter and Summer Games in the same year. They will still be held every four years, but staggered.

Among those attending the first-day ceremony were Frank Heffron, chairman of the finance committee of the U.S. Olympic Committee, which had endorsed Anchorage's bid for 1994; Rick Mystrom and Rick Nerland, chairman and executive vice president of the Anchorage Olympics committee, and Gil Wheeler II, a bobsledder who participated in the 1988 Winter Games. Joseph Caraveo, Western Region postmaster general, represented USPS. In his speech, in the fashion of skating-event judges, he awarded "a 10" to Bart Forbes for his design.

22¢ AUSTRALIAN BICENTENNIAL

Date of Issue: January 26, 1988

Catalog Numbers: Scott 2370   Minkus CM1301   USPS 4433

Colors: magenta, cyan, yellow, gray, black

First-Day Cancel: Washington, D.C. (Australian Embassy)

FDCs Canceled: 523,465

Format: Panes of 40, square, 8 across, 5 down. Gravure printing cylinders of 160 subjects (10 across, 16 around).

Perf: 11 by 10.9 (Eureka off-line perforator)

Selvage Markings: ©United States Postal Service 1987, Use Correct ZIP Code®

Designer: Roland Harvey of Fitzroy, Victoria, Australia

Art Director: Jack Williams (USPS)

Modeler: Ronald Sharpe (BEP)

Printing: 7-color Andreotti gravure press (601)

Quantity Ordered: 146,500,000
Quantity Distributed: 145,560,000

Cylinder Number Detail: One group of 5 cylinder numbers over/under corner stamps.

Cylinder Number Combination: 11111, 12111

Tagging: block over vignette

Printing Base Impressions: Magenta: 1(918,608)
Cyan: 1(131,307), 2(787,301)
Yellow: 1(918,608), 1(1,396,208)
Gray: 1(918,608), 1(1,396,208)
Black: 1(918,608)

The Stamp

A notable development in U.S. philately in the past 30 years has been the proliferation of joint stamp issues. These are stamps issued by the United States and a foreign country, usually very similar in design, to mark an event of common interest.

It began in 1959 when the United States and Canada produced matching stamps commemorating the opening of the St. Lawrence Seaway. Since then, the two North American neighbors have issued stamps jointly on three other occasions, and the United States has participated in similar programs twice each with Sweden, France, Ireland and Italy and once each with Mexico, Spain, the Soviet Union, the Netherlands, West Germany and Morocco.

On January 26, 1988, the 11th country — Australia — and 19th joint issue was added to that list. The occasion was Australia's 200th birthday.

The Australian half of the joint issue was slightly larger than the U.S. stamp and bore different typography.

Ceremonies in both Washington and Sydney accompanied the issuance of the two stamps, the U.S. 22¢ and the Australian 37¢ (which sold for 27¢ in U.S. coin). As is customary on such occasions, each country's stamp was available at the other's ceremony so that first-day covers bearing both could be prepared.

The central design of both stamps was a cartoon showing an Australian koala and an American eagle, linked arm-in-wing and waving their hats in celebration. It was the work of Roland Harvey of Fitzroy, Victoria, widely known in Australia as an illustrator of children's books and greeting cards.

In addition, each country produced a maximum card and a folder or "stamp pack" carrying a block of four of both stamps. The U.S. card, which sold for 50¢, and folder, which sold for $4, were designed by Pat Oliphant, the Pulitzer Prize-winning newspaper cartoonist who is a native of Australia.

The light-heartedness of the stamp design in no way reflected the circumstances of the event it commemorated. Australia's settlement was a grim affair indeed.

English justice in the 18th century was harsh, and its prisons badly overcrowded. For decades, authorities kept the pressure within acceptable limits by transporting prisoners overseas. Many were sent to America as indentured servants.

But the American Revolution and American independence closed off that outlet. In 1786 the Cabinet under William Pitt decided to use Australia, half a world away from the British Isles, as a dumping ground for surplus prisoners.

"Never had a colony been founded so far from its parent state, or in such ignorance of the land it occupied," Robert Hughes wrote in his best-selling history, *The Fatal Shore.* "There had been no reconnaissance. In 1770 Captain James Cook had made landfall on the unexplored east coast of this utterly enigmatic continent, stopped for a short while at a place called Botany Bay and gone north again. Since then no ship had called . . .

"Now this coast was to witness a new colonial experiment, never tried before, not repeated since. An unexplored continent would become a jail. The space around it, the very air and sea, the whole transparent labyrinth of the South Pacific, would become a wall 14,000 miles thick."

On January 26, 1788, the First Fleet — 11 vessels under Captain Arthur Phillip of the Royal Navy — landed at Sydney Cove in what was then called New South Wales. "It had been one of the great sea voyages in English history," Hughes wrote. Eight months earlier, these ships had set sail from England with 736 convicts, including 188 women, crammed aboard. These involuntary colonists ranged in age from 9 to 82, and were serving terms of seven to 14 years, many for the pettiest of petty thefts. Forty of them had died en route — a low number, considering the abominable conditions aboard.

The early years were desperate, and starvation threatened the colony. "No country offers less assistance to first settlers," Phillip reported. Expecting supplies and help, Phillip was dismayed to see the second fleet — three ships — loaded with few provisions but with many more prisoners. That voyage had been a disaster; on one ship alone, death en route had claimed 158 of the 499 convicts who had set sail.

Under Phillip's leadership, however, the colony gradually took root. Many of the convict-colonists were freed as they completed their terms and were given small plots of their own. With the last convict ship's arrival in 1868, some 162,000 men and women had been transported. Over the years, immigration of free settlers gradually increased, and new colonies were settled and won self-government.

A philatelic footnote: That settlement in Sydney Cove whose bicentennial was commemorated in 1988 also had been postally remembered 100 years earlier, on its centennial!

In 1888, New South Wales had issued a set of eight anniversary stamps, one penny to £1, which is considered the world's first set of commemorative adhesive postage stamps issued by a government postal administration. Unlike modern commemoratives, these remained on sale in the colony for several years, undergoing several changes of color, watermark and perforations. Australia Post, as part of its bicentennial observance, issued a special 37¢ stamped envelope July 29, 1988, bearing reproductions of these century-old stamps.

The Design

Three different artists submitted essays for the Australia Bicentennial commemorative, adapting the lighthearted approach requested by CSAC. Eagles and emus, kangaroos, koalas and cassowaries, platypuses, Uncle Sam and even Donald Duck got into the act.

Australian postal officials offered Roland Harvey's stamp design to USPS with the suggestion that both countries use it — or, at least, that both use the whimsical approach that it embodied.

The Citizens' Stamp Advisory Committee agreed that the approach should be lighthearted, but before it settled on Harvey's design it examined a number of concept sketches from three American artists. Such sketches are commissioned under an art visualization contract calling for submission of a selection of graphic ideas. "We gave them the general theme, told them to use eagles or Uncle Sam plus typical Australian images, and then wing it!" said Jack Williams, program manager for philatelic design.

The result was an interesting and imaginative assortment. The committee studied the sketches critically. On one, for instance, the American symbol was deemed too small; another, which showed a kangaroo

The Pat Oliphant design used on the maximum card also was reproduced on a folder carrying blocks of four of both the U.S. and Australian stamps.

riding on the American eagle's back, seemed to imply that the United States was "carrying" Australia.

In the end, the committee opted for the Harvey design and uniformity. In fact, it tried for complete uniformity by hiring a Washington calligrapher to do the lettering in the same kind of script used on the Australian stamp. But the members decided after seeing the result that they preferred conventional type.

The designs of the two stamps were disclosed in both countries November 23, 1987.

Roland Harvey's cartoon koala wears a striped football jumper of green and gold, Australia's official colors, and holds a bush hat. The American eagle wears a vest of Stars and Stripes and waves a top hat of matching national colors.

The U.S. stamp is square, the design 1.075 inches to a side, the entire stamp 1.225 inches to a side, a format last used for the 1985 stamp that advance-promoted AMERIPEX. It was printed in five-color gravure on the BEP's Andreotti press and sold in panes of 40, five stamps down and eight across — one stamp narrower than the standard pane.

The 40-stamp format was "an experiment in retail speed and convenience," said Gordon C. Morison, assistant postmaster general for philatelic and retail services. He explained that it's easier for postal employees and customers to count and keep up with a product that comes in multiples of five or 10.

The Australian version of the stamp, also in square format but somewhat larger, bore the words "Happy Bicentenary!" in a curved line of script across the top. In two rows at the bottom it displayed the official symbol of the Australian Bicentennial Authority and the words "AUSTRALIA 37c" and "Joint stamp issue with USA."

Exclamation points, such as the one on the U.S. version, are no longer unusual on U.S. postage. In the past they were used sparingly, appearing first in 1975 ("Merry Christmas!") and next in 1981 ("Alcoholism/You Can Beat It!"). In 1987 all eight of the Special Occasions booklet stamp messages were punctuated in this manner.

Whimsy wasn't new to U.S. stamps, either. Peter Max's "Cosmic Jumper" had adorned the EXPO 74 commemorative; the ZIP Code stamp of 1974 was done in a cartoon-poster style, and Smokey the Bear and McGruff the Crime Dog made their stamp debuts in 1984. Nevertheless, the design of the U.S. Australia stamp drew mixed reviews from collectors.

Writers of letters to *Linn's Stamp News* used phrases such as "below the dignity of a sovereign nation," "ridiculous cartoon" and "worst design." But others countered by calling the design "delightful and refreshing," a good way to promote stamp collecting among children, and "an attractive and witty evocation" of "a particular kind of joy in living" that is shared by Australians and Americans.

(Both New Zealand and Israel got into the same whimsical spirit with their stamps saluting the Australian bicentennial. The New Zealand 40¢ stamp — which, like the U.S. stamp, was part of a joint issue designed by Roland Harvey — depicted a New Zealand kiwi and Australian koala by a campfire, toasting friendship and prosperity. Israel's 1-shekel stamp showed two kangaroos holding a candle-laden birthday cake.)

First-Day Facts

The koala and eagle characters used in the stamp design were also incorporated in pictorial first-day cancellations.

The U.S. cancellation, with its Washington postmark, pictured the eagle's head, vest, left wing and top hat, along with the words "HAP-

PY BICENTENNIAL/AUSTRALIA!/FIRST DAY OF ISSUE." Its Aussie counterpart pictured the koala and the words: "26 JANUARY 1988/SYDNEY NSW 2000/FIRST DAY OF ISSUE."

Both postmarks were available in Washington and Sydney on January 26 to service first-day covers containing both stamps. Because of the time difference, the Sydney ceremony preceded the one in Washington by about 12 hours.

The Washington ceremony was held at the Australian Embassy, 1601 Massachusetts Avenue Northwest, before an audience of some 400 people.

Postmaster General Preston R. Tisch was on hand at the embassy to declare that despite the vast geographic distance between the two nations, "two of the world's most efficient and effective postal systems" were at work to help bridge it. Other participants included Robert B. Lansdown, chairman of the Australian Postal Commission; John C. Whitehead, deputy U.S. secretary of state, and F. Rawdon Dalrymple, Australia's ambassador to the United States.

In Sydney, thousands lined up at the general post office to buy both stamps. (They were there also to obtain a set of five se-tenant Australian stamps that would complete a 21-stamp continuing series tracing the progress of the First Fleet from its departure from England in May 1787 to its arrival in Sydney Cove.) The post office — which was one of only a handful of post offices open on Australia Day, the national holiday — sold out its stock of the U.S. stamp by 3 p.m. on the first day. All the first-day covers were sold out by the next day, and there were no blank covers left to service mail orders.

Bill Hayden, Australia's foreign minister, and Lawerence Lane Jr., U.S. ambassador, were the main speakers at the ceremony. Both men personally handstamped the first first-day cover, then cut a ribbon on the doors of the general post office and declared it open for business.

Australia participated in two more joint issues — with Great Britain and New Zealand — to mark its bicentenary. The stamps were issued June 21, 1988.

22¢ JAMES WELDON JOHNSON

Date of Issue: February 2, 1988

Catalog Numbers: Scott 2317   Minkus CM1302   USPS 4434

Colors: magenta, yellow, cyan, black, line black

First-Day Cancel: Nashville, Tennessee (Fisk Memorial Chapel, Fisk University)

FDCs Canceled: 465,282

Format: Panes of 50, vertical, 10 across, 5 down. Gravure printing cylinders of 200 subjects (10 across, 20 around) manufactured by Roto Cylinder (Palmyra, New Jersey).

Perf: 10.9 (L perforator)

Selvage Markings: ©United States Postal Service 1988, Use Correct ZIP Code®

Designer: Thomas Blackshear of Novato, California

Art Director: Jerry Pinkney (CSAC)

Typographer: Bradbury Thompson (CSAC)

Modeler: Richard Sennett (Sennett Enterprises) for American Bank Note Company.

Printing: Stamps printed and sheeted out by American Bank Note Company on a leased gravure press (J.W. Fergusson and Sons, Richmond, Virginia) under the supervision of Sennett Enterprises (Fairfax, Virginia). Perforated, processed and shipped by ABNC (Chicago, Illinois).

Quantity Ordered: 97,300,000
Quantity Distributed: 97,300,000

Cylinder Number Detail: One group of 5 cylinder numbers preceded by the letter "A" over/under corner stamps

Cylinder Number Combination: A11111

Tagging: block over vignette

Printing Base Impressions: A11111 (560,670)

The Stamp

In 1939 the novelist Carl Van Vechten wrote to President Franklin D. Roosevelt about the planned Famous Americans series of stamps:

"Don't you think the time has come when some Negro, Frederick Douglass, Crispus Attucks, Booker T. Washington or James Weldon Johnson, might be represented on a stamp?"

James Weldon Johnson, a man of multiple achievements and a close friend of Van Vechten, had been killed the summer before in a car-train collision.

As it turned out, Booker T. Washington was indeed included in the Famous Americans series of 1940, the first black man to be postally honored by the United States. Douglass was pictured on a 25¢ definitive in 1967.

But it wasn't until 1988, in the 50th anniversary year of his death, that James Weldon Johnson finally got the stamp Van Vechten had asked for. A man who attained distinction as an author, lyricist, lawyer, diplomat, educator and civil rights worker, Johnson was depicted on a 22¢ commemorative in the Black Heritage series.

The Johnson stamp was announced July 20, 1987, in the first Postal Service news release on the 1988 stamp and stationery program. It was issued February 2 in Nashville, Tennessee, where Johnson had been a professor of creative literature at Fisk University from 1930 until his death.

Johnson was born in Jacksonville, Florida, June 17, 1871. After graduating with a Bachelor of Arts degree from Atlanta University in 1894, he became principal at the Colored High School in Jacksonville. Meanwhile, he studied law, and in 1897 he left teaching to become the first black to be admitted to the Florida bar. He later received a Master of Arts degree from Atlanta (1903) and Doctor of Literature degrees from Talladega College in Alabama (1917) and Howard University (1923).

From 1901 to 1906 he collaborated with his composer brother Rosamond on some 200 songs for musical comedies and light opera, including *Congo Love Song, Oh! Didn't He Ramble* and *Since You Went Away*. James was a charter member of the American Society of Composers, Authors and Publishers (ASCAP) in 1914, along with such luminaries as Irving Berlin, Jerome Kern and Victor Herbert.

By far the brothers' best-known song was *Lift Ev'ry Voice and Sing*, which they wrote for a chorus of schoolchildren to perform at a Lincoln's birthday celebration in 1900. This hymn of faith and hope later became known as "the Negro national anthem." "Nothing that I have done has paid me back so fully in satisfaction as being the part creator of this song," James Johnson wrote in his 1933 autobiography. "My brother and I . . . have often marveled at the results that have followed what we considered an incidental effort, an effort made under stress and with no intention other than to meet the needs of a particular moment. The only comment we can make is that we wrote better than we knew."

The musical team was broken up when President Theodore Roosevelt named James U.S. consul at Puerto Cabello, Venezuela, in 1906. Later he served as consul in Corinto, Nicaragua. From 1916 to 1930 he worked with the National Association for the Advancement of Colored People, first as secretary and later as executive secretary. He was a militant crusader for federal anti-lynching legislation.

In Johnson's prose and verse, said *The New York Times* in his obituary, "he became the unofficial spokesman for the American Negro, and his influence is credited with loosing of the flood of Negro self-expression that reached its peak in the late 1920s." His works include *The Autobiography of an Ex-Colored Man*, written anonymously in 1912; *Fifty Years and Other Poems*, 1917; two collections of spirituals, and *Black Manhattan*, 1930. *God's Trombones*, written in 1927, set down as poetry the inspirational sermons of old Negro preachers and so helped ensure the survival of a great oral tradition. Carl Sandburg said of it: "The cunning rhythms, the graphic language, the figures of speech join in a work that is of the realm of art."

Johnson was killed June 26, 1938, at the age of 67 when his car collided with a train in Wiscasset, Maine.

The James Weldon Johnson stamp was the 11th in the Black Heritage series, which has appeared at the rate of one stamp a year since 1978. Like most of its predecessors in the series, it was issued in February to coincide with Black History Month. Those honored previously were Harriet Tubman, Martin Luther King Jr., Benjamin Banneker, Whitney Moore Young, Jackie Robinson, Scott Joplin, Carter G. Woodson, Mary McLeod Bethune, Sojourner Truth and Jean Baptiste Pointe Du Sable.

The Design

One of the Yale University photographs of Johnson from which artist Thomas Blackshear worked.

The Johnson stamp was designed by Thomas Blackshear, a 32-year-old artist and illustrator of growing reputation from Novato, California. Art director was Jerry Pinkney, design coordinator for CSAC.

Pinkney had designed the first nine stamps of the Black Heritage series; the 10th, 1987's Du Sable stamp, was designed by Blackshear. The James Weldon Johnson stamp was Blackshear's second assignment for the Postal Service.

The vertically oriented design contains a full-face portrait of Johnson. Like most stamps in the series, it also includes a design element, representative of an important aspect of the subject's life — in this case, a musical staff, across the bottom of the image in black, containing 2½ bars along with the title line of *Lift Ev'ry Voice and Sing.*

Tom Blackshear created the design based on photographs in the Johnson Collection of the Beinecke Rare Book and Manuscript Library at Yale University.

Thomas Blackshear made this sketch prior to developing a finished stamp design.

The stamp as printed was a disappointment to the Postal Service because of a "fuzzy" quality in the facial features. Donald McDowell, manager of the Stamps Division, said the division and the CSAC hadn't visualized how the gravure press would reproduce Blackshear's soft acrylic rendering, done on a textured surface. Gravure prints from tiny color cells whose edges don't touch, rather than with a continuous tone, as in offset; McDowell likens the gravure effect to "stenciling with Cheerios." Thus a lack of definition in the original art — a failure to define individual hairs in a mustache, for example — tends to be exaggerated in the finished product.

Said McDowell: "One of the really intriguing things that happens to you in 'excellence' programs such as we have at USPS is that as you get better your flaws can be more apparent. With U.S. gravure stamp printing even up to 1982 or 1983 it didn't really matter whether the design image was sharp or not. The product was going to be fuzzy, because that's all we could make gravure do.

"As we've gotten better, now the process can discriminate between fuzz and sharpness. And with James Weldon Johnson, from his nose to his collar the art is fuzzy, and the press faithfully printed it."

In an effort to deal with the problem, the printers used a screen finer than the normal 180 lines per inch, and also used a double-coated gravure paper. "It helped it, but it didn't solve it," McDowell said. "But we learned enough in the process that we saw how we could use the fine screen and double-coated paper to very great advantage with the (later) Cats stamps." One of the benefits the changes produced, however, was an enhancement of clarity in the words and notes of the musical excerpt below the portrait.

Artist Blackshear had used the same painting technique with his Jean Baptiste Pointe Du Sable design in 1987, McDowell said, but that stamp had been successful because the portrait was a strong profile with color behind it, not a full face, and had strong highlights in the facial flesh.

After the Johnson stamp was released, USPS brought Blackshear east for a short course in designing for gravure. One of his coaches was Richard Sennett, who had previously supervised stamp production as an American Bank Note Company vice president before establishing his own firm, Sennett Enterprises Inc., and entering into a contract with ABNC to arrange for printing of stamps under ABNC's own long-term contract with the Postal Service.

First-Day Facts

The first-day ceremony was held February 2 in the Fisk Memorial Chapel on the campus of Fisk University in Nashville. Principal speakers to a standing-room-only crowd were Dr. Henry Ponder, president of Fisk; Dr. Reavis Mitchell, university historian and executive assistant to the president, and Assistant Postmaster General Elwood A. Mosley, who promised that USPS would continue the Black Heritage stamp series "in the years ahead." The Fisk Jubilee Singers performed several songs, including, of course, *Lift Ev'ry Voice and Sing*.

An unofficial "second day of issue" ceremony — unofficial in that it wasn't organized by USPS headquarters — was held February 3 in Johnson's place of birth, Jacksonville, Florida. The site was the gymnasium of the James Weldon Johnson Seventh Grade Center. Presiding was Marjorie M. Brown, director of marketing and communications for the Jacksonville District of the USPS.

22¢ CATS (BLOCK OF FOUR)

Date of Issue: February 5, 1988

Catalog Numbers: Scott 2372-75 (stamps) Minkus CM1303-06
Scott 2375a (block of 4) USPS 4438

Colors: magenta, yellow, cyan, gray, black

First-Day Cancel: New York, New York (Winter Garden Theatre)

FDCs Canceled: 872,734

Format: Panes of 40, horizontal, 5 across, 8 down. Gravure printing cylinders of 160 subjects (10 across, 16 around).

Perf: 10.9 (L perforator)

Selvage Markings: ©United States Postal Service 1987, Use Correct ZIP Code®

Designer: John Dawson of Hailey, Idaho

Art Director and Typographer: Howard Paine (CSAC)

Project Manager: Jack Williams (USPS)

Modeler: Richard Sennett (Sennett Enterprises) for American Bank Note Company.

Printing: Stamps printed and sheeted out by American Bank Note Company on a leased gravure press (J.W. Fergusson and Sons, Richmond, Virginia) under the supervision of Sennett Enterprises (Fairfax, Virginia). Perforated, processed and shipped by ABNC (Chicago, Illinois).

Quantity Ordered: 158,556,000
Quantity Distributed: 158,556,000

Cylinder Number Detail: One group of 5 cylinder numbers preceded by the letter "A" alongside corner stamps

Cylinder Number Combination: A11111

Tagging: block over vignette

Printing Base Impressions: A11111 (562,670)

The Stamps

Cat lovers were pleased when USPS, in its continuing search for topical stamp subjects, finally got around to their favorite pets. Ever since 1984, when a se-tenant block of four stamps was issued depicting eight American dog breeds, feline fanciers had been waiting for equal treatment.

It came on February 5, 1988, when a block of four 22¢ stamps featuring domestic cats was placed on sale at the Winter Garden Theatre in New York City. The choice of the Winter Garden was another demonstration of the current USPS affinity for whimsical or offbeat first-day sites; the theater was home to the long-run musical *Cats*.

The stamps were announced July 20, 1987, in the first USPS news release about the 1988 stamp and stationery program. Later, details were provided, including the breeds chosen for illustration: Siamese cat and Exotic Shorthair cat, upper left stamp; Abyssinian cat and Himalayan cat, upper right; Maine Coon cat and Burmese cat, lower left; and American Shorthair cat and Persian cat, lower right.

Eight breeds were needed so the Cat block would match the Dog block, with two breeds per stamp, explained Jack Williams, project manager for the Cat stamps. CSAC obtained lists of most popular breeds from the Cat Fanciers' Association, which is the world's largest registry of pedigreed cats, and other sources, and selected eight that would provide a satisfactory variety of appearance.

The stamps were printed by the American Bank Note Company on its leased gravure press at the J.W. Fergusson Company in Richmond, Virginia. They were in the same 40-to-a-pane "semi-jumbo" horizontal format used for the Dogs stamps and for a 1985 se-tenant block depicting American horses. It was the first 40-subject stamp pane manufactured by ABNC, which previously had produced stamps for USPS only in the standard, 50-to-a-pane commemorative format.

Though ABNC got generally good reviews for the stamps, it drew unexpected criticism for one feature — the flavor of the gum.

The dry, matte-finish adhesive used by ABNC was intended to minimize curl, but it tasted awful, according to one letter writer to *Linn's Stamp News*, who went on to ask: "Do you know if the cats had a hand in its production?" A *Washington Post* reader suggested that "whoever did it should be made to lick 10,000 of the adulterated stamps and then destroy the offending chemical and its formula."

Cats previously had been seen infrequently on U.S. stamps. The 8¢ 100th Anniversary of Mail Order commemorative of 1972 had shown a house cat as part of the country-store scene. A non-domesticated member of the family, a puma, was shown on the Wildlife booklet pane of 1981, and a mountain lion and bobcat were included in the 1987 American Wildlife pane of 50.

Artist John Dawson submitted this set of roughs showing the cats in the "bust" configurations that were adopted.

However, the domestic cat has been one of the most popular topical subjects on the stamps of other countries. One of the earliest and best-known examples is Poland's 1964 set of 10 large-size stamps bearing cat portraits. Albania, Dominica, Fujeira, Guinea Bissau, Hungary, Laos, New Zealand, Nicaragua and Romania, among others, have also issued handsome extended sets.

USPS, in announcing its own Cat stamps, reported that although more American homes include dogs than cats, more cats are kept overall: 57.8 million, compared to about 50 million dogs. The cat's relative popularity has grown with the spread of urban areas and the consequent reduction in average living space.

The domestic cat, in its travels to all parts of the world, has been transformed into a species of great variety. Environmental conditions played a part, as did interbreeding of domestic and wild felines, which resulted in the tabby — or striped — markings of many cats today.

The Siamese is now the most popular shorthair breed. Favored for its lithe form and playful disposition, it is easily identified by its points, or colored mask, ears, paws and tail, combined with a paler body and piercing blue eyes.

The Exotic Shorthair and Persian are related (note the similar, no-nonsense facial expressions of the specimens shown on the stamps).The Exotic Shorthair's coat is as full as the Persian's, but shorter; the specimen illustrated had cream-colored markings on a gray, or "blue," coat.

Pencil sketch using full-body treatment. A refinement of the previous rough sketch.

Artist's rough composition sketch, full-body, of a Siamese cat and a Burmese.

The Abyssinian, like many old breeds, is of obscure origin. Many theorize that the breed is the closest link to the first domesticated cats, but with its sleek build and burnished coloring it retains the distinctly wild appearance of a small mountain lion. The Himalayan, on the same stamp, is the striking result of attempts to establish Siamese-patterned cats of Persian coat and body type.

The Maine Coon is one of the oldest natural breeds of North America. A legend has it that it developed from cats mating with raccoons — a biological impossibility. With its rugged build and thick coat, the Maine Coon can withstand the harshest winters, and commonly was kept on New England farms to keep down rodents. Its stamp companion, the Burmese, sports a rich sable coat and golden eyes.

The Persian, with its snub nose and long, glossy coat, ranks as the most popular longhair breed. Originally bred in the Middle East, the Persian was introduced to North America about a century ago, and quickly supplanted the Maine Coon as the most popular attraction at cat shows. It is well-known for its gentle temperament.

The American Shorthair that is depicted is the best-known kind, the silver tabby. Like their European cousins, non-pedigree cats in America earned their keep as hunters of vermin long before owners began systematically breeding and showing them. Though still dismissed as "alley cats" by some, American Shorthair show cats have been carefully developed for generations and rival any other breed in the eyes of cat fanciers.

Pencil sketch using full-body treatment of a Himalayan Longhair and Persian Longhair. On the stamps, these breeds were paired with other cats.

USPS was proud of the Cat stamps and used the block as the focus of its 10th annual winter-spring promotion of stamp collecting, particularly topicals. The promotion was called, in an excess of cuteness, "Cuddlesome Collectibles." For several weeks after the Cat stamps went on sale, post offices displayed a poster featuring the designs, and USPS philatelic publications and mint sets were widely stocked.

The Designs

CSAC solicited designs from two artists, supplying them with the list of breeds and some photo material and ultimately asking them to prepare full paintings for one stamp and pencil idea sketches for the other three stamps.

Artist's final pencil sketch of the Siamese-Exotic Shorthair design that became Stamp No. 1 on the block.

On the basis of these submissions, the job went to John Dawson, 51, a well-known wildlife artist from Hailey, Idaho. It was his first job for USPS. "I had been wanting to do a stamp for a long time," he said.

Dawson, a San Diego native and a graduate of the Art Center College of Design in Los Angeles, and his wife Kathleen moved to Idaho's Wood River Valley in 1977 to escape big-city life. He has done illustrations for *Audubon Magazine, Reader's Digest*, the National Wildlife Federation, the National Park Service, Time-Life Books, Random House — and *National Geographic Magazine*, whose art director, Howard Paine, is a Citizens' Stamp Advisory Committee design coordinator and was art director for the Cat stamp block. Among Dawson's commercial assignments — and proof of his ability to "do" cats

— were a Morris the Cat painting for 9-Lives cat food and the cat that graces the label of Alley Cat cat food.

Dawson originally submitted pencil sketches and color sample roughs showing full-body treatments of the cats. Later, he submitted sketches and roughs of close-ups. The committee had decided that with the Cat stamps, unlike the Dog stamps, it wanted to dispense with pictorial backgrounds, come in closer and tighter on the animals and get more facial expression.

"Dogs give you a better image with the full body," said Jack Williams. "But the committee wanted to show the fineness of the cats' fur and the impressive look of their eyes." The eyes, Don McDowell had specified, should be "big enough so they would be more than one gravure dot wide" — a concern based on long and occasionally disappointing experience with gravure printing.

Artist's rough composition sketch (full-body treatment) showing an American Shorthair (which made it to the finished block of stamps) and an American Wirehair (which didn't).

The acrylic painting of the Abyssinian-Himalayan pair that Dawson had submitted for the competition was used, with a few changes, for the stamp. The artist then proceeded to adapt his sketches of the other three stamps to finished paintings.

His original artwork was fine-tuned by American Bank Note Company on a Scitex computer scanner. One change made at this point was the addition of a dark background that gradually shaded to white from top to bottom. Some of the cats' whiskers were widened by a minute amount to make them more visible. After the changes were made, stamp-sized color photographic prints were sent to Idaho for Dawson to examine and approve.

One alteration that was accomplished by the artist rather than on the scanner, however, was a color change on the Siamese cat. CSAC had specified that the Siamese be a sealpoint. Dawson, however, had made it a bluepoint. This, in combination with the blue of the Siamese's eyes and the blue-gray of the Exotic Shorthair's coat, caused that particular stamp to be "too blue." At the committee's request, Dawson repainted the cat.

Explained Don McDowell: "Rather than just tell the scanner operator to make that cat brown — we weren't sure about the exact color of sealpoint — we decided, let's go back to the painter and let him identify how brown 'brown' is. Let's not sit here and try to make eyeball judgments and do something that looks right to us but will cause a cat fancier to complain.

"It was a quick and easy thing for the artist to do. Once he had done it, it was electronically married up with everything that had been done before and scanned right into the design."

For technical guidance USPS relied on one of its employees, Seymour Lazerowitz of the Market Research Division. Lazerowitz had been president of three Washington-area cat clubs, and was an experienced show judge. He was consulted on all aspects of the cats' appearance — color, attitude, facial characteristics and other details.

For maximum fidelity to the artist's work, the printer used a double-coated, high-bright paper, with extra-fine screening (300 lines per inch). This combination had been used earlier by ABNC and USPS in an attempt to improve the quality of the image on the James Weldon Johnson stamp.

First-Day Facts

The first-day ceremony at the Winter Garden Theatre offered some unusual attrations.

Laurie Beechman, who was currently playing the role of Grizabella in *Cats*, sang without accompaniment the National Anthem and *Memory*, the hit song from the show.

On stage was a live example of each of the eight breeds shown on the stamps. Donald Williams, president of the Cat Fanciers' Association, handled each of the animals and described it to the audience.

Postmaster General Preston R. Tisch, in one of his last official acts before his departure from office, was featured speaker at the first-day ceremony. (Tisch confessed that he didn't own a cat — "yet.")

Also on hand from Idaho to autograph stamps and covers was artist John Dawson. One week later Dawson would perform the same service in a much different setting — a reception at the post office in his hometown of Hailey. Friends and collectors could affix the Cat stamps to an envelope bearing a Dawson-designed cachet — a line drawing of the eight breeds of cat shown on the stamps — and have the stamps canceled with a special "cat's paw," dated February 12, which Dawson had also designed.

USPS honored mail-order requests for first-day covers bearing blocks of four or single stamps. Selection of singles was random, however, and requests for specific designs weren't honored.

22¢ MASSACHUSETTS STATEHOOD

Date of Issue: February 6, 1988

Catalog Numbers: Scott 2341   Minkus CM1307   USPS 4435

Colors: red, blue, black

First-Day Cancel: Boston, Massachusetts (State House, House Chamber)

FDCs Canceled: 412,616

Format: Panes of 50, vertical, 10 across, 5 down. Printing sleeve of 400 subjects (10 across, 40 around).

Perf: 11.1 (Eureka off-line perforator)

Selvage Markings: ©United States Postal Service 1987, Use Correct ZIP Code®

Designer: Richard Sheaff of Needham Heights, Massachusetts (CSAC)

Project Manager: Jack Williams (USPS)

Engravers: Edward Archer (BEP, vignette)
Gary Slaght (BEP, lettering and numerals)

Modeler: Esther Porter (BEP)

Printing: 3-color intaglio unit of the offset/intaglio D press (902)

Quantity Ordered: 156,125,000
Quantity Distributed: 102,100,000

Sleeve Number Detail: One intaglio sleeve number over/under corner stamps

Sleeve Number: 1

Tagging: block over vignette

The Stamp

The sixth stamp in the Statehood Bicentennial series honored Massachusetts and was issued February 6, 200 years to the day after the Bay State's convention ratified the Constitution.

In the creation of that document, Massachusetts had played a strong role.

Three of its four delegates to the Philadelphia convention, Elbridge Gerry, Nathaniel Gorham and Rufus King, were ranked by historian Clinton Rossiter as among the 11 influentials there. King and Gorham were members of the Continental Congress, and Gorham was its past president; at Philadelphia, Gorham had the highly visible role of chairman of the convention when it sat as a committee of the whole.

The most interesting delegate was Gerry, 43, a merchant, shipowner, signer of the Declaration of Independence and Articles of Confederation, and newly married to a beautiful young bride. When the convention threatened to break up over the issue of legislative representation, Gerry chaired the committee assigned to the task of working out a compromise — which turned out to be the compromise that saved the Constitution. He was deeply involved, as well, in dozens of other convention debates and decisions.

But Gerry was, in the words of historian Carl Van Doren, "captious and inconsistent," a man who was "in the habit of opposing any proposal . . . which he had not made himself." In the end Gerry refused to sign the completed Constitution, giving a laundry list of objections.

Fortunately for the federalists, Gerry wasn't a delegate to the state's ratifying convention, which met at the State House in Boston January 9, 1788. That convention found itself sharply divided.

Numerically, the antis had a slight edge, but in debate, the pros had all the heavy artillery, including Gorham, King and Caleb Strong, who had been the fourth Massachusetts delegate to Philadelphia, and ex-Governor James Bowdoin. The respected governor, John Hancock, was won over to the Constitution by King's assurance that if George Washington's Virginia didn't ratify, which was "problematical," then Hancock would be the "only fair candidate for president."

The federalists managed to get the convention moved to a church with room in the gallery for friendly crowds (the Constitution was strongly supported by Boston's artisans and tradespeople, most notably Paul Revere). They also persuaded the delegates to take up the document paragraph by paragraph, giving them a chance to gradually build their case for it.

In the end, John Hancock saved the day by offering a series of amendments — not as conditions, but as earnest proposals to the new government — that were designed to "remove the fears and quiet the apprehensions" of the people. On February 6, ratification was voted by the narrow margin of 187-168.

Ironically, Gerry, the Constitution's great critic, went on to serve in the new government as a member of the House in the first Congress and later as vice president under President James Madison.

Many Massachusetts events have been memorialized on U.S. postage, some of them more than once. These include the landing of the Pilgrims at Plymouth, the establishment of the Massachusetts Bay Colony, the founding of the Boston Latin School, the beginning of American printing at Cambridge, the Boston Tea party, the battles of Lexington, Concord and Bunker Hill, and Bell's invention of the telephone in Boston. The *U.S.S. Constitution* ("Old Ironsides"), docked in Boston Harbor, has been depicted, as have the Charles Bulfinch-designed State House, old North Church ("one if by land . . ."), the Bunker Hill Monument, Henry Hobson Richardson's Trinity Church in Boston and the Walter Gropius House in Lincoln.

Massachusetts-born men and women whose faces have appeared on U.S. stamps include Presidents John Adams, John Quincy Adams and John F. Kennedy and First Lady Abigail Adams; Ben Franklin, who was shown on the very first U.S. stamp and has been a frequent repeat visitor ever since; Samuel Adams, John Hancock, Paul Revere, Isaiah Thomas, Rufus Putnam, John Chapman (Johnny Appleseed), Eli Whitney, Francis Parkman, Henry David Thoreau, Ralph Waldo Emerson, Nathaniel Hawthorne, John Greenleaf Whittier, James Russell Lowell, Adolphus W. Greely, Clara Barton, Lucretia Mott, Lucy Stone, Mary Lyon, Emily Dickinson, Frances Perkins, Paul Dudley White, John Singleton Copley, James A.M. Whistler, Elias Howe, Horace Mann, Mark Hopkins, Charles W. Eliot and Justice Oliver Wendell Holmes.

A future Massachusetts-born stamp subject some day: President George Bush.

The Design

The Massachusetts stamp was designed by a resident, Richard Sheaff of Needham Heights, a design coordinator for CSAC. Sheaff had developed the standard design format used on all 13 Statehood

This essay for the Massachusetts Statehood stamp featured another view of the old State House in Boston.

Bicentennial stamps (see the Georgia Statehood chapter) and had designed several other commemoratives as well.

From the beginning, Sheaff said, he felt that the Commonwealth's first public building — the old State House, where the ratifying convention first met — was the right subject for the Massachusetts stamp.

As art director, he commissioned a Boston artist to prepare a treatment of the building as it looks today, in a style Sheaff described as "hard-edge simplified," with the tall modern buildings that surround it suggested by planes of color. But he also prepared some other sketches using 18th-century period engravings.

Sheaff and CSAC finally settled on an engraving titled *A Southwest View of the State House, in Boston*, attributed to "S. Hill," that first appeared in the *Massachusetts Magazine* of 1793. Originals of the engraving, and research on the design subject, were provided by The Society for the Preservation of New England Antiquities and by The Bostonian Society.

This modern treatment of the old State House, with planes of color suggesting the tall buildings that now surround it, was commissioned by Richard Sheaff but not used.

The main design is dominated by the three-tiered spire of the Old State House, as viewed from an angle at one end of the structure. The adjacent streets are busy with carriages, men on horseback and persons chatting.

A comparison of the stamp with the original shows that the BEP's engraver, Edward Archer, removed a seated woman and standing child by the State House door, a woman leading a horse in the foreground and several carriages behind the building. "The Bureau was given leeway to leave out clutter that wouldn't reproduce well and would work against it being a clean design," Sheaff said.

The Old State House originally was a wooden building erected in 1658 to serve as Boston's Town House or town hall. It burned in 1711, and its brick replacement was gutted by fire in 1747. The rebuilt building, shown on the stamp, now 239 years old, served variously as Massachusetts' seat of government, county courthouse and merchants' exchange.

It was the site of the Boston Massacre in March 1770, when British soldiers fired into a mob and killed five persons, causing troops quartered in the city to be removed and fueling the campaign for independence. Six years later, from its steps, the Declaration of Independence was first read to the people of Boston.

The Massachusetts stamp was the only one of the 11 Statehood Bicentennial stamps issued through 1988 to be printed by intaglio only. It was produced on BEP's D press, which has a multicolor offset capability, but that feature wasn't used. Instead, the shading effects, cloud texture and other refinements were provided by Archer's finely detailed intaglio work, reproduced in blue in the stamp's vignette.

BEP had actually tested the effect of adding tints of offset color behind the engraving, Sheaff said, "but basically, time ran out before they could get it right, and we all said, 'look, they haven't solved the problem aesthetically, let's just run it as it was designed to be in the first place — a straight engraved piece.'

"There are always those who feel — who 'know,' in fact — that the world prefers multicolored stamps. So the urge was there to 'colorize' it, if you will. It fell flat, and I was delighted that it came out a straight engraving," Sheaff said.

First-Day Facts

The first-day ceremony took place at the House chamber of the present State House on Beacon Hill. It had originally been announced for Boston's historic Fanueil Hall.

Thomas J. Berry, a native Bostonian who was executive assistant to Postmaster General Preston R. Tisch, was the principal speaker. In the absence of Governor Michael Dukakis, who was off preparing for the Iowa Democratic presidential caucuses that were two days away, House Speaker George Cevarian represented the Commonwealth.

Berry, in his speech, noted the large number of Massachusetts natives who had been honored on stamps, and added that the Statehood stamp indirectly saluted four persons who had never been so depicted — the state's delegation to the Constitutional Convention. "Perhaps no other state delegation proved to be possessed of such overall high quality," he said.

Berry added that sending the first souvenir album to President Ronald Reagan, as was traditional, was especially appropriate because the date, February 6, was the president's birthday.

22¢ MARYLAND STATEHOOD

Date of Issue: February 15, 1988

Catalog Numbers: Scott 2342   Minkus CM1308   USPS 4439

Colors: red, yellow, blue, green, gray (offset); red, black (intaglio)

First-Day Cancel: Annapolis, Maryland (St. John's College)

FDCs Canceled: 376,403

Format: Panes of 50, vertical, 10 across, 5 down. Offset printing plates of 200 subjects (10 across, 20 around); intaglio printing sleeve of 400 subjects (10 across, 40 around).

Perf: 11.1 (Eureka off-line perforator)

Selvage Markings: ©United States Postal Service 1987, Use Correct ZIP Code®

Designer: Stephen Hustvedt of Annapolis, Maryland

Art Director: Derry Noyes (CSAC)

Project Manager: Jack Williams (USPS)

Typographer: Bradbury Thompson (CSAC)

Engravers: Joseph Creamer (BEP, vignette)
Dennis Brown (BEP, lettering and numerals)

Modeler: Esther Porter (BEP)

Printing: 6-color offset, 3-color intaglio D press (902)

Quantity Ordered: 103,800,000
Quantity Distributed: 103,325,000

Plate/Sleeve Number Detail: Left-side panes: one group of 5 offset plate numbers over/under corner stamps; one intaglio sleeve number over/under adjacent stamps. Right-side panes: offset/intaglio numbers in reverse positions.

Plate/Sleeve Number Combination: 11111-1, 11211-1

Tagging: block over vignette

The Stamp

Maryland, the seventh state to ratify the Constitution, was honored on the seventh stamp of the Statehood series celebrating the bicentennials of the original 13 states of the Union. The 22¢ commemorative was issued in Annapolis, the state capital, February 15.

At the Constitutional Convention, Maryland's small delegation played a mixed role.

On the one hand, in Luther Martin, state attorney general, it provided one of the most vigorous and colorful critics of the convention's entire thrust toward a strong central government. Martin wasted no time attacking the Virginia plan, which called for just such a government, and one that the larger states would dominate.

Martin was "so extremely prolix," in the view of Georgia's William Pierce, "that he never speaks without tiring the patience of all who hear him."

In the end, a disgusted Martin left town before the convention ended. But other Maryland delegates, James McHenry, Dan of St. Thomas Jenifer and Daniel Carroll, signed the Constitution and campaigned strongly for it back home when Maryland elected its convention to consider the ratification question.

That election settled the issue. The voters were enthusiastically pro-Constitution, particularly the shipbuilders, merchants, mechanics and sailors of Baltimore, who believed the new general government, by encouraging commerce, would make them prosperous.

They chose delegates who met April 21 at the State House and took just five days to ratify, 63-11. The supporters signed the instrument of ratification April 28, 1788.

Maryland events and institutions that have been postally commemorated include the establishment of the colony in 1634, the founding of Annapolis; the U.S. Naval Academy, in that city; the establishment of the District of Columbia on land ceded to the federal government by Maryland; Latrobe's Baltimore Cathedral; the granting of a charter to the Baltimore and Ohio Railroad by the Maryland Legislature, and the first telegraph message, sent from Washington to Baltimore.

Marylanders whose portraits or works have been shown on U.S. stamps and postal cards have included founding fathers Charles Carroll and John Hanson; Robert Morris, the "financier of the Revolution"; Stephen Decatur and Winfield Scott Schley, naval officers; writer Edgar Allan Poe; environmentalist Rachel Carson; painter Charles Willson Peale; architect Benjamin Henry Latrobe; Montgomery Blair, Lincoln's postmaster general, and Benjamin Banneker, astronomer and mathematician. Francis Scott Key, who wrote the words to *The Star Spangled Banner* while watching the British bombardment of Fort McHenry in Baltimore Harbor, has been honored by two stamps. (The Fort McHenry flag also has been depicted.)

The Design

In size and format the Maryland stamp resembles the others in the Statehood Bicentennial series.

The central vignette is a watercolor painting by Stephen Hustvedt of Annapolis — his first assignment for USPS — and shows a view of Annapolis from across the city harbor on the Severn River. In the foreground, sailing on the water, is a skipjack sailboat, No. 48. Ashore in the background is the dome of the historic Maryland State House on the right and St. Anne's Church on the left.

For a long time, an Alexandria, Virginia, historian named Frederick Tilp had been urging USPS to issue a stamp depicting a skipjack, a type of ship that has been carrying oystermen on Chesapeake Bay for a century. A low, shallow-draft wooden vessel with a V-shaped hull, ranging in length from 30 to 45 feet, it has a single tall mast, two sails and a large, tapered spar extending forward from the bow. The Citizens' Stamp Advisory Committee agreed with Tilp that the skipjack was potentially a good stamp subject, possibly for a Transportation coil.

Stephen Hustvedt, 62, a specialist in marine art, heard of CSAC's interest and submitted some skipjack stamp designs. These were filed away for future reference by Jack Williams, USPS program manager for stamp design. In 1987, when CSAC took up the matter of a Maryland commemorative, someone suggested that a skipjack be depicted — possibly with the mighty Chesapeake Bay Bridge in the background — and Williams invited Hustvedt to try his hand at some sketches.

Hustvedt's reaction: "Lo and behold, there are still some government agencies whose files still work."

He developed several sketches containing skipjacks, including variations on the Annapolis waterfront or the bay's Thomas Point Lighthouse. The committee chose the one that became the stamp.

Hustvedt received a design fee of $3,000. He said he got so much satisfaction from the assignment that he offered another stamp idea to USPS — a se-tenant block or pane depicting fireplugs, painted in the decorative patterns that some communities display. (This proposal was duly filed away, for possible future consideration, by CSAC.)

The Maryland stamp, like the Connecticut and Massachusetts stamps just before it, was printed on BEP's offset/intaglio D press and perforated on the Eureka off-line perforator.

Intaglio was used for the lettering and numerals and the design details: the sailboat, including the shading on the sail; waves on the river, and the dome, spire and roofs of the buildings onshore. The dome and spire are printed over appropriately shaped white cutouts in the offset blue of the sky. However, when a sheet is slightly out of register, the white cutout moves away from the engraving, detracting from the effectiveness of the design.

USPS and BEP officials, after looking at trial press impressions of the stamp, made a decision to enhance the yellow offset color by increasing the size and number of the tiny printing dots. "We concluded that we could bring out the detail, the crispness overall, by kicking the yellow 15 percent," said Don McDowell, Stamps Division manager. "But you can't kick it selectively. You boost the yellow, you boost the yellow.

"So we made a tradeoff. We decided that we would let the sail on the skipjack go a little bit yellower than it was designed to be. Our consensus was that the detail in the town would really snap, crackle and pop if we strengthened the yellow."

The two buildings featured in the stamp design are links to Maryland's early history. St. Anne's Church was founded in 1692 as a state church and originally was supported by taxes. The building that is shown was built in 1859 and is the third on the same site. The State House, also the third on its site, was built in 1772 and is the oldest state capitol in the United States still in legislative use.

The skipjack shown on the stamp, No. 48, is the *Clarence Crockett,* a 45-footer built in 1908 and still in use at the time the stamp was issued. The *Crockett* made the news in two different ways after the stamp's design was unveiled late in December.

The first splash came when Frederick Tilp — prime promoter of a skipjack stamp — was quoted in Virginia newspapers as saying USPS had made what he termed a "boo-boo" because the *Crockett* had been built not in Maryland, but in Deep Creek, Virginia. If a Maryland-built boat had been shown on a Virginia stamp, Tilp asserted, "there would be another Civil War."

Postal officials took the criticism in stride; after all, they had heard similar complaining over the appropriateness of the ship they had shown on the previous Statehood stamp, for Connecticut. Dickey Rustin, manager of USPS's Stamp Information Branch, said the skipjack on the stamp represented the Maryland oyster industry, regardless of where it happened to be built.

Much more serious was the disaster that befell the *Clarence Crockett* barely a month after the stamp was issued. The *Crockett,* on its way home from oystering in the upper Chesapeake March 17, hit a channel marker in Tangier Sound and sank.

The ship's owner, Paul Holland, 40, and his two crew members clung to a line marker for 14 hours in 20-degree weather before they were rescued by a uniformed official of the state's Department of Natural Resources. The Deal Island watermen saved themselves by talking to keep each other awake so that no one would fall from his two-inch-wide ledge into the icy water.

On April 1 it was reported that the *Crockett* had been partially lifted with air bags and floated back to port for repairs. It ran briefly aground on a sandbar en route.

First-Day Facts

USPS originally announced the first-day date as February 6 and later revised it to February 15.

The stamp was available for sale during the day of issue at the Maryland State House. The by-invitation-only dedication ceremony was held at 8 o'clock that evening during a joint session of the General Assembly. Governor William D. Schaefer and U.S. Senator Paul Sarbanes were among those on hand to hear Senior Assistant Postmaster General Mitchell H. Gordon deliver the principal address.

Mitchell, a Bethesda, Maryland, resident who grew up in Prince Georges County, used the occasion to gently lobby the legislators to "help finance the cleanup of Chesapeake Bay and get my beloved stripers back."

22¢ KNUTE ROCKNE

Date of Issue: March 9, 1988

Catalog Numbers: Scott 2376   Minkus CM1309   USPS 4440

Colors: cyan, tan, brown, yellow, green, gold (offset); brown, blue (intaglio)

First-Day Cancel: Notre Dame, Indiana (University of Notre Dame)

FDCs Canceled: 404,311

Format: Panes of 50, vertical, 10 across, 5 down. Offset printing plates of 200 subjects (10 across, 20 around); intaglio printing sleeve of 400 subjects (10 across, 40 around).

Perf: 11.1 (Eureka off-line perforator)

Selvage Markings: ©United States Postal Service 1988, Use Correct ZIP Code®

Designers: Peter Cocci and Thomas Hipschen (BEP)

Art Director: Jack Williams (USPS)

Engravers: Thomas Hipschen (BEP, vignette)
Gary Slaght (BEP, lettering and numerals)

Modeler: Peter Cocci (BEP)

Printing: 6-color offset, 3-color intaglio D press (902)

Quantity Ordered: 97,300,000
Quantity Distributed: 97,300,000

Plate/Sleeve Number Detail: Left-side panes: one group of 6 offset plate numbers over/under corner stamps; one intaglio sleeve number over/under adjacent stamps. Right-side panes: offset/intaglio numbers in reverse positions.

Plate/Sleeve Number Combination: 111111-1

Tagging: block over vignette

Printing Base Impressions: Offset Cyan: 1(589,500)
Offset Tan: 1(589,500)
Offset Brown: 1(589,500)
Offset Yellow: 1(589,500)
Offset Green: 1(589,500)
Offset Gold: 1(589,500)

The Stamp

Presidents seldom attend first-day ceremonies for postage stamps, but this one was a natural. The stamp marked the 100th anniversary of the birth of a legendary football coach with a muscular name — Knute Rockne. The site was the field house of Notre Dame University in Notre Dame, Indiana, where Rockne built his powerful teams of the 1920s. And the president was the man who, as a film actor in 1940, played the part of Notre Dame football player George Gipp in a movie about Rockne. Gipp's dying plea to his coach (played by Pat O'Brien) to tell some future team to "win just one for the Gipper" is one of Hollywood's most famous lines.

So it was virtually a sure bet that Ronald Reagan would be on hand for the Rockne stamp first-day ceremonies. In fact, the first-day ceremony at the Joyce Athletic and Convocation Center was moved from

Ronald Reagan played George Gipp and Pat O'Brien was Rockne in the 1940 Warner Brothers film **Knute Rockne, All American.**

March 4 (Rockne's birthday), the original announced date, to March 9 to accommodate the president's schedule.

The 22¢ Rockne commemorative was announced by USPS July 20, 1987, as part of the 1988 stamp program. Details, along with the revised issue date, were supplied February 9, 1988.

The stamp was the sixth in the American Sports series (Babe Zaharias, Bobby Jones, Babe Ruth, Jim Thorpe and Roberto Clemente had been honored earlier) and was the third U.S. commemorative to be directly related to the game of football. The first was a 1969 6¢ marking the centenary of the first intercollegiate football game, between Princeton and Rutgers. The second was the 1984 20¢ Sports series stamp depicting Jim Thorpe of Carlisle Indian School and early professional teams, who is considered by many to have been the finest all-around player in the game's history.

Several other persons shown on stamps have had a football connection, however. President Theodore Roosevelt personally intervened in 1905 to force college officials to change the rules of the game to reduce the high number of deaths and serious injuries it was producing. President Woodrow Wilson, as a young professor in the 1880s, coached the Wesleyan University team in Middletown, Connecticut. President John F. Kennedy's much publicized games of touch football at the family home in Hyannisport did much to popularize that gentler version of the game. And Jackie Robinson, postally honored in 1982 as the man who broke organized baseball's color line, had also excelled in football at UCLA and first broke into professional sports as a football player in Hawaii.

The Rockne stamp was on sale for 25 days until the first-class letter rate increased to 25¢, making it necessary to add 3¢ postage to the envelope in order to use the stamp.

A news story in *The Washington Post* on the eve of the stamp's issuance implied that the commemorative had been ordered by President Reagan himself after a Notre Dame alumnus had written to him urging " 'the Gipper' to win one for Rockne." However, USPS denied that the White House was involved in any way in the selection of this stamp subject.

Who first proposed it? USPS declines to say, as it customarily does with such questions. CSAC often receives similar stamp suggestions from many different people over a long period of time, and USPS officials say it would be difficult, and perhaps unfair, to try to single out any one person for credit.

Knute Kenneth Rockne was born in Voss, Norway, in 1888 and came to America with his parents at the age of 5. After attending high school, he worked four years as a mail dispatcher at the Chicago Post Office, where he earned enough to enroll at Notre Dame, a small, relatively unknown Catholic institution. Here he went out for football.

The game was evolving from a sport of brute force to one of speed, agility and teamwork, thanks to several rules changes, including one revolutionary addition — the forward pass. In 1913, in a game at West Point, right end Rockne and quarterback Gus Dorais staged a dazzling exhibition of this weapon and led their team to a 35-13 upset of mighty Army. In one afternoon Notre Dame had been put on the national football map to stay.

Rockne followed his playing days with a 13-year career as head coach that spanned the "golden era" of sports in the 1920s. His colorful personality and style of play captured the public's attention, but most impressive was his record of success.

With such players as George Gipp and the 1924 backfield known as the "Four Horsemen," his Irish teams recorded five unbeaten and untied seasons and won the 1925 Rose Bowl game. He won the last 19 games he coached, bringing his winning percentage to .881 (105-12-5), the best in history for a coach in either college or professional football. An innovator, he developed the Notre Dame backfield shift, and was the first to substitute entire teams (which he called "shock troops") during a game, a forerunner of modern platooning.

Among Rockne's assets was a gift for inspirational rhetoric and a keen sense of psychology. He wasn't above bending the truth if he deemed it necessary. Once he told his players that his son, Jackie, was desperately ill and needed a Notre Dame victory, although the son was perfectly healthy at the time. The fired-up team won the game.

Even the great George Gipp deathbed story is suspect. In 1928 Notre Dame was locked in a 0-0 tie with Army at halftime, and Rockne told his team how Gipp, dying of pneumonia eight years earlier, had left with him a plea to some future Irish team to "win just

The Knute Rockne stamp was reproduced in color on tickets for Notre Dame's 1988 home football games.

one for the Gipper." Notre Dame went out, fell behind 6-0, then rallied to win 12-6, holding the cadets at bay on the one-yard line when time ran out. Unfortunately, no one besides Rockne had heard Gipp's deathbed message — and Rockne had had several chances before 1928 to use it to good effect, but had not done so.

"It's one of those things you just hope really happened," a Knute Rockne biographer said.

Rockne's career ended tragically with his death March 31, 1931, in a plane crash in Kansas. Twenty years later, when the National Football Foundation selected its first inductees for its College Football Hall of Fame, Rockne was one of them.

The Design

Notre Dame University supplied USPS with several photographs of Rockne. One, showing the coach in a business hat, had later been used as the basis for a painting that was hanging in the athletic offices. Another showed him in sweatshirt. These were worked up into some vertical sketches for CSAC to examine.

The committee members were unenthusiastic. To some of them, the portrait with the hat looked disconcertingly like Al Capone. Also, the sketches that used that portrait had no quickly recognizable association with football. The stamp design with the sweatshirt portrait did have a gridiron and goalposts, but the committee didn't like the portrait itself.

At this point, the committee decided to turn the project over to the Bureau of Engraving and Printing to see what its designers could come up with, using the electronic Design Center. "The Postal Service didn't know what was going to be the result, and to some degree neither did we," recalled Leonard Buckley, BEP foreman of designers.

Using yet another photo supplied by Notre Dame, a candid picture of a smiling Rockne standing on a practice field holding a football in both hands, BEP designer Peter Cocci and engraver Thomas Hipschen worked together to develop an image that could be printed in combination offset/intaglio on the D press.

Some CSAC members thought this picture of a hat-wearing Rockne looked too much like Al Capone.

An obvious problem with this proposed design was that it contained no reference to football.

The elements of the design, the Rockne photo and the lettering, were electronically scanned and input to the Design Center's computer memory. Cocci, using the design work station with its color video monitor, manipulated the elements and their colors to prepare a concept sketch featuring the Rockne photo in the stamp format. From this reference, Hipschen hand-engraved the portrait image, which was then scanned. With this image, Cocci composed the final lettering and worked out the coloration on the monitor.

What resulted was a waist-up portrait of Rockne, in gray sweatshirt, with face and hands in fleshtone, standing on a green football gridiron with goal posts in the distance against a dark green background. The inscription "22 USA" appears in the upper left. Across the bottom are the words "KNUTE ROCKNE" in blue above a metallic gold bar. The lettering and numerals are in a block style similar to that used on athletic jerseys.

The gold bar — which with the blue of the lettering represents Notre Dame's school colors — was a late addition. A decision to change the lettering style opened up some space at the bottom of the stamp into which the bar could be inserted as a strong base for the design. It was printed over a process-yellow offset base to strengthen the effect of the metallic ink.

Because the stamp was designed electronically, there was no painting that could be blown up to poster size and used in the first-day ceremony. For this purpose the Postal Service had to order a painting made from the stamp itself — an unusual reversal of sequence.

In the fall of 1988, the design of the Rockne stamp, in full color, was

CSAC didn't find this portrait of Rockne satisfactory.

reproduced on tickets for all of Notre Dame's home football games. The idea was that of Mike Bobinski, associate business manager of Notre Dame's athletic department. Each year, he said, the department tries to use its tickets to mark a university-related anniversary or special event.

First-Day Facts

The first-day program was President Reagan's second. He had previously taken part in a closed ceremony for the Hispanic Americans stamp on October 31, 1984, a few days before his re-election to a second term.

The president told his audience of some 10,000:

"I know that to many of you today, Rockne is a revered name, a symbol of greatness and, yes, a face on a postage stamp. But my generation, well, we actually knew the legend as it happened — we saw it unfold. And we felt it was saying something important about us as a people and a nation."

The legend, he said, "stood for fair play and honor, but you know, it was thoroughly American in another way. It was practical; it placed a value on devastating quickness and agility and on confounding the opposition with good old American cleverness. But most of all, the Rockne legend meant this . . . that on or off the field, it is faith that makes the difference, it is faith that makes great things happen."

The president reminisced about how he had battled to win the role of Gipp, "a young actor's dream," in the film, *Knute Rockne, All American*. A Warner Brothers executive had said he was too skinny, but he got the part with the help of Pat O'Brien and with photographs of himself as a Eureka College football player.

He concluded by advising the students, in a recital of the familiar lines from the film, to take a cue from the Gipper "when all of those around you are ready to give up."

"Some time when the team is up against it and the breaks are beating the boys, tell them to go out there with all they've got and win just one for the Gipper."

"I don't know where I'll be then, but I'll know about it and I'll be happy."

Reagan then unveiled a replica of the new stamp. The ceremony ended when he was given a plaque bearing the words of the school song, *Notre Dame, Our Mother*. He sang along softly as the song echoed through the fieldhouse.

The original USPS announcement had specified South Bend, Indiana, as the first-day city. South Bend is the customary dateline for newspaper reports of Notre Dame football games. The announcement was later corrected after postal officials realized that Notre Dame was an independent post office and not a South Bend branch.

The authorized first-day cancellation featured a stylized football and the words "FIRST/DAY OF/ISSUE" between two horizontal bars. However, a number of first-day covers received machine-applied cancellations with a standard first-day design (four killer bars with "First Day of Issue" in the center) instead. Although the standard cancellations were applied in error, USPS said on July 21 that it would make them available to all customers wanting them. Collectors were instructed to send their payment or prestamped envelopes to the Philatelic Sales Division in Washington for this purpose.

Rockne's birthplace, Voss, Norway, also marked his centennial with a special March 4-5 postmark containing his portrait.

25¢ SOUTH CAROLINA STATEHOOD

Date of Issue: May 23, 1988

Catalog Numbers: Scott 2343   Minkus CM1310   USPS 4436

Colors: red, gray, yellow, green, black

First-Day Cancel: Columbia, South Carolina (State House)

FDCs Canceled: 322,938

Format: Panes of 50, vertical, 10 across, 5 down. Gravure printing cylinders of 200 subjects (10 across, 20 around) manufactured by Roto Cylinder (Palmyra, New Jersey)

Perf: 10.9 (L perforator)

Selvage Markings: ©United States Postal Service 1988, Use Correct ZIP Code®

Designer: Bob Timberlake of Lexington, North Carolina

Art Director: Derry Noyes (CSAC)

Project Manager: Jack Williams (USPS)

Typographer: Bradbury Thompson (CSAC)

Modeler: Richard Sennett (Sennett Enterprises) for American Bank Note Company.

Printing: Stamps printed and sheeted out by American Bank Note Company on a leased gravure press (J.W. Fergusson and Sons, Richmond, Virginia) under the supervision of Sennett Enterprises (Fairfax, Virginia). Perforated, processed and shipped by ABNC (Chicago, Illinois).

Quantity Ordered: 162,045,000
Quantity Distributed: 162,045,000

Cylinder Number Detail: One group of 5 cylinder numbers preceded by the letter "A" over/under corner stamps.

Cylinder Number Combination: A11111

Tagging: block over vignette

Printing Base Impressions: A11111 (895,468)

The Stamp

The first commemorative stamp to bear the new 25¢ first-class rate honored South Carolina on the 200th anniversary of its ratification of the Constitution. It was the eighth in the series marking the statehood of the original 13 states, and was issued in Columbia, the capital, on the exact anniversary date: May 23, 1988

Like most of the other 1988 stamps printed by the gravure process, this one was produced by the American Bank Note Company.

South Carolina sent a strong delegation to the Constitutional Convention in 1787. The members were John Rutledge, the state's Revolutionary War governor and member of the Continental Congress; Charles Pinckney, not yet 30, from New York, who had also served in Congress; his cousin, Charles Cotesworth Pinckney, British-educated and a brigadier general by brevet in the Continental Army, and Pierce Butler, an ex-British Army major.

The foursome vigorously defended the slave trade, which they said was essential to their state's economy. However, they acceded to the compromise that prohibited the trade after 1808.

All four signed the Constitution and afterward strongly defended it during debate in the state legislature. Leading the opposition there was Rawlins Lowndes, former president of the state, who represented the anti-federalist "upcountry" against the pro-Constitution "low country" representatives. Lowndes belittled the Constitution as "an experiment" and defended the Articles of Confederation as having "stood the test of time."

Pondering the conflicting arguments, the legislature called a convention, which met in the Hall of the Exchange in Charleston May 12. Here Charles Pinckney ably argued the merits of the Constitution. On May 21 General Thomas Sumter moved unsuccessfully to adjourn until October. Two days later the convention voted 149-73 to ratify. The action brought the number of states endorsing the Constitution to eight — one short of the total needed to bring it to life.

South Carolina events and subjects that have been postally commemorated include the first permanent settlement at Albemarle Point in 1670; the colonists' move to the site of Charleston in 1680; Lafayette's landing at Charleston in 1777; the Revolutionary War campaigns of General Francis "Swamp Fox" Marion, and the important battles of Kings Mountain (on the North Carolina border), Cowpens and Eutaw Springs; the locomotive *Best Friend of Charleston*, which in 1830 provided the country's first scheduled train service, and the firing on Fort Sumter by South Carolina troops in 1861, precipitating the Civil War.

Mary McLeod Bethune, a native South Carolinian, was pictured on a Black Heritage stamp. And a scene from George Gershwin's opera *Porgy and Bess*, which was set on Charleston's Catfish Row, was shown on a 1973 stamp honoring the New York-born composer.

Interestingly, one of South Carolina's most famous historical figures, Vice President and later Senator John C. Calhoun, has never been postally honored. Calhoun was a strong pro-slavery state's-rights advocate in the bitter decades leading up to the Civil War. (He was depicted on a 1¢ stamp of the Confederacy, although the stamp was never officially issued by the Confederate government.)

The Design

Among the design sketches that CSAC considered were some views of the state capitol at Columbia flanked by palmettos, the state tree. In the end, the committee opted for a painting of three palmettos standing alone, done by Bob Timberlake of Lexington, North Carolina.

Timberlake, a self-taught realist painter, had previously designed the 1980 Christmas stamp picturing toys in a window. As official artist of Keep America Beautiful, he also provided the painting used on that organization's National Enviromental stamp in 1982.

The artist had spent part of his boyhood in Myrtle Beach, South Carolina, and had hunted and fished the length of the South Carolina coast. For the South Carolina stamp, he submitted three different studies — actually, finished paintings in watercolor and gouache — to CSAC. One showed an arrangement of jasmine, the state flower. Another depicted a live oak tree; Timberlake was unaware that Greg Harlin had also painted a live oak for the Georgia Bicentennial stamp.

But the artist's own "first, best and only" choice, as he put it, was the painting of the three palmettos against a gray coastal sky, with sea oats waving in the foreground. The committee quickly agreed that this was the design to use.

"The palmetto is recognizably South Carolina," Timberlake explained. "It's probably the first thing the settlers saw. It's the state tree, with a lot of state history and folklore associated with it."

Timberlake's painting wasn't done from life, but from his own lifelong familiarity with the palmetto (*Sabal palmetto*), a fan-leaved palm tree that grows in low regions throughout the Southeast. The most common variety is called the cabbage palm. Some may reach 50 feet or more in height.

Two other state trees had been featured on recent Statehood Anniversary stamps: the live oak on the Georgia stamp, and the white pine on the Michigan Sesquicentennial commemorative of 1987.

In the Battle of Sullivan's Island in 1776, during the Revolutionary War, South Carolina forces fought the attacking British from a fort made of palmetto logs, which were ideal for the purpose because their soft wood absorbed shot without splintering or shattering.

The South Carolinians won, and the palmetto became the symbol of this victory. The following year the state incorporated the tree in the design of its flag. The palmetto also appears in the state seal, towering over an uprooted oak tree, which symbolizes the oaken ships of the British.

The palmetto, as part of the flag design, had been shown on stamps twice before: on the South Carolina stamp in the 50 State Flag pane of 1976, and on the 1970 6¢ marking the 300th anniversary of the Albemarle Point settlement. In addition, palmettos appear on the 2¢ stamp of 1930 that commemorated the 250th anniversary of the colonists' move to Charleston.

First-Day Facts

The first-day ceremony for the stamp was held in the House of Representatives chamber of the South Carolina capitol. Governor Carroll Campbell and Johnny Thomas, Eastern regional postmaster general, were the principal speakers. Designer Bob Timberlake was on hand to sign autographs.

As happened with the Knute Rockne stamp, a number of first-day covers bearing the South Carolina stamp received machine-applied cancellations with a standard first-day design (four killer bars with "First Day of Issue" in the center) instead of the authorized pictorial postmark. Although these were applied in error, USPS announced July 21 that it would make the standard cancellations available through the Philatelic Sales Division in Washington.

25¢ FRANCIS OUIMET

Date of Issue: June 13, 1988

Catalog Numbers: Scott 2377   Minkus CM1311   USPS 4444

Colors: magenta, yellow, cyan, black, black line

First-Day Cancel: Brookline, Massachusetts (Country Club)

FDCs Canceled: 383,168

Format: Panes of 50, vertical, 10 across, 5 down. Gravure printing cylinders of 200 subjects (10 across, 20 around) manufactured by Roto Cylinder (Palmyra, New Jersey).

Perf: 10.9 (L perforator)

Selvage Markings: ©United States Postal Service 1988, Use Correct ZIP Code®

Designer: M. Gregory Rudd of Trumbull, Connecticut

Art Director: Jack Williams (USPS)

Typographer: Bradbury Thompson (CSAC)

Modeler: Richard Sennett (Sennett Enterprises) for American Bank Note Company

Printing: Stamps printed and sheeted out by American Bank Note Company on a leased gravure press (J.W. Fergusson and Sons, Richmond, Virginia) under the supervision of Sennett Enterprises (Fairfax, Virginia). Perforated, processed and shipped by ABNC (Chicago, Illinois).

Quantity Ordered: 153,045,000
Quantity Distributed: 153,045,000

Cylinder Number Detail: One group of 5 cylinder numbers preceded by the letter "A" over/under corner stamps

Cylinder Number Combination: A11111

Tagging: block over vignette

Printing Base Impressions: A11111 (869,138)

The Stamp

As sportswriter Red Smith told it, one day in 1912 Theophilus England Niles, managing editor of *The New York Evening Mail*, called assistant sports editor Francis Albertani into his office and asked why golf got no space in *The Mail*.

"It's an important game," Niles said, "very popular with the Wall Street crowd."

"Then put it on the financial page," Albertani said.

A year later, a 20-year-old American named Francis Ouimet amazed and excited Americans by beating two veteran English professionals, Harry Vardon and Ted Ray, for the United States Open Championship at The Country Club in Brookline, Massachusetts. That victory by a "common man" over two of the world's greatest players changed forever Americans' perception of the game as a pastime for the privileged.

Within a few years, wrote Red Smith, Ouimet, along with two other young men named Walter Hagen and Bobby Jones, "would put golf in headlines even on the sports pages of *The Evening Mail*."

On June 13, 1988, at The Country Club, where the U.S. Open had returned in the 75th anniversary year of the great upset of 1913, USPS issued a 25¢ stamp in its American Sports series to honor Francis DeSales Ouimet.

It was the seventh stamp in the Sports series, and the second of 1988. In March a 22¢ stamp had depicted Notre Dame football coach Knute Rockne.

In the design, Ouimet is identified as "US Open Champion, 1913." This addition of a descriptive phrase — the first time it was done on a Sports series stamp — was an acknowledgement that Ouimet, despite the key role he played in popularizing golf, is a relatively unfamiliar figure to modern-day Americans.

The stamp had been requested by the Francis D. Ouimet Caddie Scholarship Fund. The Fund credited the success of its three-year effort to the persistence of its commemorative committee chairman, Robert M. Jenney.

Jenney obtained the help of the seven living charter members of the World Golf Hall of Fame: Patty Berg, Ben Hogan, Byron Nelson, Jack Nicklaus, Arnold Palmer, Gene Sarazen and Sam Snead. They signed a petition for the stamp, which was forwarded to the postmaster general by former President Gerald Ford — an enthusiastic, if sometimes erratic, golfer himself — along with Ford's own letter of support. Former House Speaker "Tip" O'Neill also lent his influence, as did Representative William D. Ford of Michigan, who as chairman of the House Post Office and Civil Service Committee was able to get USPS' attention when he cleared his throat.

Gene Sarazen, for one, credits Ouimet's 1913 Open victory for inspiring his own great career. "I was then only a boy of 13, and I was

Young Francis Ouimet as he appeared when he won the 1913 U.S. Open.

caddying," he wrote. "I remember hearing about Ouimet and deciding right then and there to follow in his footsteps." Sarazen had plenty of company. In 1913 fewer than 350,000 Americans played golf; 10 years later, two million were playing — and the game has continued to grow in popularity ever since.

Francis Ouimet (pronounced "WE-met"), son of a French-Canadian immigrant gardener, was born May 8, 1893, in Brookline, and lived across the street from the old 17th green of The Country Club. His interest in the game was piqued by the stray balls found as he crossed the fairways on the way to school.

Ouimet won scholastic and amateur tournaments as a teenager and entered the U.S. Open in 1913, the year it came to his home course. A slightly gawky young man who played in a white shirt with four-in-

69

hand tie, a checkered cap, rumpled jacket and unpressed trousers, he attracted no attention when he teed off for the first of two days of qualifying play.

The large field was divided for this purpose, and Vardon and Ray each led his division, as expected. But Ouimet finished only one stroke behind Vardon. The tournament proper consisted of 72 additonal holes, 36 each day. After 54 holes in intermittent rain, Vardon and Ray were tied at 225 — but with them, at the same score, was the young man from across the road.

At the end of the final round the two Englishmen were still tied, at 304. Ouimet had run into trouble early, and after 12 holes was 10 over par. But he got the two birdies he needed on the last six to score his own 304 and elbow his way into the next day's playoff.

It was chilly and drizzling at 10 a.m. when the threesome left the first tee. Each man shot 38 for the first nine. The break came on the 10th, when Ouimet took a one-stroke lead. On the twelfth, he doubled it. Vardon won back a stroke on 13, but on 15 Ray's double-bogey six left him three shots behind, and Ray fell back another stroke on 16.

On 17 it was Vardon's turn to falter. He drove into a fairway trap (it's still known as the "Vardon bunker"), took two more shots to the green and two-putted. But on the 18th green Ouimet sank a short putt for a 72 and the victory, five strokes under Vardon, six under Ray. The game's leading historian, Herbert Warren Wind, would later describe that playoff, September 20, 1913, as "the most important round of golf ever played."

The Country Club granted its former caddy "the privilege of the golf course without dues for a year," and the waiver was renewed annually until he was elevated to formal membership. Ouimet never won the Open again, but he did win the U.S. Amateur title in 1914 and again 17 years later, when he was thought to be past his prime.

In 1963, in the 50th anniversary year of Ouimet's Open victory, the Open was again held at Brookline — just as it would be in the 75th anniversary year of 1988. Ouimet, then 70, was honorary chairman. He died four years later of a heart attack on September 2, 1967.

His name is perpetuated in the Ouimet Caddie Scholarship Fund, founded in 1949. Golfers all over Massachusetts buy and display annual bag tags, with all proceeds going to the fund. In its 39 years of existence, the fund has granted more than 7,800 college scholarships, amounting to $4.7 million, to hundreds of high school graduates.

The Ouimet stamp was the fourth golf item issued by USPS. A stamped envelope in 1977 commemorated the game itself, and the first two stamps in the American Sports series, in 1981, honored golf stars Babe Zaharias and Bobby Jones.

The Design

The Ouimet stamp was involved in an unprecedented mid-course change in printers and printing methods by USPS.

Original plans for 1988 called for the Ouimet stamp to be printed by offset/intaglio on the BEP's D press, and the Virginia Statehood Bicentennial stamp to be printed on the American Bank Note Company's leased gravure press in Richmond, Virginia.

However, Pierre Mion's Virginia design "just wasn't working" in gravure, Jack Williams said. The gravure printing cells weren't defining the human and animal figures in the foreground clearly enough. Meanwhile, at BEP, it was decided that it wouldn't be necessary to use intaglio to bring out facial details and the checkerboard pattern of the cap, as some had thought.

Fortuitously, both stamps — whose scheduled issue dates were only 12 days apart — were at approximately the same stage of development. Once the idea occurred to USPS officials to switch Ouimet to ABNC's gravure press and Virginia to BEP's D press, it was fairly simple to accomplish.

Artist Gregory Rudd of Trumbull, Connecticut, based the smiling portrait of Ouimet in the top half of the stamp design on photographs taken at the time of his 1913 victory. The lower portion shows the golfer as "the old-timer" — as he had come to be known at the age of 38 — driving from the tee on his way to victory in the 1931 U.S. Amateur Championship.

First-Day Facts

The Country Club, founded in 1882 and the site of a golf course since 1893, is said to be the oldest country club in the world, and the source of the generic name for such organizations.

The 5 p.m. invitation-only first-day ceremony was held on its indoor tennis courts following the first day of practice for the 1988 Open, which was to begin later in the week.

Deputy Postmaster General Michael S. Coughlin was the principal speaker. Platform guests included Ouimet's two daughters, Mrs. Barbara Mclean and Mrs. Janice Salvi; William C. Battle, president of the U.S. Golf Association; William C. Campbell, captain of the Royal and Ancient Golf Club of St. Andrews; ex-Speaker O'Neill; Representative Ford, and representatives of the Ouimet Caddie Scholarship Fund.

Golfer Ben Crenshaw, in town for the Open, was in the audience. Stamp designer M. Gregory Rudd was also on hand to autograph stamps and covers. The Worcester Kiltie Bagpipe Band performed at the ceremony.

The first-day postmarks bore the name of Brookline, which is a branch of the Boston post office. Its name was used because of its close association with Ouimet, The Country Club and the U.S Open. USPS had originally announced Boston as the first-day city, but reported the change in plan January 8.

Commemorative covers were sold by the Francis Ouimet Caddie Scholarship Fund, with proceeds going to the fund.

25¢ NEW HAMPSHIRE STATEHOOD

Date of Issue: June 21, 1988

Catalog Numbers: Scott 2344   Minkus CM1312   USPS 4445

Colors: magenta, yellow, cyan, black

First-Day Cancel: Concord, New Hampshire (State House)

FDCs Canceled: 374,402

Format: Panes of 50, vertical, 10 across, 5 down. Gravure printing cylinders of 200 subjects (10 across, 20 around) manufactured by Roto Cylinder (Palmyra, New Jersey).

Perf: 10.9 (L perforator)

Selvage Markings: ©United States Postal Service 1988, Use Correct ZIP Code®

Designer: Thomas Szumowski of Waltham, Massachusetts

Art Director and Typographer: Richard Sheaff (CSAC)

Project Manager: Jack Williams (USPS)

Modeler: Richard Sennett (Sennett Enterprises) for American Bank Note Company.

Printing: Stamps printed and sheeted out by American Bank Note Company on a leased gravure press (J.W. Fergusson and Sons, Richmond, Virginia) under the supervision of Sennett Enterprises (Fairfax, Virginia). Perforated, processed and shipped by ABNC (Chicago, Illinois).

Quantity Ordered: 153,295,000
Quantity Distributed: 153,295,000

Cylinder Number Detail: One group of 4 cylinder numbers preceded by the letter "A" over/under corner stamps

Cylinder Number Combination: A1111

Tagging: block over vignette

Printing Base Impressions: A1111 (871,137)

The Stamp

The framers of the U.S. Constitution provided in Article VII the "the ratification of the conventions of nine States shall be sufficient for the establishment of this Constitution between the States so ratifying the same."

New Hampshire ratified on June 21, 1788 — the ninth state to do so. At that moment the Constitution sprang to life. It has been alive and evolving ever since.

On the 200th anniversary of its historic action, New Hampshire, "the state that made us a nation," was honored with a 25¢ commemorative stamp in the Statehood Bicentennial series.

A 1955 commemorative marked the 150th anniversary of the discovery of the Great Stone Face.

Its central vignette showed the state's best-known natural wonder, the Great Stone Face, a granite formation shaped like a man's profile that overlooks the highway through Franconia Notch. First-day ceremonies were held in Concord, the state capital, on the anniversary date, June 21.

The American Bank Note Company was the printer, using its leased six-color Champlain gravure press.

The stamp is closely related to two older stamps, each of which also had a June 21 issue date.

The first was a 3¢ stamp issued 50 years earlier — June 21, 1938 — to mark the 150th anniversary of the action by New Hampshire's ratification convention that made the Constitution official.

Because the stamp's purpose was to celebrate the action of nine states, not just one, it made no mention of New Hampshire. It bore the legend "The States Ratify the Constitution," and pictured a generic colonial-era meeting house with messengers on horseback about to

A view of Mount Chocura, with autumn foliage in the foreground, was one of the designs considered for the New Hampshire Statehood stamp.

ride away to spread the news. The designer based his illustration on a picture of the old Court House at Williamsburg, Virginia.

The second antecedent was a 3¢ green stamp issued June 21, 1955, to commemorate the 150th anniversary of the discovery of the Great Stone Face. Like the 1988 Statehood issue, it was vertically arranged, and the two views of the profile are very similar.

Its issuance was the result of a direct appeal by Senator Norris Cotton, an influential Republican senator from New Hampshire, to President Dwight D. Eisenhower. Senator Cotton pointed out that New Hampshire had never been honored with a stamp, and a sympathetic Ike instructed his postmaster general to remedy that situation.

The 1955 stamp's inscription read, "The Old Man of the Mountains." This is an alternative name for the landmark, used interchangeably with "The Old Man of the Mountain" (singular), which is what USPS called it in its announcement of the 1988 stamp.

The striking formation, consisting of five layers of granite ledge 40 feet in height, juts out near the crest of Profile Mountain. Nathaniel Hawthorne wrote of it in a celebrated short story: "It was a happy lot for children to grow up to manhood or womanhood with the Great Stone Face before their eyes, for all the features were noble, and the expression was at once grand and sweet, as if it were the glow of a vast, warm heart, that embraced all mankind in its affections, and had room for more. It was an education only to look at it."

The profile was discovered in 1805 by Nathaniel Hall, a member of

Art Director Richard Sheaff prepared this essay from a 19th-century engraving of the Profile seen from a distance.

a road-building crew. Early one morning he shouldered his gun and left camp to hunt for partridges. As he crept along the shore of a small lake, he happened to glance up — and for a moment was stunned by what he would call "the most wonderful face" he had ever seen.

News of the discovery spread rapidly through New England. The road on which Hall was working was pushed through the Notch. Men and women came on horseback, by stage, carriage and cart. The popularity of the Great Stone Face was one of the factors that led to the building of a railroad through the Franconia region.

In 1916 hotel owners hired a quarry engineer to secure a 25-ton portion of the forehead that was slipping out of place. The heavy steel pins, rods and turnbuckles that were used to knit the Old Man's brow are invisible from below.

New Hampshire's role in the drafting of the Constitution of 1787

This proposed design featured a Revolutionary War symbol from a New Hampshire regimental flag, showing a circle of linked states.

June 21, 1788
New Hampshire

was less significant than the unique part it played in ratifying it. The Revolution left New Hampshire deeply in debt, with no money to send delegates to Philadelphia. It was nine weeks after the Constitutional Convention got under way before the colony's representatives, John Langdon and Nicholas Gilman, arrived. Langdon, a wealthy merchant, had finally decided to pay their expenses himself. The two men missed the "Great Compromise," which resolved the question of how the states would be represented in Congress — a critical issue for small states like New Hampshire.

In the end, however, thanks to the geographical arrangement of signatures, Langdon and Gilman were the first to sign the document.

New Hampshire's ratification didn't come easily. A convention to consider the matter was called in Exeter in February, but after 10 days of debate, the opposition was so strong that the convention leaders adjourned to rally pro-Constitution forces rather than risk a decisive vote. Among the objections of the anti-federalists was the failure of the Constitution to cut off the slave traffic or to give the central government the power to abolish slavery.

However, when the convention reassembled at Concord June 17, eight states had ratified, the mood was different, and New Hampshire was aware of its chance to make history. Four days later it did so, by vote of 57 to 46. Just in case Virginia might have ratified on the same day, to be in a position to challenge New Hampshire's claim to be the ninth state, the time of ratification — 1 p.m. — was specifically noted.

New Hampshire natives who have appeared on postage stamps include Franklin Pierce, 14th president; Chief Justice Harlan F. Stone; sculptor Daniel Chester French and Daniel Webster, statesman and orator. One stamp that pictured Webster also honored New Hampshire's most distinguished educational institution; it was the 1969 6¢ commemorative for the 150th anniversary of the Supreme Court's landmark decision in the Dartmouth College case.

The Design

Art director Richard Sheaff of Needham, Massachusetts, a design coordinator for CSAC who had lived in New Hampshire for 15 years, showed the committee a few idea sketches he had made himself. One was a Revolutionary War symbol, showing a circle of linked states that had been used as a device on a New Hampshire regimental flag. Two others were photographic views of New Hampshire's Mount Chocorua with autumn foliage flaming in the foreground.

But Sheaff and the committee concluded, in his words, that "the Great Stone Face is really the only thing that New Hampshire folk consider a symbol of the state."

The committee considered two different Stone Face designs prepared by Sheaff and based on 19th-century artwork: an engraving showing the profile from a distance, and a painting depicting the formation from a closer vantage point but bare of foliage. "We liked that view, but it was colorless, so we decided to redo it and put a little life into it," Sheaff said.

Artist Thomas Szumowski of Waltham, Massachusetts, was hired to do the original acrylic painting that was used for the final design. Szumowski was familiar with gravure printing requirements, having previously designed the 18¢ coil stamp of 1985 depicting George Washington and the Washington Monument. He knew the mountain from frequent visits, and he used his own photographs as the basis for his painting.

First-Day Facts

New Hampshire is a small state, but it has one of the world's largest legislatures. Thus the State House Chamber of Representatives Hall, where the first-day ceremony was held, accommodated without difficulty the more than 500 people who attended.

25¢ VIRGINIA STATEHOOD

Date of Issue: June 25, 1988

Catalog Numbers: Scott 2345   Minkus CM1313   USPS 4446

Colors: magenta, yellow, cyan, black (offset); red, black (intaglio)

First-Day Cancel: Williamsburg, Virginia (Capitol Building)

FDCs Canceled: 474,079

Format: Panes of 50, vertical, 10 across, 5 down. Offset printing plates of 200 subjects (10 across, 20 around); intaglio printing sleeve of 400 subjects (10 across, 40 around).

Perf: 11.1 (Eureka off-line perforator)

Selvage Markings: ©United States Postal Service 1988, Use Correct ZIP Code®

Designer: Pierre Mion of Lovettsville, Virginia

Art Director: James Dean (CSAC)

Project Manager: Joe Brockert (USPS)

Engravers: Thomas Hipschen (BEP, vignette)
Michael Ryan (BEP, lettering and numerals)

Modeler: Peter Cocci (BEP)

Printing: 6-color offset, 3-color intaglio D press (902)

Quantity Ordered: 160,250,000
Quantity Distributed: 160,245,000

Plate/Sleeve Number Detail: Left-side panes: one group of 4 offset plate numbers over/under corner stamps; one intaglio sleeve number over/under adjacent stamps. Right-side panes: offset/intaglio numbers in reverse positions.

Plate/Sleeve Number Combination: 1111-1, 2222-1, 2223-1, 3223-1, 3323-1, 3333-1

Tagging: block over vignette

Printing Base Impressions: Offset Yellow: 3(88,000)
Offset Cyan: 3(298,000)
Offset Black: 2(220,000), 3(298,000)

The Stamp

Virginia, the 10th state to ratify the Constitution, was appropriately honored on the 10th stamp in the series commemorating bicentennials of statehood. The 25¢ stamp was issued June 25, 1988, on the anniversary of the ratification by the Virginia convention.

Although the stamp depicts a scene in Williamsburg, and the first-day ceremony was held in that restored colonial capital, the ratifying convention actually had met in Richmond, to which the capital had been moved in 1779.

At the time of the Constitutional Convention, Virginia was the largest of the states, with at least one-fifth of the total population of the United States. The leadership role it played in the creation of the Constitution was commensurate to its size and influence.

Two of Virginia's most distinguished sons, George Washington and James Madison, led the political maneuvering that brought about the convention. The Virginia Assembly was the first to choose delegates. Once the convention began, Washington was named presiding officer. Madison was the author of the Virginia Plan, a detailed proposal laid before the delegates as deliberations began for a new central government to replace the Articles of Confederation. And it was Madison whose detailed journal of the proceedings, published after his death in 1836, gave the world the fascinating story of how the great document was assembled.

Other distinguished Virginia delegates included Edmund Randolph, the 33-year-old governor; George Mason, author of the state's famous Declaration of Rights, and George Wythe, a law professor and signer of the Declaration.

All through the convention the Virginians were in the thick of the debate. In the end, though, only Washington, Madison and John Blair, a judge of the state's high court of chancery, signed the document. Randolph and Mason, for their part, thought it gave the national government too much power, and objected to the take-it-or-leave-it basis on which it would be submitted to the states.

The Virginia ratifying convention met at Richmond June 2, 1788. The delegates knew that New Hampshire might become the ninth state to ratify and thereby put the Constitution into effect, but they were also aware that a United States that excluded their powerful state would be a weak and divided entity. Their convention was evenly divided, and debate was intense.

Dominating the debate for the anti-federalists was the fiery Patrick Henry, who had refused even to be a delegate to the Constitutional Convention. (Asked why he hadn't lent his aid to making a Constitution that pleased him, he would say only: "I smelt a rat.") Now Henry was particularly bitter about the defection to the federalist side of Governor Randolph, who had refused as a delegate to sign the Constitution but who now asserted that its ratification by eight states had changed the picture.

Others speaking against the Constitution included George Mason, William Grayson and future President James Monroe; its proponents included Madison, George Nicholas, Henry ("Light Horse Harry") Lee and future Chief Justice John Marshall. When the vote came June 25, the Constitution was ratified 89-79. Amendments, including a Bill of Rights, were recommended — but not put forth as conditions of ratification, as Mason and others had wished.

It was only after the convention had adjourned that the Virginians learned they had lost to New Hampshire, by four days, the honor of being the ninth state to ratify.

Not surprisingly, a history as rich as Virginia's has been reflected in many U.S. stamp issues. The 1607 settlement at Jamestown, the founding there of the U.S. shipbuilding industry, the establishment of the city of Alexandria, the Revolutionary War victory at Yorktown and the French fleet's victory at the Virginia Capes that made Yorktown possible, the Civil War Battle of the Wilderness and Lee's surrender at Appomattox, the final encampment of the United Confederate Veterans in 1951, the international naval review in 1957 — all have been the subjects of stamps.

Among Virginia's sons and daughters who have been postally depicted have been the eight presidents born there (Washington, Jefferson, Madison, Monroe, William Henry Harrison, Tyler, Taylor and Wilson), plus George Mason, Patrick Henry, Martha Washington, John Marshall, George Wythe, George Rogers Clark, Winfield Scott, Robert E. Lee, Stonewall Jackson, Cyrus Hall McCormick, Dr. Walter Reed, Dr. Ephraim McDowell, Meriwether Lewis, William Clark, Richard E. Byrd and Willa Cather.

Noted Virginia buildings and landmarks that have been pictured on stamps include Mount Vernon, Monticello, Jefferson's Virginia Rotunda, Gunston Hall, Stratford Hall, Washington and Lee University, Wolf Trap Farm Park and the Dulles International Airport terminal.

The Design

Pierre Mion of Lovettsville, Virginia, designed the stamp, which depicts the old Capitol building in Williamsburg, with a horse and carriage in the foreground. Mion also created the design for the Blair House postal card issued a few weeks earlier.

Another artist had also submitted concept sketches for the stamp.

This close-up of the tower of the Capitol at Williamsburg wasn't considered recognizable enough for the stamp.

This artist proposed a montage of portraits of famous Virginians — Washington, Jefferson, Madison — but the sketches "didn't seem to say Virginia," according to a CSAC spokesman.

Mion went to Williamsburg with his camera and took pictures of the restored buildings and their landscaping. From these, he worked up a number of sketches for CSAC's consideration.

A design featuring the Governor's Palace was turned down because of the "royal image" it conveyed, and the red-brick Capitol was chosen instead. The building depicted is a 1934 reconstruction of what was the first of two buildings on the site. Work on that structure had begun in 1701, and until it was destroyed by fire in 1747, it served as home of the colony's legislature, the House of Burgesses.

Several CSAC members liked a close-up of the top of the Capitol, but others felt it wasn't readily recognizable. The design finally decided upon showed the entire building from a point slightly left of center. In his watercolor rendering, Mion added a two-horse carriage, with passenger and driver, similar to some of the carriages that now transport tourists along Williamsburg's Duke of Gloucester Street. He exercised further artistic license by removing a tree that was in the foreground of his photograph and adding leaves to the autumn-bare trees behind the building.

USPS originally planned to have the stamp printed by the American Bank Note company on its gravure presses. But gravure turned out to be an unsatisfactory process for this particular detailed image.

"We were absolutely pulling our hair on this one," said Don

This view by Pierre Mion of the Governors' Palace at Williamsburg was turned down by the Citizens' Stamp Advisory Committee because it conveyed a "royal image."

With modifications, this Pierre Mion painting became the stamp design. The tree in front of the Capitol was removed and foliage added to the other trees.

McDowell, general manager of the Stamps Division. "It's not all predictable. Sometimes those little gravure cells just don't want to perform the way you want them to. You're like a lion tamer with a chair and a whip trying to make them jump through the hoop, but sometimes they won't.

"So this was one where the artist worked very hard doing and redoing, trying to make what we picked in the committee — the 'icon' representing Virginia — work and reproduce. This was one where we used up all our lead time, and we were right down to the wire and still tinkering."

"We asked the artist to give us an alternative approach," explained Joe Brockert, the stamp's project manager. "We asked him to crop the original image, come in tighter on the building and carriage, make it more like a poster with simple flat colors of the kind that reproduce well in gravure. But we didn't like the result, and neither did the printers and the artist."

In the end, the solution, as described earlier in this volume, was to send the stamp to BEP's intaglio-offset D press and give the Francis Ouimet stamp, which had been scheduled for the D press, to ABNC to be printed in gravure.

USPS was pleased with the Virginia stamp that resulted. The horse-and-carriage design element were engraved, as were two seagulls flying overhead, and printed in black over a background printed in offset magenta, yellow, cyan and black. The lettering and numerals at the bottom were also printed by intaglio.

The artist tried close-up views of the Capitol in an effort to make the gravure printing process work more effectively.

First-Day Facts

Announcement of Williamsburg as the first-day city was made by the Postal Service March 17, 1988. The June 25 issue date had been announced earlier.

The first-day ceremony was held at the Capitol building shown on the stamp. Senior Assistant Postmaster General David H. Charters, a graduate of the University of Virginia Law School, was among the principal speakers.

The ceremony kicked off a two-day "Liberty Summit" celebrating religious freedoms in America. The conference was funded by the non-profit Williamsburg Charter Foundation of Washington.

25¢ NEW YORK STATEHOOD

Date of Issue: July 26, 1988

Catalog Numbers: Scott 2346   Minkus C1315   USPS 4447

Colors: green, yellow, purple, black (offset); blue, black, red (intaglio)

First-Day Cancel: Albany, New York (State Museum)

FDCs Canceled: 385,793

Format: Panes of 50, vertical, 10 across, 5 down. Offset printing plates of 200 subjects (10 across, 20 around); intaglio printing sleeve of 400 subjects (10 across, 40 around).

Perf: 11.1 (Eureka off-line perforator)

Selvage Markings: ©United States Postal Service 1988, Use Correct ZIP Code®

Designer and Typographer: Bradbury Thompson (CSAC)

Art Director: Joe Brockert (USPS)

Engravers: Edward Archer (BEP, vignette)
Michael Ryan (BEP, lettering and numerals)

Modeler: Jack Ruther (BEP)

Printing: 6-color offset, 3-color intaglio D press (902)

Quantity Ordered: 184,040,000
Quantity Distributed: 183,290,000

Plate/Sleeve Number Detail: Left-side panes: one group of 4 offset plate numbers over/under corner stamps; one intaglio sleeve number over/under adjacent stamps. Right-side panes: offset/intaglio numbers in reverse positions.

Plate/Sleeve Number Combination: 1111-1, 2111-1, 2131-1, 2232-1, 2242-1

Tagging: block over vignette

Printing Base Impressions: Offset Yellow: 1(91,000), 2(350,500)
Offset Purple: 3(39,500), 4(326,500)
Offset Black: 1(200,500)
Intaglio Sleeve: 1(530,500)

The Stamp

On July 26, 200 years to the day after New York became the 11th state to ratify the Constitution, USPS issued a 25¢ stamp in the Statehood Bicentennial series to mark the anniversary.

Although the ratification being celebrated had taken place in Poughkeepsie, the first-day ceremony was held in Albany, to the north on the Hudson River, and the stamp depicted a scene in New York City, to the south.

But, then, New York's role at the Constitutional Convention itself had been unusual. It sent three delegates. Two of them, John Lansing Jr., youthful speaker of the state assembly and mayor of Albany, and Robert Yates, a justice of the New York Supreme Court, were members of the state's dominant political faction led by its governor, George Clinton. The Clintonians were opposed to a strong national government. They saw their state as having the best chance of any to succeed on its own and were determined to resist any loss of its sovereignty that would also mean a diminution of their own power.

The third delegate was the brilliant Alexander Hamilton, only 30 years old, former aide to George Washington and a dedicated nationalist. Hamilton, though an active and outspoken member of the convention, was consistently outvoted by his two colleagues, who aligned New York with the smaller states in several early tests. Later, Lansing and Yates abandoned the convention to return to Albany, leaving Hamilton alone and unable to vote because of New York's rule requiring a quorum of the delegates.

After the convention concluded its work, New Yorkers lobbied vigorously both for and against ratification. Governor Clinton led the campaign to reject the Constitution, while Hamilton and John Jay, with James Madison's help, authored *The Federalist*, a series of pro-Constitution essays published in New York newspapers.

If Virginia was essential to the new Union that had already been secured by the ratification of nine states, New York was equally so.

At the Poughkeepsie ratifying convention, which began June 17, the upstate anti-federalists had a two-to-one edge. The gathering turned out for the most part to be an extended debate between Hamilton and Melancton Smith, an anti-federalist lawyer and merchant. Smith argued with logic and sharpness, a witness wrote, but he was no match for Hamilton, whose experience at Philadelphia and in writing *The Federalist* had armed him with "an exhaustless store of argument and illustration." Concluded historian Carl Van Doren: "The New York convention was a triumph for Hamilton as no other state convention was for any other man."

Still, New York's ratification vote on July 26 was close — 30-27 — and was accompanied by 32 recommended amendments and a circular letter to the other states calling for a second general convention. The second convention, of course, was never held.

More than any other state, New York has seen its treasure of history, scenes and personalities poured out as subject matter for stamps.

These include events during and after the American Revolution (the Battles of Oriskany, Fort Stanwix, Saratoga, White Plains and Brooklyn, General Sullivan's expedition against the Iroquois, Washington's proclamation of peace at Newburgh, Washington's first inauguration); buildings and institutions (Sagamore Hill, Hyde Park, New York University, Columbia University, the Metropolitan Opera, Bellevue Hospital, the United Nations, "Lyndhurst" at Tarrytown, the New York City skyline, ASCAP, the American Museum of Natural History); landmarks (the Statue of Liberty, Niagara Falls, three different bridges at Niagara and two in New York City); manmade waterways (the St. Lawrence Seaway, the Erie Canal); New York City events (its founding, its consolidation into five boroughs, the introduction of the first American streetcar); upstate events (the landing of the Walloons at Fort Orange, the travels of the locomotive *Brother Jonathan*, the invention of baseball at Cooperstown, the first women's rights convention at Seneca Falls, the 1932 and 1960 Winter Olympics at Lake Placid, and the fictitious ride of the Headless Horseman); shows (the Pan-American Exposition, Hudson-Fulton Celebration and two New York World's Fairs); and Lindbergh's flight to Paris from Roosevelt Field, Long Island.

Persons born in or associated with New York included Presidents Martin van Buren, Millard Fillmore and the Roosevelts, Theodore and Franklin D.; First Lady Eleanor Roosevelt; Alexander Hamilton, John Jay, Albert Gallatin, Robert Fulton, Sojourner Truth, Dr. Mary Walker, Washington Irving, James Fenimore Cooper, Julia Ward Howe, Herman Melville, Bret Harte, Horatio Alger, Edith Wharton, Edna St. Vincent Millay, Eugene O'Neill, Belva Ann Lockwood, Elizabeth Blackwell, Elizabeth Cady Stanton, Dr. Bernard Revel, Edward MacDowell, Victor Herbert, George M. Cohan, George Gershwin, Jerome Kern, Duke Ellington, Enrico Caruso, Igor Stravinsky, Frederic Remington, Horace Greeley, Admiral William T. Sampson, Joseph Pulitzer, Adolph S. Ochs, George Eastman, Edwin Armstrong, Horace Moses, George W. Goethals, Babe Ruth, Ralph Bunche, Whitney Young — and two great 20th-century politicians, Governor Alfred E. Smith and Mayor Fiorello La Guardia.

The Design

How do you choose a design theme that will best represent a state of great geographic, cultural, commercial and historical diversity? This

A ground-level view of Wall Street, with Federal Hall at the right and Trinity Church in the background.

was a problem for USPS with several of the Statehood Bicentennial series stamps, but most of all with New York.

Through most of 1987 CSAC and the Stamps Division wrestled with the problem. Four different artists at one time or another tried their hands at concept sketches based on ideas furnished by USPS officials. Niagara Falls, the New York City skyline, Niagara superimposed over the New York City skyline (which impolitically suggested, a CSAC member observed, that New York was "going over the falls," the Erie Canal, the New York State Seal, a detail from the Seal, a dramatic Hudson River School painting of the river itself, even the "I (heart) New York" slogan and the "Big Apple" symbol for New York City — all these ideas were tried and rejected.

"We knew we had to separate out New York City from New York State," recalled Joe Brockert, project manager and art director for the stamp, "and at the same time we didn't want to ignore the city as being such a big part of the state."

Eventually Brockert and his associates did turn to the city for their solution — but to the city historic, the city that served as a national capital during the time when the Constitution was being written and ratified. And that brought them to Federal Hall.

Federal Hall, on Wall Street in lower Manhattan, was originally New York's City Hall. The Congress of the Confederation met here,

This frontal view of Federal Hall was rather dull compared to the angled view finally chosen.

beginning in January 1785. In expectation that New York would be the permanent capital of the new nation, Major Pierre L'Enfant was commissioned to remodel the building in 1788 for this purpose.

It was on its balcony that George Washington took the oath of office April 30, 1789, as first president — a scene reproduced on a 3¢ stamp of 1939 that commemorated the inauguration's sesquicentennial.

Federal Hall was demolished in 1812. It is now the site of the Subtreasury Building, built in 1842 as a custom house and remodeled in 1862 for use as a subtreasury. The Federal Reserve Bank used it until 1925, and since then it has housed various federal agencies.

USPS began looking for pictures of Federal Hall. Several were obtained, and Bradbury Thompson, CSAC design coordinator, worked some of them into stamp essays. The one that the USPS staff and CSAC found most appealing was a perspective from an elevation, looking up Wall Street toward Broadway, with Federal Hall on the right and Trinity Episcopal Church in the distance.

This particular picture was found in the files of the Federal Hall National Memorial, run by the Department of Interior. It was a photograph of a newspaper clipping, which in turn reproduced the Wall Street scene, which Mark Drucker, Federal Hall curator, believes was a lithograph. Thus it was two steps removed from the original.

Not a shred of identifying information accompanied the photo in the file. The identity of the newspaper or its date was unknown.

Drucker said he had never seen another view from quite this perspective, with the horizon line even with Federal Hall's rooftop. Most views of the building are seen from the eye level of someone on the street, he said.

Brockert took the photo to other experts, at the New York Historical Society and the Museum of the City of New York. No one could identify it. Nothing like it appears in *Stokes' Iconography*, a six-volume compedium of New York City images, maps and information

These essays featured the New York State Seal and a detail from it, showing the Hudson River.

87

assembled between 1909 and 1919 — although that work contains several other lithographs and engravings of Federal Hall.

Mark Drucker personally suspects the unknown original is fairly recent, possibly done in the 1930s, when the Washington bicentennial had stirred interest and research in early federal architecture. The detailing on the building is more precise and accurate than is found in many 19th-century renderings, he said.

If the work is in fact that modern, other copies may exist accompanied by identifying information, Drucker speculated.

Drucker places the period depicted in the lithograph as between 1789, when the Trinity Church exterior was completed, and 1810.

Even though the illustration's pedigree was uncertain, USPS decided to base the stamp design upon it, and to use the equipment best equipped to reproduce it — BEP's offset/intaglio combination D press. BEP's experts were given an unusual amount of latitude in converting the picture to a postage stamp.

"We told the Bureau to create an image based primarily on this engraving, using for reference all the other perspectives of Federal Hall we had available, and to take whatever other artistic license needed to be taken," Brockert said. "Basically, they created a total new engraving."

The modeler, V.J. Ruther, and engraver, Edward Archer, cropped the image to emphasize the two historic buildings and create a strong diagonal along Wall Street. ("I was very impressed," said Drucker. "It produced a much more powerful effect than I thought it would.")

The angle of sight was slightly altered so the cupola on Federal Hall would conceal a second tower behind it. Some of the pedestrians were deleted, as was a horse and carriage, and another carriage was moved. The bare branches of the trees were given foliage. The clouds were reshaped and centered.

BEP personnel then added background colors, refining them on the electronic Design Center, to create the delicate effect of an engraving hand-tinted in 19th-century fashion.

"We kept a close eye on the project," Brockert said, "and gave them

This picture of Federal Hall, from an unknown source, was used with extensive modifications to produce the finished stamp. The picture was cropped, street traffice was reduced, foliage added, clouds modified and an extraneous tower behind Federal Hall removed.

some guidance, saying, 'no, that purple is too strong, try something weaker,' and 'that yellow is too overpowering' — things like that."

The end result was a striking-looking stamp. Its engraved portions are the foreground scene in black, the sky and certain building details in blue, and the words "New York" in red. Offset colors are green, yellow and purple for the illustration, and black for the date and "USA 25." BEP used the combination process to achieve an unusual chiaroscuro effect. A patch of golden sunlight bathes the facade of Federal Hall, the street in front of it and the church building in the distance, and purple shadows cover the areas concealed from the sun.

The Trinity Church building pictured on the stamp hadn't been built on the ratification date featured in the design. According to Trinity archivist Phyllis Barr, the old church had burned in 1776, and the cornerstone of its replacement wasn't laid until August 21, 1788, a few weeks after the date given on the stamp. (That date can be seen on the cornerstone itself. It is preserved in an interior wall of the present church structure, which dates to 1846.)

The apparent anachronism — showing a church that didn't yet exist — was pointed out to USPS by a local New York historian, John Tauranac. Tauranac complained to *The New York Times* that the stamp, by suggesting that the scene depicted was how Wall Street actually looked on July 26, 1788, "will go far in miseducating the public, which is a grave disservice — one might even say, an engraved disservice."

However, Jack Williams of USPS explained to *The Times* that the image was meant to be "reminiscent of the era" and not supposed to depict New York on a given date. And, added designer Bradbury Thompson, Wall Street "would hardly be recognized if Trinity Church weren't in it."

The fact that the New York stamps' design is from an unknown source makes it unusual, but not unique. At least two other U.S. commemoratives have designs whose originals can't be traced: the 2¢ Jamestown Exposition issue of 1907, showing English colonists wading ashore on Jamestown Island in 1607 (Scott 329), and the 1¢ Lexington-Concord Sesquicentennial issue of 1925, depicting Washington at Cambridge (Scott 617).

First-Day Facts

The first-day ceremony was held in the State Museum on Empire State Plaza in Albany. Featured speakers included New York State historian Paul J. Scudiere and Northeast Regional Postmaster General William R. Cummings.

For the general sale of the stamp that began the next day, July 27, USPS authorized a pictorial cancellation to be used on that date at 26 New York post offices. The cancellation included the seal of the state, the slogan "We the People" and the inscription "1788-1988" and "Bicentennial Station." The deadline for receipt of mail orders for covers was the cancellation date.

In addition, a second-day ceremony was held at the present Federal Hall, 26 Wall Street, New York. John M. Nolan, general manager/postmaster of the New York division of USPS led the ceremony. Other scheduled speakers were Sol Wachtler, chief judge for the state of New York and the state chairman of the commission on the bicentennial of the U.S. Constitution, and Comer S. Coppie, senior assistant postmaster general, Finance and Planning Department. Stamp designer Bradbury Thompson was also on hand.

25¢ SUMMER OLYMPICS

Date of Issue: August 19, 1988

Catalog Numbers: Scott 2380   Minkus CM1317   USPS 4449

Colors: light brown, red, green, purple, dark brown

First-Day Cancel: Colorado Springs, Colorado (Olympics Sports Complex)

FDCs Canceled: 402,616

Format: Panes of 50, horizontal, 5 across, 10 down. Gravure printing cylinders of 200 subjects (10 across, 20 around).

Perf: 11.2 by 11.1 (Eureka off-line perforator)

Selvage Markings: ©United States Postal Service 1988, Use Correct ZIP Code®

Designer: Bart Forbes of Dallas, Texas

Art Director: Jack Williams (USPS)

Typographer: Bradbury Thompson (CSAC)

Modeler: Peter Cocci (BEP)

Printing: 7-color Andreotti gravure press (601)

Quantity Ordered: 157,250,000
Quantity Distributed: 157,215,000

Cylinder Number Detail: One group of 5 cylinder numbers alongside corner stamps.

Cylinder Number Combination: 12111

Tagging: overall

Printing Base Impressions: Red: 2(1,282,000)
Dark Brown: 2(264,000)

The Stamp

On August 19, USPS issued its postal tribute to the 1988 Summer Olympic Games that would open in Seoul, South Korea, a month later: a single 25¢ commemorative stamp.

It was a precedent of sorts. In the past, whenever the United States had postally honored the Summer Olympics, it had been with sets of two or more varieties, beginning with the 3¢ and 5¢ stamps it had produced for the Los Angeles Games of 1932.

As noted in the Winter Olympics chapter, U.S. postal Olympimania reached an all-time high for the Winter and Summer Games of 1984. Of the 28 postal items issued for those two events, 22 were exclusively for the Summer Games — which were again held in Los Angeles.

The Citizens' Stamp Advisory Committee requested these travel-poster-type designs as a new approach to Olympic stamp art, but in the end settled for the old approach.

Issuing only a single stamp for the 1988 Summer Olympics constituted a 180-degree change of course, like a swimmer's kick-turn at the end of the pool.

The Games of the XXIVth Olympiad spanned 16 days, from September 17 to October 2, 1988.

Security was at a record high level in and around Seoul, because of fears of disruption by North Korea — which had refused to send a team — or by terrorist groups. There were problems in boxing (where at least six of the 12 gold-medal decisions were considered questionable) and with drug use by athletes (which led to the most sensational disqualification in Olympic history — that of 100-meter-dash winner Ben Johnson of Canada, after he had tested positive for steroids).

On the whole, however, events ran so smoothly that the president of the International Olympic Committee, Juan Antonio Samaranch, was able to declare at the end: "These were the best and most universal Games in history."

An all-time high of 160 countries sent nearly 10,000 athletes who participated in 23 official sports, three demonstration sports and one exhibition sport, bowling. For the first time since 1972, no superpowers and no large blocs of countries boycotted the Games.

The Soviet Union ended up with 132 medals, 55 gold, the most ever in a Summer Games with full participation. East Germany had 102 medals, 37 gold, and the United States collected 94, 36 gold. Host South Korea was fourth in gold medals, with 12.

The Games produced many memorable individual performances. U.S. diver Greg Louganis repeated his feat of 1984 by winning golds in both platform and springboard events — despite hitting his head during a dive, an accident that required some quick surgical stitching at poolside. Two U.S. sisters-in-law, sprinter Florence Griffith Joyner and heptathlete-long jumper Jackie Joyner-Kersee, between them collected five gold medals and one silver plus two world, three Olympic and three American records.

Other standout performers included American sprinter Carl Lewis, Soviet pole vaulter Serge Bubka, the U.S. men's volleyball team and women's basketball team, the Soviet men's basketball team, Soviet and Rumanian gymnasts, Portuguese marathoner Rosa Mota, East German swimmer Kristin Otto and U.S. swimmers Matt Biondi and Janet Evans.

The Design

Bart Forbes of Dallas, who had previously created the vertically oriented artwork for the U.S. Winter Olympics commemorative,

One of Bart Forbes' travel-poster designs, showing a statue of a warrior-king in Seoul.

This essay by Forbes showed a high jumper clearing the bar using the "Fosbury flop" method.

completed his year's assignments for USPS with a horizontal design for the Summer Games stamp.

Like the earlier one, the Summer Games stamp was printed by gravure. However, this one was done by the Bureau of Engraving and Printing instead of by the American Bank Note Company.

Forbes' painting portrayed a male gymnast performing on the rings. The gymnast was suspended horizontally in mid-swing, a dramatic image of strength and grace against a dark brown background.

The original painting had a mottled background that BEP officials decided wouldn't reproduce well on the gravure press. Rather than changing it on BEP's Design Center, USPS asked the artist to repaint it in solid color. "We're not going to let the scanners and computers replace the designer," explained Jack Williams, project manager and art director for the stamp.

Early essays for the Summer Olympics stamp, like those for the Winter Olympics, included some that focused on site rather than sports. One showed a Korean pagoda; another, a statue of a warrior king in Seoul. In the end, the committee concluded, as it had done with the Winter Games, that a sports image would provide a more recognizable connection with the Games than a travel-poster design.

A working sketch of a gymnast.

As sometimes happens, the *Postal Bulletin* beat the Stamp Information Branch to the punch on a postal design. The *Bulletin* for July 14 carried a picture of the Summer Olympics stamp, 12 days before the Information Branch officially released an illustration to the public.

The Olympics made 1988 a busy year for Bart Forbes. Chosen by the South Korean Olympic Committee as official artist for the Summer Games, he was commissioned to paint two- by three-foot oil sketches of each sport, plus the opening and closing ceremonies — 31 paintings in all. The artwork was destined for an Olympic museum in Seoul.

First-Day Facts

The first-day ceremony was held at the 34-acre Olympic Complex in Colorado Springs, Colorado, where the U.S. Olympic Committee is headquartered and where some 14,000 athletes train yearly as guests of USOC.

Discus thrower Al Oerter, the only athlete ever to win gold medals in the same event in four consecutive Olympics (1956 through 1968), was the keynote speaker. He was a last-minute replacement for Joan Benoit Samuelson, 1984 marathon gold medalist and a stamp collector, who had to bow out because of an inner-ear infection.

25¢ CLASSIC CARS BOOKLET

Date of Issue: August 25, 1988

Catalog Numbers: Scott 2381-85 (stamps)
Scott 2385a (pane of 5)   Minkus CM1318-22
USPS 6637

Colors: magenta, yellow, cyan, black, phosphor (offset); red (intaglio)

First-Day Cancel: Detroit, Michigan (STAMPSHOW 88, Cobo Hall)

FDCs Canceled: 875,801

Format: Four panes of 5 different horizontal stamps each. Offset printing plates of 240 subjects (20 across, 12 around); intaglio printing sleeve of 480 subjects (20 across, 24 around).

Perf: 10 (Goebel booklet machine stroke perforator)

Selvage Markings: Sleeve number and registration markings on each pane binding stub. ©UNITED STATES POSTAL SERVICE 1988 inside front cover. Universal Product Code (UPC) and proof of purchase notation printed on outside of back cover.

Designer: Ken Dallison of Indian River, Ontario, Canada

Art Director: Howard Paine (CSAC)

Project Manager: Jack Williams (USPS)

Typographer: Bradbury Thompson (CSAC)

Engravers: Gary Chaconas (BEP, vignettes of Scott 2381, 2382, 2385)
Kenneth Kipperman (BEP, vignettes of 2383, 2384)
Michael Ryan (BEP, lettering and numerals)

Modeler: Peter Cocci (BEP)

Printing: Stamps printed on the 6-color offset, 3-color intaglio D press (902). Covers printed and booklets formed on Goebel booklet forming machine.

Quantity Ordered: 32,000,000
Quantity Distributed: 32,667,900

Plate/Sleeve Number Detail: One intaglio sleeve number on each pane binding stub

Sleeve Number: 1

Tagging: offset printed tagging block on bottom half of each stamp

The Stamps

Like many U.S. stamp issues, the Classic Cars booklet of 1988 represented the fruition of an idea that had been around for several years and had been approached in different ways.

Mary Ann Owens, chairman of the Topical Subcommittee of the Citizens' Stamp Advisory Committee, recalled that when she joined CSAC in 1979, artwork was already in hand for a proposed set of stamps showing historic American automobiles.

Later, according to Howard Paine, a design coordinator for CSAC, the committee commissioned two different artists to prepare sketches for two se-tenant blocks of four.

One of these pictured early horseless carriages: an 1899 Stanley Steamer, 1903 Ford, 1903 curved-dash Oldsmobile and 1903 Duryea. The other featured luxury cars of the 1920s and 1930s: Duesenberg, Locomobile, Packard and LaSalle.

The blocks of four were never issued. In 1985, however, the Stanley Steamer (a 1909 model) was pre-empted for a Transportation series coil, and in the same year the Transportation series also claimed a car

This pane, photographed under ultraviolet light, shows how the cut-away tagging in the white area of the stamps traces the wheel and body type of each car.

that would have fit nicely into the second proposed block — a 1933 Stutz Bearcat.

At about this same time, CSAC decided to go ahead with a Classic Cars set — not in sheet format but as a booklet, similar to the topical booklets it had already approved for fish (issued in 1986) and locomotives (1987).

Fortuitously, a new member with expertise in automotive subjects had become a member of CSAC and was assigned to join Mary Ann Owens on the Topical Subcommittee. He was John Foxworth, national business management manager for the Chevrolet Motor Division of General Motors.

Owens and Foxworth were assigned to do the necessary research and recommend makes of car to be included in the booklet. To save USPS from the charge of commercial favoritism, cars made by companies that were still active were eliminated in advance.

(That rule, had it been in effect earlier, would have blocked Oldsmobile and Ford from consideration for the se-tenant blocks. It also would have eliminated LaSalle; as John Foxworth could testify, GM, which made the car, was still very much in business.)

The two CSAC members reported back with a list of a dozen makes, and the committee chose the five that would end up in the Cars stamp booklet.

These were from the classic period, identified by collectors as the years from 1925 to 1942, when the luxurious fast motorcar emerged, flourished and — after the Depression arrived — declined. The five included three of the makes that had been proposed for that earlier se-tenant block.

As they appeared on the pane, chronologically from top to bottom, they were a 1928 Locomobile, 1929 Pierce Arrow, 1931 Cord, 1932 Packard and 1935 Duesenberg.

The booklet was announced July 20, 1987, in the first listing of USPS' 1988 stamp and stationery program. In the detailed schedule that was released April 4, 1988, it was disclosed that the booklet would be issued August 25 at the American Philatelic Society's STAMPSHOW 88, to be held in Detroit, America's motor city.

Still later the details were published, including the list of cars to be shown and the fact that the booklet would contain four panes (20 stamps) and sell for $5.

Old cars — particularly those from the 1920s, 1930s and 1940s — are fascinating artifacts of a simpler age. For stamp collectors, automobile stamps are a popular topical subject, and many countries, including Great Britain, have obliged by issuing sets depicting vintage vehicles.

USPS, in its 1988 *Guide to U.S. Stamps*, provided a list of 24 U.S. postal issues that had featured automobiles and trucks in their designs. Many of these were generic rather than actual models, although the first one of all — the 4¢ Pan American Exposition commemorative of 1901 (Scott 296) — showed a real Columbia electric car rolling past the U.S. Capitol.

The elegant cars of the booklet pane were mobile symbols of status and style. Though conservative in basic design, the large, fast cars of the 1920s and '30s featured lavish appointments and advanced engineering. Most were limited-edition production models, with exclusive styling and individual touches reflecting the tastes and personalities of the owners.

Far from being multipurpose vehicles in the modern sense, these cars were built and bought to serve two basic purposes: to transport people in elegance over city streets, or to carry them in comfort, privacy and speed from city to vacation playground.

1928 Locomobile: One of the first companies to enter the classic market was Locomobile, a Bridgeport, Connecticut, firm that earned a reputation for scrupulous detail.

After buying the Stanley brothers' steam-car design rights in 1899, J.B. Walker and A.L. Barber did brisk business with a small Locomobile steam runabout before moving up to gasoline-powered cars.

The Locomobile Book, available in dealer's showrooms, expressed the firm's pride with statements like these: "The rear seat cushion and back are provided with upholstery 10 inches thick . . . the foot rest is a brass rod lightly knurled to prevent slipping . . . the four-speed transmission with its manganese bronze case and alloy steel shafts never gives trouble."

One of the firm's last and finest products was the 1928 model shown on the top stamp.

1929 Pierce-Arrow: In 1865, George N. Pierce founded a company in Buffalo, New York, to manufacture bird cages, iceboxes and other household items. By the time he introduced his Pierce-Arrow motorcar in 1909, his reputation for fine craftsmanship was such that supply would never sufficiently meet public demand.

Studebaker Corporation bought the firm in 1928 and added styling to its reputation for quality. Acceleration and the ability to climb hills

Maximum card, 1928 Locomobile.   *Maximum card, 1929 Pierce-Arrow.*

in high gear were among the points stressed in the advertising. The 1929 model included innovative standard equipment, such as shatterproof glass and an adjustable driver's seat.

The Pierce-Arrow could be recognized by its distinctive fender-mounted headlights, a feature that dates from 1914, and the kneeling archer hood ornament, or mascot. Today these hood ornaments are popular automotive collectibles.

1931 Cord L-29: Erret Lobban Cord began as a car salesman, converting Model T Fords and, later Moon Motor Cars into sportier models that found a ready market. At 30 he reorganized the failing Auburn Motor Company of Auburn, Indiana, put it back on its feet and took it over.

Later, as Auburn thrived, Cord bought the Lycoming Aircraft Company and the Duesenberg car-making operation, and in 1929, at age 35, he introduced a new front-wheel-drive car bearing his name.

The first Cord, the L-29, was a handsome sedan with a Lycoming eight-cylinder engine that featured America's first production front-wheel-drive system. The absence of a drivetrain permitted a lower chassis and body that lent extra elegance. The car used a de Dion front axle on four quarter-elliptic springs.

The 1931 L-29 was one of the sportiest cars of its era. Its handsome grill was followed by the longest hoodline in the industry.

1932 Packard: James Ward Packard's first car was a single-cylinder device and with it began his company's reputation for reliability and excellence.

By the early 1920s Packards were the American car to own, with Lincoln the only other real choice and Cadillac just moving into contention. The Packard was a favorite of royalty abroad; in 1931, for instance, Prince Eugene of Belgium used two Packard Series Eights as personal transport for his trip across the Sahara Desert. Packards were over-engineered, with components that were bigger, stronger and more precisely machined than necessary, and were credited with contributing more than 1,000 innovations to the automotive industry.

The 1932 "Light Eight" model was distinguishable by the broad

Maximum card, 1931, Cord.   *Maximum card, 1932 Packard.*

forward sweep of the bottom portion of its V-shaped grill. The car had a silent synchro-mesh transmission, finger-control steering, shatterproof glass in every window and full insulation. Ride-control shock absorbers, adjustable from the dashboard, were standard equipment.

1935 Duesenberg SJ: The car that gave the language the slang term "doozy," the Indianapolis-made Duesenberg was the most admired American car of all time. Even today it remains one of the most coveted of all collectibles.

Frederick and August Duesenberg loved engines, and they spent their early years developing racing cars for the Indianapolis 500. A

Maximum card, 1935 Duesenberg.

Duesenberg was the first — and so far the only — American racing car to score a victory in the French Grand Prix.

In time, the brothers' company was acquired by E.L. Cord, who directed Duesenberg to build the fastest road car available to the American buyer. The result was the Model J, with a Lycoming straight-eight engine with dual overhead cams and four valves per cylinder. It delivered 265 horsepower which gave the two-seat tourer an almost unusable top speed of 116 mph. The Model J featured chassis lubrication by an onboard oil pump, plus dashboard warning lights for oil and battery levels.

Duesenberg sold only the chassis and engine; the bodies were built to order by custom coach builders like Murphy, Le Baron and Derham. The Model J was replaced by the even more costly SJ, capable of about 130 mph. The chassis with engine was priced at about $15,000, and a custom coach could add as much or more again.

Royalty — both the actual and Hollywood kind — provided a market for these elegant chariots. Among the celebrities who flaunted Duesenbergs were Clark Gable, Al Jolson, Gary Cooper, Mae West and William Randolph Hearst.

The Designs

The Classic Cars stamps were in the same long horizontal format introduced with the Flag over Capitol booklet of 1984 and used for three subsequent five-stamp commemorative booklets: the Fish of 1986 and the Drafting of the Constitution and Locomotives of 1987.

Ken Dallison of Indian River, Ontario, was chosen to do the artwork. A frequent contributor of U.S. stamp designs, Dallison also had extensive experience in automotive art, having worked for 20 years for *Car and Driver* and another 15 years with *Road and Track*. His most recent USPS assignment had been the 45¢ Langley airmail stamp issued May 14, 1988.

Dallison was given the makes of car selected by the Citizens' Stamp Advisory Committee, and allowed to choose the model years he considered best for design purposes. He based his pen-and-ink-wash designs on archival and personal photographs.

All the cars face to the right, but from the top car to the bottom on the pane the viewing points move gradually from side to front, giving a fanning effect to the five vehicles. This was art director Howard Paine's idea, and it makes the full pane much more interesting visually than the 1987 Locomotives pane or a similar se-tenant block of four of 1983 showing streetcars, on which all the vehicles are shown in full profile.

Like the Locomotives, the Classic Cars were printed by BEP by offset/intaglio combination on the D press. The way the combination process was used was unusual, however.

The automobiles were first hand-engraved, then photographed and converted for use by offset printing. This technique produces a sharper image than that generally found on stamps produced by offset or photogravure. The year dates and makes of the cars also were engraved, but these were actually printed in intaglio.

The Classic Cars stamps also differ from the Locomotives and Streetcars in that each subject is silhouetted against a black background that suddenly fades to white near the center of the stamp. On the Locomotive and Streetcar stamps, the vehicles had floated on white backgrounds.

"The committee decided that wouldn't happen again," said Jack Williams, project manager. "The locomotives in particular looked as if they were hanging out in space when the stamp was mounted on an envelope.

"With the white background, there were no strong corners, no edges, no real lines of definition around each design. Collectors had this quandary: Is it a well-centered stamp or not?

"Here, on the Classic Cars, we've got two strong corners. We couldn't figure out a way to block out the other two corners, short of putting in an artificial rule along the bottom, and that would look awfully odd, we thought. So we stayed with two corners."

The black backgrounds were added by BEP's Peter Cocci, using the electronic Design Center. Here Cocci also made final adjustments in the colors of the automobiles themselves.

BEP used an unusual kind of tagging on this issue. Because taggant only works effectively when placed on a light surface, it was applied in a cut-away fashion to the white portion at the bottom of each stamp.

Thus the tagging was basically customized for each car, with the upper edge of the taggant tracing the vehicle's underside and wheels.

Although USPS had announced that the booklet-pane tabs would contain four single-digit offset numbers and one intaglio number, the tabs as issued contained only the intaglio number, in red.

A footnote to the set is that its production marked the return of BEP engraver Kenneth Kipperman to active stamp production.

Kipperman — who engraved the vignettes for the Cord and Packard from which the offset plates were made — had been suspended without pay after involvement in a bizarre incident in Washington June 17, 1987. He had threatened to detonate a bomb to protest plans to raze an old building next door to BEP in order to build the United States Holocaust Museum.

In March 1988 Kipperman pleaded guilty (by arrangement) to making a misdemeanor and unauthorized entry. He was sentenced to two suspended 30-day jail terms and 100 hours of community service.

Kipperman was better known for his unauthorized addition of a Star of David into the beard of his engraving of Hebrew educator Bernard Revel while making the die for the $1 definitive of 1986.

A BEP spokesman would say only that Kipperman was back performing his security engraving work, and that a review of all stamps issued during the previous 10 years had disclosed no anomalies in the dies other than the Revel secret mark. The spokesman said the BEP had taken "appropriate action" of an undisclosed nature to discipline its employee.

The booklet cover, printed in red and black, showed a portion of the fender and hood of a Duesenberg, with the distinctive hood ornament, a headlight and the four right-side header pipes. The back and inside of the cover contained promotional material on the USPS Commemorative Stamp Club.

First-Day Facts

The booklet was dedicated in Detroit's Cobo Hall just before the beginning of STAMPSHOW 88, the 102nd annual convention of the American Philatelic Society.

A display of the five gleaming classic cars, each one parked beside a poster-size reproduction of the appropriate stamp, served as a backdrop for the ceremony.

Postmaster General Anthony M. Frank, who owns a rare car himself — a 1957 Volkswagen van, the oldest one imported into the United States — gave the main address.

The official logo of STAMPSHOW bore a line drawing of an antique automobile as a salute to Detroit, the Motor City. The logo was used as a cachet on first-day covers and also appeared on the show's souvenir card, whose most prominent feature was a reproduction of that 4¢ Pan-American stamp depicting the electric automobile.

At the first-day ceremony, USPS also introduced a set of five maximum cards picturing the five automobiles on the booklet pane. Each of the full-color cards showed an enlarged version of Dallison's art, but against an all-white background. There was no lettering; names and descriptive information were printed on the reverse of the cards.

A set of five was offered for $2.50 mint and $3.75 with the appropriate stamp affixed to the front of the card and postmarked with the August 25 first-day cancellation.

USPS also made available for sale, on a test basis, a 24- by 36-inch poster featuring the classic cars theme. The price was $10.

As usual with first-day events, USPS urged first-day cover collectors to prepare their own covers for cancellation during the grace period. This period, originally set at the normal 30 days, was later extended an additional 45 days to November 8.

For covers that the Postal Service serviced, full panes only were affixed at a $1.25 (face value) charge.

25¢ ANTARCTIC EXPLORERS (BLOCK OF FOUR)

Date of Issue: September 14, 1988

Catalog Numbers: Scott 2386-89 (stamps)   Minkus CM1323-26
Scott 2389a (block of 4)   USPS 4448

Colors: magenta, yellow, blue, process black, line green, black

First-Day Cancel: Washington, D.C. (National Geographic Society)

FDCs Canceled: unavailable

Format: Panes of 50, horizontal, 5 across, 10 down. Gravure printing cylinders of 200 subjects (10 across, 20 around) manufactured by Roto Cylinder (Palmyra, New Jersey).

Perf: 10.9 (L perforator)

Selvage Markings: ©United States Postal Service 1988, Use Correct ZIP Code®

Designer: Dennis Lyall of Norwalk, Connecticut

Art Director and Typographer: Howard Paine (CSAC)

Project Manager: Jack Williams (USPS)

Modeler: Richard Sennett (Sennett Enterprises) for American Bank Note Company.

Printing: Stamps printed and sheeted out by American Bank Note Company on a leased gravure press (J.W. Fergusson and Sons, Richmond, Virginia) under the supervision of Sennett Enterprises (Fairfax, Virginia). Perforated, processed and shipped by ABNC (Chicago, Illinois).

105

Quantity Ordered: 162,142,500
Quantity Distributed: 162,142,500

Cylinder Number Detail: One group of 6 cylinder numbers preceded by the letter "A" alongside corner stamps

Cylinder Number Combination: A111111

Tagging: block over vignette

Printing Base Impressions: A111111 (1,027,151)

The Stamps

When the U.S. Postal Service produced a se-tenant block of four stamps in 1986 to honor Arctic explorers, it was inevitable that another would eventually follow to commemorate explorers at the other end of the world — Antarctica.

The anticipated block was included in the initial announcement of the 1988 stamp program, and was issued September 14. Portraying four U.S. Antarctic explorers — Nathaniel Palmer, Charles Wilkes, Richard E. Byrd and Lincoln Ellsworth — it made an attractive companion piece to the earlier quartet.

Both blocks were designed by the same artist, Dennis Lyall of East Norwalk, Connecticut. Both followed the same design style, with each stamp containing a head-and-shoulders portrait of the individual, an appropriate illustration and a polar-projection map showing his route of discovery.

Both were printed by the American Bank Note Company on its Champlain gravure press. Where the predominant color of the Arctic block had been a cold blue, the color of the new block was an equally icy blue-green.

Antarctica, the fifth largest continent, is the remotest, the coldest (with temperatures in the interior as low as 125 degrees below zero) and the highest (average elevation 8,000 feet). It has been glaciated for about 170,000 years. Ice still blankets 90 percent of its surface. Only the lowest forms of vegetation cling to its frozen rocks, but its seas and shores are home to whales, seals, fish, penguins, petrels and terns.

There is no permanent human settlement. The first recorded landing on the mainland didn't occur until 1895. But increasingly over the years scientific expeditions from many countries have visited Antarctica and established bases.

In 1959 the 12 nations then actively exploring the continent signed a treaty pledging to use the Antarctic for peaceful purposes. Full inspection of all bases was authorized, and territorial claims were placed in abeyance. In 1971 an 8¢ U.S. stamp bearing an outline map of Antarctica was issued to commemorate the 10th anniversary of the date the treaty took effect.

Nathaniel Palmer: Who first sighted the mainland of Antarctica is disputed by historians. Some assign credit to an 1820 British expedition under Edward Bransfield. The Soviet Union has made a belated claim on behalf of Thaddeus von Bellingshausen, captain of the Imperial Russian Navy, who voyaged near the continent in the same period. And some believe the honor belongs to a 21-year-old Yankee from Stonington, Connecticut, named Nathaniel Brown Palmer.

Palmer unquestionably was the first American to sight the southern continent. Commanding the tiny sloop *Hero*, part of a sealing expedition from Stonington, young Palmer sailed out of the South Shetland Islands in November 1820 scouting for seals. The weather was fine and clear, and as they bore south they sighted land on the horizon.

At 4 a.m. November 18, Palmer's log tells us, they "made sail in shore and Discovered — a strait — Tending SSW & NNE — it was Literally filled with Ice and the shore inaccessible we thought it not Prudent to Venture in ice — Bore away to the Northerd & saw 2 small islands and the shore every where Perpendicular." The peninsula he had sighted, where the mainland thrusts north of the Antarctic Circle, still bears the name Palmer Land.

Charles Wilkes: In the 1820s, an increasing number of New England sailors ventured into the Antarctic Ocean in search of whales, seals and fish. Many ships were wrecked on unreported islets or foundered on unmarked reefs. Pressure grew for a government-sponsored voyage to chart and survey these dangerous waters.

Lieutenant Charles Wilkes, U.S. Navy, was named to command the first American exploring expedition. In August 1838 he set sail aboard the sloop-of-war *Vincennes*, flagship of a six-vessel squadron. The expedition would spend two Antarctic summers (the winter months in the Northern Hemisphere) probing the southern ocean, and would later venture the length and breadth of the Pacific, finally heading westward to complete a circumnavigation of the globe.

On December 26, 1899, The *Vincennes* left Sydney, accompanied by three other vessels, to sail as far south as possible. On January 11 they reached what Wilkes was to call "the icy barrier" — floes, drifting icebergs and a white frozen cliff to the south. They turned west, searching for a path through the pack ice. The weather was bad, and although land was reported by each vessel at several points, it was rarely seen distinctly. For six weeks Wilkes sailed to the west, naming mountains and headlands beyond the ice.

Although some of his discoveries were later challenged, explorations in the 20th century revealed the coast essentially as he described it. Charles Wilkes was the first explorer to see a major segment of Antarctica, and the first to call it the Antarctic Continent.

Wilkes would later attract international attention in a different way. As commander of the *USS San Jacinto* during the Civil War, he precipitated a crisis with Great Britain by stopping a British mail packet, the *Trent*, on the high seas and removing two Confederate commissioners, James Mason and John Slidell. President Abraham Lincoln agreed to resolve the so-called "Trent affair" by sending the two men back.

Richard E. Byrd: In modern times, the man whose name is most closely linked to Antarctica is Richard Evelyn Byrd, whose 100th birth anniversary fell in October 1988, only a month after the stamp depicting him was issued. The career naval officer made five expeditions to the Antarctic, each more ambitious than the one before.

But Byrd's first polar expedition was to the north, not the south, and was remarkable enough to have qualified him to appear on one of the Arctic Explorers stamps as well. In 1926, with Floyd Bennett as pilot, Byrd navigated the first plane to fly over the North Pole.

His initial visit to Antarctica, in 1928-30, was the first American expedition since that of Wilkes 90 years earlier. He established a base — Little America — on the Ross Ice Shelf, and he mapped a vast territory, which he named Marie Byrd Land, for his wife. He also completed an extraordinary "double" by making the first airplane flight to the South Pole.

In 1933-35 Byrd returned to resume exploring and research. He proved that no strait linked the Weddell and Ross Seas and that Antarctica was a single continent. To study weather inland he spent the dark winter months by himself in a hut 123 miles south of Little America. Here he nearly perished from carbon monoxide from his stove and a malfunctioning generator. Profoundly ill, Byrd was rescued by a party pushing through the polar night from Little America in a Citroen tractor-car. Later he wrote of his ordeal in the book *Alone*.

This second Byrd expedition was commemorated by a 3¢ blue stamp of 1933 with a design devised by President Franklin D. Roosevelt himself. It showed a globe with the explorer's expeditions marked by dotted lines. The stamp was intended for letters mailed through the Little America post office, but was valid for general use.

On his third expedition (1939-41) Byrd made important discoveries. In 1946-47 he commanded the Navy's Operation High Jump, with more than 4,700 men, 13 ships and 23 aircraft, and introduced new technology — radar, magnetometers, helicopters, modern icebreaker vessels — to Antarctic exploration. Finally, he took part on Operation Deep Freeze (1955-59), a U.S. contribution to the International Geophysical Year. After its first phase was completed, Byrd returned home to Boston, where he died March 11, 1957, at age 68.

Lincoln Ellsworth: Lincoln Ellsworth was unique among Antarctic explorers: He was rich. As the son of an American millionaire he could have made a name for himself financing expeditions and sharing in their prestige. But Ellsworth wanted to be part of the action.

In 1926 he supported an Arctic expedition of Roald Amundsen, the Norwegian who had discovered the South Pole 14 years earlier, and flew over the North Pole with him in a dirigible. By 1933 he was ready for what he called the last great adventure in Antarctic exploration — a flight across the continent, from the Ross Sea to the Weddell Sea and back. His pilot would be Bernt Balchen, who had piloted Byrd's South Pole flight.

Ellsworth set sail for the Antarctic. With him was the *Polar Star*, the plane Northrop had custom-made for him — a low-wing, metal monoplane with skis for landing gear. But a series of misfortunes would force Ellsworth to postpone his attempt for nearly two years and to change his route plans and his pilot.

Finally, in November 1935, with pilot Herbert Hollick-Kenyon at the controls, Ellsworth took off in the *Polar Star* from Dundee Island at the tip of the Palmer peninsula on course for Little America 2,300 miles away. They landed several times to escape bad weather — one such break, to sit out a blizzard, lasted eight days — and finally were forced down, out of gas, and had to head on foot for the abandoned Byrd camp. They reached it on December 15, 22 days after leaving on what they thought would be a 14-hour flight.

Ellsworth made another long flight over the continent in 1939. His deeds proved that two men could fly freely about the Antarctic and that with care they could land and take off anywhere, instead of having to operate from prepared bases.

The Designs

The four stamps were arranged chronologically by subject in the block, with the earliest explorer, Palmer, at upper left and the most recent, Ellsworth, at lower right. Each portrait was accompanied by a picture of the explorer's ship or aircraft.

Artist Dennis Lyall based his portrait of Palmer on a Samuel Waldo

In Lyall's original painting, Wilkes wore a close-fitting cap with earflaps.

painting owned by the Old Lighthouse Museum of Stonington, Connecticut, the explorer's hometown. His sailing ship, *Hero*, is based on a line drawing by John Leavitt, also provided by the museum.

This enlarged detail from the Wilkes stamp shows how the white line tracing the explorer's route passes, paradoxically, in front of the ship's bow.

The portrait of Lieutenant Wilkes is based generally on an 1870 painting by Samuel Bell Waugh, provided by the National Portrait Gallery. The rendering of Wilkes' ship, the *Vincennes*, comes from National Geographic Society reference materials.

Admiral Byrd's likeness is a composite based on National Portrait Gallery photographs by Seymour Stone and Woolf (only name shown). Ellsworth's portrait is also a composite, taken from several photographs from the Library of Congress. The Byrd and Ellsworth planes are based on National Geographic Society photographs.

Only a few changes were made in the artwork Lyall submitted to the Citizens' Stamp Advisory Committee.

In the original version of the Wilkes portrait, the lieutenant wore a close-fitting cap with earflaps. Research by Helen Wadsworth, a USPS consultant, established that a regulation Naval officer's cap would have been a more appropriate headgear, and Lyall made the change. The cap in the final design, part of an Navy lieutenant's "undress" (other than full-dress) uniform, was illustrated in the book *Military Uniforms in America: Years of Growth, 1796-1851*, published by the Company of Military Historians.

The designer also deleted a tiny flag he had shown flying from the stern of Wilkes' ship. "It looked as if it was growing out of Wilkes' ear, and it wouldn't have shown as a flag in stamp size anyhow," explained Jack Williams, USPS project manager for the stamps.

Some additional lines were painted into the explorers' fur collars to provide more texture. And the lines tracing their routes near and on the Antarctic continent were changed from black to dropout white to give them better visibility.

Even with all the fine-tuning, a design oddity emerged on the printed stamps. The white line on the Wilkes stamp tracing the explorer's route is seen going behind the rigging near the bow of the ship, as it should — but then it continues in front of the bow itself. (The paradox thus created was reminiscent of one on the Boston Tea Party se-tenant block of 1973, in which the ship's rigging appears to pass behind the crescent moon.)

Varieties

A single pane of the stamps was found October 21 with the black completely missing. As a result, the stamps lacked the explorers' names, map markings, ships' rigging and windows on the airplanes, as well as the black "1" from the group of gravure cylinder numbers in the margin.

The discoverer of the pane, Carolanne Tramz of Diamond Bar,

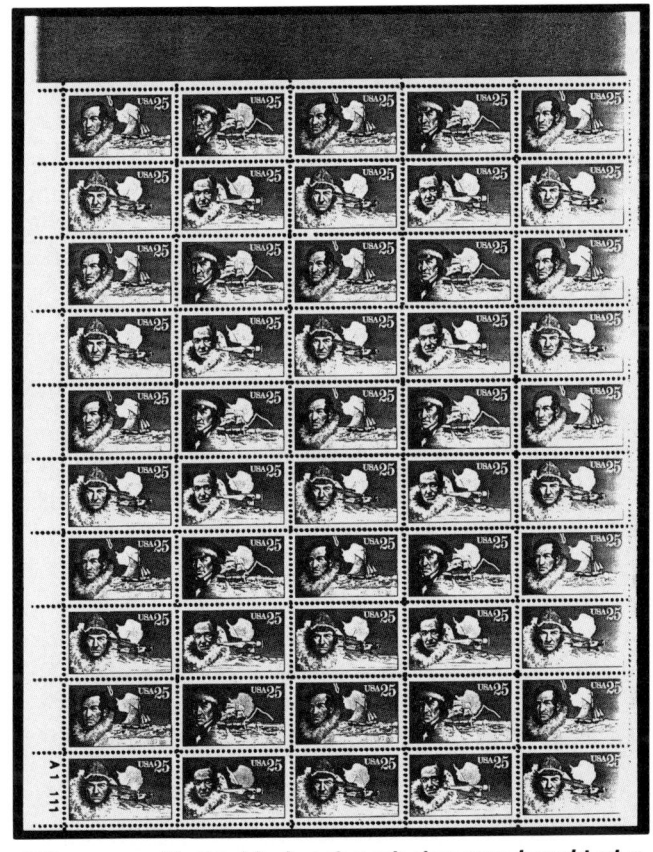

This pane with the black color missing was bought at a post office by a California collector.

California, bought it in a Covina area post office. Tramz, a 30-year collector who specializes in full panes and plate number strips, was purchasing only the plate strip of the pane when she spotted the error and bought it intact.

In theory, three other panes from the same sheet should exist with the same flaw.

First-Day Facts

The issue date of the Antarctic block was first announced as September 13 and later put back one day.

The first-day ceremony took place in the Gilbert H. Grosvenor Auditorium at the National Geographic Society in Washington, with Gilbert M. Grosvenor, president of the organization, and Postmaster General Anthony M. Frank taking part. The ceremony marked not only the issuance of the stamps but also the centennial of the 10.5 million-member National Geographic Society and its many contributions to science and education.

A sad footnote to the first-day ceremony was the death of Richard Byrd Jr., the only son of the polar explorer, who set out by train from Boston to Washington to attend the ceremony honoring his father and never arrived.

Three weeks later, on October 3, the body of Byrd was found in a vacant warehouse in Baltimore, dead of malnutrition and dehydration. He was 68 — the same age at which his father died. He was wearing what appeared to be green workman's clothes and one shoe.

It was undetermined why he had left the train at Baltimore, what he had done in the days that followed or how he had come to be in the warehouse. Byrd's family told Baltimore authorities that he sometimes became confused and on occasion had problems remembering events, but had never wandered away.

As usual with first-day events, USPS encouraged customers mailing in self-addressed covers for first-day postmarks to affix their own stamps. The Postal Service offered to affix blocks or singles, but its selection of single stamps was random, and requests for specific designs weren't honored.

Because of the large number of philatelic items issued in 1988, USPS announced on September 2 that collectors would be given additional time to obtain first-day cancellations for five new issues. For the Antarctic Explorers block, the deadline was extended from October 14 to November 28.

A second-day-of-issue ceremony was held September 15 at the National Museum of Natural History in Washington, where a special exhibition honoring Wilkes had been assembled. The principal speaker was Gordon C. Morison, senior assistant postmaster general.

25¢ CAROUSEL ANIMALS (BLOCK OF FOUR)

Date of Issue: October 1, 1988

Catalog Numbers: Scott 2390-93 (stamps)   Minkus CM1327-30
Scott 2393a (block of 4)   USPS 4450

Colors: *yellow, orange, *yellow, red, blue, green (offset); brown, black (intaglio)

First-Day Cancel: Sandusky, Ohio (Cedar Point Amusement Park)

FDCs Canceled: unavailable

Format: Panes of 50, vertical, 10 across, 5 down. Offset printing plates of 200 subjects (10 across, 20 around); intaglio printing sleeve of 400 subjects (10 across, 40 around).

Perf: 11.1 (Eureka off-line perforator)

Selvage Markings: ©United States Postal Service 1988, Use Correct ZIP Code®

Designer: Paul Calle of Stamford, Connecticut

Art Director: James Dean (CSAC)

Typographer: Bradbury Thompson (CSAC)

Engravers: Thomas Hipschen (BEP, vignettes)
Dennis Brown (BEP, lettering and numerals)

113

Modeler: Clarence Holbert (BEP)

Printing: 6-color offset, 3-color intaglio D press (902)

Quantity Ordered: 303,425,000
Quantity Distributed: 305,015,000

Plate/Sleeve Number Detail: Left-side panes: one group of 6 offset plate numbers over/under corner stamps; one intaglio sleeve number over/under adjacent stamps. Right-side panes: offset/intaglio numbers in reverse positions.

Plate/Sleeve Number Combination: 111111-1, 111121-1, 222232-1, 323232-1, 323243-1

Tagging: block over vignette

*Same yellow ink used twice. One plate to fill in with yellow ink the seam area of the second plate that printed the yellow frame and vignette areas of the design.

The Stamps

USPS launched its eighth annual Stamp Collecting Month October 1 by issuing a block of four stamps commemorating a romantic American art form, the hand-carved carousel.

It was the third issue of 1988 designed to appeal to the topical collector, following February's Cats block of four and August's Classic Cars booklet.

The first-day ceremony was held at one of the country's great old amusement parks: Cedar Point Amusement Park in Sandusky, Ohio, home to four hand-carved carousels — and to one of the four wooden steeds pictured on the stamps.

Announcement of the block, a part of the American Folk Art series, was made July 20, 1987, in USPS' first disclosure of its 1988 program. On November 25, the date and place of issue were announced.

Design information was released July 1, 1988, three months ahead of the issue date, in order to give USPS plenty of time to promote the issue in national advertising and articles in publications that don't customarily use philatelic news.

Later in the summer USPS made available to 115 post offices a machine cancellation illustrating the Stamp Collecting Month theme. It showed a carousel horse with the slogan "For the ride of a lifetime — collect stamps."

And on October 3 the Bureau of Engraving and Printing opened a special exhibit, to run through the early spring of 1989, on the Carousel Animals block. It included a replica of the Cedar Point carousel horse shown on the block, on loan from the amusement park; the dies used to make the stamps; photos of the engravers working on them, and full printing sheets showing progressive colors.

Carousel animals were an interesting addition to a series that started with the 1977 Pueblo Pottery issue and has featured — all in se-tenant blocks — such folk arts as quilts, Pennsylvania Toleware, Indian masks, duck decoys, Navajo blankets, woodcarved figurines and lacemaking.

At the same time the Carousel Animals block was issued, USPS placed on sale a new mint set called "Folk Art and Crafts: An American Collection." It contained all the stamps in the Folk Art series except the first block, Pueblo Pottery — presumably because the supply of these stamps in the USPS "posterity stock" had run low.

The mint set contained 32 stamps with a face value of $6.24 and sold for $9.95. A deluxe hardbound version was marketed later for $16.50. In all, 100,000 sets were created.

The periodic appearance of the Folk Art stamps has coincided with a growing popular interest in Americana. Hand-carved carousel animals have attracted their share of appreciation.

Fiberglass and aluminum imitations abound, but many collectors have sought the wooden originals, rescued them from decay and neglect, researched and classified them, and honored them in amusement parks, homes and museums. Today, some 300 handcrafted carousels are in operation across the country.

"Carousel animals are a lovely part of our heritage," wrote *New York Times* art critic David L. Shirey, "showing as much vision as many of our most respected sculptures."

Prancing horses, roaring lions, menacing sea serpents and whimsical frogs are only a few species in the menagerie. Such creatures were carved in the late 19th and early 20th centuries by European immigrants who brought with them the skills essential to the art.

The founder of the American carousel industry was a young cabinetmaker named Gustav Dentzel, who came to Philadelphia from Germany in 1864, built a carousel and took it to nearby towns selling rides, just as his father had done in the old country.

In 1875 another new arrival from Germany, Charles I.D. Looff, carved a menagerie of animals from scrap wood from the Brooklyn furniture company where he worked. He opened a shop and soon had turned out two carousels, which he installed at Coney Island.

In the Buffalo area, James Armitage, Allan Herschell and Edward Spillman carved horses that were small and simple, made for traveling shows or small county fairs.

The four stamps in the se-tenant block represent the work of three of the masters or their pupils.

At the upper left is a graceful deer carved in 1895 by Gustav Dentzel. It features a rack of real antlers, and is finished in an antique glaze that emphasizes the detailed carvings of the fur. The deer, restored by Bill Carlone, is now in Charlotte Dinger's private collection in New Jersey, one of the most comprehensive in the country.

At lower right is a rare, long-horned goat, circa 1880, the work of Charles Looff. It is part of the Jean and Noel Thompson collection.

Looff's company also produced the bejeweled gold camel at lower left, circa 1917. A camel was among the animals Looff had carved for his first carousel in 1875, and was the only one of that group to remain a standard figure throughout his career. This one last graced a carousel in Long Beach, California, where Looff had moved his factory.

Finally, at upper right, is the most ornate and sought-after creature on any carousel: the "lead" or "king" horse. This magnificent standing stallion was created to commemorate the 50th anniversary of the Dentzel Company by one of the world's finest carvers, Daniel C. Muller, who learned his trade under Gustav Dentzel. With intricate armor, draped coverlet and meticulous ornaments, Muller's king horse is considered one of the rarest and most beautiful of all carousel creatures. It is now on the Kiddieland carousel at Cedar Point, site of the stamps' first-day ceremony.

The Design

The Carousel block of four was printed by offset/intaglio on BEP's D press, and the result was widely acclaimed for its craftsmanship and vivid colors.

Paul Calle, veteran stamp designer from Stamford, Connecticut, studied photographs of many carousel figures before narrowing the field of candidates to a handful for which he prepared essays.

His principal sources were two elaborate picture books: *The Art of the Carousel* by Charlotte Dinger with photographs by Richard C. Carter and others (Carousel Art Inc., Green Village, New Jersey, 1983), and *The Carousel Animal* by Tobin Fraley with photographs by Gary Sinick (Zephyr Press, 1983).

At the time CSAC decided on carousel animals as a stamp series subject, it hadn't chosen the form the stamps would take. So some of

This frog in human apparel was made around 1915 by the Herschell-Spillman Company, the only carousel manufacturer to produce such an animal.

A hippocampus, or sea horse, from the Smithsonian Institution's collection — an example of the kind of bizarre creatures included in carousel menageries.

Calle's sketches were for stamps in sheet format, while others were in the long, shallow booklet-stamp configuration.

After it was decided to make the set a se-tenant block of four, the committee still had to choose among a variety of subjects and styles.

Paul Calle prepared a full-view sketch of Cedar Point's Dentzel lead horse.

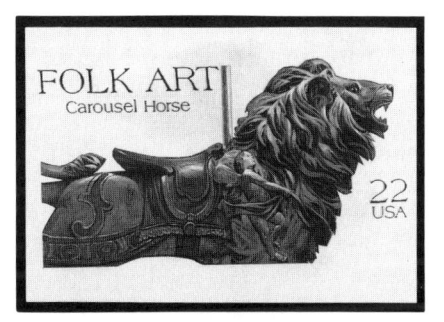

Dentzel's lions are considered the finest of that type of beast.

Calle sketched horses, frogs, sea serpents, deer and other creatures, all from the side, and all facing right. (American carousels, unlike their European counterparts, rotate counterclockwise, enabling riders to grasp for a brass ring with the right hand.) One design option showed the creatures' entire bodies; another, utilizing the vertical format, zoomed in on the heads and necks.

The committee decided that the close-ups had greater visual impact. The figures were set against a white background, and as a final touch, each stamp was framed in a gold border that bled across the perforations to the edge of the adjacent stamp design.

To make maximum use of the design space, wording such as "Folk Art" and "Carousel Horse" was eliminated. "The committee felt that was superfluous," explained Jack Williams. "These were obviously carousel beasts, from their appearance and from the vertical poles rising from their backs."

When the committee had made its final choices for the four stamp subjects, the Postal Service arranged for purchase of the design rights. Three of the subjects were from Charlotte Dinger's book: the horse

A Dentzel tiger, not used.

117

(pages 114 and 119), the deer (page 200) and the goat (page 73). With the latter, Calle exercised minor artistic license, angling one horn back so that both horns would be visible. The fourth animal — the camel — is in the Tobin Fraley volume (page 87).

First-Day Facts

Although Cedar Point Amusement Park was closed for the season, two hand-carved carousels were in operation on the day of the ceremony, which fortunately was sunny and warm. Admission and parking were free, but visitors had to pay a 50¢ state road toll.

Featured speakers were William Manns, a carousel enthusiast and co-author of *Painted Ponies,* and Senior Assistant Postmaster General Gordon C. Morison. Morison's speech was interrupted — according to plan — by the spiel of a carnival barker, adorned in white tie and tails, inviting "children of all ages" to come to the carousel.

The Daniel Muller king horse depicted on one of the stamps had been removed from the Kiddieland carousel for the day and set up at the ceremony site in the Midway. Children were invited to climb onto its ornate saddle.

In addition to the standard first-day postmark, a special pictorial cancel showing a prancing carousel horse also was available in Sandusky.

Collectors were originally given 30 days after the issue date to submit mail requests for first-day covers, but on September 2 USPS announced they would get an additional month and a half — until December 5 — for this purpose.

SPECIAL STAMPS

Special stamps are a relatively recent addition to the list of philatelic categories. They differ from commemorative stamps in that they are issued for use on specific occasions and not to honor persons, places or events. They differ from definitive stamps in that they don't remain on sale for many years at a time or until they are rendered obsolete by a rate change.

The first of the special stamps was the Christmas stamp of 1962. It proved to be the forerunner of an annual series that has continued unbroken to this day and seems likely to go on as long as USPS uses stamps to indicate prepayment of postage.

In 1973 came the first Love stamp, for Valentines, wedding invitations and any other mail on which a little added sentiment was appropriate. There was no reason to think that it would be more than a one-time phenomenon. But nine years later another Love stamp was issued, and beginning in 1984, "Love for Sale" became an annual song for the Postal Service.

The newest type of recurring special issue is called Special Occasions. Special Occasions made its debut in 1987 as a booklet pane carrying eight different messages of the affectionate, upbeat variety. A second booklet was a belated addition to the 1988 stamp program, and USPS said a third one would appear in 1989.

The special stamps of 1988 incorporated several innovations. The two Christmas stamps were issued in a new size and pane layout; with one of them, the so-called "traditional," BEP appropriately returned to a traditional method of production, intaglio. Two Love stamps were issued rather than one, the second being at the two-ounce rate. And with Special Occasions, USPS offered a new look in booklets. These changes will be discussed in detail in the appropriate chapters.

25¢ LOVE

Date of Issue: July 4, 1988

Catalog Numbers: Scott 2378   Minkus CM1314   USPS 5528

Colors: pink, red, yellow, green, gray

First-Day Cancel: Pasadena, California (Rose Bowl)

FDCs Canceled: 399,038

Format: Panes of 100, vertical, 10 across, 10 down. Gravure printing cylinders of 400 subjects (20 across, 20 around).

Perf: 11.2 by 11.1 (Eureka off-line perforator)

Selvage Markings: ©UNITED STATES POSTAL SERVICE 1988, USE CORRECT ZIP CODE®

Designer and Typographer: Richard Sheaff of Needham Heights, Massachusetts (CSAC)

Art Director: Jack Williams (USPS)

Modeler: Peter Cocci (BEP)

Printing: 7-color Andreotti gravure press (601)

Quantity Ordered: 900,000,000
Quantity Distributed: 841,240,000

Cylinder Number Detail: One group of 5 cylinder numbers alongside corner stamps

Cylinder Number Combination: 11111

Tagging: overall

The Stamp

The 1988 Love stamp was the seventh in this popular series — but only the second to be issued after Valentine's Day. The reason this time, as in 1985, was a postal rate change early in the year that quickly would have made obsolete a Love stamp that appeared before the February 14 lovers' holiday.

No problem, said USPS; Love stamps are intended not just for Valentine mail but for year-round use, on any correspondence where an extra affirmation of affection was appropriate. Thus a Love stamp would be perfectly useful even if issued on the Fourth of July — which, as it happened, this one was.

The first two Love stamps were printed in 1973 and 1982. Since 1984, USPS has issued a new variety every year. 1988 brought a new development: a second Love stamp, at the 45¢ two-ounce first-class rate, issued August 8, to accommodate wedding invitations that enclose RSVP cards and envelopes.

The initial announcement of 1988 stamp plans from USPS, however, mentioned only the standard Love stamp at the basic first-class rate. And that was the stamp that was unveiled in Washington, D.C., on New Year's Eve.

For the fifth consecutive year, the countdown to midnight and the coming of the new year in Washington culminated with the lowering of a huge image of the forthcoming Love stamp from the Old Post Office clock tower on Pennsylvania Avenue. While thousands of celebrants counted down the final seconds of 1987, the stamp came to rest at the tower's base, signaling the arrival of 1988 in the nation's capital.

Later in the day, the stamp design was featured again, this time on the other side of the continent at the Tournament of Roses Parade in Pasadena, California. As a salute to the 1988 centennial of that annual New Year's Day pageant, USPS also chose Pasadena to host the first-day ceremony, which it scheduled for July 4.

The stamp design shown in Washington and Pasadena bore no figure of value, because at that time the new first-class rate anticipated for early in the year hadn't been established. Later, a revised picture of the stamp was released, with the denomination "25" included.

Use of Love stamps by the public has steadily increased over the years. The 1973 prototype saw final sales of 320 million. In 1988, the initial print order for Love stamp No. 7 was 900 million. In all, more than 36 billion Love stamps have been produced.

The Design

Two of the numerous rose photographic essays in various sizes, arrangements and colors that Richard Sheaff prepared for CSAC's consideration.

Once again, the subject was roses.

For its 1988 Love stamp theme, USPS returned to a flower it had featured on stamps three times in the recent past — the domestic rose. Roses had appeared on a booklet pane in 1978, one stamp in a se-tenant Flowers block of four in 1981 and the International Peace Garden commemorative of 1982. In addition, wild roses were shown on three stamps of the State Birds and Flowers pane in 1982. But the planned tie-in of the new Love stamp with the Tournament of Roses centennial made another rose design almost inevitable.

The Citizens' Stamp Advisory Committee asked Richard D. Sheaff of Needham Heights, Massachusetts, one of its design coordinators, to provide a selection of design choices based on studio photographs of roses. Sheaff has been designing stamps since 1985 and, earlier in 1988, had created the Old State House design for the 25¢ Massachusetts Statehood Bicentennial commemorative.

When he was given the Love stamp assignment, Sheaff recalled, USPS and BEP held out the possibility that the stamp would be printed in combination offset and intaglio on BEP's D press. Later, however, it was assigned to the Andreotti gravure press.

Sheaff hired Robert Schlowsky, a Boston photographer, to make the required pictures, and Schlowsky and his wife obtained a quantity of roses and went to work. From the ensuing photo sessions, Sheaff presented CSAC with approximately 20 different stamp essays, showing roses red, pink, yellow and variegated, as buds, bouquets and formal and informal arrangements. He made them up in definitive, commemorative and square formats, each with an overlay of type.

Based on the committee's likes and dislikes, a second photo session was held, and then a third. In all, Sheaff said, some 40 essays were prepared as the choices were narrowed and refined.

CSAC ultimately picked an appealingly shaped single blossom against a green leafy background for a definitive-size stamp. The only problem was that the rose was yellow and the committee wanted a pink flower.

The decision was finally made to let BEP artificially convert the yellow rose to pink on its electronic equipment. This was done, although it turned out to be a very difficult task for the Bureau's technicians, and neither Sheaff nor CSAC members were completely satisfied with the result.

Stamp collectors and rose fanciers, not knowing about the electronic legerdemain involved, pressed for information on what specific variety of rose was depicted — and got differing answers.

Linn's Stamp News reported, in answer to one query, that the stamp was "based on a photographic essay showing a bloom of the Tournament of Roses variety, according to the Postal Service." However, *The San Francisco Chronicle* (as quoted in *Stamp Collector*) declared: "Although the Postal Service says the rose is of the Color Magic variety, there are some who would disagree. It is a pink rose, but not Color Magic, said one rose society president."

"We were trying specifically not to make it any one rose variety," Sheaff said. "We checked to see if there was one variety that is the 'official' U.S. rose. There isn't. If there had been, we would have used it. We also asked the Tournament of Roses people if they had a preference. They said it didn't matter, as long as it was a rose."

Some stamp collectors noted a similarity between the design and that of the nine gravure-printed Rose stamps issued by New Zealand in 1975 (Scott 584-92).

First-Day Facts

The first-day ceremony was part of the Independence Day celebration in the Rose Bowl in Pasadena on the evening of July 4.

Associate Postmaster General Kenneth J. Hunter and John Biggar III, president of the Tournament of Roses, were the speakers. Hunter saluted the Rose Parade as "an inseparable part of our national heritage" and suggested that Love stamps, too, had become an annual tradition that he expected "will continue well into the 21st century."

As Hunter finished, a large reproduction of the stamp was unrolled behind him. Later, during the fireworks exhibit, a replica of the Love stamp in fireworks blazed forth on the field of the Rose Bowl.

45¢ LOVE

Date of Issue: August 8, 1988

Catalog Numbers: Scott 2379   Minkus CM1316   USPS 5521

Colors: red, yellow, green, black

First-Day Cancel: Shreveport, Louisiana (American Rose Center)

FDCs Canceled: 121,808

Format: Panes of 50, vertical, 10 across, 5 down. Printing cylinders of 200 subjects (10 across, 20 around).

Perf: 11.1 (Eureka off-line perforator)

Selvage Markings: ©United States Postal Service 1988, Use Correct ZIP Code®

Designer, Art Director and Typographer: Richard Sheaff of Needham Heights, Massachusetts (CSAC)

Project Manager: Jack Williams (USPS)

Modeler: Ronald Sharpe (BEP)

Printing: 7-color Andreotti gravure press (601)

Quantity Ordered: 250,000,000
Quantity Distributed: 169,765,000

Cylinder Number Detail: One group of 4 cylinder numbers over/under corner stamps

Cylinder Number Combination: 1111

Tagging: overall

Printing Base Impressions: Red: 1(1,571,000)
Yellow: 1(1,571,000)
Green: 1(1,571,000)
Black: 1(1,571,000)

The Stamp
During the design stage of the Love stamp of 1988, USPS decided to proceed with a project that had been under consideration: the issuance of a second Love stamp at the two-ounce first-class rate.

Accordingly, when the full 1988 stamp and stationery program was announced on April 4, it included a 45¢ Love stamp, to be issued August 8, five weeks after the basic 25¢ version had made its debut.

USPS said the added starter was created in response to many requests for a stamp for mailing wedding invitations. Most invitations include at least two envelopes and often an RSVP card as well, putting them well over the one-ounce weight.

In the past, USPS said, a bride-to-be and her family had two choices: Use a Love stamp with an unrelated issue, or use two Love stamps and overpay the postage. The new stamp would provide the correct double-rate amount with a single stamp.

It also would pay the charge for the increasing number of greeting cards too large to qualify for a single 25¢ stamp. Any envelope that measures more than 11½ by 6½ inches, or is more than ¼ inch thick, requires 45¢, whether or not it weighs more than an ounce, according to postal officials. Coincidentally, the 45¢ Love stamp also met the overseas airmail rate.

The Postal Service meant the stamp to be used for its intended purpose, however. *The Washington Post* noted that postmasters were cautioned "to restrict sales to collectors and to customers mailing greeting cards and wedding invitations." For more mundane correspondence, USPS had plenty of 45¢ Harvey Cushing Great Americans and 45¢ Samuel P. Langley airmail stamps available.

The Design
For Richard Sheaff of Needham Heights, Massachusetts, the job of designing the 45¢ Love stamp was simply an extension of his earlier assignment to prepare the 25¢.

After the latter design had been chosen — a single flower in the definitive stamp size — CSAC asked Sheaff and photographer Robert Schlowsky to "go back and shoot another round of pictures, with multiple roses in a commemorative format," the artist said. The new stamp, like the earlier one, was scheduled to be printed by gravure on BEP's Andreotti press.

CSAC looked over Sheaff's essays and selected a vertically arranged design showing a cluster of 10 roses — five red, five yellow — against a green leafy background.

As with the first stamp, the roses were intended to be generic rather than represent specific varieties. And, again, BEP technicians used the electronic Design Center to alter the coloring — although not to the extent they had done with the 25¢ stamp. The purpose was to lighten the shaded areas and make the photographic image more compatible with gravure reproduction.

But BEP "ran out of time," Sheaff said. The roses on the finished stamp had a flatness to them that contrasted with the sharp, crisp image in the color transparencies of the stamp design that USPS had released to the philatelic press beforehand.

Sheaff used identical typography on both Love stamps: the word "LOVE" in dropout white Roman capitals, numerals of the same size for the denomination, and "USA" in slightly smaller letters.

First-Day Facts

The first-day ceremony was held at the American Rose Center in Shreveport, Louisiana, which USPS described as "the world's largest rose garden and clearinghouse for registering all new roses." It contains more than 15,000 rose bushes in more than 40 gardens.

Howard Goldstein, executive director of the Rose Center, was among the guests. The featured speaker was John R. Wargo, assistant postmaster general, who traced the history of the rose in America back to a flower that left its fossilized imprint on a slate deposit in Colorado 40 million years ago. A sailor with Columbus picked a rose branch from the sea, inspiring the explorers to continue their search for land, Wargo said. "Pilgrims planted roses," he continued. "George Washington is credited with growing what may have been the very first hybrid rose. And today, a tradition which began in Miami more than 30 years ago rewards every newly naturalized American citizen with a single red rose."

The August 8 first day provided collectors with a unique cancellation. The date, translated numerically, read 8-8-88 (although that wasn't the way it appeared in a postmark, of course).

USPS also placed on sale in Shreveport a philatelic Love folder. The folder, priced at $4.50, contained a block of four of both 1988 Love stamps (face value $2.80). The text was based on Elizabeth Barrett Brownings's verse from *Sonnets from the Portuguese*, which begins: "How do I love thee? Let me count the ways . . ." Pictures and text evoked the many aspects of love. Beginning August 9, the folder was available by mail order and at philatelic centers.

25¢ CHRISTMAS GREETINGS

Date of Issue: October 20, 1988

Catalog Numbers: Scott 2400   Minkus 909   USPS 5547

Colors: blue, green, red, brown, black

First-Day Cancel: Berlin, New Hampshire (Berlin Middle School Auditorium)

FDCs Canceled: unavailable

Format: Panes of 50, horizontal, 5 across, 10 down. Gravure printing cylinders of 300 subjects (15 across, 20 around).

Perf: 11.25 (Eureka off-line perforator)

Selvage Markings: ©UNITED STATES POSTAL SERVICE 1988, USE CORRECT ZIP CODE®

Designer: Joan Landis of New York, New York

Art Director and Project Manager: Jack Williams (USPS)

Typographer: Bradbury Thompson (CSAC)

Modeler: Ronald Sharpe (BEP)

Printing: 7-color Andreotti gravure press (601)

Quantity Ordered: 1,037,855,000
Quantity Distributed: 1,030,850,000

Cylinder Number Detail: One group of 5 cylinder numbers alongside corner stamps on 4 external panes. One group of 5 cylinder numbers over/under corner stamps on 2 internal panes.

Cylinder Number Combination: 11111

Tagging: overall

Printing Base Impressions: Blue: (1,247,000)
Green: (1,247,000)
Red: (1,247,000)
Brown: (1,247,000)
Black: (1,247,000)

The Stamp

With its 1988 Christmas contemporary stamp, USPS attempted something almost without precedent. It sought to pay postal tribute to a living American — even though, under its own rules, individuals cannot be depicted on stamps until they have been dead 10 years.

Thus the tribute had to be paid obliquely. In fact, it turned out to be so oblique that nobody — simply by looking at the stamp itself — could possibly have any idea what was going on.

The person was Irving Berlin, the legendary creator of the words and music to *White Christmas* and dozens of other songs that have become popular classics. Berlin turned 100 on May 11, 1988.

One of the songwriter's most devoted fans was Postmaster General Anthony M. Frank, who had made headlines early in his term of office by proposing a stamp for another contemporary music figure, Elvis Presley (see Year in Review).

"Irving Berlin is 100 years old, he deeply deserves to be honored and yet obviously he made a miscalculation 10 years ago and kept on living," Frank told *The Los Angeles Times.*

"So I've got a dual problem. I've got somebody who's dead (Presley) who's alleged to be alive, and I've got somebody alive (Berlin) that I want to honor that's not dead."

Frank tried to solve the latter problem, at least, with the 1988 Christmas contemporary stamp, issued October 20. Planned for issuance in 1990, the design was moved up two years on the schedule.

It depicted a snowy holiday scene, with an 1890s-style couple riding in a horse-drawn sleigh in the foreground. Because Irving Berlin was still alive, his name wasn't included in the design. And, in keeping with USPS practice, as the contemporary Christmas stamp it didn't even carry the word "Christmas."

But, said Frank, because the stamp featured "a house in the snow with trees and smoke and so on, we hope it gets through to people that this is *White Christmas.*"

As an added touch, however, the postmaster general said, "I'll be dedicating the stamp in — are you ready? — Berlin, New Hampshire."

"Well," he added, "it's a reach."

This "reach" was even longer than that made by the U.S. Post Office Department in 1927, when it yielded to popular demand for a stamp honoring another man who then was very much alive — Charles A. Lindbergh.

Lindbergh had just thrilled the nation with his solo flight from New York to Paris. The Post Office couldn't put his portrait on postage, but it did the next best thing. It put his plane, the *Spirit of St. Louis,* on a 10¢ airmail stamp.

Then — openly bending the spirit of the law — it added his name, "Lindbergh," to the design.

Fifty years later, with a commemorative stamp marking the 50th anniversary of that flight, USPS was much more conservative.

It again pictured the *Spirit of St. Louis*, flying low over the choppy Atlantic Ocean, but this time it didn't include Lindbergh's name — or in any other way identify him in the stamp design. To many collectors, the omission was baffling in that Lindbergh by now was actually dead (although the 10 years necessary to make him eligible for a portrait hadn't passed).

That same kind of official restraint was at work in 1988 in the inferential honor paid to Irving Berlin.

How Berlin felt about all this can only be guessed. The songwriter, whose active career spanned six decades, withdrew from the public's view in the 1970s and since then has declined all public appearances and interviews. He bars visits from friends and associates, and communicates by telephone with only a favored few.

His 100th birthday was celebrated with television and radio retrospectives and a star-studded concert sponsored by the American Society of Composers, Authors and Publishers (ASCAP), which he had helped found in 1914. But Berlin participated in none of them.

The song, *White Christmas*, whose opening eight notes, all in half-steps, constitute one of the world's most familiar melodic phrases, was introduced by Bing Crosby in the 1942 movie *Holiday Inn*. It has sold more than six million copies of sheet music and is said to be the most valuable musical copyright of all time.

Daniel Webster, music critic of *The Philadelphia Inquirer*, wrote of it: "Snow and Christmas; noncontroversial, a visual image that rings with nostalgia for something that never was for people in the Sun Belt, for people who live in urban sprawl and for whom snow is a transportation hazard. Its melody is as naive and easily sung as 'Happy Birthday,' and it is a nearly perfect popular song."

The Design

New York artist Joan Landis did her horizontally arranged design in a two-dimensional primitive style. Smoke rose from the chimney of a two-story gray house with a red barn behind it. A bright green wreath decorated the front door and evergreens flanked the yard and lined the snow-covered hills in the background.

The finished stamp, printed by gravure on BEP's Andreotti press, was reminiscent of various generic holiday designs used in the past on Christmas seals sold by the National Tuberculosis Association, partic-

The 1942 National Tuberculosis Association Christmas seal, whose design and colors resemble those of the 1988 Christmas Greetings postage stamp.

ularly the 1942 seal.

Like the 1988 traditional Christmas stamp, the contemporary stamp was printed in a new size, between definitive and commemorative, in response to complaints that the 1986 and 1987 Holiday stamps were too small.

Like the traditional, it was sheeted out in 300-subject sheets and guillotined into panes of 50 stamps each. Also like the traditional, it offered six distinctive plate-number block configurations.

But because the stamp was gravure-printed, it had only one group of five numbers per pane, located in the top, bottom or side selvage opposite one of the pane's corner stamps. ZIP and copyright markings appeared on the same side of each pane as the plate numbers, at the opposite end of the selvage. (See diagram.)

Varieties

A spectacular cutting error resulting in a pane of stamps with two plate numbers and a full gutter was reported to *Linn's Stamp News* by a collector in eastern Pennsylvania. The same collector also reported that two more such panes had been sold to other collectors in his town.

Apparently the printing sheet of 300 of which the panes were a part was rotated 90 degrees after printing and perforating but before being sliced into panes of six. The resulting pane shown to *Linn's* contained 42 full stamps and parts of 14 others, with what should have been the long side of the pane emerging as the short side, and vice versa. The full vertical gutter included in the pane showed the "color ladder" in the middle.

Miscut pane caused by a 90-degree rotation of the sheet after printing and perforation but before being sliced into six panes.

Shown are two constant production varieties found on the Christmas Greetings stamp. The stamp on the left shows the partially missing curlicue; the stamp on the right the missing curlicue.

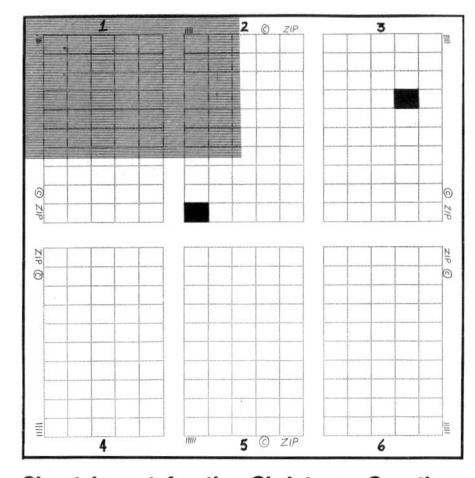

Sheet layout for the Christmas Greetings stamp. Plate number positions are (1) upper-left, (2) center-top, (3) upper-right, (4) lower-left, (5) center-bottom, and (6) lower-right. The shaded area represents the location of the miscut pane to the printing sheet of 300. The solid-colored areas represent the locations of the gravure-cylinder curlicue varieties. Each 300-stamp sheet is sliced into six 50-stamp panes.

    The largest part of the miscut pane was from the upper left pane of the printing sheet, and the rest was from the top center pane.

    Dealer Jacques Schiff of Ridgefield Park, New Jersey, reported the existence of similar miscut panes from the lower left area of the printing sheet.

    Two cylinder varieties of the Christmas stamp have been discovered by collectors. They both involve the curlicue on the front runner of the sleigh. One is completely missing; the other is partially missing.

    The BEP checked its printing cylinders and found these varieties present. This means that every sheet from the positions shown should contain these varieties.

The partially missing curlicue appears on stamp No. 46 from the top-center panes; the missing one from position No. 19 of the upper-right panes bearing cylinder No. 11111.

First-Day Facts

To get to Berlin, the northernmost city in New Hampshire, for the October 20 first-day ceremony, USPS officials from Washington had to fly to Portland, Maine, then travel 2½ hours by car.

In the spirit of the occasion, Berlin kicked off its Christmas season early. A parade was held on the eve of the first-day ceremony, and Senior Assistant Postmaster General Gordon C. Morison joined Mayor Roland Couture in lighting the community Christmas tree.

The day of the stamp ceremony opened with a stirring event — an unusual New Hampshire earthquake that registered 4.6 on the Richter scale. Though it knocked out power in some areas, the quake didn't interfere with the 11 a.m. events at Berlin Middle School.

Morison delivered the main address, in which he asserted that the 1.5 billion Christmas stamps printed in 1987, if stacked one on top of another, would make "a pile stretching 166 miles high!"

Although USPS had notified Berlin of its intention to honor him through this stamp, the reclusive centenarian sent no representative to the first-day ceremony.

25¢ CHRISTMAS MADONNA AND CHILD

Date of Issue: October 20, 1988

Catalog Numbers: Scott 2399   Minkus 910   USPS 5548

Colors: red, yellow, pink, blue, gold (offset); brown (intaglio)

First-Day Cancel: Washington, D.C. (National Gallery of Art)

FDCs Canceled: unavailable

Format: Panes of 50, vertical, 10 across, 5 down. Offset printing plates of 300 subjects (15 across, 20 around) and intaglio printing sleeve of 600 subjects (15 across, 40 around).

Perf: 11.25 (Eureka off-line perforator)

Selvage Markings: ©UNITED STATES POSTAL SERVICE 1988, USE CORRECT ZIP CODE®

Designer and Typographer: Bradbury Thompson (CSAC)

Project Manager: Jack Williams (USPS)

Engravers: Thomas Hipschen (BEP, vignette)
Michael Ryan (BEP, lettering and numerals)

Modeler: Peter Cocci (BEP)

Printing: 6-color offset, 3-color intaglio D press (902)

Quantity Ordered: 844,200,000
Quantity Distributed: 821,285,000

Plate/Sleeve Number Detail: Left-side external panes: one group of 5 offset plate numbers over/under corner stamps; one intaglio sleeve number over/under adjacent stamps. Right-side external panes: offset/intaglio numbers in reverse positions. Internal panes: one group of 5 offset plate numbers alongside corner stamps; one intaglio sleeve number alongside adjacent stamps.

Plate/Sleeve Number Combinations: 11111-1, 22222-2, 22323-2, 22333-2, 32333-2, 32433-2, 42433-2, 42443-2, 42444-2, 43444-2, 43454-1, 53454-1, 53554-1, 63554-1, 63554-2, 63565-2, 63665-2

Tagging: block over vignette

Printing Base Impressions: Offset Red: 1(163,500)
Offset Yellow: 1(163,500)
Offset Pink: 1(163,500)
Offset Blue: 1(163,500)
Offset Gold: 1(163,500)
Intaglio Brown: 1(171,000)

The Stamp

In 1986 and 1987, the U.S. Postal Service issued its annual Christmas stamps in the definitive, rather than commemorative, size. That way it got twice as many stamps from the Bureau of Engraving and Printing for the same outlay of paper, gum and ink. With total print orders for the stamps at a billion and a half units, this constituted no small saving.

But the public wasn't pleased.

Many holiday mailers complained that the stamps were too small to adequately portray the design, and that the numbers and typography were hard to read. An Illinois woman wrote the postmaster general early in 1988:

"When I saw ads for the (1987) Christmas stamps, I was delighted, as I thought they were the prettiest in many years; the lovely branch with colored ornaments as well as the beautiful Madonna. When my order came I was so very disappointed I could have cried...

"The Christmas stamps were so tiny that they looked lost on the envelopes... Christmas stamps should show the joy and happiness of the season and not need a magnifying glass to see them."

Responding to the complaints — but still keeping budget needs in mind — USPS and BEP jointly developed a new stamp size, about 50 percent larger than the previous year's Christmas stamps.

The image area was 0.77 by 1.05 inches; the overall size, perf to perf, was 0.91 by 1.19 inches. Full sheets consisted of 300 stamps. Instead of being divided into four panes, as was customary, they were divided into six panes each containing 50 stamps (5 by 10).

Both Christmas stamps for 1988 — the traditional, which, as usual, depicted a Madonna and Child from the National Gallery of Art, and the contemporary, a winter scene — were issued in this size and plate layout. Future special issues, including Love stamps, would follow the same patterns, USPS said.

The source of the 1988 traditional design was the painting *Madonna and Child* by Italian master Sandro Botticelli (1445-1510), one of the foremost artists of the Florentine Renaissance.

A similar Botticelli Madonna, from the Art Institute of Chicago, was used on a small-format Christmas stamp in 1981. And the artist's painting *Primavera*, or *Allegory of Spring,* was the source of the design of the 1940 U.S. stamp commemorating the 50th anniversary of the founding of the Pan-American Union. As adapted for the stamp, the painting's dancing female figures — the Three Graces — represented North, Central and South America.

Today the annual Christmas stamps are an established part of the U.S. holiday season. In their early years, however, they ran into some heavy criticism.

It all began in 1962 when the Post Office announced its intention to help Americans celebrate the Yuletide with a special 4¢ stamp. (It didn't announce, however, that one of its motivations was to encourage mailers to use first-class postage on their Christmas cards rather than the 3¢ that was still permissible for unsealed envelopes.)

Anxious to offend no one with its new venture, the Post Office chose for the design candles and a holly wreath. It adopted similar themes for its 1963 and 1964 Christmas stamps. This caused some citizens, including U.S. Representative Melvin Laird of Wisconsin, to complain that the religious origin of Christmas was being unjustly ignored.

The Post Office yielded to this argument in 1965 and produced a stamp reproducing Hans Memling's *Madonna and Child*. Predictably, protests then came from the other direction, the American Civil Liberties Union and the American Jewish Congress.

When the same picture was used in a larger format the next year, it also generated a lawsuit from Protestants and Others United for Separation of Church and State, which contended that the design had a pro-Roman Catholic bias. A federal court refused to issue the requested injunction.

Finally, in 1970, the Post Office introduced the compromise approach of giving customers a choice between religious and secular designs. Since then there has been little public antagonism to the Christmas stamps expressed. Beginning in 1980, the contemporary stamp has carried a neutral "Season's Greetings" or merely "Greetings."

The Design

Another change in 1988 was the decision of USPS to print the traditional stamp by combination offset/intaglio on the D press rather than by less-costly gravure. Not since the 1969 "Winter Sunday" issue

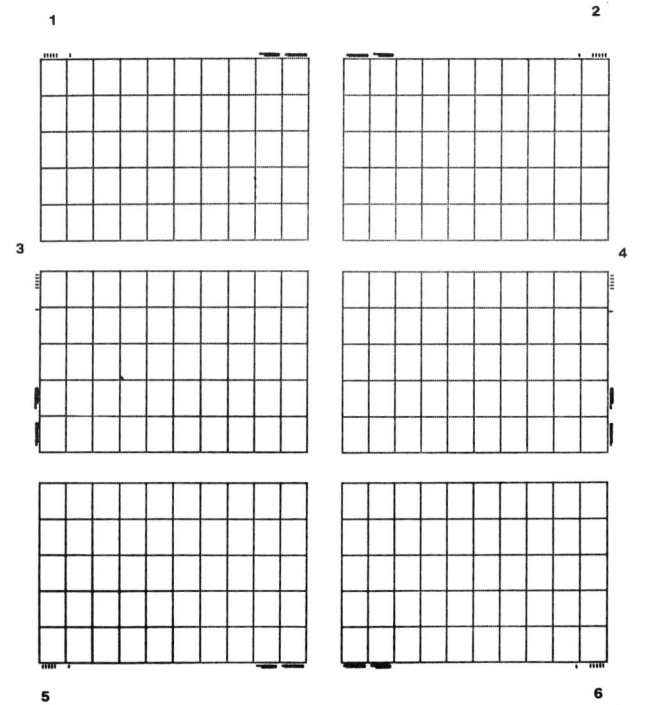

Sheet layout for the Christmas Madonna stamp. Plate number positions are (1) upper-left, (2) upper-right, (3) center-left, (4) center-right, (5) lower-left and (6) lower-right.

had the public been offered a hand-engraved Christmas stamp.

"The committee decided that you really need intaglio to bring out the detail in the Old Masters' paintings," said Jack Williams, USPS project manager for both 1988 Christmas stamps.

That lesson, on occasion, had been hard-learned. Officials still wince when they recall the 1976 traditional stamp, with a nativity scene by John Singleton Copley, on which the facial features of the infant Jesus disappeared altogether. The problem: The gravure printing cells were too large to show the necessary detail.

It didn't happen this time. Botticelli's faces, fashioned into a stamp design by Bradbury Thompson, engraved by one of BEP's top craftsmen, Thomas Hipschen, and printed in brown intaglio ink, were clear and strong. A lustrous effect was achieved by the use of a metallic gold as the offset color behind the halos.

The new plate layouts used for the Christmas stamps — 300 subjects divided into six panes of 50 — provided one set of plate numbers for each pane. For the traditional stamp, a set consisted of five offset numbers on the selvage of the corner stamp and, on the selvage of the adjacent stamp, a single intaglio number.

Each of the six panes had its plate block in a distinctive position:

upper left, upper right, lower left, lower right, left side or right side. (See diagram.) ZIP and copyright markings appeared on the same side of each pane as the plate numbers, at the opposite end of the selvage.

Varieties

A number of panes were printed and distributed with a gold offset ink omitted by mistake. The error was first reported by Main Line Coin and Stamp Inc. of Ardmore, Pennsylvania, which bought three

Left, a plate block from a normal pane of the Christmas Madonna stamp; right, a plate block from a pane completely missing the gold offset ink. (Note missing right-hand plate number and missing top color bar.)

panes from a collector. The panes were said to have been bought initially by a postal worker in a rural southern post office in October. Error panes were also reportedly sold at two stations in Greensboro, North Carolina.

First-Day Facts

The first-day ceremony for the stamp was held October 20 in the Main Auditorium of the National Gallery of Art's East Building in Washington, D.C.

Deputy Postmaster General Michael S. Coughlin was the featured speaker.

USPS permitted collectors to submit combination covers bearing both the traditional and contemporary Christmas stamps for either the Washington first-day postmark or the Berlin, New Hampshire, cancellation used for the contemporary version. The Postal Service, on request, also would affix and cancel both stamps on a single cover.

Collectors were given an additional month — to December 19 — to submit first-day cover requests. The normal 30-day time period after the issue date would have expired November 19.

25¢ SPECIAL OCCASIONS BOOKLET

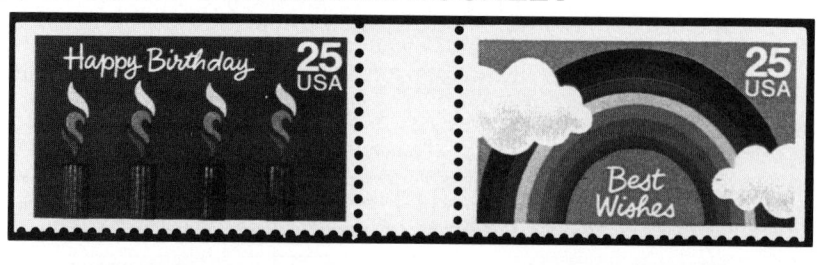

Date of Issue: October 22, 1988

Catalog Numbers: Scott 2395-98 (stamps)
　　　　　　　　　Scott 2395a and 2397a (pane of 6, 3+3)
　　　　　　　　　Scott 2396a and 2398a (pane of 6, 3+3)
　　　　　　　　　Minkus CM1331-34　　USPS 6607

Colors: magenta, yellow, cyan, purple

First-Day Cancel: King of Prussia, Pennsylvania (SEPAD stamp show, Valley Forge Convention and Exhibit Center)

FDCs Canceled: unavailable

138

Format: Two panes of 6 horizontal stamps each. Each pane folded through a center vertical gutter producing 2 pages of 3 stamps of the same design on each page. Gravure printing cylinders of 180 subjects (15 across, 12 around) manufactured by Roto Cylinder (Palmyra, New Jersey).

Perf: 10.9 (L perforator)

Selvage Markings: ©United States Postal Service 1988 and Universal Product Code (UPC) printed on outside of back cover.

Designer: Stamps: Harry Zelenko of New York, New York

Art Director and Project Manager: Donald McDowell (USPS)

Typographer: Bradbury Thompson (CSAC)

Modeler: Richard Sennett (Sennett Enterprises) for American Bank Note Company

Printing: Stamps printed and sheeted out by American Bank Note Company on a leased gravure press (J.W. Fergusson and Sons, Richmond, Virginia) under the supervision of Sennett Enterprises (Fairfax, Virginia). Booklet cover printed in yellow, magenta, cyan and black on an offset press by ABN (Chicago, Illinois). Booklets formed on standard bookbinding equipment by ABN (Chicago).

Quantity Ordered: 40,000,000
Quantity Distributed: 1,932,000

Cylinder Number Detail: One group of 4 cylinder numbers preceded by the letter "A" in the center gutter selvage of each pane.

Cylinder Number Combination: A1111

Tagging: block over vignette

The Stamps

With its second booklet of Special Occasions stamps, USPS produced the most significant change in booklet arrangement and appearance in the 88 years since an innovative assistant postmaster general named Edwin C. Madden introduced the idea of stamps between cardboard covers.

The change was made in response to complaints about the first Special Occasions booklet, issued in 1987.

That booklet, printed by BEP, had contained one pane of 10 22¢ stamps, bearing eight different personal messages. Users found that to obtain a particular message — a "Love You, Dad!" for example — all the stamps below it on the pane had to be detached with it.

The new $3 booklet, printed by the American Bank Note Company, contained only four stamp varieties, bearing the four most requested messages: "Happy Birthday," "Best Wishes," "Thinking of You" and "Love You."

Its heavy stock cover folded sideways. Inside were two se-tenant panes of six commemorative-size 25¢ stamps, each folded through a center gutter of selvage to create four pages of three stamps each. "Thinking of You" and "Love You" made up one two-page pane, "Happy Birthday" and "Best Wishes" the other. Designed like a miniature book, it permitted mailers to pick the appropriate message and easily remove any stamp without disconnecting others.

(In an apparent planning lapse, however, the covers were cut slightly short, so that when they were closed and sealed they didn't quite clear the edge of the stamp panes inside.)

The center gutter selvage on each pane bore the letter A — indicating that the printing was by ABNC — and four plate numbers, one for each of the four gravure colors used to print the stamps.

This allowed another innovation, one adopted strictly for the benefit of stamp collectors. The gutter selvage was spot-glued in three places to the booklet, securing the stamps but making it possible — at least theoretically — for collectors to peel them away for mounting in albums.

Previously, since the Goebel booklet-making machines began production at BEP in 1977, booklet-pane tabs had been glued tightly to booklet covers. To remove them intact without disturbing the gum on the stamps, collectors were obliged to apply heat (usually with an iron at a moderate setting) and a great deal of patience. Even then, they were often unsuccessful. It remained to be seen whether the new method would be an improvement.

Another complaint that had been heard about the 1987 Special Occasions stamps was that some of the messages were too specific.

An Orlando, Florida, postal clerk told a reporter for *The Orlando Sentinel:* "They're not selling much at all. They're a problem." Explained the reporter: "The problem is, people usually don't send cheery letters. They're more likely to send crisp, unemotional business letters, or checks or magazine subscription renewals. None of which are the time and place for 'Love You, Mother!' "

No doubt as a result of such reaction, the messages in the new booklet were fewer and more general.

The 1988 Special Occasions booklet was only the second U.S. stamp booklet to be made by a private contractor. It had been preceded earlier in 1988 by the 25¢ Pheasant booklet, also printed by ABNC.

But delays in printing and distribution cropped up. Late in November, more than five weeks after the issue date, *Linn's* reported that the booklet still was unavailable in many parts of the country.

The announcement of the booklet itself had come as a surprise to collectors. It wasn't on the original 1988 stamp program unveiled in

July 1987, nor on the detailed program released April 4,1988. Not until August 4 did USPS announce that Special Occasions booklet II would be issued later in the year.

On September 19 the issue date and place were provided: October 22, at SEPAD 88, the 48th annual exhibition and bourse of the Associated Stamp Clubs of Southeastern Pennsylvania and Delaware, in King of Prussia, Pennsylvania.

Hallmark Cards Inc. used the booklet in a promotion shortly after it was issued. If a customer bought a certain amount of merchandise, he was given a certificate entitling him to receive by mail a Special Occasions booklet and a metal container for other stamps.

The Designs

New York City artist Harry Zelenko developed the designs for each theme in a style that might be called "greeting-card simple." Each

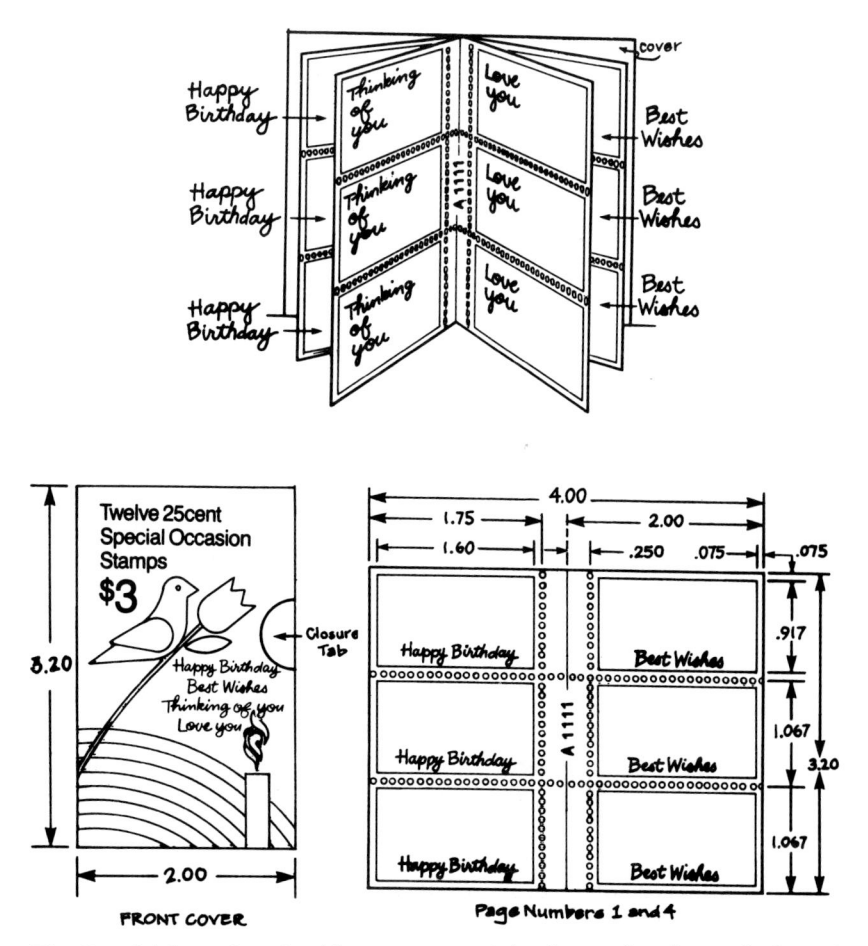

The Special Occasions booklet represented the first major change in format since U.S. stamps first appeared in booklets in 1900.

subject was shown against a different solid-color background. "Happy Birthday" featured four blazing candles, on purple; "Best Wishes," a rainbow, on sky blue; "Thinking of You," flowers, on orange, and "Love You," a bird peering from an open mailbox, on green.

The artist's original concept sketches were accepted by CSAC, with only one alteration: the lettering was changed from black to dropout white for better visibility.

Zelenko also designed the full-color front cover, which combined the elements of the designs inside — a bird perched on the stem of a flower, with a rainbow and candle beneath, and the four messages. The covers were printed by offset-lithography.

It was a first design assignment for Zelenko, a man described by Jack Williams, the project manager, as "very clever, very creative at working with small objects." Zelenko had submitted some ideas for Christmas stamps to Howard Paine, a CSAC design coordinator. Donald M. McDowell, general manager of the Stamps Division, had liked them, and the result was the Special Occasions design contract.

McDowell himself assumed the task of art director for the booklet, an unusual role for him. Zelenko prepared other designs, bearing other messages, in addition to the four that were used, and USPS put them in storage for future Special Occasions booklets.

First-Day Facts

Some 350 people attended the booklet's first-day ceremony on the second day of the SEPAD 88 exhibition in King of Prussia's Valley

The Special Occasions booklet panes distributed in the first-day ceremony program were unfolded, unlike those panes that were normally available.

Forge Convention and Exhibit Center, 1200 First Avenue. Regional Postmaster General Johnny F. Thomas was the principal speaker.

The first-day ceremony programs distributed by USPS contained something unavailable any other way — unfolded panes from the booklet. Normal booklet production folds the panes down the middle, but each first-day program contained an unfolded pane of the Happy Birthday and Best Wishes stamps, machine-glued to the bottom of the inside of the program and tied by an October 22 King of Prussia first-day cancel.

Frank Thomas of USPS' Stamp Information Branch said the normal run of 2,200 first-day programs was made, all of them using the Happy Birthday/Best Wishes pane, and several hundred were distributed at SEPAD. The balance went to the postmaster general's stock for distribution at his discretion.

Thomas said there were no plans to make unfolded panes available to collectors or commercial cover makers.

As usual, USPS encouraged first-day cover collectors to buy the stamps and affix them to their envelopes. For covers prepared by USPS, individual stamps were affixed at random, and requests for specific single stamps weren't honored. However, customers ordering a full six-stamp pane for their cover could specify which of the two different panes they wanted.

DEFINITIVES

To meet the requirements of the rate change, USPS issued a total of 24 new face-different definitive stamps in 1988. There were also coil and booklet versions of new and existing sheet stamps, plus a new precancel overprint to which USPS gave new-issue treatment. These brought the year's total to 32 different collectible varieties.

The Great Americans series was enlarged by the addition of five new faces — four men and one woman — bringing the total in its gallery to 44, and enabling it to hold onto the distinction of being the longest definitive series ever issued by the United States.

But just barely. The Transportation series of coil stamps, by getting 12 new face-different varieties, raised its total number to 43. Some would argue that because three of the earlier Transportation stamps had been later re-engraved with clear differences in appearance, they should count in the total, thereby thrusting this series into the lead.

The major news about the definitives of 1988, however, was not their number but the new policy adopted by USPS toward service-inscribed stamps — what the Postal Service calls precancels.

In the past, fractional-rate coil stamps issued for various types of bulk mailings were available in two forms.

The larger part of each issue bore an inscription, in a color other than that of the vignette, describing the service ("Bulk Rate," "Zip + 4 Presort," etc.). The inscription was either overprinted over the basic stamp or engraved as part of the design. These stamps weren't tagged because, being precanceled, they didn't go through the post offices' facer-canceler machines.

At the same time, a second variety was issued, minus the precancel but with tagging added. Its market was primarily made up of stamp collectors. Because USPS rules required collectors who wanted plate number specimens of fractional coil stamps to buy strips of as many as 60 in order to get them, collectors could be expected to — and did — use many of their excess stamps on ordinary mail. Hence the need for tagging.

This dual procedure with each stamp complicated things for the BEP, particularly in the case of the more recent issues on which the service inscriptions were engraved. These required two completely different printing sleeves for the two versions, not merely one sleeve and a flexographic plate applying an overprint.

Furthermore, in practice many stamp collectors collected both the precanceled and non-precanceled versions anyway.

The obvious step — one generally beneficial to both USPS and stamp collectors — was taken in 1988.

On April 4, when USPS released its list of forthcoming rate-change definitives, it specified that the nine brand-new Transportation series coils that were intended for various bulk-mail categories would be issued in service-inscribed form only. The same was true for a 10th variety, the existing 10.1¢ Oil Wagon stamp on which a new precancel would be overprinted.

"There's no real need of the unprecanceled versions," said Dickey Rustin, manager of the Stamp Information Branch. By printing only one variety of each stamp, he said, USPS would save on the cost of printing and of accounting for stamp quantities.

(For the record: When all possible varieties of the Transportation series were added in, the count for the series by year's end had reached 71. This included all 43 design-different stamps; the three that had been re-engraved; three other stamps originally printed on the Cottrell press that were adapted for the B press, slightly altering the size of the printed area; 19 stamps that had been issued as non-precanceled, tagged versions, in addition to their precanceled counterparts; the new precancel overprint on the 10.1¢ Oil Wagon, and two additional types of precancel on the 17¢ Electric Auto.)

The first reaction of collectors and the philatelic press to the new policy on service-inscribed or precanceled stamps was to ask the Postal Service for a clarification of its rules on the use of such stamps by the general public.

The clarification was necessary because many postal clerks weren't aware of two-year-old USPS rules that permitted the public to use precancels on ordinary mail. The clerks were refusing letters that had been prepared in accordance with these rules.

Before July 10, 1986, collectors hadn't been allowed to prepay ordinary mail with precanceled postage, even philatelic covers. Any cover submitted for philatelic cancellation had to bear enough mint, non-precanceled stamps to cover the first-class rate, even if it already bore an equivalent amount in precancels.

But after that date, collectors submitting covers for first-day or special commemorative cancellations could use any combination of unused precanceled stamps so long as they added up to the first-class rate. They didn't need a permit to use precancels, because USPS considered itself the mailer in such cases.

The 1986 policy change also set forth a way for stamp collectors to use up the excess precancels they were obliged to buy in order to obtain plate numbers.

As published in *Postal Bulletin 21547*, the new rules were:
1. Although precanceled stamps typically are used to pay postage on bulk mailings, they also may be used on single-piece or limited-size mailings as long as the proper amount of postage is paid. Bulk rate discounts do not apply under such usage.

2. All users of precanceled stamps must have an approved permit Form 3620, *Permit to Use Precanceled Stamps or Envelopes,* on file.*

3. Those who do not have permits may purchase precanceled stamps only for philatelic purposes.

4. Mail bearing precanceled stamps may not be deposited in street collection boxes. All such mail must be presented to authorized postal employees at weigh units, window units, or detached mail units of the post office where the mailer's permit is held. When such use is not part of the qualifying bulk mailing, stamps should be canceled with a dated device by the accepting clerk.

5. A mailer may use precanceled stamps along with regular stamps on the same mailpiece for full payment of postage. In this event, a permit must also be on file and mail must be presented as in item 4.

6. Unless a bulk mailing is being made, it is not necessary to complete a Form 3602 PC, *Statement of Mailing With Bulk Rate,* simply because a mailer uses precanceled stamps.

7. Precanceled stamps bearing endorsements such as "Presorted First Class" may be used in any mailing as long as the appropriate amount of total postage is reflected on each piece.**

* Possession of this permit does not require a fee. A fee must be paid only when mailing in bulk at discount rates.

** Unless an item is part of a qualified bulk mailing, the total postage must equal or exceed the First-Class rate, regardless of the type of endorsement.

These rules were restated in a USPS news release July 6, 1988. Some philatelic periodicals reprinted the text of the announcement so collectors could clip it and show it to postal clerks who still weren't aware of the two-year-old USPS policy.

3¢ CONESTOGA WAGON

Date of Issue: February 29, 1988

Catalog Numbers: Scott 2252   Minkus 883   USPS 7761

Color: maroon

First-Day Cancel: Conestoga, Pennsylvania (Main Street Fire Hall)

FDCs Canceled: 155,203

Format: Coils of 100, 500 and 3,000. Printing sleeve of 936 subjects (18 across, 52 around).

Perf: 9.75 (Goebel stroke perforator on coils of 100; Huck rotary perforator on coils of 500 and 3,000).

Designer: Richard Schlecht of Arlington, Virginia

Art Director: Jack Williams (USPS)

Typographer: Bradbury Thompson (CSAC)

Engravers: Thomas Hipschen (BEP, vignette)
Dennis Brown (BEP, lettering and numeral)

Printing: 3-color intaglio B press (701)

Quantity Ordered: Coils of 100 - 134,800
Coils of 500 - 115,800
Coils of 3,000 - 20,768

Quantity Distributed: Coils of 100 - 134,400
Coils of 500 - 112,200
Coils of 3,000 - 20,096

Sleeve Number Detail: One sleeve number every 52nd stamp

Sleeve Number: 1

Tagging: block over vignette

The Stamp

The first of the long procession of definitive stamps for 1988 was a 3¢ coil stamp depicting a Conestoga wagon, the graceful, high-wheeled vehicle on which Americans rolled into the Ohio Valley.

The stamp was the 32nd face-different variety in the popular Transportation series, which was inaugurated in 1981. It was placed on sale February 29 in Conestoga, Lancaster County, Pennsylvania. USPS researchers reported that it was the first postal item ever to be issued on this date, which occurs only in Leap Year.

The Conestoga was printed in maroon on BEP's B intaglio press in coils of 100, 500 and 3,000. It replaced another Transportation series stamp, the 3¢ Railroad Handcar of 1983, which was a product of the Bureau's old Cottrell press.

USPS first announced the stamp's subject, denomination and first-day date and place November 25, 1987. Design details and other information were furnished January 14, 1988.

With the official adoption of the new 25¢ first-class postal rate — 3¢ more than the old rate — it became obvious that the new coil would see a lot of use as makeup postage for postal customers with leftover 22-centers.

The Conestoga wagon, as a stamp subject, was a "people's choice." In April 1987, John M. Hotchner, author of the U.S. Notes column in *Linn's Stamp News*, invited his readers to send their ideas for new Transportation series stamps to W.L. "Pete" Davidson, director of the USPS Office of Stamps and Philatelic Marketing, and to forward copies to him. Of 194 different conveyances suggested, the Conestoga wagon was "clearly the winner," Hotchner reported.

Davidson was "delighted" at the response, the columnist added, and had promised that many of the ideas would be used, "some as early as 1988." Davidson was as good as his word. Besides the Conestoga wagon, the suggested subjects that turned up on 1988 Transportation series coils included the tugboat, ore (coal) car, elevator, cable car and police patrol wagon.

The characteristics of the Conestoga wagon were a rounded bed with upturned front and rear, high side walls, oversized wheels and extended wooden bows framing the white canvas cover. The side-rear view of the wagon shown on the stamp emphasized these features.

The date reference on the stamp is "1800s," which refers to the first half of the 19th century, rather than merely its first decade. The vehicle, in fact, was in use for roughly 100 years.

It was invented by the Pennsylvania Dutch of the Conestoga Valley of Pennsylvania around 1750 to haul their produce to fairs and farmers' markets behind teams of four to six horses, but it soon became the primary vehicle for overland freight hauling to new settlements in the Ohio Valley.

The boatlike shape of the wagon was practical as well as aesthetically pleasing. The high front, rear and side walls helped in floating the wagon across streams as well as improving its handling and maneuverability, an important feature to settlers facing rough roadways — or no roadways at all — on their way west. The broad wheel rims resisted bogging down in mud.

The Conestoga wagon was almost never used west of the Missouri River except by freighters along the Santa Fe trail. Thus, modern illustrations that show Conestogas taking settlers across the prairies to

In 1987, several Linn's Stamp News *readers suggested that the Conestoga Wagon be shown on a Transportation series coil. These sketches accompanied two of their letters.*

the West are in error. The Conestoga was much too heavy for the long pull to Oregon or California, and the covered wagons that actually made that trip were smaller and lighter descendants. Those few Conestogas that were ill-advisedly taken westward almost always had to be abandoned somewhere along the road.

The generic covered wagon was once a common design element in U.S. stamps. During the 1930s, 1940s and 1950s, it seemed that no commemorative stamp connected with the settling of the West was complete without a "prairie schooner." One of its most recent philatelic appearances was on the 1974 Fort Harrod (Kentucky) Bicentennial commemorative.

The Design

All designs for the Transportation series are prepared as black line drawings, and artists use either black pencil or black ink, as they prefer, to guide the engraver in his interpretation.

To maintain the "series look," typographer Bradbury Thompson prepares type overlay in advance, including, when necessary, space for an endorsement like "Bulk Rate" or "Nonprofit." The designer fits his art into the available space.

"This wasn't the case in the early days of the series, when type was added almost as an afterthought," said Jack Williams, USPS program manager for philatelic design and the project manager and art director for the Conestoga Wagon stamp.

"The Motorcycle stamp (of 1983) is a good example of the artwork being too small, thus making the type much too large."

Richard Schlecht of Arlington, Virginia, based his design for the Conestoga Wagon stamp on a photo from the book *Conestoga Wagon 1750-1850*, by George Shumway. Schlecht completed the design as-

This early essay for the Conestoga Wagon stamp separated the date from the vehicle designation, something that isn't done in the Transportation series.

signment in April 1987.

"It's a nice little stamp you can really get graphic with," the artist told *The Washington Post*. Other stamps, such as the typical commemorative, "get a little 'painterly,' " he said.

Schlecht, 51, had worked in the Washigton area since 1960. A native of Denver who came to the capital as an Army illustrator, he said he was perhaps best known for the historical scenes he had painted for the National Geographic Society and National Park Service.

For USPS, Schlecht had previously designed the 1985 Junipero Serra airmail stamp, the 1985 Flying Cloud postal card, and the 1983 German Immigration and 1982 Wolf Trap Farm Park commemoratives. The volume of stamp work he does, he said, is one of the "real advantages of living just 10 minutes, just across the bridge," from USPS headquarters.

Varieties

A vertical plate crack, starting at the top of the letter W in "Wagon" and extending down through the vignette, was found in rolls of 500 purchased at a Memphis, Tennessee, philatelic center. It appears in postition 41 of rolls with plate number 1 — the 11th stamp to the left of the stamp with the number.

First-Day Facts

The stage for the first-day ceremony February 29 was the bed of an authentic 16-foot Conestoga wagon, parked in the Fire Hall on Conestoga's Main Street.

More than 500 people heard talks by Assistant Postmaster General Peter A. Jacobson and Arthur L. Reist, teacher, author and wagon expert, among others. Also on hand was designer Richard Schlecht. (When Schlecht, who is well over six feet tall, stood up in the wagon, his head extended above the framing hoops, from which the canvas cover had been partially removed.)

As is customary, a presentation album of the new stamps was sent by Express Mail to President Reagan at the White House. On this occasion, however, the album was carried from the first-day ceremony to the Conestoga post office in another authentic Conestoga wagon, drawn by a team of horses.

Several different cachets were on sale. The Lancaster County philatelic and historical societies sponsored an official one, whose central motif was an end view of a wagon, similar to that on the stamp. The Keystone Federation of Stamp Clubs sponsored a cachet in red or blue featuring a side view.

At least 19¢ additional postage had to be affixed to a first-day cover bearing a Conestoga Wagon stamp to make up the 22¢ first-class rate. On customer-addressed envelopes that were submitted along with remittance for stamps, USPS affixed four 3¢ Conestoga Wagons and one 10¢ Canal Boat Transportation series coil of 1987.

E (25¢) SHEET STAMP

Date of Issue: March 22, 1988

Catalog Numbers: Scott 2277   Minkus 884   USPS 1098

Colors: red, blue, yellow, black

First-Day Cancel: Washington, D.C. (no first-day ceremony)

FDCs Canceled: 363,639 (includes all E stamps and E Savings Bond envelope)

Format: Panes of 100, vertical, 10 across, 10 down. Printing cylinders of 400 subjects (20 across, 20 around)

Perf: 11.2 by 11.1 (Eureka off-line perforator)

Selvage Markings: ©UNITED STATES POSTAL SERVICE 1986, USE CORRECT ZIP CODE®

Designer: Robert McCall of Paradise Valley, Arizona

Art Director and Typographer: Bradbury Thompson (CSAC)

Project Manager: Jack Williams (USPS)

Modeler: Esther Porter (BEP)

Printing: 7-color Andreotti gravure press (601)

Quantity Ordered: 1,479,750,000
Quantity Distributed: 1,473,900,000

Cylinder Number Detail: One group of 4 cylinder numbers alongside corner stamps

Cylinder Number Combinations: 1111

Tagging: block over vignette

Printing Base Impressions: Red: 2(11,000), 2(2,098,000)
Blue: 1(4,495,400), 1(3,063,800), 2(11,000)
Yellow: 1(4,495,400), 1(2,113,800)
Black: 2(11,000), 2(2,098,000)

The Stamp

Since 1978, USPS has accompanied each change in the first-class letter rate with the issuance of non-denominated sheet, coil and booklet stamps — prepared long in advance — on which a letter of the alphabet represented the new rate. These were meant to meet customer demand until permanent new definitives bearing the actual rate designation could be printed and distributed

Thus we had the A stamp in 1978 (15¢), the B in 1980 (18¢), the C in 1981 (20¢) and the D in 1985 (22¢). All four were single-color stamps sharing a common design — the Postal Service's stylized eagle.

A few months after the 22¢ rate had become effective in early 1985, USPS made preparations for the advance printing of an E stamp for the next rate increase. This time, however, the Citizens' Stamp Advisory Committee decided on a design change.

"Aside from expressing distaste for non-denominated stamps in general, mail users and collectors alike told us that the A, B, C and D stamps were drab in appearance," said Jack Williams, E stamp project manager. "In response to those observations, we determined that the E stamp (and its successors, if necessary) would be more appealing to the eye."

CSAC decided to link the subject of the stamp with the letter E. Bradbury Thompson, a design coordinator, chose from the dictionary several words that evoked usable images and were of the right length to fit comfortably on a stamp, including Eagle (already thoroughly worked over as a subject), Egret — and Earth. Pete Davidson, director of stamps and philatelic marketing, spoke strongly on behalf of the Earth, and the members agreed that that was their topic.

"Earth made us think of NASA photographs from space, and space led us immediately to Bob McCall, who had done almost all of our Space stamps," Williams said.

Design work began in September 1985, and production of some six billion E stamps took place over a period of several months in 1986. (1986 was the copyright number appearing on the margin of the panes.) There were two shipments of stamps — 57 tractor-trailer truckloads — to USPS' huge underground storage facility carved out of limestone near Kansas City, Missouri: one in September 1986 and the other in February-March 1987.

USPS unveiled the E design February 18, 1988, and announced that the stamp would be issued to correspond with the new first-class rate "expected to be implemented this spring."

The actual issuance in three formats — sheet, coil and booklet — came without advance notice in Washington March 22, in conjunction with the special meeting of the USPS Board of Governors, which approved the new 25¢ first-class letter rate effective April 3.

By now many post offices across the country had already received the E stamps, but didn't know until the last minute when they were to be released.

At a press conference after the governors' meeting, Postmaster General Anthony M. Frank purchased the first E stamps — three booklets, for $15 — using the USPS Stamps by Phone service, as reporters listened to the conversation.

It wasn't until two days later, on March 24, that USPS published the formal announcement of the new stamps' issuance and gave ordering details for first-day covers.

As before, USPS emphasized that non-denominated stamps were for use in the United States only. Universal Postal Union regulations require denominated postage on international mail. However, Canada Post announced in its April 4 *Bulletin* that the E stamps would be honored on mail to Canada as a courtesy extended to a neighbor.

"Therefore," the *Bulletin* said, "no deficient postage should be collected from addressees unless the item bears a T stamp (postal marking) affixed by the USPS indicating postage due."

When the notice was published, Canada Post was unaware that U.S. rates to Canada were to be higher than domestic rates. In spite of this, said Brenda Adams of Canada Post, the policy would remain the same. Unless a postage-due marking appeared on the mail item, deficient postage wouldn't be collected.

Adams said the same policy had been in effect for the U.S. C series and D series non-denominated stamps as well. In 1981 Canada itself had issued an A series non-denominated stamp; it wasn't honored in the United States.

The Design

With the E stamp, printed in four colors on BEP's Andreotti gravure press, USPS gave collectors an attractive stamp with a popular topical theme — space.

Robert T. McCall's dramatic and colorful moon's-eye view of the Earth shows blue oceans and a burnt-orange North America seen

If "E for Eagle" instead of "E for Earth" had been chosen, this design might have been adopted.

through swirls of white clouds covering the planet. The backdrop of outer space is represented by layered colors — a center band of yellow, blending above and below into red and then to blue, with a few white stars appearing at the top.

The "E" at upper left and "Earth" at lower left are in white dropout lettering and the words "Domestic" in red and "USA" in blue appear on a white background beneath the stamp image.

McCall, a veteran Space-stamp designer from Paradise Valley, Arizona, based his painting on composite photographs provided by the National Aeronautics and Space Administration (NASA).

His previous stamp credits include the 1971 Space Achievement Decade se-tenant pair, 1974 Skylab, 1975 Pioneer 10, 1975 Apollo-Soyuz se-tenant pair, 1978 Viking Mission and 1981 eight-stamp se-tenant Space Achievement block of 1981. A non-Space stamp designed by McCall was the 1984 Hispanic Americans commemorative.

"It (the E stamp) was a highly popular, beautiful stamp which has brought us many compliments," said USPS' Jack Williams. "The only complaints have been that the definitive size is too small; that is, we should have printed it in the larger, more expensive commemorative size."

Although a few collectors disagreed and pronounced the stamp "ugly" in letters to the editor, others praised it.

One, writing to *Linn's*, likened the globe in the E stamp design to "a beautiful multicolored aggie that I used in the early 1920s when we youngsters knuckled down for a game of marbles." Another noted its "3-D-like appearance" that "makes it a very interesting stamp." A third commended USPS for "getting out of the rut" and added: "It is fascinating to consider that the E stamp's design, which had its inspiration from the actual photos of Earth from outer space, could not have been rendered only a quarter century ago, except in the imagination of an artist."

The same could have been said of earlier stamps depicting Earth as seen from space, including those commemorating Project Gemini (1967), Apollo 8 (1969), the Apollo 10 Moon Landing (1969), Apollo 15 (1971), Skylab (1974), Apollo Soyuz (1975) and the entire range of U.S. Space Achievements (1981), plus the Campaign Against Pollution (1970).

First-Day Facts

There was no first-day ceremony for the E sheet stamp. Because it was issued with no advance notice, first-day cover collectors were given 60 days rather than the usual 30 to submit self-addressed covers to the postmaster in Washington for first-day cancellations.

E (25¢) COIL STAMP

Date of Issue: March 22, 1988

Catalog Numbers: Scott 2279   Minkus 885   USPS 7706

Colors: red, blue, yellow, black

First-Day Cancel: Washington, D.C. (no first-day ceremony)

FDCs Canceled: 363,639 (includes all E stamps and E Savings Bond envelope)

Format: Coils of 100, 500 and 3,000. Printing cylinders of 432 subjects (18 across, 24 around)

Perf: 9.75 (Goebel stroke perforator on coils of 100; Huck rotary perforator on coils of 500 and 3,000).

Designer: Robert McCall of Paradise Valley, Arizona

Art Director and Typographer: Bradbury Thompson (CSAC)

Project Manager: Jack Williams (USPS)

Modeler: Esther Porter (BEP)

Printing: 7-color Andreotti gravure press (601)

Quantity Ordered: Coils of 100 - 24,826,400
Coils of 500 - 1,070,400
Coils of 3,000 - 58,496

Quantity Distributed: Coils of 100 - 24,826,400
Coils of 500 - 1,070,000
Coils of 3,000 - 58,528

Cylinder Number Detail: One group of 4 cylinder numbers on every 24th stamp

Cylinder Number Combinations: 1111, 1211, 1222, 2222

Tagging: block over vignette

Printing Base Impressions: Red: 2(2,237,000)
Blue: 2(2,237,000)
Black: 2(2,237,000)

The Stamp

The existence of the E stamps first came to light when *Linn's* reported in its November 24, 1986, issue that a coil had turned up in a Hollywood, Florida, post office vault during a routine inventory. None of the stamps was sold.

The parallel white lines on the beginning stamps of each roll were tape residue.

The coil version of the 25¢ non-denominated stamp was printed on the BEP's Andreotti gravure press from a 432-subject cylinder (18 across by 24 around). This meant that number collectors could expect to find one group of four cylinder numbers on every 24th stamp.

The numbers were so tiny, and the yellow color so pale, that the yellow cylinder number was extremely difficult to distinguish, even under strong magnification. Difficult became impossible on a used copy of the stamp when the cancellation touched the yellow number.

Collectors noted that up to three stamps at the beginning of each roll bore parallel white lines across the design, slightly raised from the surface and with a bit of a gritty feel. These lines were residue from the white tape used to keep the coils from unrolling. The tape had been in place for two years while the stamps awaited the call to service and, during that time, had adhered to the paper and dried out.

Varieties

An imperf pair of E coil stamps.

All four of the earlier non-denominated coils had been found in imperforate form, and a few weeks after the E coil was issued the first such variety for this one was reported.

Robert E. Tallon of Fort Worth, Texas, said he found a strip of 32 without perforations in a roll he purchased at the main post office in Fort Worth. Others later reported similar finds. The imperfs were in rolls with cylinder numbers 1111 and 1211.

E (25¢) BOOKLET STAMP

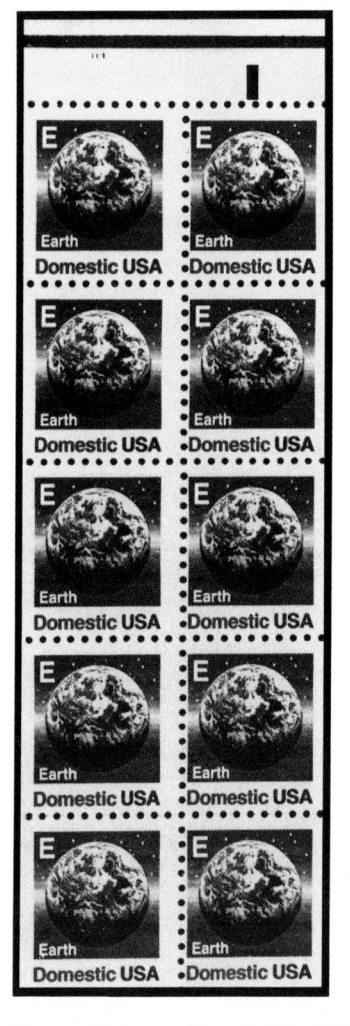

Date of Issue: March 22, 1988

Catalog Numbers: Scott 2282 (stamp)   Minkus 886   USPS 6603
Scott 2282a (pane of 10)

Colors: red, blue, yellow, black

First-Day Cancel: Washington, D.C, (no first-day ceremony)

158

FDCs Canceled: 363,639 (includes all E stamps and E Savings Bond envelope)

Format: Two panes of 10 stamps each arranged 2 by 5. Printing cylinders of 480 subjects (20 across, 24 around).

Perf: 10 by 9.75 (Goebel booklet machine stroke perforator)

Selvage Markings: 4 cylinder numbers and registration markings on each pane binding stub. ©UNITED STATES POSTAL SERVICE 1986 on inside of booklet cover.

Designer: Robert McCall of Paradise Valley, Arizona

Art Director and Typographer: Bradbury Thompson (CSAC)

Project Manager: Jack Williams (USPS)

Modeler: Esther Porter (BEP)

Printing: Stamps printed on the 7-color Andreotti gravure press (601). Covers printed and booklets formed on Goebel booklet machine.

Quantity Ordered: 80,000,000
Quantity Distributed: 83,713,000

Cylinder Number Detail: One group of 4 cylinder numbers on each pane binding stub.

Cylinder Number Combinations: 1111, 2122, 2222

Tagging: block over vignette

Printing Base Impressions: Blue: 2(1,148,000)
Yellow: 2(2,098,000)

The Stamp

The E stamp booklet panes were printed on the Andreotti gravure press from 480-subject cylinders (20 across by 24 around). Two panes of 10 stamps each were glued into each $5 booklet.

One group of four cylinder numbers appeared on the booklet tabs. As with the coil stamps, the tiny, pale yellow cylinder numbers were extremely difficult to distinguish.

The booklet covers were printed in blue. In keeping with the theme of the stamp itself, the front of the cover depicted a circle representing a globe with lines of longitude and latitude, along with the inscription "TWENTY U.S. STAMPS/Meets First-Class Letter Mail Rate/E SERIES/DOMESTIC MAIL ONLY." An explanatory paragraph about the E stamps was included on the inside of the cover.

As with the sheet and coil versions, no first-day ceremony was held. For first-day covers on which the customer asked USPS to affix the stamps, only full panes of 10 were used, and $2.50 remittance was required for each cover.

25¢ PHEASANT BOOKLET

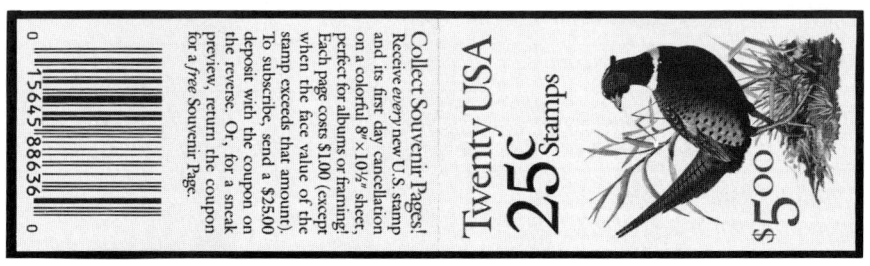

Date of Issue: April 29, 1988

Catalog Numbers: Scott 2283 (stamp)   Minkus 887   USPS 65636
Scott 2283a (panes of 10)

Colors: magenta, yellow, cyan, black

First-Day Cancel: Rapid City, South Dakota

FDCs Canceled: 167,053

Format: Two panes of 10 stamps each, arranged 2 by 5. Gravure printing cylinders of 400 subjects (20 across, 20 around) manufactured by Roto Cylinder (Palmyra, New Jersey).

Perf: 10.9 (L perforator)

Selvage Markings: Cylinder numbers printed on each pane binding stub. ©UNITED STATES POSTAL SERVICE 1988 printed on inside front cover. Universal Product Code (UPC) printed on outside back cover.

Designer: Chuck Ripper of Huntington, West Virginia

Art Director: Jack Williams (USPS)

Typographer: Bradbury Thompson (CSAC)

Modeler: Richard Sennett (Sennett Enterprises) for American Bank Note Company

160

Printing: Stamps printed and sheeted out by American Bank Note Company on a leased gravure press (J.W. Fergusson and Sons, Richmond, Virginia) under the supervision of Sennett Enterprises (Fairfax, Virginia). Booklet cover printed in yellow, magenta, cyan and black on an offset press by ABN (Chicago). Booklets formed on standard bookbinding equipment by ABN (Chicago).

Quantity Ordered: 160,000,000
Quantity Distributed: 107,081,027

Cylinder Number Detail: One group of 4 cylinder numbers preceded by the letter "A" on each pane binding stub.

Cylinder Number Combinations: A1111, A3111, A3222

Tagging: block over vignette

Printing Base Impressions: A1111 (6,050,348)
A3111 (1,400,095)
A3222 (2,149,286

The Stamp

A significant trend in U.S. stamp production is the increase in the number of stamps in booklets relative to those produced in other forms. The year 1987 marked the first time more stamps were produced in booklets (25 percent) than in sheets or panes (24 percent). The remaining 51 percent took the form of coils.

During the next few years, USPS officials say, booklet production will increase even more.

The 1988 rate increase stimulated that trend. With the first-class rate at 25¢, the smallest coil of 100 stamps costs $25. Booklets could be — and were — conveniently priced at $1.50, $3 and $5.

Distributional convenience also has become a factor. During 1988, the stamps on consignment program grew, with a growing number of supermarkets offering booklets at the checkout counter — in some cases, at a discount.

For many months before 1988, the Bureau of Engraving and Printing had operated its Goebel booklet-forming machines around the clock. During the last year of the 22¢ first-class rate, BEP was unable to satisfy USPS' requirement of 600 million booklets of 22¢ stamps. It produced the $4.40 Flag with Fireworks booklet on other equipment to make up a 40 million booklet production shortfall.

In 1988, the demand for booklets again led USPS to take extraordinary measures.

It contracted with the American Bank Note Company for production of the first stamp booklet made by a security printer other than BEP — and the first booklet made specifically for the 25¢ rate.

This was the $5 Pheasant booklet. Its 20 gravure-printed stamps featured one of America's handsomest birds, the male ring-necked pheasant, rising in flight against a deep blue sky from a field resplendent in autumnal red, gold and orange.

The stamp was designed to appeal to mailers who had expressed a preference for more color and variety in booklets, USPS said. "In general," it added, "a greater variety of stamp booklets will be available in the future than was previously the case."

But a serious drawback — one that some Citizens' Stamp Advisory Committee members acknowledged — was that the small size of the stamp image area (0.81 inches across by 0.72 inches deep, the standard definitive size arranged horizontally) didn't show artist Chuck Ripper's pheasant painting to best advantage. The details of the bird's plumage were too small to be readily appreciated in that size, and they disappeared in a blur whenever the gravure colors were even minutely out of register.

The modest dimensions were the result of a cost-conscious decision to include 10 stamps to a pane, two panes to a booklet. Unfortunately, Ripper had created his design with a larger stamp size in mind, as will be explained later.

At some point, USPS decided that the visual effect would be improved if the blue of the sky was made less intense. ABNC was asked to "back off a little on the blue" when making the next batch of printing cylinders, in the words of Don McDowell, general manager of USPS' Stamps Division.

In the original version of the stamp, the dot pattern of the sky was composed of two different colored screens. One was blue and the other a gradated red dot pattern. The two colors blended to form the deep blue sky color.

But after receiving USPS' request, ABNC took the red out of the top part of the design and changed the screening, leaving only the light blue color — and a sky noticeably different from what it was before.

The deletion of color from an entire area of the stamp design constituted a major collectible and listable variety, entitled to the same catalog status of any other re-engraved or reworked stamp design.

The discovery of the new variety was made by Wayne L. Youngblood, a staff writer at *Linn's Stamp News*, who examined the stamps under magnification and determined the reason for the altered color. He then queried McDowell at USPS for confirmation.

The stamp's design was unveiled at a news conference at USPS headquarters March 22 after the Board of Governors had approved the rate schedule recommended by the Postal Rate Commission. Postmaster General Anthony Frank used a full-color enlargement as an example of a new 25¢ stamp.

The first-day ceremony was held in Rapid City, South Dakota, on April 29. South Dakota's official bird is the ring-neck (*Phasianus colchicus*), and hunters flock to the state during the pheasant season. A standing pheasant was featured on the South Dakota stamp of the 1982 Birds and Flowers issue.

The earliest known use of the light-sky variety was October 31, 1988.

The ring-necked pheasant isn't a native of America. Attempts to import pheasants were unsuccessful until 1881, when Owen H. Denny, consul general at Shanghai, shipped 21 Chinese ring-necks to his brother's farm near Corvallis, Oregon. In 10 years their progeny had spread through the Willamette Valley.

Ring-necks were released during the next few decades in at least 10 states. Today the big birds are found all across the upper portion of the continental United States and lower Canada.

The Design

A male ring-neck is an attractive subject for an artist. The black of the head and neck glossed with iridescent green and violet and topped

This later printing has only one colored dot pattern. The red has been completely eliminated from the sky, leaving only the light blue color.

by ear tufts; the bright red naked patch, combining comb and wattle, around the yellow eye and on the cheek; the narrow white collar ringing the base of the neck; the body, a blend of brown, copper and russet tones; the smoothly tapering, buff-brown, black-barred tail plumes that make up at least half of the mature bird's 2½-foot to 3-foot length — this is definitely not the plumage of the back-yard sparrow.

Artist Chuck Ripper of Huntington, West Virginia, had no difficul-

"Light sky" variety.

ty with the assignment. He had plenty of photographs of ring-necks available from sporting magazines and other sources. Besides, he said, as a boy in Pennsylvania he "grew up with ring-necked pheasants."

Ripper had originally submitted a painted rough of his pheasant design at the request of USPS as part of its preliminary planning for a priority mail stamp (a project that is still unrealized). USPS suggested that the bird be shown in flight, Ripper said, explaining: "For a priority mail situation, they didn't want it under a shade tree, asleep!"

USPS liked the design — but decided to use it in a booklet instead. Ripper was asked to change the proportions of the artwork to fit a booklet-sized stamp, and to prepare a finished painting.

Chuck Ripper is one of the first artists USPS thinks of when it has a wildlife subject in mind. Besides the 1987 American Wildlife pane — which won that year's stamp popularity polls of both *Linn's Stamp News* and *Stamp Collector* — the 58-year-old West Virginian also designed the 1980 Coral Reefs block of four, the 1981 Wildlife Habi-

What appears to be a vertical line on this blowup of a stamp from the original printing is actually a slight color misregistration where the red and blue screen patterns meet. The blue-only pattern is at the extreme right.

tats block of four, the 1982 Christmas Kitten-and-Puppy stamp, the 1984 Louisiana World Exposition commemorative and the 1986 booklet pane of five different Fish stamps.

He has a reputation as a fine craftsman who is known for the painstaking research he conducts before putting brush to paper. He worked for a dozen years for a printing company before going freelance, and fully understands the capabilities and limitations of gravure printing.

"We've never had a Ripper wildlife issue that wasn't popular, that wasn't well done and that didn't print well," said Don McDowell, manager of the USPS Stamps Division.

A Ripper painting was also used for the cover for the booklet, depicting a pheasant standing in tall grass. The wording, stamp denomination and booklet price are in the same typeface used on the stamp.

The cover, the first booklet cover to feature full color, was printed by ABNC at its Chicago plant on white card stock by offset-lithography in the same four process colors as the stamp — magenta, yellow, cyan and black.

Varieties

In October 1988, it was reported that an employee of a waste firm that disposed of material for the American Bank Note Company had been arrested after offering a strip of 10 attached booklets from the company's waste to Robert M. Weisz of Stamp King of Chicago.

The booklets had been printed and attached to the cover stock, but remained as an intact strip of 10. The stamps themselves appeared in imperforate vertical pairs where the finished booklets would have been slit. The entire strip had been creased through the center.

The strip was confiscated by the Postal Inspection Service, presumably for eventual destruction.

It wasn't the first time that printer's waste had escaped from ABNC. Several years ago, a large quantity of waste from the Benjamin Banneker and John Paul Jones issues made its way through ABNC security. Much of the material remained on the market.

First-Day Facts

Jerry K. Lee, Central regional postmaster general, was principal speaker at the first-day ceremony in Rapid City.

In his speech he cited the Pheasant stamp booklet as an example of USPS "responsiveness to customer wants and needs" — convenience, color, and a popular wildlife theme.

A portion of a strip of 10 unsevered $5 Pheasant stamp booklets that was determined to be printer's waste.

25¢ JACK LONDON BOOKLET ($1.50 and $3)

Date of Issue: May 3, 1988

Catalog Numbers: Scott 2197 (stamp)   Minkus 888   USPS $1.50 6605
Scott 2197a (pane of 6)   USPS $3 6614

Color: blue

First-Day Cancel: San Francisco, California (no first-day ceremony)

FDCs Canceled: 94,655 (all three Jack London booklets)

Format: One pane of 6 stamps ($1.50 booklet)
Two panes of 6 stamps each ($3 booklet)
Printing sleeves of 864 subjects (18 across, 48 around).
Stamp Size: 0.87 by 0.96 inches. (Original Jack London sheet stamp size was 0.84 by 0.99 inches.)

Perf: 10 by 9.8 (Goebel booklet machine stroke perforator)

Selvage Markings: Sleeve number and registration markings appear on each pane binding stub. ©UNITED STATES POSTAL SERVICE 1988 printed on inside front cover of booklet. Universal Product Code (UPC) printed on outside back cover.

Stamp Designer: Richard Sparks of Norwalk, Connecticut
Cover Designer: Frank Waslick (BEP)

Typographer: Bradbury Thompson (CSAC)

Engravers: Thomas Hipschen (BEP, vignette)
Dennis Brown (BEP, lettering and numerals)

Printing: Stamps printed on the 3-color intaglio C press (901). Covers printed and booklets formed on Goebel booklet forming machine.

Quantity Ordered: $1.50 booklet - 24,000,000
$3 booklet - 57,000,000
Quantity Distributed: $1.50 booklet - 21,386,100
$3 booklet - 27,289,800

Sleeve Number Detail: One sleeve number on each pane binding stub

Sleeve Numbers: $1.50 booklet - 1
$3 booklet - 1

Tagging: block over vignette

25¢ JACK LONDON BOOKLET ($5)

Date of Issue: May 3, 1988

Catalog Numbers: Scott 2183 (stamp)   Minkus 888   USPS 6634
Scott 2183a (pane of 10)

Color: blue

First-Day Cancel: San Francisco, California (no first-day ceremony)

FDCs Canceled: 94,655 (all three London booklets)

168

Format: Two panes of 10 stamps each. Printing sleeve of 800 subjects (20 across, 40 around).

Stamp Size: 0.84 by 0.96 (Original Jack London sheet stamp size was 0.84 by 0.99.)

Perf: 11.2 by 11.1 (Eureka off-line perforator)

Selvage Markings: Sleeve number on binding stub of each pane. Electric-eye mark remnants on 10% of all pane binding stubs. ©UNITED STATES POSTAL SERVICE 1988 on inside of front cover. Universal Product Code (UPC) printed on outside back cover.

Stamp Designer: Richard Sparks of Norwalk, Connecticut
Cover Designer: Frank Waslick (BEP)

Typographer: Bradbury Thompson (CSAC)

Engravers: Thomas Hipschen (BEP, vignette)
Dennis Brown (BEP, lettering and numerals)

Printing: Stamps printed on the 3-color intaglio unit of the 8-color gravure/intaglio A press (702).
Covers printed on the Goebel offset Optiforma press (043) in red, blue and black.
Booklets formed on standard bookbinding equipment.

Quantity Ordered: 82,000,000
Quantity Distributed: 53,122,800

Sleeve Number Detail: One sleeve number on each pane binding stub

Sleeve Numbers: 1, 2

Tagging: block over vignette

The New Stamp

On March 17, 1988, two and a half weeks before the scheduled increase in the first-class rate, USPS announced plans for its first new denominated definitives to meet the need for 25¢ postage.

These turned out to be adaptations of a stamp that was more than two years old and had seen relatively little use until then. It was the 25¢ Jack London stamp in the Great Americans series, which had been issued in sheet form January 11, 1986.

The London stamp made its reappearance May 3, 1988 — one month after the new rate went into effect — in three separate booklet formats. It was the first, and so far the only, of the many Great Americans stamps to be made available in booklets.

The first-day city was San Francisco, birthplace of the popular novelist depicted on the stamp. No first-day ceremony was held, but collectors were able to obtain cancellations at the main San Francisco Post Office and by mail order.

The three booklets sold for $1.50 (one pane of six stamps), $3 (two panes of six) and $5 (two panes of 10). Adapting the stamps for booklet production required the Bureau of Engraving and Printing to manufacture two new intaglio press sleeves, one for six-stamp panes and the other for 10-stamp panes.

The two smaller booklets provided collectors with a major new collectible variety. Both these booklets were printed on BEP's C and D presses (which are used interchangeably and whose products cannot be distinguished one from the other). They were then perforated and formed on the Goebel booklet-forming machine. The perforation measure was 10 by about 9.8, as contrasted to the perf 11.25 of the sheet stamp.

The $5 booklet stamps, like the sheet stamps, were printed on the A press and perforated 11 on the off-line Eureka perforator. They were formed into booklets on equipment that had been assembled in 1987 to make booklets out of the 22¢ Flag with Fireworks sheet stamps.

The process is a proprietary one, meaning that BEP didn't choose to disclose details.

Improvisation was necessary, as USPS explained in 1987, because production was falling behind demand by some 40 million booklets a year, even with the Goebel equipment operating at full capacity.

Original sheet version of London stamp from 1986.

In all three of the Jack London booklets, each stamp had a straight edge on one or two sides. Since the sheet-version stamps are fully perforated, a straight edge on a London stamp is a sure indication that it comes from a booklet. Telling whether it is from one of the two smaller booklets or from the larger one requires a perforation gauge, of course.

The image size in all booklets is identical to that of the sheet stamp — 0.71 by 0.82 inches. However, the overall sizes of the stamps varied between booklets.

The original sheet stamps measured .84 by .99 inches overall. As announced by USPS, the $1.50 and $3 booklet stamps measured 0.87 by 0.96 inches; the $5 booklet stamps were slightly narrower, measuring 0.84 by 0.96 inches. (Actually, these latter dimensions were unreliable. Booklet-forming processes allow for a wide range of individual stamp sizes from pane to pane.)

The *Scott Specialized Catalogue of United States Stamps* recognized the perf 10 by 9¾ London booklet stamp as a major variety and assigned it a new number (2197). This was a departure from Scott's treatment of other perforation varieties on modern U.S. stamps, most of which had gotten a minor letter listing or no listing at all.

The $5 booklet, whose stamps had a perforation measurement the same as the sheet stamp's, received a minor listing (Scott 2183a).

The $1.50 and $3 London booklets were printed on the C and D presses from 864-subject cylinders arranged 18 subjects across by 48

These photographically cropped booklet panes of the Jack London stamp are shown in their positions relative to one another on the original printing sheet. The short markings on the tabs are thought to be the tips of longer marks printed on the strips of paper between the panes that are trimmed away during booklet processing.

around. This meant that if spread out, the cylinder would be six booklet panes tall by 24 around. It printed the equivalent of 144 booklet panes per revolution.

The $5 booklet panes, like the sheet stamps, were printed by 400-subject cylinders that were 20 subjects wide by 20 around, divided into quadrants 10 subjects by 10 subjects each.

To this extent, the operation was similar to that which produces 1987's Flag With Fireworks booklet stamps.

However, unlike the Flag with Fireworks — which was issued in 20-stamp booklet panes — the Jack London booklet stamps were issued in panes of 10 stamps each. This required that the layout of subjects on the printing cylinder be different from that for the sheet stamps. For the booklets, horizontal rows six through 10 and 16 through 20 were inverted in relation to the remaining rows. (See diagram).

This made it possible for the large gutters that were left between the quadrants on the printed sheets to be sliced through to become the stubs that attached the panes to the booklet covers.

The differences between full-sized booklet panes are obvious. The $1.50 and $3 booklets had panes of six stamps with a plate number, cross register and length register markings on the binding stub.

This marking took the form of a blue rectangle, diagonal or parallelogram at the left or right edge. These were believed to be the tips of longer marks printed in that portion of the sheet selvage between the panes that is termed "gutter waste." The gutter waste is trimmed away during booklet processing.

The Design

The original Jack London stamp was designed by Richard Sparks of Norwalk, Conneticut, with Howard Paine as art director and Bradbury Thompson as typographer. Thomas Hipschen engraved the vi-

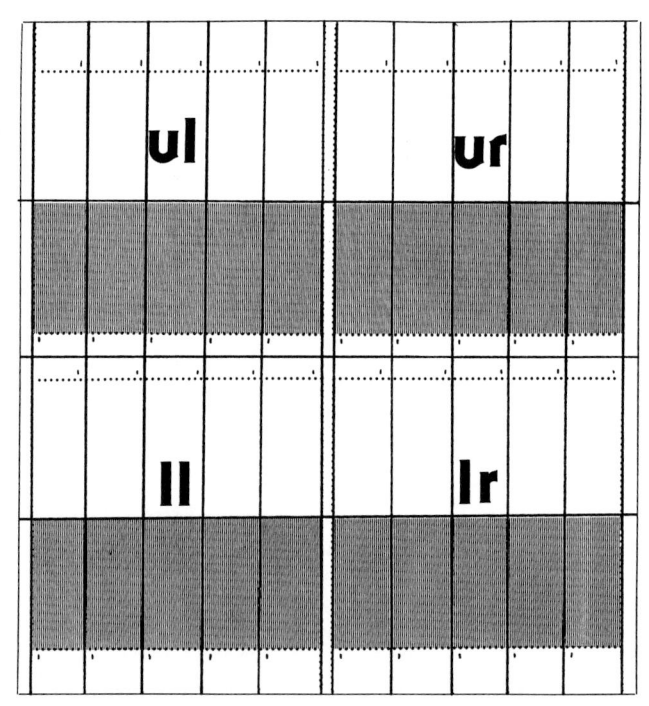

This illustration shows the positioning of the 40 booklet panes printed by one revolution of the A-press cylinder. The shaded portions are inverted in relation to the white portions. The subject layout is similar to that used for sheet stamps, except for the inverted areas.

gnette and Dennis Brown the lettering and numerals.

The booklet covers for the three London booklets bore identical artwork but differed in color and references to the booklet value and number of stamps included.

The common design, created by Frank J. Waslick of the BEP, featured a wolflike animal in the foreground watching a dog team pulling a sled. The animal, according to Belmont Faries, chairman of the Citizens' Stamp Advisory Committee, was Buck, the "hero" of London's best-known novel *The Call of the Wild*. Buck was a half-St. Bernard dognapped in California and taken to Alaska to be trained as a sled dog. Unbroken by his cruel trainers, he escaped, managed to survive in the frozen wilderness and became the leader of a pack of wolves.

The $1.50 and $3 covers were printed in two-color offset, blue and brown. The $1.50 cover had a solid blue background with Buck in brown and the sled, dog team, driver, distant treeline and lettering in dropout (white). The $3 cover had a light background with the lettering in blue and the remainder in brown.

The $5 cover was printed by four-color process (magenta, yellow, cyan and black), giving it a multicolored appearance.

All three versions bore the Universal Pricing Code, making them convenient items for sales in supermarkets and other outlets.

The $5 booklet had a relatively short life. Its original printing of 35 million was quickly snapped up, and a new printing ordered. In the meantime, the Bureau of Engraving and Printing filled requisitions with the Owl and Grosbeak booklet.

25¢ FLAG WITH CLOUDS SHEET STAMP

Date of Issue: May 6, 1988

Catalog Numbers: Scott 2278   Minkus 889   USPS 5535

Colors: light blue, red, dark blue, gray

First-Day Cancel: Boxborough, Massachusetts (Sheraton Boxborough)

FDCs Canceled: 131,265

Format: Panes of 100, horizontal, 10 across, 10 down. Printing cylinders of 400 subjects (20 across, 20 around).

Perf: 11.1 by 11.2 (Eureka off-line perforator)

Selvage Markings: ©UNITED STATES POSTAL SERVICE 1988, USE CORRECT ZIP CODE®

Designer, Typographer and Modeler: Peter Cocci (BEP)

Art Director: Joe Brockert (USPS)

Printing: 7-color Andreotti gravure press (601)

Quantity Ordered: 2,700,000,000
Quantity Distributed: 1,065,300,000

Cylinder Number Detail: One group of 4 cylinder numbers over/under corner stamps

Cylinder Number Combinations: 1111, 1222, 2222, 2131

Tagging: overall

Printing Base Impressions: Dark blue: 1(1,391,900)

The Stamp

During the first 110 years of U.S. stamp production, the American flag, when it appeared on stamps at all, was shown only as an incidental part of the design. It was never displayed prominently.

This changed, however, when the BEP obtained its first modern multicolor printing equipment.

The first stamp printed on the BEP's new Giori press was a commemorative, issued July 4, 1957, depicting the Stars and Stripes in red, white and blue with the motto "Long May It Wave."

It has been followed in the intervening years by a parade of commemoratives and definitives on which the American flag (in one historical version or another) has constituted a major design element.

In fact, beginning in 1963 a full-color Flag definitive in the first-class rate has always been available, providing post-office clerks with a sure-to-please item to offer customers inclined to be critical of other available stamps.

On May 6, 1988, the 15th in this series of definitive flag designs made its appearance in Boxborough, Massachusetts, on a sheet stamp in the new 25¢ first-class rate. It showed a tethered Old Glory waving against a light blue sky filled with billowing cumulus clouds.

It stirred little comment, pro or con. Flag stamps have long since ceased to arouse controversy. But when those first few flags were run up the postal flagpole — particularly the very first one, back in 1957 — the saluting was far from universal.

Letter writers to the Post Office Department and philatelic periodicals that year argued that to subject the flag to postal cancellation would be disrespectful.

Gridley Adams, director general of the United States Flag Foundation, deplored the notion that "upward of a hundred thousand ex-GIs, now working in the 40,000 post offices," would be forced "to smear with their daubing brushes or canceling machines that very flag for which they once offered their lives." Adams asserted further that a Flag stamp would violate the criminal codes of virtually every state, which barred the use of the flag on business envelopes or articles for carrying merchandise.

The Post Office ignored the criticism, and the "Long May It Wave" stamp proved popular. So did a 1959 stamp commemorating the debut of the 49-star flag (signaling Alaska's admission to the Union) and a 1960 issue for the 50-star flag (Hawaii).

In January 1963 the first Flag definitive appeared, to meet the new 5¢ first-class rate. It depicted the flag over the White House, thus establishing the "flag over something" pattern that continues to the present day.

It was also unique among U.S. stamps in that it carried only the denomination — no "US," no "postage." Obviously the Post Office felt that the American flag in full color provided national identification enough. Nevertheless, this design treatment — the ultimate in simplification — has never been repeated.

Since then, as the first-class rate has ratcheted ever upward, definitives have shown the flag in a variety of settings: over the White House again (6¢, 8¢); in colonial and modern versions, crossed (10¢); over Independence Hall (13¢); over the Capitol (13¢, and again at 22¢); as it looked when it inspired *The Star Spangled Banner*, with 15 stars and 15 stripes (15¢); over purple mountain majesties, amber waves of grain and shining sea, accompanied by appropriate lines from *America the Beautiful* (18¢); over the Supreme Court building (20¢), and against a night sky, with fireworks (22¢).

The Fireworks stamp, issued in sheets in May 1987 and in an improvised booklet form later in the year, was the first Flag definitive to be printed by money-saving gravure instead of intaglio.

USPS followed this precedent in 1988 with the Flag with Clouds stamp — which was also its first definitive produced specifically for the new 25¢ rate. Said USPS in its April 4 announcement:

"Like the previous issue, its full-color design is a reflection of the Postal Service's intention to use brighter colors on many regular issues expected to receive widespread use."

At the same time the sheet stamp was announced, USPS announced that a booklet version would be issued July 5 in Washington.

The Design

The Flag with Clouds design was created and modeled for gravure printing on the Andreotti press by Peter Cocci of the BEP. Four process colors — blue, red, light blue and gray — were used.

Cocci also had designed the Flag with Fireworks stamp. His previous credits included the 15¢ Organized Labor stamp of 1980; the three 18¢ Flag and *America the Beautiful* designs of 1981 issued in sheet, coil and booklet form, and the 6¢ Circle of Stars booklet stamp that was part of the set; the 22¢ Migratory Bird Stamp Act commemorative of 1984, and the five Seashells booklet stamps of 1985.

The artist fine-tuned his design by scanner and computer in the BEP Design Center.

First-Day Facts

The May 6 first-day ceremony at the Sheraton Boxborough was held in conjunction with Philatelic Show 88, sponsored by the Northeastern Federation of Stamp Clubs. It was the first of five such ceremonies to be held at stamp shows in 1988.

Northeastern Regional Postmaster General William R. Cummings, the principal speaker, said the Flag with Clouds stamp and its predecessor, the Flag with Fireworks stamp, were issued in response to survey findings that postal customers wanted "something different" in their Flag stamps.

Another speaker noted that the date, May 6, was the 148th anniversary of the world's first postage stamp, Great Britain's Penny Black.

Because of the relative lateness of the stamp's announcement, collectors wishing to order first-day covers were given an additional 30 days to do so. The deadline date, July 5, was the same day the booklet version of the stamp was issued in Washington.

25¢ FLAG WITH CLOUDS BOOKLET

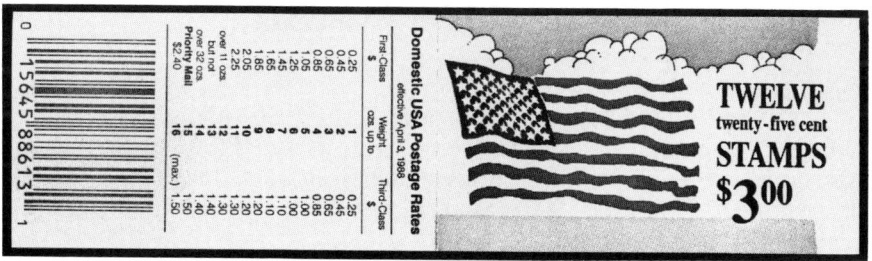

Date of Issue: July 5, 1988

Catalog Numbers: Scott 2285A (stamp)   Minkus 890E   USPS 6613
Scott 2285c (pane of 6)

Colors: light blue, red, dark blue, gray

First-Day Cancel: Washington, D.C. (no first-day ceremony)

FDCs Canceled: 117,303

Format: Two panes of 6 stamps each. Printing cylinders of 360 subjects (15 across, 24 around)

Perf: 9.8 by 10 (Goebel booklet machine stroke perforator)

Selvage Markings: Cylinder numbers and registration markings on all pane binding stubs. ©UNITED STATES POSTAL SERVICE 1988 on inside of front cover. Proof of purchase notation on inside of back cover.

Designer, Typographer and Modeler: Peter Cocci (BEP)

Art Director: Joe Brockert (USPS)

Printing: 7-color Andreotti gravure press (601)

Quantity Ordered: 39,000,000
Quantity Distributed: 9,741,600

177

Cylinder Number Detail: One group of 4 cylinder numbers on each pane binding stub.

Cylinder Number Combinations: 1111

Tagging: overall

The Stamp

The booklet version of the 25¢ Flag with Clouds stamp was issued July 5 in Washington, D.C. Each booklet contained two panes of six stamps each and sold for $3.

The issue was the seventh booklet to appear in 1988, in keeping with USPS' promise to make a variety of stamps available in that format. It was preceded by the E stamp, Pheasant and Owl-and-Grosbeak booklets, each costing $5, and three different Jack London booklets, at $1.50, $3 and $5.

The Flag booklet stamp was produced by BEP, using the Andreotti press and Goebel booklet-forming equipment. The image size and perforation measure for the booklet version were the same as for the sheet stamp. Of course, individual stamps from booklets, unlike those from sheets, have one or two straight edges.

The tabs that attached the panes to the booklet contained a group of four cylinder numbers, one for each gravure color — blue, light blue, red and gray.

The front of the cover, like the stamp, showed a fluttering flag against a cloud background. The flag was a larger version of the one inside, but without the pole or line. However, the clouds were in a different configuration and more stylized. Beside the flag were the words "TWELVE/twenty-five cent/STAMPS/$3.00."

The rest of the cover, inside and outside, contained the same postal information found on the Owl-and-Grosbeak booklet cover, plus a proof-of-purchase form.

First-Day Facts

There was no first-day ceremony, but collectors were able to get cancellations on a handback basis at the main Washington post office and the Philatelic Center in USPS headquarters.

Those ordering covers by mail were urged to prepare their own stamped and addressed envelopes. Upon request, USPS affixed single panes of six stamps on addressed envelopes at $1.50 each.

25¢ FLAG OVER YOSEMITE

Date of Issue: May 20, 1988

Catalog Numbers: Scott 2280 Minkus 890 USPS 7737 (100s)
USPS 7725 (500s)
USPS 7726 (3,000s)

Colors: red, blue, green

First-Day Cancel: Yosemite National Park, California (Yosemite Village post office)

FDCs Canceled: 144,339

Format: Initially in coils of 500 and 3,000; later in coils of 100. Printing sleeves of 936 subjects (18 across, 52 around) and printing sleeves of 960 subjects (20 across, 48 around).

Perf: 9.75 (Goebel stroke perforator on coils of 100; Huck rotary perforator on coils of 500 and 3,000.)

Designer and Modeler: Peter Cocci (BEP)

Art Director: Joe Brockert (USPS)

Typographer: Bradbury Thompson (CSAC)

Engravers: Thomas Hipschen (BEP, vignette)
Dennis Brown (BEP, lettering and numerals)

Printing: Initially printed on the 3-color intaglio B press (701); later printed on the 3-color intaglio C press (901).

Quantity Ordered: Coils of 100 - 41,000,000
Coils of 500 - 3,367,970
Coils of 3,000 - 165,854

Quantity Distributed: Coils of 100 - 3,752,800
Coils of 500 - 1,176,450
Coils of 3,000 - 109,408

Sleeve Number Detail: One sleeve number on every 48th (C press) or 52nd (B press) stamp.

Sleeve Numbers: 1, 2, 3 - B press
4, 5 - C press

Tagging: block over vignette

The Stamp

For its second 25¢ American Flag definitive of 1988 — and 16th face-different stamp in the continuing Flag series that began in 1963 — USPS went back to a long-established pattern: an intaglio (engraved) product displaying Old Glory over a national landmark.

These landmarks had mostly been Washington buildings: the Capitol, the White House, the Supreme Court. This time, however, USPS reached across the continent to California and depicted Half Dome, a granite formation that rises some 4,850 feet from base to crown in Yosemite National Park.

The stamp's closest precedent was the America the Beautiful sheet, coil and booklet trio of 1981, designed by the same person, the Bureau of Engraving and Printing's Peter Cocci. Those stamps also pictured the flag over landscape scenes.

The Yosemite stamp was issued in coil form only. It had its first-day sale May 20 in front of the Yosemite Village Post Office.

Gordon C. Morison, assistant postmaster general for philatelic and retail services, said in the announcement of the stamp that it was a response to a challenge from postal customers and stamp collectors to make stamps "more colorful and creative."

Criticism came from an unexpected quarter, however — Yosemite's postmaster, Leroy (Rusty) Rust.

Rust, 67, a veteran of 26 years in the job, had long advocated that a commemorative be issued in October 1990 for the park's centennial. A commemorative, being larger than a definitive, would have ample room to display Half Dome or some other symbol of Yosemite.

The Flag Over Half Dome Coil "is being issued because they want to shut us up," Rust told the *San Francisco Chronicle.*

Dickey Rustin, manager of stamp information for USPS, disagreed. "One of the highest honors for a locale," he told the newspaper, is "to be depicted on what is to become a regular stamp."

Later, Rust changed his mind. He informed *Linn's Stamp News* that the definitive would see much more use than a commemorative and would be good for the park. It "will probably be around until the next rate change," he said.

Years earlier Yosemite had, in fact, been featured on a commemorative. The 1¢ value of the National Parks series of 1934 showed El Capitan, another of the park's granite landmarks, towering above the placid waters of the Merced River.

In its April 4 announcement of the Yosemite Flag stamp, USPS placed the date of issue on May 13. Later the issue date was pushed back one week. The stamp's design was first made public through publication in USPS' *Postal Bulletin* of April 14, and was officially released April 27.

The Yosemite Valley, on the western slope of the Sierras about 150 miles from San Francisco, is a worthy subject for a stamp design. It contains some of America's most spectacular landscape.

Carved over the course of millions of years by glaciers and rivers acting upon periodic upheavals of the earth, it features enormous rock formations such as Half Dome, El Capitan and Cathedral Rocks; spectacular waterfalls gushing from hanging valleys, and great stretches of pine forest and flowering meadows.

Half Dome, marking the valley's east end, is exactly what its name indicates — a dome of rock, split as if by a colossal cleaver by the scouring of glaciers. (One of the most frequent questions asked at the park visitor's center is: "What became of the other half?")

The monolith appears barren, but lizards and squirrels find a living on its bald summit. Legend holds that it is an Indian wife who was turned to stone as she fled from her husband, and that the dark streaks down the sheer face of the cliff are her tears.

Dimensions throughout the park are prodigious. El Capitan has the volume of four Gibraltars and the height of nearly three Empire State Buildings. Yosemite's Upper Falls, 1,430 feet high, exceeds nine Niagaras end on end. A series of lesser falls drop an additional 995 feet. The earthquakelike tremors from the downpour can be felt for half a mile.

Armed settlers discovered the valley in 1851 while pursuing Tenaya, leader of the Yosemite (grizzly bear) Indians, and his warriors. Thirteen years later Abraham Lincoln signed an act of Congress setting aside the land, along with the nearby Mariposa Grove of giant sequoias, as a trust to be administered by California.

In 1890 Congress established Yosemite National Park around the state-run areas, and in 1906, with the state's concurrence, the valley and grove were added to the park.

The Design

The stamp, in red, blue and green, was first printed on the BEP's three-color intaglio B press, in 500- and 3,000-stamp rolls. Later it was also produced on the C press in rolls of 100.

The two versions are distinguishable only in the number of stamps between plate, or sleeve, numbers. On the C press, the number appears at 48-stamp intervals; on the B press, at 52-stamp intervals.

Peter Cocci's design features the U.S. flag in the top half of the stamp, billowing above Half Dome. The vertical cliff face appears in any icy blue, climbing from a dense blue-green forest of ponderosa pines standing beside the Merced River. The line of treetops rises from lower left to upper right, where it almost touches Old Glory.

After Cocci submitted his original sketch to the Citizens' Stamp Advisory Committee, only slight modifications were requested. The flag was made wider, the shoreline was altered somewhat, and some of the type elements were rearranged.

The flag closely resembles the one Cocci used on the Flag with Clouds sheet stamp issued two weeks earlier, but it is unattached to a pole or line, and a close inspection shows that the rippling curves of the stripes are discernibly different on the two stamps.

Varieties

As with most recent U.S. coil stamps, imperforate examples of the Yosemite stamp were found. These exist with both Plates 2 and 3, according to *Coil Line*, the official journal of the Plate Number Coil Collectors Club.

First-Day Facts

The first-day ceremony was held outdoors at Yosemite's post office against a spectacular waterfall backdrop. Taking part were Regional Postmaster General Joseph Caraveo; Representative Tony Coelho, D-California; Robert Setrakian, a member of the USPS Board of Governors, and Stanley T. Albright, Western regional director for the National Park Service.

The ceremony was open to the public, and some 700 people attended. A $5 entrance fee was charged those without a 1988 Golden Eagle pass. The pass, which cost $25, allowed its purchaser unlimited access to any national park during the year.

Free shuttle bus service was provided between the day-use parking lot at Curry Village inside the park and the ceremony site.

25¢ OWL AND GROSBEAK BOOKLET

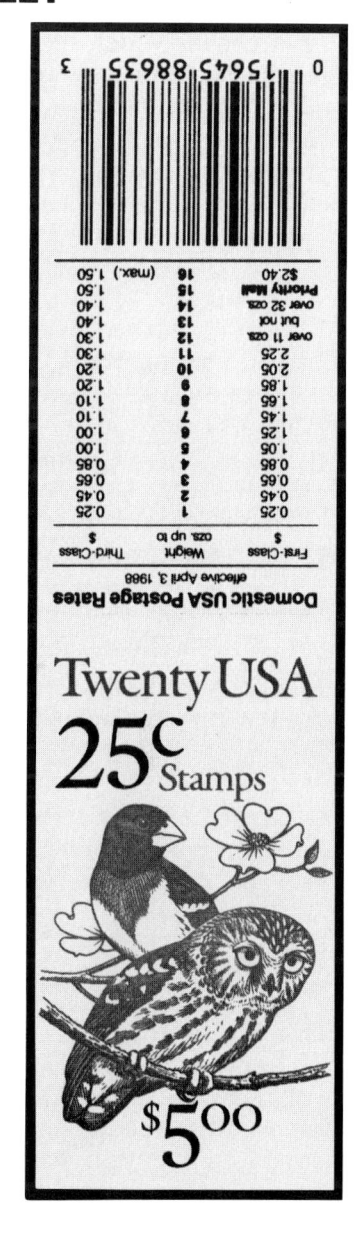

Date of Issue: May 28, 1988

Catalog Numbers: Scott 2284-85 (stamps)   Minkus 892-93   USPS 6635
Scott 2285a (pane of 10)

Colors: magenta, cyan, yellow, black

183

First-Day Cancel: Arlington, Virginia (NAPEX stamp show, Sheraton National Hotel)

FDCs Canceled: 272,359

Format: Two panes of 10 stamps, vertical, 5 Owl and 5 Grosbeak stamps per pane in a checkerboard pattern with the two designs se-tenant vertically and horizontally. Printing cylinders of 480 subjects (20 across, 24 around).

Perf: 10 by 9.8 (Goebel booklet machine stroke perforator)

Selvage Markings: Cylinder numbers and registration markings on each pane binding stub. ©UNITED STATES POSTAL SERVICE 1988 printed on inside front cover. Universal Product Code (UPC) printed on outside back cover.

Stamp and Cover Designer: Chuck Ripper of Huntington, West Virginia

Art Director: Jack Williams (USPS)

Typographer: Bradbury Thompson (CSAC)

Modeler: Ronald Sharpe (BEP, stamp and cover)

Printing: 7-color Andreotti gravure press (601). Covers printed and booklets formed on Goebel booklet forming machine.

Quantity Ordered: 350,000,000
Quantity Distributed: 85,345,800

Cylinder Number Detail: One group of 4 cylinder numbers on each pane binding stub.

Cylinder Number Combinations: 1111, 1112, 1211, 2111, 2122, 2221, 2222, 3233, 3333

Tagging: overall

The Stamps

The second in a series of stamp booklets that USPS had promised would feature "more color and variety" was issued May 28 in Arlington, Virginia. Containing 20 25¢ stamps and selling for $5, it featured two different designs, each showing an American bird in full color: the rose-breasted grosbeak and the saw-whet owl.

The format of the two 10-stamp panes was unique for a U.S. booklet. The stamps were se-tenant in a checkerboard pattern. The grosbeak was at the left of the top row and the owl was at the right, and the arrangement was reversed in each succeeding horizontal row.

The booklet followed by less than a month another colorful $5 Bird booklet, this one showing a pheasant in flight. Both were designed by Chuck Ripper, veteran wildlife artist and stamp designer from Huntington, West Virginia. However, the Pheasant booklet had been printed by the American Bank Note Company; for the Owl and Grosbeak, USPS returned to its traditional booklet supplier, BEP.

The booklet marked the second appearance on a U.S. stamp for the saw-whet owl, which was pictured in flight on a 15¢ stamp of 1978, part of a se-tenant block of four featuring American owls.

After he had designed the Pheasant booklet, Ripper said, USPS told him it wanted to issue another booklet featuring a bird with "punch and color." He was asked to suggest a subject that hadn't appeared on either the American Wildlife pane of 1987 (which he had also designed) or the State Birds and Flowers pane of 1982.

"I kind of kicked it around," Ripper said. "I customarily submit two different sketches to give them a choice. The two I submitted this time were the owl and the grosbeak, and after thinking about it, they decided they would use two designs instead of one. So that was a bit of serendipity there.

"I've always been interested in owls. In hindsight, I found out that that block of four owls they had done before had a saw-whet owl on it, so probably I should have used something else, but they didn't complain...

"The rose-breasted grosbeak is a bird that we get here in Huntington in the spring and summer. It's snappy and doesn't have a lot of detail that's going to get lost on a small stamp.

"Why we pick the things we pick is strange, because there's a gourmet's list of birds, but with some of the species that are sort of dainty you get the feeling they might get lost, they're just too small.

"These two birds make a good pairing. Although the owl is much chunkier, they are about the same size as far as length goes. That surprises most people, who have never seen a saw-whet owl and don't realize how tiny they are."

The rose-breasted grosbeak, a member of the finch family, is concentrated mainly in the Northeast. The familiar bright colors, including the rose breast, are restricted to the males; the females wear drab plumage. Partial to wooded areas, the birds feed on seed, fruit and, occasionally, insects. The name "grosbeak" refers to the large, conical bills common to all members of that family.

The saw-whet owl is one of the smallest birds of prey and is sometimes called "the night watchman of our gardens." It has a wide range, and generally prefers the cover of forests and wooded swamps. Its well-developed senses include binocular vision and extremely keen hearing, which it can fine-tune, using external ears similar to those of many mammals. Its fluffy plumage, which makes the bird seem larger than it actually is, enables it to fly silently. This species of owl gets its name from the resemblance of its harsh cry to the sound made by filing a saw.

With this booklet, USPS made use of the cover to publicize the recent rate change. The inside and outside contain a table of 1988 domestic postage rates for first-class, third-class and Express Mail, and facts about various types of security mail services available.

Also new to booklet covers was a proof-of-purchase form buyers could sign, making it unnecessary for those who needed a receipt to go to a window rather than use a lobby vending machine. As with previous booklets, the Universal Product Code was imprinted, for electronic reading of the price at checkout counters.

The decision to include this information was made at the eleventh hour, after a cover model had been made containing the standard promotional paragraph and coupon for the USPS souvenir pages subscription program. (This original model was illustrated in the May 10 USPS news release announcing the booklet.)

USPS officials estimate that rate-change information has a useful life of only about six months, and at first they left open the possibility that the cover would be changed in the future, creating a new variety for booklet collectors. Later, however, the decision was made to stay with the "rates" cover for the life of the booklet.

How to allocate the valuable advertising space on stamp booklets is a continuing issue within USPS. On this occasion, the Office of Stamps and Philatelic Marketing yielded it in order to help publicize the new postal rates. Among the planned uses of booklet covers in 1989 will be the promotion of World Stamp Expo 89, just as 1986 covers promoted AMERIPEX 86.

The Designs

The stamps were printed in four colors — magenta, yellow, cyan and black — by 480-subject (20 across, 24 around) gravure printing cylinders on BEP's Andreotti press. The two-color booklet covers were produced on the Goebel six-color, webfed Optiforma press.

To assure authenticity in his work, Chuck Ripper never misses a chance to photograph or sketch actual specimens, and he also relies upon his large file of published photos. "I just get the whole table full of every bit and piece I can," he says.

For the grosbeak, he used snapshots he had taken of a "window casualty" — a bird that had perished crashing against a pane of glass. The Owl stamp was designed from photos and sketches Ripper had made at a roadside wildlife exhibit near Bar Harbor, Maine, which included a cage containing several saw-whet owls.

"These were birds that had been hit by cars and injured and the people had patched them up as best they could, but they couldn't be released. It was sort of a wildlife rehabilitation center," Ripper said. "I just had a field day with my camera and sketch pad."

Both birds are depicted in similar attitudes, perched on branches and facing to the left with heads turned slightly toward the viewer. The grosbeak is shown on a flowering dogwood bough against a solid blue background; the owl, its large yellow eyes unblinking, clings to the branch of an eastern hemlock, with the sky behind colored blue, gold and mauve by a rising or setting sun.

Ripper's original painted rough had shown the owl against a nocturnal blue-green background. However, CSAC asked that the background be changed to a sunrise or sunset to provide better contrast and more effectively silhouette the bird.

Ripper also designed the booklet cover, which showed the two birds perched on branches, the grosbeak partly concealed by the owl. Because the picture was in red only, he executed this design as a pen-and-ink line drawing rather than a painting.

As was the case with the Pheasant booklet earlier in the year, there was no identification of the species of bird on either the stamp design or booklet cover. Obviously the small size of the stamps had a bearing on this decision by CSAC. Also, ring-necked pheasants and rose-breasted grosbeaks are reasonably well-known birds.

The saw-whet owl, however, is another matter. It's unlikely that one postal customer out of 100 could go further than simply "owl" in identifying that specimen.

First-Day Facts

When the booklet was first announced on April 4, the first-day city was given as Washington. Later it was changed to Arlington so the ceremony could launch the annual show of the National Philatelic Exhibitions of Washington (NAPEX) at the Sheraton National Hotel. The ceremony concluded with the official cutting of a stamp coil to open the exhibition.

Assistant Postmaster General Gordon C. Morison, the principal speaker, said the introduction of colorful definitive stamps in booklet form was only one of several changes in store for stamp collectors and stamp users.

Also participating in the ceremony were Milton Mitchell, NAPEX president, and the Forest Service's anti-pollution expert Woodsy Owl, noted for his slogan: "Give a hoot, don't pollute."

Many of the 400 to 500 persons who attended the first-day ceremony were unable to obtain programs, although USPS brought 1,200 copies. This problem was one of the specific cases that led to USPS' later decision to begin selling first-day ceremony programs by subscription, beginning in 1989.

USPS encouraged collectors to prepare their own covers for first-day cancellation. On request, USPS affixed stamps to self-addressed covers, but only in full 10-stamp panes at $2.50 each.

15¢ BUFFALO BILL CODY

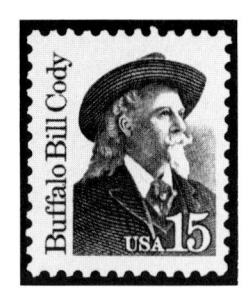

Date of Issue: June 6, 1988

Catalog Numbers: Scott 2178   Minkus 981   USPS 1062

Color: maroon

First-Day Cancel: Cody, Wyoming (Buffalo Bill Historic Center)

FDCs Canceled: 356,395

Format: Panes of 100, vertical, 10 across, 10 down. Printing sleeves of 800 subjects (20 across, 40 around).

Perf: 11.2 by 11.1 (Eureka off-line perforator)

Selvage Markings: ©UNITED STATES POSTAL SERVICE 1988, USE CORRECT ZIP CODE®

Designer: Jack Rosenthal of Casper, Wyoming (CSAC, after an engraving)

Art Director and Typographer: Bradbury Thompson (CSAC)

Project Manager: Jack Williams (USPS)

Engravers: Thomas Hipschen (BEP, vignette)
Michael Ryan (BEP, lettering and numerals)

Printing: Initially on the 3-color intaglio unit of the 8-color gravure/intaglio A press (702); later on the 3-color intaglio unit of the 9-color offset/intaglio D press (902).

Quantity Ordered: 800,000,000
Quantity Distributed: 699,300,000

Sleeve Number Detail: One sleeve number alongside corner stamps.

Sleeve Numbers: 1 (A press)
2 (D press)

Tagging: overall

The Stamp

More than half a century ago, a postage stamp was first seriously proposed for William F. "Buffalo Bill" Cody, hunter, scout, showman and raconteur of the Wild West.

It happened in 1935, when Michael L. Eidsness Jr., former superintendent of the Post Office Department's Division of Stamps, wrote two much-discussed articles for *Stamps* listing 135 American "heroes of peace" who in his opinion deserved postal honors. Buffalo Bill was on that list.

In the decades that followed, dozens of the men and women Eidsness nominated did turn up on postage stamps. Finally, in 1988, Cody's turn arrived.

By then, the strongest push for a Cody stamp was coming from the Buffalo Bill Historical Center in Cody, Wyoming. Beginning around 1977, officials there made three separate pitches to CSAC, enlisting the aid of such influential ex-members of the Center's board as former Governor Milward Simpson and his son, U.S. Senator Alan Simpson, the Senate's Republican whip.

But they got nowhere until 1985, when Jack Rosenthal, a Casper, Wyoming, television executive, stamp collector and Western history buff was appointed to CSAC. Rosenthal's arrival coincided with the museum's fourth letter to the committee, and he began working on Buffalo Bill's behalf.

"The committee very clearly has a heavy Eastern orientation," Rosenthal said. "There was a brief period where I was the only member who lived in other than the Eastern and Central Time Zones. There isn't the understanding of the West that there might be.

"Knowing that that void existed, I concentrated on trying to educate the other members on the need for greater geographic distribution of the subject material.

"A lot of the stereotypes that had been applied to Buffalo Bill precluded his being favorably considered prior to this. For instance, 'wanton killer of buffaloes.' But in his time the top priority in the nation was building a transcontinental railroad, and the only way to feed the construction crew with fresh meat was to kill buffalo.

"He was never one of those that let the bones yellow out in the sun. He was very prudent in his approach to it, and in fact was active with Gifford Pinchot in the environmental movement.

"I tried to dispel concerns over some of those stereotypes, and I brought in information showing how he was perceived as the embodiment of the United States in foreign countries. His Wild West show was important enough to be staged at the opening ceremonies for the Eiffel Tower. He was one of the few performers that really captured the imagination of Queen Victoria, and was invited to perform at her Golden Jubilee.

"So it was really an education job."

Within a year Rosenthal had persuaded the committee of the merits of a Cody stamp. (On the day the stamp was issued, Rosenthal would send each of his fellow committee members a commemorative Buffalo Bill T-shirt, using the new stamps to frank the parcels.)

CSAC originally had in mind a commemorative for issuance in late 1986 or early 1987. Later, after it became clear that 1988 would be a rate-change year, the committee decided, at Rosenthal's recommendation, to use Buffalo Bill's stamp for that purpose and make it a definitive in the Great Americans series. As such, the stamp was listed in the basic 1988 program announced by USPS July 20, 1987.

"A commemorative usually goes 110 to 160 million and is gone from post offices in 45 days in some cases," Rosenthal explained. "A

This engraving from a railroad dining car menu turned out to be the ideal portrait.

definitive, in an important denomination like the postcard rate, will probably go three or four billion before it's over. Even though a definitive is smaller, and you don't have the room for as much message, so to speak, my feeling was we should opt for the quantity, and we did."

Further information reached the public in installments: on November 25, that the stamp would have first-day sale in Cody, Wyoming; on March 17, that it would be issued June 7, 1988, in the new postcard-rate denomination; on March 22, that this rate would be 15¢, and on April 4, that the issue date would be June 6 instead of 7.

Finally, the design of the stamp (without denomination) was shown in the May-June *Philatelic Sales Catalog*, published by the USPS

Philatelic Sales Division, before it was formally distributed (with denomination) to accompany a May 27 news release.

The stamp was the 40th face-different variety in the Great Americans series that began in 1980, and the first of the 15¢ denomination. (The 15¢ Dolley Madison miniature stamp of 1979 was the Great Americans design prototype, but isn't considered a part of the series.) As the postcard-rate stamp, Buffalo Bill replaced the 14¢ Julia Ward Howe definitive of 1987.

William Frederick Cody, like a handful of other men pictured on U.S. stamps — Casey Jones, Daniel Boone, Johnny Appleseed — was a real-life character whose deeds have taken on the aura of legend. He participated in many of the dramatic events that helped push back the frontier: the gold rushes, the brief life of the Pony Express, the Indian wars, the building of the railroads.

Cody was born on a farm in Scott County, Iowa Territory, February 26, 1846. As a teenager he worked as a horse wrangler, a mounted messenger for a wagon-freight firm, a prospector in the Colorado gold rush and, at 14, a Pony Express rider. During the Civil War, Cody served the Union as cavalry scout in a campaign against Kiowa and Comanche Indians, and was a U.S. Army scout during Tennessee and Missouri military operations.

In 1866 he obtained the job that, as Jack Rosenthal said, would appall conservationists of the next century. He became a buffalo hunter for a firm under contract to provide food for railroad construction crews. Using a .50-caliber breech-loading Springfield rifle, he killed (by his own count) 4,280 buffaloes (bisons) in 17 months, and won his enduring nickname, "Buffalo Bill."

Later Cody served as chief of scouts in the Army's campaigns against the Indians. In 1876, in one of his most famous exploits, he killed Yellow Hand, a Cheyenne chief, in a duel. Both men were unhorsed, and in hand-to-hand combat, Cody drove his hunting knife into his opponent's heart. "Jerking his war bonnet off," Cody recounted afterward, "I scientifically scalped him in about five seconds."

A popular dime-novel press gave varying accounts of this duel, which stirred the reading public. Hundreds of dime novels, in fact, were written by Ned Buntline (pen name of E.Z.C. Judson) and others featuring exploits of "Buffalo Bill, King of Border Men." In 1872 Cody took the leading role in a play based on his adventures; it was a critical failure but a popular hit.

Cody made a fortune with the Wild West Show he organized but invested his money unwisely. On January 10, 1917, at the age of 70, the survivor of countless hazardous escapades died of uremic poisoning at the home of his sister in Denver. Typical of the tributes that poured in was one from former President Theodore Roosevelt, who called Cody "the most renowned of those men, steel thewed and iron nerved, whose daring opened the West to settlement and civilization."

Cody was buried in a tomb hewn out of rock on Lookout Mountain, near Golden, Colorado.

The Design

Like other recent Great Americans issues, the Cody stamp was printed by BEP on the intaglio section of its A press. Its design featured a classic engraved profile of the subject, instantly identifiable by his white mustache and goatee, flowing hair, and distinctive hat, coat, vest and tie.

CSAC had looked at some designs in commemorative size worked up by Bradbury Thompson, but the members weren't satisfied. Final-

When the design was being developed, CSAC was thinking in terms of a commemorative rather than a definitive.

ly, they asked Jack Rosenthal, Cody's champion on the committee, to have a try at a design.

Rosenthal asked the Buffalo Bill Historical Center to find some portraits and other materials for him. Included in what was sent was an engraving of Cody that had once been used on a dining car menu for a special Chicago, Burlington and Quincy train from Denver to Cody, Wyoming.

"I took all the material back and worked on it for about a month and did about four or five pasteups," Rosenthal said. "I played with things like using his signature, all kinds of ideas.

"But when I saw the steel engraving from the menu, it just seemed to be a natural for the Great Americans series. It was such a great face and such a great engraving that the image would carry itself and we wouldn't have to add anything extra."

The CB&Q railroad's successor, the Burlington Northern, granted the necessary copyright release for the portrait. Typographer Bradbury Thompson arranged the name "Buffalo Bill Cody" vertically at the left and placed the inscription "USA 15" in heavily outlined dropout characters at the lower right.

The maroon color shows to excellent advantage the intaglio work of the BEP's Thomas Hipschen (vignette) and Michael J. Ryan (lettering and numerals). The depth of Hipschens's engraving was such that the

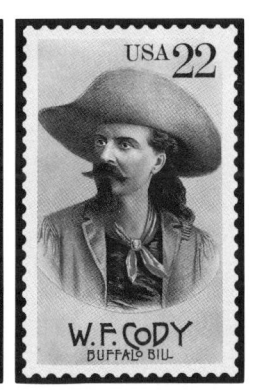

Jack Rosenthal created these essays for the Cody stamp from Buffalo Bill's show posters and other sources.

raised ink lines on the stamp can readily be felt with the fingertip. Bill McAllister, stamp columnist for *The Washington Post*, called the result "a philatelic winner — a fine, hand-engraved stamp that looks more like a bank note than a flashy travel poster."

First-Day Facts

Cody is a town in northwest Wyoming and one of the gateways to Yellowstone National Park. It was founded by its namesake in the 1890s when he was trying his luck as a land developer. The Historical Center — which is one of the nation's leading museums and almost certainly its most isolated — includes the C.V. Whitney Gallery of Western Art, the Winchester arms collection and the Plains Indian Museum, and offers excellent facilities for historical research.

The outdoor ceremony at the Center, originally scheduled for noon, was moved to 10 a.m. so Washington visitors could catch a plane. This was fortunate, because the temperature that day reached 90 degrees, unusual for the high plains in June.

A large crowd heard the speakers, including Governor Mike Sullivan; U.S. Senators Alan Simpson and Malcolm Wallop; Jerry K. Lee, regional postmaster general from Chicago, and Jack Rosenthal. On hand were Buffalo Bill's grandson, Bill Cody, and great-grandson, Bill Garlow Jr.

Jerry Lee canceled the first first-day cover, addressed to President Reagan at the White House, and dispatched it by a special Pony Express rider to the Cody airport. The cover was carried in a mochila, or leather saddle skirt fitted with mail pouches, which was draped over the saddle before the rider mounted. This one was a replica of Buffalo Bill's own copy, owned by the Historical Center and on display there.

At the airport, the returning congressional delegation took custody of the mochila and contents and carried them with them to Washington. The cover in the mochila contained an invitation to the First Family to attend a Frederic Remington art exhibition opening at the Historical Center June 17.

45¢ HARVEY CUSHING

Date of Issue: June 17, 1988

Catalog Numbers: Scott 2188   Minkus 895   USPS 1046

Color: blue

First-Day Cancel: Cleveland, Ohio (Amasa Stone Chapel, Case Western Reserve University)

FDCs Canceled: 135,140

Format: Panes of 100, vertical, 10 across, 10 down. Printing sleeve of 800 subjects (20 across, 40 around).

Perf: 11.2 by 11.1 (Eureka off-line perforator)

Selvage Markings: ©UNITED STATES POSTAL SERVICE 1987, USE CORRECT ZIP CODE®

Designer, Art Director and Typographer: Bradbury Thompson (CSAC)

Engravers: Gary Chaconas (BEP, vignette)
Michael Ryan (BEP, lettering and numerals)

Modeler: Ronald Sharpe (BEP)

Printing: 3-color intaglio unit of the 8-color gravure/intaglio A press (702)

Quantity Ordered: 350,000,000
Quantity Distributed: 272,300,000

Sleeve Number Detail: One sleeve number alongside corner stamps

Sleeve Number: 1

Tagging: block over vignette

The Stamp

Following a special request by First Lady Nancy Reagan, USPS issued a Great Americans definitive stamp June 17, 1988, to honor Dr. Harvey Williams Cushing.

However, USPS says many other people, including numerous physicians, also had asked for a stamp for Dr. Cushing, who is often called the "father of neurosurgery" and was pronounced by the *New England Journal of Medicine* a few months before his death "perhaps the foremost physician produced by the United States."

Mrs. Reagan's father, Dr. Loyal Davis, also a neurosurgeon, was a volunteer assistant to Dr. Cushing in 1923 and 1924 and admired him greatly. Dr. Davis died in 1982.

The basic design of the stamp, a portrait of Dr. Cushing based on a 1924 charcoal drawing by American artist John Singer Sargent, was unveiled April 8, 1987 — the surgeon's birthday — by President Ronald Reagan and Postmaster General Preston R. Tisch in a ceremony in the White House Rose Garden. On hand were the First Lady and Dr. Cushing's daughter Betsey (Mrs. John Hay Whitney).

The design then bore no denomination. USPS announced at the time that it would be a rate-change issue, to be released in connection with the anticipated postal rate increase, whenever it might come.

The revision occurred April 3, 1988, and on May 23, USPS announced that the Cushing stamp would be 45¢, to meet the new first-class rate for two ounces. For that purpose it replaced the 39¢ Grenville Clark stamp of 1985. At 45¢ it also covered the new basic international airmail letter rate.

The stamp was the 41st face-different issue in the Great Americans series, and the second in the series in 1988. A 15¢ stamp depicting Buffalo Bill Cody had made its debut 11 days earlier, on June 6.

Harvey Cushing was born April 8, 1869, in Cleveland, Ohio, the son and grandson of physicians. As a boy he collected coins, butterflies, birds' eggs — and postage stamps.

He received his B.A. degree at Yale University, studied medicine at Harvard, interned at Massachusetts General Hospital, and went to The Johns Hopkins Hospital as assistant resident surgeon. Here he studied with Dr. William S. Halsted, from whom he learned his exquisite operating technique.

Cushing worked in Baltimore until 1912, becoming the first American to concentrate entirely on neurosurgery. Losing all his early cases, he applied himself to reducing the hazards of brain operations. He learned to control bleeding by cranial tourniquet and silver clips, and devised other technical aids. He developed the method of operating with the use of local anesthesia. In 1926 he introduced electrocautery into brain surgery, attacking many previously inoperable cases.

In 1912 Cushing became professor of surgery at Harvard Medical School and was the first surgeon-in-chief of the Peter Bent Brigham Hospital. Except for World War I service in France, he remained at the hospital until his retirement in 1932. From 1933 to 1937 Cushing was Sterling Professor of Neurology at Yale.

During his career Cushing reduced mortality in brain operations to 8.4 percent, while European surgeons were reporting 38 to 50 percent mortality. "By devoting his life to neurological surgery and its problems," said his biographer, Elizabeth Thomson, "he made operations on the brain of little more hazard than those involving the abdomen." His reputation understandably drew patients and students from all over the world.

Despite his responsibilities as adminstrator, teacher and surgeon, Cushing found time to write 25 books and more than 300 papers, many of them on the history of medicine. His two-volume biography of Sir William Osler, with whom he had worked at Johns Hopkins, won the Pulitzer Prize, and his war diary, *From a Surgeon's Journal*, was widely read. He was also a talented artist who illustrated many of his own works.

Cushing died October 8, 1939, in New Haven, Connecticut, at the age of 70. He was buried in Cleveland, his birthplace.

Design

Like most of the Great Americans stamps, the Cushing stamp was printed by intaglio on the BEP's A press.

This essay shows a younger, pensive Cushing, and incorporates a middle initial in his name.

CSAC reviewed two sets of designs: one by Bradbury Thompson, design coordinator for the committee, based on the John Singer Sargent charcoal drawing, and the other by a second artist based on photographs of a younger Harvey Cushing. In accordance with USPS policy to show designs in advance to surviving family members, Mrs. John Hay Whitney, Dr. Cushing's only surviving offspring, was shown both versions and favored the Sargent charcoal used in the Thompson sketches.

"We couldn't lose," said Jack Williams. "Both sets of designs were excellent."

Another portrait that was considered was this profile.

USPS described the color of the Cushing stamp as Yale blue, appropriate for a portrait whose original hangs in the Yale University Art Gallery and depicts a Yale graduate. It is a brighter, richer blue than the shade used on two other recent Great Americans stamps, the 3¢ Paul Dudley White of 1986 and the 2¢ Mary Lyon of 1987.

First-Day Facts

The first-day ceremony was held in the Amasa Stone Chapel of Case Western Reserve University in Cleveland. Among the scheduled speakers were Dr. Cushing's granddaughter, Mrs. Ronald Wilford; Dr. George T. Tindall, president of the American Association of Neuro-

The Great Americans stamp for a distinguished physician inspired a variety of first-day covers — including one made from a tongue depressor.

logical Surgeons; Dr. Robert G. Ojemann, past president of the AANS; and Gordon Morison, acting senior assistant postmaster general.

Dr. Cushing's daughter, Mrs. John Hay Whitney, also spoke briefly, reminiscing about her father.

Dr. Richard Davis, Nancy Reagan's brother, was in the audience. On her behalf he accepted a presentation album for this issue from Gordon Morison.

10.1¢ OIL WAGON (NEW PRECANCEL)

Date of Issue: June 27, 1988

Catalog Numbers: Scott 2130   Minkus 837   USPS 7903

Colors: blue (intaglio), red (flexography)

First-Day Cancel: Washington, D.C. (no first-day ceremony)

FDCs Canceled: 136,428

Format: Coils of 500 and 3,000. Printing sleeve of 936 subjects (18 across, 52 around). Flexographic plates for red overprint.

Perf: 9.75 (Huck rotary perforator)

Designer: James Schleyer of Burke, Virginia

Art Director: Mary Margaret Grant (USPS)

Project Manager: Joe Brockert (USPS)

Typography: Bradbury Thompson (CSAC)

Engravers: Edward Archer (BEP, vignette)
Robert Culin, Sr. (BEP, lettering and numerals)

Printing: 3-color intaglio B press (701)

Quantity Ordered: Coils of 500 - 145,000
Coils of 3,000 - 100,000
Quantity Distributed: Coils of 500 - 123,100
Coils of 3,000 - 46,240

Sleeve Number Detail: One sleeve number on every 52nd stamp

Sleeve Number: 2

Tagging: untagged

The Stamp

In addition to the dozen new Transportation series coil stamps USPS produced in 1988, it also issued a third variety of an old one — the 10.1¢ Oil Wagon stamp.

The Oil Wagon stamp, printed on BEP's intaglio B press, was first released April 18, 1985, and was overprinted "Bulk-Rate." The stamp was simultaneously issued in a collectors' version — tagged and minus the overprint.

At that time, and until the rate change of 1988, 10.1¢ paid the rate for third-class mail presorted to five-digit ZIP codes.

The cost of this classification rose to 13.2¢ April 3, 1988. But in the same revision, the rate for third-class mail presorted to the carrier route went from 8.3¢ to 10.1¢ — a rate conveniently met by the Oil Wagon stamp.

On June 27, the Oil Wagon was re-released, untagged and bearing a new two-line overprint in red: "Bulk Rate/Carrier Route Sort." It was produced in rolls of 500 and 3,000 stamps.

Previously, the 10.1¢ Oil Wagon stamp had been issued with an overprint reading "Bulk-Rate" and with no overprint (tagged).

Its new overprint was larger and better placed for visibility than the old "Bulk-Rate" inscription, which was printed in black between two horizontal lines on the body of the oil truck. This one was positioned on the white background between the denomination and the vignette.

The fact that the inscription was overprinted by a flexographic plate on an engraved stamp, rather than being engraved itself, made this stamp a throwback to an earlier kind of precancel.

Beginning with the 5.5¢ Star Route Truck coil of November 1986, and with only one exception since then (the 8.5¢ Tow Truck of 1987), USPS and BEP have used a new method of creating the precancel versions of the Transportation series stamps. Instead of applying the service inscription over the top of the printed stamp, they engraved it on the printing sleeve along with the design.

The precanceled versions were then produced as two-color intaglio products with the use of inking-in rollers. The inscription was printed in a different color from that of the vignette.

USPS continues to call these all-intaglio products "precancels," since the service inscription has the same purpose, whether engraved or overprinted: to bar the re-use of the stamp once it has carried the mail. However, collectors refer to them alternatively as "service-inscribed," to distinguish them from the overprinted kind.

To date, the *Scott Specialized Catalogue of United States Stamps* has made no distinction. It terms both kinds "untagged (bureau precancel)" and lists them as sub-varieties of the tagged mint varieties.

The new 10.1¢ Oil Wagon stamp was produced as an overprint because the engraving of the vehicle wasn't originally made with a service inscription in mind. There wasn't enough room on the design area to allow for one.

Of all the fractional-rate Transportation series coils issued in 1988, this was the only one with the old-fashioned kind of precancel.

However, it was heralded by the Postal Service as a new issue. Although no first-day ceremony was held, Washington first-day cancellations were provided.

That was unprecedented. Never before had a precancel overprint even been announced, let alone given first-day treatment.

When the first announcement of the stamp was made on April 4, no issue date was given. That information, along with the first illustration of the new variety, appeared in the June 9 issue of the USPS publication *Postal Bulletin*.

The stamp that it replaced for purposes of paying the carrier-route presort rate was the 8.3¢ Ambulance coil of 1985.

Collectors of precancels remembered that a situation similar to that which led to the new Oil Wagon variety had occurred before, with the 7.9¢ stamp of the Americana series. That stamp, depicting a drum, was originally issued April 23, 1976, in two versions: mint and bearing a city-state bureau precancel. The "bulk rate" service inscription was part of its design.

The stamp was removed from sale after its rate was no longer valid. But on August 13, 1982, more than six years after its original issue date, the stamp was reissued with the overprint "CAR-RT SORT" instead of the city-state designation.

This new printing of the Drum stamp appeared on recognizably different paper and with dull gum. However, it was not listed as a variety by the catalogs. A mint version of the new printing was issued in USPS' 1982 Definitive Mint Set.

The Design

No change was made in the basic stamp design, showing an 1890s oil wagon in slate blue. The designer was James Schleyer of Burke,

A straight line has been drawn beneath the overprint on the Oil Wagon stamp on the left to show how its height differs from that of its neighbor. This is a form of "gap" that precancel specialists collect.

Virginia, who had designed eight other Transportation series coils and the seven higher values of the Americana series.

First-Day Facts

First-day cancellations could be ordered until August 26, 60 days after the issue date.

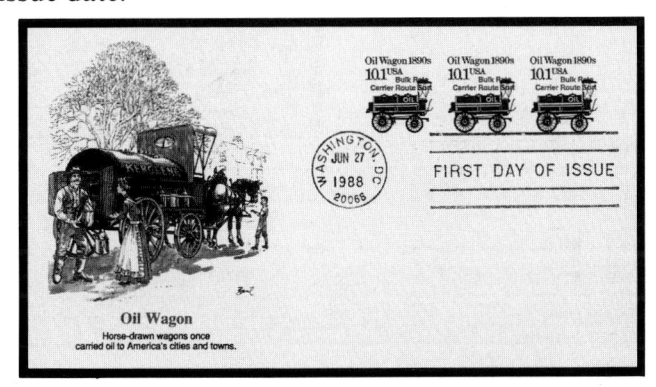

This Oil Wagon stamp was the first precancel ever to receive first-day cover treatment.

Collectors affixing their own stamps were reminded that at least 14.9¢ additional postage was needed to meet the minimum first-class letter rate. On covers on which USPS affixed the stamps, 26¢ was charged, and two Oil Wagon stamps were used, along with one 4.9¢ Buckboard (Transportation series) stamp of 1985. Thus, on each cover USPS collected nine-tenths of a cent more than the face value of the stamps affixed.

As a limited-use item, the precancel wasn't universally available at postal retail outlets. However, it was sold at all philatelic centers.

16.7¢ POPCORN WAGON (PRECANCELED)

Date of Issue: July 7, 1988

Catalog Numbers: Scott 2261   Minkus 898   USPS 7960A (500s)
USPS 7961A (3,000s)

Colors: red, black (precancel)

First-Day Cancel: Chicago, Illinois (State of Illinois Center)

FDCs Canceled: 117,908

Format: Coils of 500 and 3,000. Printing sleeve of 936 subjects (18 across, 52 around)

Perf: 9.75 (Huck rotary perforator)

Designer: Lou Nolan of McLean, Virginia

Art Director: Jack Williams (USPS)

Typographer: Bradbury Thompson (CSAC)

Engravers: Gary Chaconas (BEP, vignette)
Dennis Brown (BEP, lettering and numerals)

Modeler: Ronald Sharpe (BEP)

Printing: 3-color intaglio B press (701)

Quantity Ordered: Coils of 500 - 362,000
Coils of 3,000 - 143,000
Quantity Distributed: Coils of 500 - 342,350
Coils of 3,000 - 117,600

Sleeve Number Detail: One sleeve number on every 52nd stamp

Sleeve Number: 1

Tagging: untagged

The Stamp

The 33rd face-different stamp in the Transportation series, and the first to be issued only in service-inscribed (precanceled) form, was a 16.7¢ coil depicting a 1902 popcorn wagon.

The stamp, placed on sale in Chicago July 7, paid the basic bulk mail rate, replacing the 14¢ Iceboat coil of 1985. More than 500 million stamps for this rate are purchased each year, USPS reported.

One collector, writing to *Linn's Stamp News,* questioned the premise that the popcorn wagon was a "transportation" vehicle. Popcorn, he reasoned, is added after the vehicle has arrived at the site of the vending operation.

In any event, popcorn is now a basic part of Americans' snack diet, essential to moviegoing and regularly consumed at home. Chicago's Popcorn Institute reports that 11.9 billion quarts of popped corn is eaten annually in the United States, or 48 quarts for each person. Its high fiber content, the Institute explains, makes it appealing to the health-conscious.

The industry is a native one that traces its roots back to 15th-century Indian tribesmen who cooked corn by tossing the ears into the ashes of their campfires and waiting for the kernels to pop out.

The father of the modern popcorn business was Charles C. ("C.C.") Cretors of Chicago, manufacturer of the wagon shown on the stamp. As a young man who combined the talents of tinkerer and businessman, he set up a one-man shop in 1885 making steam-powered peanut roasters that could also handle coffee, popcorn and chestnuts.

Previously, vendors had popped corn by holding a wire basket over an open flame. At best, the result was a hot, dry, unevenly cooked product. The Cretors machines popped corn in a mixture of one-third clarified butter, two-thirds lard, and salt — a mixture that could withstand the 450-degree temperature needed to detonate the kernels, and do so without producing much smoke.

A fire under the boiler created steam that drove a small engine, which in turn drove the gears, shaft and agitator that stirred the corn and also powered the "Tosty Rosty Man." Tosty Rosty, a little red-suited mechanical clown that cranked the tumbler full of peanuts, was a standard fixture on all Cretors peanut roasters, and later became virtually a company trademark.

Over the next few years, C.C. developed a variety of models of roasters for specific customers and purposes. Each was meticulously handcrafted and was rich in eye-appealing elements: deep red paint with gilt accents, copper tanks, brass trim and tubing, bevel-edged French plate glass.

In 1893, C.C. broke new ground with his No. 6, the first model to display the popcorn area more prominently than the peanut compartment — and the first model that a storekeeper could easily move indoors and out. In the same year, C.C. created his first popcorn wagon, the No. 1, which was a completely self-contained unit that could go wherever its owner wanted to take it. If customers weren't buying at one location, it could simply be moved to a better spot.

C.C. took No. 1 to the Midway of the World's Columbian Exposition to try his luck. But wary showgoers were disinclined to pay to sample this snack food that was still relatively little-known.

On the third day, the businessman tried a daring ploy: He offered his popcorn free to develop a market for it. "This event, as much as anything else, marks the start of the popcorn industry," according to the 1985 centennial history of the Cretors company.

Today C. Cretors & Company sells about $8 million worth of popcorn makers each year. Its customers include all the major movie theater chains, such as Cineplex and General Cinema. Retail machines can make 50 pounds of popcorn an hour, but that output is modest compared to the 1,000-pound-an-hour capacity of the big popcorn poppers.

The Design

Lou Nolan of McLean, Virginia, who has been a free-lance artist since 1952, designed the stamp. It shows a side view of the Cretors No. 1 Wagon, Model 1902, from a catalog picture provided by C. Cretors & Company.

A glass case at the right of the wagon encloses the popcorn pan, suspended above a mound of freshly popped corn. Under the canopy at the left, the Tosty Rosty clown turns the crank to rotate the cylindrical peanut roaster.

The photograph from which Nolan worked shows a detachable handle lying on the ground between the two front wheels; this was eliminated in the image on the stamp.

"It was difficult to draw something that appeared to be popcorn and have it work when the design was reduced four or five times," Nolan said. "You have a tendency to put in a lot of detail, and when you get photostats of it and reduce them down to stamp size you realize that a lot of the detail fills in, and you have to go back and simplify it even more."

Nolan had previously designed the 3.4¢ School Bus, 17¢ Dog Sled and 5¢ Milk Wagon stamps of the Transportation series, and the 22¢ Certified Public Accountants commemorative and 14¢ Take Pride in America postal card of 1987.

The Popcorn Wagon stamp was printed on the Bureau of Engraving and Printing's intaglio B press. The vignette and text are in ruddy red, and the service inscription is in black.

First-Day Facts

The July 7 dedication ceremony took place in the lobby of Chicago's Main Post Office, 433 West Van Buren Street. It was moved there from the State of Illinois Center at 100 West Randolph Street, the site originally announced.

Participating were Thomas J. Fritsch, assistant postmaster general, Delivery Services Department; Charles D. Cretors, president of C.

The first-day programs, with corners cut, were designed to look like a popcorn box.

Cretors & Company, and his father, C.J. Cretors, retired president of the firm and grandson of founder C.C. Cretors.

Several vintage popcorn vehicles were on display, including a 1902 Cretors wagon that was essentially the same as the one on the stamp. A modern popper, also furnished by Cretors, produced a steady supply of hot popcorn, which was distributed free to the public in folding cardboard cups of antique design. Even the first-day program was designed like a red-and-white striped popcorn box, with corners cut to give it a three-dimensional look and with the inscription "Popcorn Wagon Stamp" in the middle. Booths along the lobby, where collectors could obtain cacheted envelopes and affix stamps, had striped canopies to give them a carnival look.

For first-day covers, collectors were reminded that an additional 8.3¢ was necessary to make up the first-class letter rate. On covers prepared by USPS, the 8.3¢ Ambulance stamp was used for this purpose, and the price was 25¢ per cover.

15¢ TUGBOAT

Date of Issue: July 12, 1988

Catalog Numbers: Scott 2260   Minkus 899   USPS 7963

Color: purple

First-Day Cancel: Long Beach, California (*Queen Mary*)

FDCs Canceled: 134,926

Format: Coils of 500 and 3,000. Printing sleeve of 936 subjects (18 across, 52 around).

Perf: 9.75 (Huck rotary perforator)

Designer: Richard Schlecht of Arlington, Virginia

Art Director and Project Manager: Jack Williams (USPS)

Typographer: Bradbury Thompson (CSAC)

Engravers: Gary Chaconas (BEP, vignette)
Dennis Brown, (BEP, lettering and numerals)

Modeler: Clarence Holbert (BEP)

Printing: 3-color intaglio B press (701)

Quantity Ordered: Coils of 500 - 400,000
Coils of 3,000 - 43,000
Quantity Distributed: Coils of 500 - 305,550
Coils of 3,000 - 40,992

Sleeve Number Detail: One sleeve number on every 52nd stamp

Sleeve Number: 1

Tagging: block over vignette

The Stamp

A 15¢ Tugboat stamp, issued in Long Beach, California, July 12, was the 34th face-different variety in the Transportation series.

The stamp provided customers a definitive in coil form to meet the current postcard rate. For that purpose it replaced the 14¢ Iceboat coil of 1985. A strip of three Tugboats also made up the 45¢ needed for international airmail letters and first-class letters weighing between one and two ounces.

When the stamp was announced by USPS April 4, the date and place of issue were unspecified. Later the date of issue was given as September 14; still later, it was moved to July 12. Long Beach was chosen, it was explained, because tugboats are extensively used in Los Angeles area harbors.

The stamp was issued in coils of 500 and 3,000.

Tugboats — which are midgets compared to some of the vessels they assist — keep traffic flowing smoothly and safely in the crowded waters of the world's seaports. Agile and powerful, they help larger ships with docking and sailing, tow barges, rescue ships in distress, accompany fireboats to burning piers and haul away endangered vessels, do salvage work and assist in ship refueling.

Before the American Revolution, rowboats manned by eight or ten men each were used as tugs. Until the turn of the century, along canals and rivers, barges were towed by teams of mules walking on land. The first engine-powered tugs were sidewheelers resembling old-time Mississippi River boats. Most tugs are now diesel-powered.

The first recorded commercial towing was done in 1815 by the small steamer *Enterprise* on a trip from the Gulf of Mexico up the Mississippi River to New Orleans. The first propeller-driven tug in America was the *Robert Stockton*, built in 1839.

The Design

The Tugboat stamp was printed in purple on BEP's intaglio B press. Richard Schlecht of Arlington, Virginia, a prolific supplier of designs for the Postal Service, provided this one as well — his third of 1988. Earlier he had designed the Conestoga Wagon coil and the Yorkshire postal card.

His line drawing of a tugboat was based on his review of several historical photographs supplied by the Smithsonian Institution. The vessel represented a tugboat type common at the turn of the century,

The "phantom plate number."

with a prominent single smokestack and a heavily guarded hull. The inscription "Tugboat 1900s" — referring to the decade, not the century — is centered above the vessel.

Varieties

One consistent plate flaw has been found on the Tugboat stamp: a tiny circle or semicircle, possibly from a dropped tool, punched into the plate two millimeters below the tugboat. Dubbed the "phantom plate number," the mark appears on the ninth stamp to the right of the stamp that shows the actual plate number, in this case plate No. 1.

The postcard that bore the stamp with the plate flaw.

Because the B-press cylinders contain 18 rows of subjects, the flaw appears on only one of every 18 rolls of stamps produced by plate 1.

First-Day Facts

An elaborate first-day ceremony, complete with brass band, was held on the aft deck of the *Queen Mary* in Long Beach harbor.

Presiding was William J. Good, general manager/postmaster at Long Beach. Keith Kambak, vice president and general manager of the *Queen Mary*, gave the welcome. Speakers were Richard J. Sargent, president of the Long Beach Centennial Committee; Joseph F. Prevratil, executive director of the Port Of Long Beach, and Joseph R. Caraveo, regional postmaster general, who likened USPS to a tugboat ("a friend every day, through bad weather and good") and presented guests with souvenir folders.

Collectors ordering first-day covers by mail and affixing their own stamps were reminded that their self-addressed envelopes must carry at least 25¢ in postage. Postcards, of course, could be submitted bearing only a single Tugboat stamp. When USPS affixed the stamps to envelopes, a 10¢ Canal Boat stamp of 1987 — the only other Transportation series stamp to depict a watercraft — was added to make up the first-class rate.

13.2¢ RAILROAD COAL CAR (PRECANCELED)

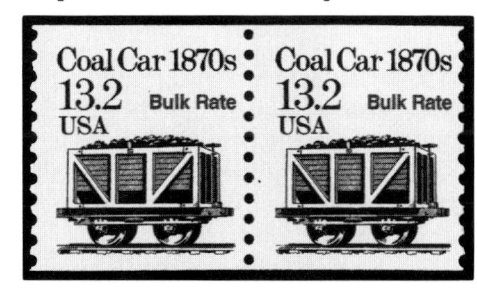

Date of Issue: July 19, 1988

Catalog Numbers: Scott 2259   Minkus 900   USPS 7957A (500s)
USPS 7958A (3,000s)

Colors: dark green, red (precancel)

First-Day Cancel: Pittsburgh, Pennsylvania (Mellon Science Center, Duquesne University)

FDCs Canceled: 123,965

Format: Coils of 500 and 3,000. Printing sleeve of 936 subjects (18 across, 52 around).

Perf: 9.75 (Huck rotary perforator)

Designer: Richard Schlecht of Arlington, Virginia

Art Director: Jack Williams (USPS)

Typographer: Bradbury Thompson (CSAC)

Engravers: Thomas Hipschen (BEP, vignette)
Michael Ryan (BEP, lettering and numerals)

Printing: 3-color intaglio B press (701)

Quantity Ordered: Coils of 500 - 344,000
Coils of 3,000 - 198,000
Quantity Distributed: Coils of 500 - 315,350
Coils of 3,000 - 98,112

Sleeve Number Detail: One sleeve number on every 52nd stamp

Sleeve Number: 1

Tagging: untagged

The Stamp

On July 19, USPS issued a coil stamp in the Transportation series depicting a coal mining car. First-day sale was in Pittsburgh, Pennsylvania, whose location atop the vast Pittsburgh Coal Bed was a major factor in making it one of the world's great industrial cities.

The 13.2¢ denomination met the rate for a single item presorted to five-digit ZIP codes. For this purpose it replaced the 10.1¢ Oil Wagon stamp of 1985.

(The Oil Wagon, which had previously carried a "Bulk-Rate" overprint, was reissued June 27, 1988, with a new overprint to meet the new 10.1¢ rate for third-class mail presorted to the carrier route.)

An ore car had been one of the vehicles suggested for the Transportation series in 1987 by readers of John M. Hotchner's column in *Linn's Stamp News.*

The Stamp Information Branch of USPS released a picture of the new stamp, plus details, July 5. However, as sometimes occurs, the *Postal Bulletin* had beaten the official release. It illustrated the design in its June 23 edition.

Until the mid-19th century, coal was most often hauled out of the mines by mules or by miners themselves, a slow, dangerous process.

But the development of safe and practical locomotives — themselves dependent on coal for power — proved of great benefit to mining. Soon, coal was being carried to the surface in cars pulled by an ingenious variation of the railroad.

Loading coal into cars like the 1870s-vintage model pictured on the stamp remained a manual task until the 1920s, when various mechanical devices began to appear. Since then, modern equipment has continued to add to the safety — albeit the complexity — of mining.

Today massive continuous-mining machines slice through solid coal walls. Other stations on the machines simultaneously claw the fragmented rock and shovel it onto conveyors to be transported to waiting shuttle cars. Thus the most dangerous and difficult work — cutting new, unsupported passages — is accomplished with the miner removed from the danger area.

Today's coal cars often are self-propelled by diesel or electronic engines, but the basic need to haul coal to the surface remains.

Coal has not been the dominant energy source in the United States for many years, but it remains an essential part of the nation's overall energy program. Most coal is now used by electric generating plants and for making coke for the steel industry.

The mining of anthracite, or hard coal, is limited to northwestern Pennsylvania, where huge reserves of the material remain untapped. West Virginia leads in the production of bituminous soft coal, followed by Pennsylvania, Kentucky and Illinois.

The Design

Richard Schlecht's design, showing a side view of a loaded coal car on a section of rail, was based on a photograph of a car manufactured in 1873 by the York, Pennsylvania, firm of Billmyer and Small.

The stamp was printed by BEP's intaglio B press in dark green. The

The Coal Car coil was anticipated a year earlier by a Linn's Stamp News reader.

single-line service inscription "Bulk Rate" was in red.

Schlecht's previous 1988 design assignments were the Conestoga Wagon and Tugboat coil stamps and the Yorkshire postal card.

Varieties

A few Coal Car stamps were discovered in imperforate form. In October one dealer was advertising a pair for $300.

An imperforate pair of Coal Car coil stamps.

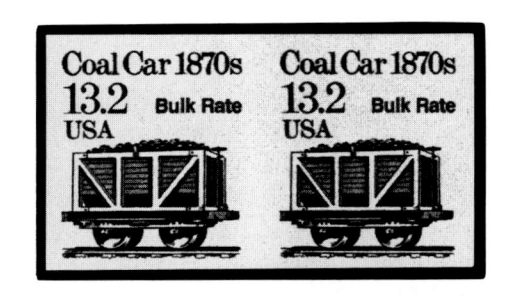

First-Day Facts

The first-day ceremony was at the Mellon Science Center of Duquesne University. Scheduled speakers included John R. Wargo, assistant postmaster general for marketing, and representatives of the coal industry and the U.S. Bureau of Mines.

For first-day covers serviced by USPS, a pair of Coal Car stamps was affixed to cover the first-class rate. The cost was 27¢ per cover.

8.4¢ WHEELCHAIR (PRECANCELED)

Date of Issue: August 12, 1988

Catalog Numbers: Scott 2256 Minkus 901 USPS 7955A (500s) USPS 7956A (3,000s)	
Colors: maroon, red (precancel)	
First-Day Cancel: Tucson, Arizona (VA Medical Center)	
FDCs Canceled: 136,337	
Format: Coils of 500 and 3,000. Printing sleeves of 936 subjects (18 across, 52 around) and 864 subjects (18 across, 48 around).	
Perf: 9.75 (Huck rotary perforator)	
Designer: Chris Calle of Ridgefield, Connecticut	
Art Director and Project Manager: Jack Williams (USPS)	
Typographer: Bradbury Thompson (CSAC)	
Engravers: Gary Chaconas (BEP, vignette) Gary Slaght (BEP, lettering and numerals)	
Printing: 3-color intaglio B press (701) and 3-color intaglio C press (901).	
Quantity Ordered: Coils of 500 - 197,000 Coils of 3,000 - 141,000 **Quantity Distributed:** Coils of 500 - 207,600 Coils of 3,000 - 72,608	
Sleeve Number Detail: One sleeve number on every 48th (C press) or 52nd (B press) stamp.	
Sleeve Numbers: 1 (B press) 2 (C press)	
Tagging: untagged	

The Stamp

An 8.4¢ coil stamp, covering the single-piece rate for third-class bulk mailings by non-profit organizations, was issued August 12 in

Tucson, Arizona.

The stamp depicted a 1920s-vintage wheelchair — or "wheel chair," as it was designated on the stamp and in some (but not all) of the relevant USPS press releases. Most current dictionaries and the Associated Press stylebook opt for one word.

It was the sixth stamp of the year in the Transportation series and 36th face-different variety in the series overall.

The denomination met the single-piece rate for third-class bulk mailings prepared by non-profit organizations, a rate previously covered by the 1987 8.5¢ Tow Truck coil precanceled with the overprint "Nonprofit Org." This rate had been lowered to 8.4¢ April 3, representing one of the few reductions in the comprehensive rate schedule adopted on that date.

Issuance of the Wheelchair stamp followed by four months the release of an 8.4¢ precanceled stamped envelope for the same purpose. The envelope, issued April 12, depicted the frigate *Constellation*.

Many well-known people have used wheelchairs for lengthy periods. Among them have been President Franklin D. Roosevelt, who as a still-young man was stricken by polio; ex-Governor George Wallace of Alabama, disabled by a bullet fired by a would-be assassin, and Stephen Hawking, mathematician and cosmologist, who pursues his search for a unified theory of creation despite being almost completely paralyzed with amyotrophic lateral sclerosis (Lou Gehrig's disease).

The principle they personify — full participation in life despite physical disability — has been the theme of three previous U.S. stamps that depicted wheelchairs.

A 4¢ commemorative of 1960 showed a man in a wheelchair operating a drill press under the slogan: "Employ the Handicapped."

In 1981, an 18¢ commemorative used a similar image to mark the International Year of the Disabled. The worker was seated at a desk, peering through a microscope, and the caption read: "Disabled doesn't mean Unable."

In between, in 1969, a 6¢ stamp proclaiming "Hope for the Crippled" showed a four-step multiple image of a boy seated in a wheelchair, standing, and walking away.

In addition, a 1983 20¢ envelope honoring paralyzed veterans bore an embossed wheelchair in the indicium. A wheelchair also appeared on the 22¢ stamp of 1985 commemorating the 50th anniversary of the Social Security Act.

A paraplegic German watchmaker has been credited with the first self-propelled wheelchair, a three-wheeled model he built for his own use in 1640. This and later versions were cumbersome and expensive, and required great strength by the user or a full-time attendant.

In the early 20th century, Herbert A. Everest, a paraplegic, found the then-available wooden wheelchairs — weighing 75 to 90 pounds — clumsy and hard to operate. With a friend, Harry C. Jennings Sr., a mechanical engineer, he designed a light metal wheelchair. Demand for the new model grew, and in 1932 they established a company to manufacture the vehicles.

Meanwhile, the population of permanently disabled persons was growing because of several factors: the return home of World War I casualties, an increasing number of traffic and industrial accidents, and life-saving improvements in medicine and surgery. The result was the development of more rehabilitative equipment in a few short years than had been made in the previous century.

Many practical design innovations were applied to the wheelchair, such as seat cushions to reduce the incidence of pressure sores, longer-lasting sealed bearings in the main wheel hub, die-cast "mag" wheels eliminating many maintenance and replacement problems, and improved motor control systems.

Among the leaders in research and development of wheelchair improvements have been the Veterans Administration and other organizations for the disabled.

The Design

The stamp was printed by intaglio with the vignette in maroon and the engraved service inscription "Nonprofit" in red.

The designer was Christopher Calle of Ridgefield, Connecticut. Although he had many other stamps to his credit — including, earlier in 1988, the Connecticut Statehood commemorative — this was his first Transportation series design.

Calle based his drawing of a 1928-model wheelchair produced by the Invacare Corporation of Elyria, Ohio, on resource material provided by the Smithsonian Institution. The chair, of wicker construction, had a single centrally mounted rear wheel and two larger front wheels. The wheels were driven by belts connected to shoulder-level hand cranks, unlike those on today's models, which are propelled by the use of attached hand rims.

The stamp was at first printed on BEP's B press and later moved to the C press, reportedly because of ink-drying problems that had slowed production. The C press version was put on sale without fanfare at the philatelic sales windows at USPS headquarters in Washington October 6.

The new version, which appeared as Plate 2, was indistinguishable from the B press version, except for the plate, or sleeve, number, which occurs at 48-stamp intervals on the C press rather than 52.

First-Day Facts

The dedication ceremony August 12 took place in the courtyard of the Veterans Administration Medical Center at 3601 South 6th Avenue, Tucson. One of more than 170 such facilities nationwide, the Medical Center serves as the central distribution point for philatelic

Charles Yeager, Washington correspondent for Linn's Stamp News, *prepared this unofficial first-day cover of the C-press version of the stamp on October 6, 1988.*

material and information regularly sent to individuals and groups of veterans interested in stamp collecting.

It was a typical Arizona August day, with the temperature close to 100 for the morning event. The stage was in the shade and the estimated 600 persons in the audience — including many patients from the hospital — were seated under canopies. Gordon C. Morison, senior assistant postmaster general for marketing and communications, was the principal speaker.

Morison pointed out that USPS actively recruits disabled employees and ensures them equal access to the workplace. All newly constructed postal facilities are designed to be accessible to the physically handicapped, he said, and when possible older ones are modified. In 1987, USPS developed plans to make its 29,000 leased facilities accessible. He also noted that 43 percent of the 760,000 Postal Service employees are veterans, including 82,000 who are disabled and nearly 17,000 severely disabled.

For mailed-in self-addressed first-day covers on which USPS affixed the postage, 26¢ was charged, and three Wheelchair stamps were used to cover the 25¢ first-class rate.

21¢ RAILROAD MAIL CAR (PRECANCELED)

Date of Issue: August 16, 1988

Catalog Numbers: Scott 2265   Minkus 902   USPS 7970A (500s)
                                                                      USPS 7971A (3,000s)

Colors: green, red (precancel)

First-Day Cancel: Santa Fe, New Mexico (Palace of the Governors)

FDCs Canceled: 124,430

Format: Coils of 500 and 3,000. Printing sleeves of 936 subjects (18 across, 52 around) and 864 subjects (18 across, 48 around).

Perf: 9.75 (Huck rotary perforator)

Designer: David Stone of Chapel Hill, North Carolina

Art Director and Project Manager: Joe Brockert (USPS)

Typographer: Bradbury Thompson (CSAC)

Engravers: Gary Chaconas (BEP, vignette)
Dennis Brown (BEP, letter and numerals)

Modeler: Clarence Holbert (BEP)

Printing: 3-color intaglio B press (701) and 3-color intaglio C press (901).

Quantity Ordered: Coils of 500 - 150,000
Coils of 3,000 - 145,000
Quantity Distributed: Coils of 500 - 146,400
Coils of 3,000 - 79,360

Sleeve Number Detail: One sleeve number on every 48th (C press) or 52nd (B press) stamp.

Sleeve Number: 1 (B press)
2 (C press)

Tagging: untagged

The Stamp

For its seventh Transportation series coil stamp of 1988, USPS paid tribute to the vehicle that made possible the rapid growth of the postal service into a swift and reliable nationwide institution — the railroad mail car.

The 21¢ service-inscribed stamp was issued August 16 in Santa Fe, New Mexico, to meet the single-piece rate for first-class mailings presorted to either the three- or five-digit ZIP code. For that purpose it replaced the 18¢ George Washington and Washington Monument coil of 1985.

It depicted a specific car still in existence: Southern Railway Postal Car No. 49, which was built in 1922 by the American Car and Foundry Company. On the side are the words "United States Mail/Railway Post Office."

At 21¢, the item also met an existing rate — for postal cards to Canada. It was a rate for which a new sheet stamp, a 21¢ Great Americans depicting Chester Carlson, would be issued two months later. However, because it was service-inscribed, it could be used only by postal patrons who had a precancel permit.

The new coil was the third railroad-related design in the Transportation series and the third to depict a postal vehicle. The earlier designs showed an 1870s locomotive, an 1890s caboose, an 1880s mail wagon and a 1910s star route truck.

But the railroad mail car itself had made its debut on stamps long before. In the 1912-1913 Parcel Post series, the 3¢ value depicted a railway postal clerk standing at the door of a mail car removing a bag of mail from the car's catching arm. The 5¢ showed a speeding mail train approaching a suspended mail bag.

Railroad mail cars combined fast transportation with in-transit mail processing to speed the distribution of mail across the continent.

Mail by rail got a boost from the Act of July 7, 1838, that constituted all U.S. railroads as post routes. Until 1862, all mail carried on trains was distributed in post offices, but in that year the postmaster of St. Joseph, Missouri, tried a system of sorting and distributing mail on a moving train between Hannibal and St. Joseph in an attempt to avoid delays in mail departures for the West.

On August 28, 1864, George B. Armstrong, assistant postmaster general of Chicago, launched an official test of a railway post-office car between Chicago and Clinton, Iowa. Its success led to establishment later that year of the Railway Post Office (RPO).

At first, traveling post offices occupied only very small sections in the end of baggage cars. But as the country became more thickly settled and the amount of mail increased, it often became necessary to use entire cars to accommodate RPOs.

At the zenith of railway mail service immediately after World War II, more than 30,000 transportation postal clerks worked on more than 4,000 RPO cars. They handled about 93 percent of all non-local mail matter as they covered some 205 million miles per year on more than 1,500 separate routes.

However, decline came quickly. It paralleled the decline in passenger train service that resulted from the increased use of the automobile and commercial airlines.

With the drop in available trains for mail transportation, RPO service began to dry up. The number of trains decreased steadily from 2,600 in 1956, to 1,400 in 1961, to 741 in 1967.

When RPO service was eliminated in 1977, only two trains survived. They ran daily between New York and Washington. Last-run ceremonies in both cities June 30, 1977, marked the end of an era for mail transportation that had lasted more than a century.

The Design

David Stone of Chapel Hill, North Carolina, designed the stamp. He was responsible for several previous stamps in the Transportation series, including the 18¢ Surrey of 1981 that inaugurated the series and the 10.9¢ Hansom Cab, 5.9¢ Antique Bicycle, 2¢ Locomotive, 1¢

The denomination, service inscription and arrangement of design elements were changed on the finished stamp, but the train picture remained the same.

Omnibus and 5.5¢ Star Route Truck. Stone also designed the 1970 Fort Snelling, 1974 Fort Harrod and 1983 Civilian Conservation Corps commemoratives and the 1987 Constitutional Convention postal card.

The artist sketched several different mail cars from three different eras: the 1870s, 1898 and the 1920s. He also experimented with the descriptive labels "railway mail car," "railway post office car" and "railway post office" before settling on "railroad mail car."

Two of the pictures from which Stone worked showed trackside devices for mail-bag pickup. He included these in his essays, but CSAC decided that this kind of accessory should be eliminated in the final design in order to focus full attention on the vehicle.

The car that was finally chosen for the stamp, Postal Car No. 49, is 64½ feet long, weighs 112,000 pounds and has a 45-foot mail distribution section equipped with 744 letter and 210 paper separations.

It was donated by the Southern Railway to the Atlanta Chapter of the National Railway Historical Society Inc., and later sold to the

Artist David Stone tried several different cards, with and without trackside mail-bag devices, and different inscriptions.

North Carolina History Corporation and moved June 13, 1979, to its present location, Spencer, North Carolina, an easy drive from artist Stone's hometown.

At the time the stamp was issued, the state of North Carolina was restoring the car to operating condition and planned to use it at the historic site for actual running demonstrations.

Bradbury Thompson's first type overlay for the finished art bore the denomination figures 20.7 and the service inscription "ZIP+4 Presort" in the lower left corner. This was the denomination USPS had originally requested for that category of mail. Later, when the rates were established, the stamp became 21¢ for first-class mail presorted to three- or five-digit ZIP codes.

The denomination was moved to the bottom and the "Presorted/First-Class" service inscription was placed in the relatively open space above the front of the car. BEP suggested the re-arrangement in order to widen the space between the intaglio green of the vignette and red of the inscription and reduce the chances that ink from one would bleed into the other.

Like the 8.4¢ Wheelchair, the Railroad Mail Car was produced by BEP on the intaglio B press (with plate numbers on every 52nd stamp) and later moved to the C press (plate number every 48th stamp).

Varieties

Imperforate copies of the Railroad Mail Car stamp were discovered on three different rolls shortly after the stamp was issued, according to *Coil Line*, the official journal of the Plate Number Coil Collectors'

An imperforate pair of the Railroad Mail Car stamp.

Club. At least 17 plate number strips exist, the periodical said, which would indicate that a large quantity of non-numbered copies would also exist.

First-Day Facts

Santa Fe was chosen as the first-day city because of its historic association with railroads, USPS said.

Ceremonies were held before some 250 people at the historic Palace of the Governors, located on the Plaza. The Palace itself was the subject of the 1¼¢ Liberty series stamp of 1960, which was issued in both sheet and coil versions.

Thomas J. Fritsch, assistant postmaster general for delivery services, reminded the audience that the presorted mail on which the Railroad Mail Car stamp would be used would be "separated in advance by customers to speed handling and reduce costs, just as its subject did years ago."

For first-day covers prepared by USPS, a pair of 2¢ Locomotive stamps was affixed to make up the 25¢ first-class rate.

7.6¢ CARRETA (PRECANCELED)

Date of Issue: August 30, 1988

Catalog Numbers: Scott 2255   Minkus 903   USPS 7953A (500s)
USPS 7954A (3,000s)

Colors: brown, red (precancel)

First-Day Cancel: San Jose, California (San Jose Historical Museum)

FDCs Canceled: 140,024

Format: Coils of 500 and 3,000. Printing sleeve of 936 subjects (18 across, 52 around).

Perf: 9.75 (Huck rotary perforator)

Designer: Richard Schlecht of Arlington, Virginia

Art Director and Project Manager: Jack Williams (USPS)

Typographer: Bradbury Thompson (CSAC)

Engravers: Edward Archer (BEP, vignette)
Gary Slaght (BEP, lettering and numerals)

Printing: 3-color intaglio B press (701)

Quantity Ordered: Coils of 500 - 136,000
Coils of 3,000 - 62,000
Quantity Distributed: Coils of 500 - 122,000
Coils of 3,000 - 27,424

Sleeve Number Detail: One sleeve number on every 52nd stamp

Sleeve Number: 1, 2

Tagging: untagged

The Stamp

The Transportation series turned regional and ethnic August 30 with a stamp depicting a primitive wooden cart used by settlers and natives in early Spanish California.

The cart — *carreta* in Spanish — was depicted on a 7.6¢ coil stamp issued to meet the rate for third-class non-profit bulk mail presorted to five digits. For that use it replaced the 7.1¢ Tractor stamp of 1987.

It was the 38th face-different Transportation variety and depicted the earliest vehicle to be featured in the series to date. In fact, the carreta, according to Mignon Gibson, director of the San Jose, California, Historical Museum, may have been the first vehicle used on the North American continent.

The Carreta stamp was the idea of Theron Fox, 83, of San Jose, a stamp collector, pioneer cachetmaker, ex-newspaperman and former chairman of the city's Historic Landmark Commission. Fox had gotten to know officials in USPS' Stamps Division in an unusual way.

In 1977, USPS had issued a 13¢ commemorative for the 200th anniversary of San Jose, the first civil settlement in Alta (Upper) California. Earl Thollander, an artist from Calistoga, California, prepared a design for the stamp, showing early farm buildings with a carreta parked in front. But there were some errors in the design.

These errors would have been perpetuated on the stamp itself except for a lucky circumstance. During the 1970s USPS issued an annual promotional folder called "The Treasury of Stamps," which illustrated the current year's issues and provided space to mount the stamps themselves. The 1977 edition went to press before the Alta California commemorative was issued, and the picture the compilers used was of Thollander's original design.

Theron Fox saw a copy of the folder at his post office in San Jose and called Jack Williams, program manager for stamp design at USPS, to point out the inaccuracies as he saw them. For one thing, the adobe building depicted was too fancy, and it flew a Spanish flag.

"They didn't bother carrying a flag in those days," Fox said. "There was nobody to impress." For another, the stamp showed a carreta with small wheels — but the actual wheels, Fox pointed out, were made from cross sections of oak trees, at least three feet across.

"So I flew out to California," Williams recalled. "I met with Theron and went over the design and got it all lined up historically. Then I went to Calistoga and met with Earl Thollander and he made the desired changes, and it came out all right in the end."

Fox stayed in touch with Williams, and after the Transportation series began rolling in 1981, he proposed that a carreta be included. Williams and CSAC thought about it and agreed to do it.

"I figured it was a completely original vehicle," Fox told the *San Jose Mercury News*. "It was strictly used in Spanish America — they had no wheelwrights here, and no metal."

The cart — used throughout the Southwest by the Spanish — was a cage on big wheels, without springs, lashed together with leather thongs. Wooden pegs held the wheels to a wooden axletree.

Though "Carreta 1770s" appeared above the vignette on the stamp, the cart was actually in use for many decades. Pulled by oxen joined by the horns, with drivers walking alongside prodding the animals, carretas were used by settlers to haul firewood and water during the week, and to carry women and children to Mass on Sundays.

The Design

The basis for the Carreta stamp design was a drawing made by Ralph Rambo of Palo Alto, California, an artist-historian who is now 94. Theron Fox had sent Rambo's artwork to USPS in 1977 to illustrate what the carreta on the Alta California stamp ought to look like.

When the time came to design the Transportation series stamp, the Rambo drawing was deemed much too detailed to serve as a guide to BEP's engravers. So Richard Schlecht of Arlington, Virginia, was assigned to reproduce the picture in a simpler style. It was Schlecht's fifth philatelic design of the year.

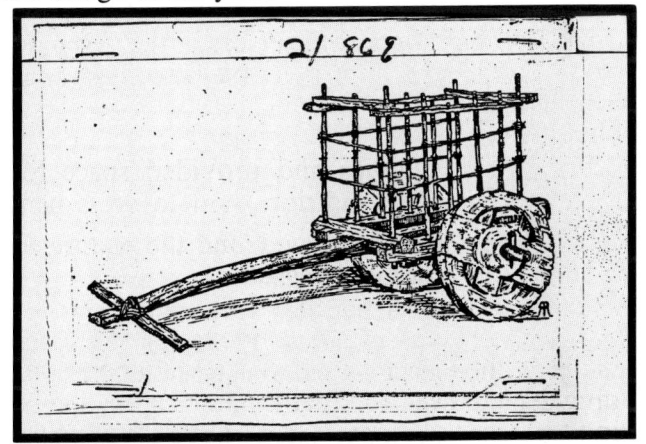

Ralph Rambo's carreta drawing on which Richard Schlecht based his stamp design.

The stamp was printed on BEP's intaglio B press. Its basic color was brown, an appropriate hue for a wooden cart. The precancel endorsement "Nonprofit" appeared in red at lower left.

Earlier in the year, Schlecht had designed the Conestoga Wagon, Tugboat and Coal Car stamps, plus the Yorkshire postal card.

He had done one previous design with a historic California theme: the 44¢ Junipero Serra airmail stamp of 1985.

First-Day Facts

The first-day ceremony took place on the grounds of the San Jose Historical Museum just outside the Pacific Hotel, which houses the museum's adminstrative offices.

Assistant Postmaster General M. Richard Porras, the principal speaker, said the stamp was an example of how stamps can "spread the word about a little-known subject to a very large audience."

25¢ HONEYBEE

Date of Issue: September 2, 1988

Catalog Numbers: Scott 2281 Minkus 905 USPS 7723 (100s)
 USPS 7900 (3000s)

Colors: cyan, magenta, yellow, PMS yellow, black (offset); black (intaglio)

First-Day Cancel: Omaha, Nebraska (Holiday Inn Central, Omaha Stamp Show)

FDCs Canceled: 122,853

Format: Coils of 100 and 3,000. Offset printing plates of 450 subjects (18 across, 25 around) and 500 subjects (20 across, 25 around) used on Goebel offset Optiforma press (043) in conjunction with C press (901) intaglio printing sleeves of, respectively, 864 subjects (18 across, 48 around) and 960 subjects (20 across, 48 around). Offset plates of 432 subjects (18 across, 24 around) and 480 subjects (20 across, 24 around) used on D press (902), respectively, with intaglio sleeves of 864 and 960 subjects.

Perf: 9.75 (Goebel stroke perforator on coils of 100; Huck rotary perforator on coils of 3,000.)

Designer: Chuck Ripper of Huntington, West Virginia

Art Director: Jack Williams (USPS)

Typographer: Bradbury Thompson (CSAC)

Engravers: Edward Archer (BEP, honeybee outline)

Modeler: Peter Cocci (BEP)

Printing: 6-color Goebel offset Optiforma press (043) and 3-color intaglio C press (901) or 6-color offset, 3-color intaglio D press (902). Flexographic tagging plates of 432 subjects (for coils of 3,000) or 480 subjects (for coils of 100).

Quantity Ordered: Coils of 100 - 90,000,000
 Coils of 3,000 - 100,000
Quantity Distributed: Coils of 100 - 20,347,000
 Coils of 3,000 - 57,120

Sleeve Number Detail: One sleeve number on every 48th stamp

Sleeve Numbers: 1, 2

Tagging: block over vignette

The Stamp

In 1980, USPS had issued a 15¢ stamped envelope depicting a honeybee hovering over a pair of orange blossoms. There was one problem with it, however. The bee was embossed without color onto the white envelope and was almost literally invisible.

This planning disaster left beekeepers bitterly disappointed, and they let the Postal Service know about it. Their message was, in effect: You owe us one.

Eight years later, USPS paid off the debt, with interest. It issued a 25¢ Honeybee coil stamp. A definitive, the stamp had an initial print order of 11.3 billion, with the potential of many additional billions. And this time, the bee, in black intaglio on a colorful offset background, stood out so prominently that you could almost hear it buzz.

The Honeybee stamp was the first combination-process coil ever issued by USPS. It was printed by two completely different procedures at the Bureau of Engraving and Printing. The first of these was a throwback to the multiple-printing method for bicolor stamps that was almost as old as the postage stamp itself.

The rolls of paper were first run through the Goebel Optiforma press, designated Press 043. This is a six-station web offset press acquired by BEP several years ago — reportedly for printing gasoline ration stamps in the event they were needed — and currently being used to produce Official Mail stamps. It applied the color portions of the design, inscription and frame.

Then the rolls, without being rewound, were taken to the C press, where the intaglio portion — the honeybee — and the phosphor tagging, by flexographic plate, was applied.

The printed webs were then perforated and processed on the Goebel and Huck coiling equipment into rolls for retail sale.

In the past, the printing of stamps in two separate steps had sometimes resulted in color inverts — most recently, on the $1 Candleholder stamp of the 1970s Americana series. There was no chance of that happening here. Inverting an entire web — not just a single sheet — would have required a blunder of unimaginable proportions.

Later, BEP moved the entire operation to its D press, which had become available for the purpose. Here, offset printing, intaglio printing and tagging could be done in one operation. This eliminated the excessive spoilage BEP had been experiencing because of the difficulty of registering the separately printed images.

When the Honeybee stamp was originally announced April 4, 1988, the date of issue was given as June 11 and the place Corpus Christi, Texas, at the TEXPEX 88 philatelic exhibition.

Then, on April 21, it was announced that the Honeybee coil had been "deferred" and a new date and site hadn't been set.

In late June, these details were announced. The stamp would appear September 2 at the Omaha Stamp Show, in Omaha, Nebraska.

(Meanwhile, as a consolation prize, TEXPEX got the first-day ceremony for the new 15¢ and 25¢ Official Mail stamps.)

One reason for the postponement, USPS officials said, was that BEP wasn't "absolutely comfortable" with the complicated, unprecedented printing procedure it first used on the Honeybee stamps. The Bureau wanted to make sure that once they were issued it could guarantee full production.

"They needed a little more leeway," a USPS spokesman said, "and since we had the 25¢ Bread Wagon and 25¢ Yosemite coils, we decided we wouldn't rush the process."

The honeybee, its admirers are quick to point out, is one of Earth's most industrious and important insects.

In 1988 more than three million beehives produced about 20 million pounds of honey in the United States alone. The task is prodigious; to produce a single pound of honey, more than 550 bees have to visit more than 2.5 million flowers.

Besides manufacturing honey and wax, honeybees provide indispensable help to farmers and fruit growers by pollinating crops and fruit trees. This service is a byproduct of their travels among flowering plants to gather nectar for the colony.

The U.S. Department of Agriculture estimates that about 3.5 million acres of fruits, vegetables and seed crops depend on insect pollination and that another 63 million acres benefit from it. Ninety percent of this work is performed by the honeybee.

The Design

Chuck Ripper of Huntington, West Virginia, who had designed the Pheasant and Owl and Grosbeak booklet stamps issued earlier in the year, produced the gouache painting used for the Honeybee stamp.

Sometimes the seam, where the two ends of the offset plates adjoin, leaves a line, or a pair of lines, as shown at the center here.

Chuck Ripper's original sketch featured a blue-and-pink color scheme and white dropout typography.

bee alighting on a bright pink flower against a blue background, with the denomination and "USA" in dropout white.

In the final painting, at the committee's request, he changed the flower to a red clover with green leaves, and made the bee more prominent in relation to the blossom. He also changed the background color to yellow to provide better contrast — which required that the lettering be black instead of white.

The stamp design was Ripper's 69th. All the others had been made for gravure printing, a process with which Ripper was intimately familiar because of his professional background, and one in which the artist's work essentially goes directly to the camera to be processed.

The honeybee painting, however, had to be interpreted by a modeler and engraver. Ripper said he made no changes in his own technique because of the new printing method, and BEP engraver Edward P. Archer's detailed rendering of the artist's honeybee turned out to be suitably lifelike.

The assignment was another first for Ripper: Though he had produced literally hundreds of wildlife paintings in his career, he had never done one in which a bee was the central subject. USPS needed the painting in the early spring of 1988, before West Virginia's bees had emerged, and so the artist had to work from photos.

"I found out that the world isn't blessed with good bee photographs," Ripper said. "I was moaning to myself that if they had just put the project off a month, I could go out in the yard and get one!"

The offset colors used in production were magenta, light yellow, yellow, cyan and black. The intaglio was black only, and the only plate number appearing on the coils was the intaglio number, which turned up at 48-stamp intervals.

No offset numbers were used, USPS explained, because the offset plate on the Optiforma press had a 25-stamp interval. Thus, because of these different repeat lengths, the two sets of numbers would have "floated" in relation to one another, and the spacing variations would have been virtually infinite.

This wouldn't have been a problem with the D press, because its offset plate units had a repeat length of 24 stamps, putting them "in sync" with the 48-stamp intaglio sleeves.

At the outset, two intaglio sleeves were used. Sleeve 1 had 864 subjects — 18 across by 48 around. Therefore the companion offset plates had to be 18 rows across as well. At 25 subjects around, each contained a total of 450 subjects.

Sleeve 2 had 20 rows across by 48 subjects around, or 960 subjects. This required offset plates of 20 by 25, or 500 subjects.

Collectors wondered at first why most of the digits on the plate 1 rolls had a decapitated appearance, with a serif at the bottom but none at the top. This was later explained by research done by Charles Yeager, Washington correspondent for *Linn's Stamp News*.

Originally, the numbers engraved on sleeve 1 were normal. But during test runs, the number was so high that a slight misregistration would thrust it into the bottom of the stamp design.

The sleeve was dechromed and sent back to siderographers in the design and engraving division of BEP to shorten the plate numbers at each of the 18 positions across the sleeve's wide dimension. But a master die with a smaller number wasn't available.

So, using a flat engraving tool, the siderographer went into the metal below the engraved image and threw up a mound of steel. He "stabbed it up, tiled it and trimmed it," according to Yeager, filling in the top portion of the existing digit.

The digits for Plate 1 of the Honeybee stamp were "decapitated" to help compensate for the effects of misregistration.

The printing sleeve was then rechromed and returned to production. In that way the plate numbers were all shortened, so that on loosely registered stamps they would still be clear of the bottom of the frameline most of the time.

But because the repair was done by hand, there was some variation from one row to the next. One or more positions had a top serif. Another had a rounded swelling at the top, while most seemed to be cleanly chopped.

On this misregistered Plate 2 coil, the plate number is entirely inside the frame of the stamp design rather than below it (see enlarged inset).

By the time sleeves 2 and 3 were prepared, the BEP had acquired smaller dies for the digits. The No. 2 Honeybee digit was only one-half millimeter tall, compared with three-fourths of a millimeter on other plate number coils.

Despite BEP's best efforts to prevent misregistration during the original, two-stage printing phase, it did occur. On sleeve 2, in particular, the plate number tended to drift — and occasionally was completely swallowed up inside the stamp design.

In those examples, of course, the bee image was elevated accordingly, rising partially out of its own background color.

Several tagging variations were also noted. On some rolls, the tagging blocks were approximately the height of the printed design but visibly narrower, ranging from 16 to 17.5 millimeters in width, with square or rounded corners; on others, the blocks were larger than the printed area in both dimensions and had rounded corners. This indicated that the tagging plates were being changed frequently and weren't of uniform manufacture.

On the test runs, the tagging appeared under the intaglio black image, rather than on top. That's because the test-run tagging was done at the unused station of the Goebel Optiforma offset press, rather than at the letterpress station of the C or D press, as on the full-production stamps.

Some collectors found pairs of Honeybee stamps displaying what looked like an intaglio joint line on the old Cottrell and Stickney rotary press coils.

These lines of color marked the edge of the offset plates. On a normal offset press run, the seam where the two ends of the plate met wouldn't show a printed impression. But as a plate wears, it can develop rough spots that repel water as effectively as the etched image. These spots pick up ink, particularly at the edge.

The image created by the wear faithfully transferred to the blanket and printed onto the paper web as readily as the stamp design itself. It's one reason why offset plates are changed so frequently.

Ken Lawrence, *Linn's* plate number coil specialist, reported that on the Goebel Optiforma-printed stamps the gutter between the adjacent stamp images at an offset plate seam was two-tenths of a millimeter wider than the 4mm spacing between the rest of the stamps, measuring frame to frame. That would help explain the many problems BEP experienced in registering the offset and intaglio images.

BEP added an electric-eye device to the intaglio C press to monitor variations in the offset images from the rolls first printed on the Goebel Optiforma press and to keep them in register.

The device activated a chill roller, which regulated the stretching or shrinkage of the paper web to keep the images in register by keeping the repeat length 21¾ inches every 25 stamps.

Varieties

Imperforate specimens of the Honeybee stamp were found in printings from plates 1 and 2, according to *Coil Line*, the official journal of

The misregistered Honeybee stamps on the left and right make the bee appear to fly toward the flower, land and take off. The center stamp is normal.

the Plate Number Coil Collectors' Club. In January 1989 a dealer was advertising imperforate pairs for $45.

One collector, John Greenwood, obtained an imperforate pair in time to get it canceled on a first-day cover during the 30-day grace period. Tom Hut, a California stamp dealer, prepared six such covers.

An unofficial souvenir card bearing an enlarged, "doctored" image of the Honeybee stamp also turned up and created some controversy.

The card was produce by the Bureau of Engraving and Printing and distributed to employees who worked on the complicated Honeybee stamp printing job. It took the place of the letter of appreciation that is normally sent out to recognize a job well done.

The text of the card, titled "BEE '88," read: "In commemoration of those employees of the Bureau of Engraving and Printing, whose shear (sic) brilliance, dedication, steadfastness, innovativeness, and technical know-how made 'Project Honeybee' a success. The Bureau salutes you."

The illustration on the card showed three BEP employees struggling to keep the bee in line on the stamp, with a group of people cheering below. The four-color process cards were printed on BEP's six-color Miller offset sheetfed press.

A BEP employee traveled, at his own expense, to Omaha, where he purchased Honeybee stamps that were then affixed to the cards and canceled "First Day of Issue."

This may be a philatelic first: an imperforate error pair on a first-day cover.

BEP sources said about 80 cards were produced and distributed internally. Some collectors outside the Bureau considered the item a collectible souvenir card, and the price for those that found their way onto the market was reportedly about $100 each. Several people called the Bureau to complain because the cards weren't made generally available.

First-Day Facts

The annual Omaha Stamp Show, hosted by the Omaha Philatelic Society, was participating for the first time in the American Philatelic Society's World Series of Philately program.

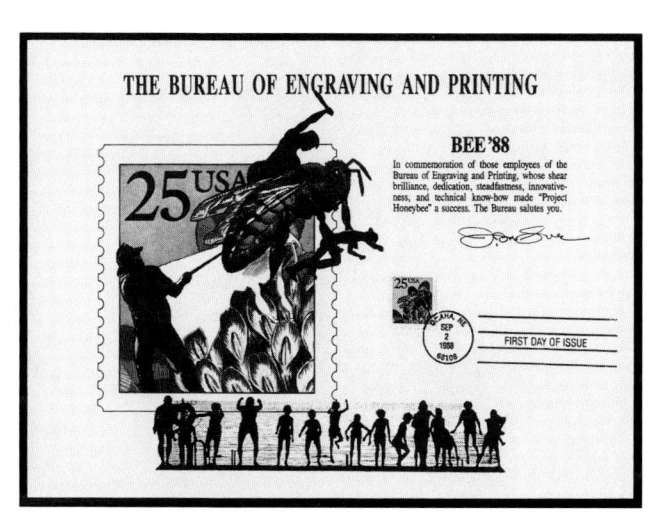

This limited-edition souvenir card was produced by BEP and distributed to its employees.

231

Its first event was the dedication of the Honeybee stamp by Postmaster General Anthony M. Frank in the JFK Room at the Holiday Inn Central, 72nd Street and I-80.

In a speech crawling with bee-related puns, Frank spoke of the importance of keeping all segments of the stamp-using public happy. Because research had shown that ordinary users and casual collectors prefer colorful gravure and offset stamps, he said, USPS produces them, in hopes of converting "the casual collector into a serious philatelist." But, he added, the Postal Service also strives to satisfy the collecting fraternity's preference for traditional engraved designs through the Transportation, Great Americans and Literary Arts series.

Afterward, Frank moved to the exhibition hall, where he cut a strip of Honeybee stamps to officially open the show.

5.3¢ ELEVATOR (PRECANCELED)

Date of Issue: September 16, 1988

Catalog Numbers: Scott 2254   Minkus 906   USPS 7951A (500s)
                                               USPS 7952A (3,000s)

Colors: black, red (precancel)

First-Day Cancel: New York, New York (Waldorf Astoria Hotel)

FDCs Canceled: unavailable

Format: Coils of 500 and 3,000. Printing sleeve of 936 subjects (18 across, 52 around)

Perf: 9.75 (Huck rotary perforator)

Designer: Lou Nolan of McLean, Virginia

Art Director: Derry Noyes (CSAC)

Project Manager: Joe Brockert (USPS)

Typographer: Bradbury Thompson (CSAC)

Engravers: Gary Chaconas (BEP, vignette)
              Dennis Brown (BEP, lettering and numerals)

Printing: 3-color intaglio B press (701)

Quantity Ordered: Coils of 500 - 150,000
                     Coils of 3,000 - 78,000
Quantity Distributed: Coils of 500 - 95,600
                         Coils of 3,000 - 77,664

Sleeve Number Detail: One sleeve number on every 52nd stamp

Sleeve Number: 1

Tagging: untagged

The Stamp

When columnist John M. Hotchner of *Linn's Stamp News* polled his readers in 1987 for new Transportation series subjects, they responded with a total of 194 different suggestions. Hotchner listed some three dozen of these in his column of July 13, 1987. He concluded his report by writing:

"Finally, there's a group of suggestions that reflect *Linn's* readers' sense of humor.

"Hardly anyone would expect to see these subjects on Transportation coils. But then again, why not? Dog catcher's truck; grocery cart (with child); 'big wheel' tricycle; garbage truck; riding lawn mower; golf cart; sedan chair; and elevator."

As it turned out, some of that sense of humor Hotchner spoke of was shared by USPS.

On April 4, 1988, in its first major listing of new definitives for the year, USPS announced that a 5.3¢ Transportation series coil would be issued September 16 in New York to meet the rate for non-profit third-class mail presorted to carrier route.

Its subject? An elevator!

USPS pointed out, however, that the choice of subject had nothing to do with Hotchner's readers' suggestions. In fact, CSAC had approved an elevator as a Transportation series subject two years earlier, in 1985.

The new stamp was necessitated by a reduction in the carrier route presort rate for non-profit organizations — one of the few postage rates that was lowered in the April 3 rate overhaul. The old rate, 5.5¢, had been met with the Star Route Truck stamp of 1986.

The choice of conveyance dramatically broadened USPS' concept of what "transportation" modes were appropriate for the series. For the first time a vehicle that didn't travel on wheels, slide on runners or float on water joined the ranks.

And although the elevator isn't unique in being confined to a prescribed track (the locomotive and ore car also fit that description), its range of travel is much more restricted than any other carrier that had been shown.

Though elevators don't go far, some collectors thought USPS had done so. Too far, in fact.

Ken Wood, editor emeritus of *Stamp Collector*, wondered why USPS had let the series stray into "marginal" areas, and descended into pundom in the process.

The Elevator stamp didn't furnish Wood "much of a lift," he wrote. He "felt a tad let down" when he heard of it. What's more, by neglecting ships and aircraft in the series, USPS was "giving the shaft" to those forms of travel.

In the same jocular mood, one collector suggested to the periodical that the stamp should have been a vertical rather than a horizontal coil. "Who ever heard of an elevator going sideways?" he asked.

Critical comments from another collector, in a letter published in *Linn's*, elicited this reply from Lawrence J. Gavrich, communication services director for the Otis Elevator Company:

"... Without the elevator, invented in 1853 by Elisha Graves Otis, cities would not have been able to grow up, as well as out. Buildings in cities without elevators would be three stories tall, no higher, and structures like the Eiffel Tower and Empire State Building would be the stuff of science fiction.

"The National Inventors Hall of Fame, operated by the U.S. Department of Commerce, recognized the vital contribution of the safe elevator by inducting Mr. Otis earlier this year . . . A stamp that recognizes the elevator's contribution is long overdue."

USPS took much the same line in its news release describing the new stamp.

Of all the vehicles in the Transportation series, USPS said, the elevator is "arguably the most significant of all in its impact."

"Besides helping to mold our urban geography, elevators have changed the very way we live and work," USPS continued. "New York City's 1977 power blackout drew that rarely considered point into very sharp focus. Cars and buses moved through the streets at a normal pace, and enough natural light existed so that some work was still possible. Yet the great metropolis stood immobilized.

"The outage had shut down the one device without which any modern city is completely helpless — its elevators."

Hoisting devices may date back as far as the pyramids. Aristotle and Archimedes both mentioned hoists in their writings, and the Colosseum in Rome, built in 80 A.D., contained crude elevators to lift the gladiators and animals to the arena.

In America in the 19th century, several businesses manufactured mechanical hoists before Elisha Otis did, but they were unsafe. When the lifting ropes or cables broke, the platforms plunged to the bottom of the shaft with men and cargo aboard.

In 1852, Otis, 41, a master mechanic for a New Jersey bedstead maker, was put in charge of building a new factory across the Hudson River in Yonkers, New York. Asked by the company owner to install a freight elevator, Otis complied — and, as a bonus, built a safety device into the mechanism.

He placed a used wagon spring on top of the hoist platform, and a ratchet bar attached to the guide rails on each side of the hoistway. The lifting rope was attached to the wagon spring in such a way that the weight of this hoist platform alone exerted enough tension on the spring to keep it from touching the ratchet bars.

But, if the cable snapped, the tension would be released from the wagon spring, and each end would immediately engage the ratchet bars, securely locking the hoist platform in place and preventing it from falling.

The idea worked, but Otis soon found himself unemployed when the bedstead manufacturer went bankrupt. As luck would have it, he got an order for two of his "safety hoisters" from a furniture maker in

New York City who had just lost two of his workers when a hoist rope snapped, sending them plunging to their death. Otis rented space in his former boss' building and went into the elevator business.

He made an advertising breakthrough at New York's Crystal Palace Exposition — America's first world's fair — in 1854. Here Otis installed a full-size working elevator in an open area, climbed aboard, had it hoisted to a height for all to see — and then ordered the hoist rope cut. Spectators gasped, but instead of falling, the elevator hung suspended in mid-air, held by the ratchet bars. To loud applause, Otis doffed his top hat and exclaimed: "All safe, gentlemen, all safe!"

In 1857 Otis installed the first passenger elevator, powered by steam, in the five-story E.V Haughwout & Company store at Broome Street and Broadway in New York City. After the inventor's death in 1861 his sons, Charles and Norton, took over the business, which grew steadily during post-Civil War boom times.

An Otis elevator was installed in the White House by President Garfield in 1881. In 1883 New York's first co-op apartment house got an elegant wood-paneled, glass and brass elevator; today residents of 34 Gramercy Park still use it. In 1889, the first successful electric elevator was installed in the Demarest Building, New York, and in 1904, the first gearless traction elevators, in the Beaver Building, New York.

Automatic elevators were introduced in residential buildings in the 1890s. In major office buildings, attendants operated the elevators until 1950, when a Dallas office structure became the first with automatic elevators.

Today, the Otis Elevator Company is the industry's largest manufacturer. It installs 25,000 new elevators and escalators each year and services an estimated 600,000. The company claims that every nine days Otis elevators move more people than populate the earth.

The Design

The stamp's designer, Lou Nolan of McLean, Virginia, produced for USPS a pen-and-ink drawing of a turn-of-the-century elevator cab with elaborate grillwork and a black and white tiled floor.

The cab was a composite, based on information and plans that the Otis company furnished the artist. Nolan added the tile floor, he said, from his own memory of old elevators, "to make the art work a little nicer, and break up that plane somewhat."

"Otis gave me layouts from their design manuals showing various grills, different tops, different scrollwork on the sides," the artist said, "and I just played around with them and put one together that I thought symbolized the old elevators the Postal Service wanted."

Using "trial and error," he developed scrollwork patterns that could be effectively reduced to stamp size. Where the background was a dark area within the elevator, he used white; where it was white, he used black. "That was the hardest thing," he said, "planning all that fine filigreed work so that when they took it down in size it would stand out."

Various arrangements of type and vignette were tried before the final arrangement, denomination and wording were decided upon.

In modeling the stamp at BEP, one early version had the cab placed at the center of the stamp. Ultimately, it was moved to the right.

The stamp was Nolan's second design assignment in the Transportation series in 1988. Earlier, he had done the artwork for the 16.7¢ Popcorn Wagon.

First-Day Facts

The Elevator stamp was issued September 16 in the Park Avenue lobby of New York City's Waldorf Astoria Hotel. Scheduled speakers were Crocker Nevin of the USPS Board of Governors, Senior Assistant Postmaster General Comer S. Coppie, and Merton D. Meeker, technical marketing director for Otis Elevator.

Coppie joked that he felt "empathy" for Otis executives because they, like USPS, "are destined to provide a service that people remember most for their lapses, however few and far between."

"Stories about the proverbial letter that took forever stand alongside tales about the time we were stuck forever in an elevator," he said. "The truth is that mail service and elevators both work remarkably well. Mailing a letter or taking an elevator should be second nature. Both systems have earned our trust and confidence."

20.5¢ FIRE ENGINE (PRECANCELED)

Date of Issue: September 28, 1988

Catalog Numbers: Scott 2264   Minkus 907   USPS 7968A (500s)
                                               USPS 7969A (3,000s)

Colors: red, black (precancel)

First-Day Cancel: San Angelo, Texas (Fort Concho National Landmark)

FDCs Canceled: unavailable

Format: Coils of 500 and 3,000. Printing sleeve of 936 subjects (18 across, 52 around).

Perf: 9.75 (Huck rotary perforator)

Designer: Chris Calle of Ridgefield, Connecticut

Art Director and Project Manager: Jack Williams (USPS)

Typographer: Bradbury Thompson (CSAC)

Engravers: Thomas Hipschen (BEP, vignette)
              Gary Slaght (BEP, lettering and numerals)

Modeler: Clarence Holbert (BEP)

Printing: 3-color intaglio B press (701)

Quantity Ordered: Coils of 500 - 95,000
                     Coils of 3,000 - 50,000
Quantity Distributed: Coils of 500 - 75,600
                         Coils of 3,000 - 21,440

Sleeve Number Detail: One sleeve number on every 52nd stamp

Sleeve Number: 1

Tagging: untagged

The Stamp

For the 10th stamp of the Transportation series in 1988, and the 40th face-different variety overall, USPS returned to a type of vehicle it had used once before in the series: a fire engine.

The stamp, issued September 28, bore the 20.5¢ denomination. It showed a 1913 truck that had been manufactured by Ahrens-Fox of Cincinnati, a well-known manufacturer of firefighting equipment.

Back in 1981, one of the earliest stamps in the Transportation series had been a 20¢ depicting a 1860s Amoskeag steam-powered fire pumper. Its color, like that of the new stamp, was — what else? — fire engine red.

However, the new coil also bore the service inscription "ZIP+4 Presort" in black. It was issued to pay the recently designated first-class rate on letters that were presorted by ZIP+4 coding and presented to the post office in batches of 500 or more.

The previous stamp for that specific purpose, the 17.5¢ Racing Car, had been issued only one year earlier. It had been the first stamp to represent the ZIP+4 presort rate, even though the rate had been available since 1985.

This suggested that there was only a limited demand for the item, and the suggestion was borne out by the experience of collectors who seek fractional coil stamps on covers showing their proper commercial use. They found the search for the Racing Car coil to be a challenge; it seemed likely that the same situation would obtain with the fire engine.

After Michael Laurence, editor of *Linn's Stamp News*, wrote that he had personally seen only one cover bearing a 17.5¢ Racing Car stamp inscribed "ZIP+4 Presort" that was obviously used to pay that rate, he received responses from more than 40 collectors, providing photocopies or other evidence to document a total of 68 Racing Car covers.

Of the 68, more than half — 35 — came from one mailer, a New Hampshire bank offering credit cards and loans. Fourteen came from a direct-mail merchant in Irvine, California, with a contest promotion.

At least 20 of the covers represented false-franking uses, posted after the ZIP+4 presort rate went to 20.5¢ April 3, Laurence reported.

False franking describes the use of a bulk-mail stamp for other than its intended purpose. Postal regulations permit it as an accommodation to large mailers, who are allowed to use certain stamps in this manner for a limited period and pay the remaining postage in cash.

Laurence concluded from his study that few mailers used the Racing Car stamp, and that when they did, they used it in quantity. Presumably, a very large mailing is needed to take full advantage of a nine-digit presort discount.

The editor deduced that mass mailers of first-class material, such as banks, utilities or merchants who regularly mail invoices to large customer lists, have no motive to use stamps on such correspondence.

Unlike mass mailers who have something to sell, they don't need to attract the recipients' attention and interest by franking the mail with stamps. Their natural inclination is to use meters or imprints.

The great majority of the mailers who do feel a need to use stamps employ third-class mail, which has its own sorting discounts and its own special stamps, at rates substantially cheaper than first class, Laurence pointed out.

The earlier Fire Pumper stamp in the Transportation series was far from being the first postal recognition granted to firefighters.

A 1948 3¢ commemorative (in the same inevitable red color) marked the 300th anniversary of volunteer fire departments. It portrayed Peter Stuyvesant, colonial governor of New York, who first appointed fire wardens to inspect homes for fire hazards and later established a fire patrol. Also shown were an early hand pumper and a contemporary fire engine modeled on one then in service at the Riverdale, Maryland, Volunteer Fire Department.

This stamp was part of the flood of Congress-mandated commemoratives that made the year 1948 singular in philatelic history. Its sponsor was Representative J. Caleb Boggs of Delaware, who was inspired to push for the stamp after volunteer firemen had put out a fire on his father's farm the preceding Christmas.

Firefighting began in America with colonial bucket brigades, but techniques and equipment steadily improved over the years. The buckets gave way to hand-powered water pumpers, hoses, steam-operated pumpers (such as the one on the earlier Transportation stamp) and self-propelled equipment that replaced horse-drawn models.

The early 20th century saw the introduction of the internal combustion engine that both drove the vehicle and powered the pump. The basic automotive hose carrier soon assumed a permanent form. It is equipped with a powerful pump, several sizes of hoses and nozzles and a water tank for use in places out of reach of fire hydrants.

Specialized auxiliaries were developed, like the ladder truck with extension ladders and the snorkel truck, introduced in Chicago in 1958, that is capable of lifting a firefighting or rescue operation up to 150 feet in the air by way of two hydraulically operated booms mounted on a turntable.

The Design

Christopher Calle of Ridgefield, Connecticut, designed the Fire Engine stamp, his second Transportation series issue in as many months. He had designed the Wheelchair coil issued August 12.

Calle based his design on a picture he found in a book entitled *Ahrens-Fox Album 1973* by John F. Sytsma a fire engine buff from Medina, Ohio. The photo, from the collection of Richard Henrich, depicted Model AC No. 516 engine, a vehicle that had been purchased by the city of San Angelo, Texas. "C" in the model designation indicates that the apparatus was equipped with a chemical tank.

Calle also roughed out some designs based on pictures of fire engines supplied by the Smithsonian Institution, but both he and CSAC

Two sketches of a 1926 vintage fire engine done by Christopher Calle for a possible 10.1¢ stamp from pictures supplied by the Smithsonian Institution.

preferred the San Angelo vehicle.

"The committee thought this one had a better shape, and liked the arrangement of bells and wheels," said Jack Williams, art director and project manager for the stamp.

USPS researchers were unable to find the actual Model AC No. 516 in a museum or collection, and concluded that it had been junked somewhere along the line.

Charles McDaniel, assistant fire chief of San Angelo and a veteran of 37 years in the department, told *Linn's Stamp News* he had heard the truck was sold for scrap in 1946. He said the oldest firefighting vehicle in San Angelo was a 1928 Seagrave, used now by the local firefighters' association in parades.

First-Day Facts

The first-day ceremony took place on the parade grounds of the Fort Concho National Historic Landmark in San Angelo, Texas, where the fire engine pictured on the stamp saw its service.

Coincidentally, San Angelo is the residence of a CSAC member, Dr. Virginia Noelke, professor of history at Angelo State University. Neither she nor the other committee members knew, when they chose this particular fire engine for the stamp, of its connection to her home city because the name San Angelo didn't show in the picture.

Dr. Noelke spoke briefly at the first-day ceremony. The principal speaker was W.L. "Pete" Davidson, director of USPS' Office of Stamps and Philatelic Marketing. More than 100 youthful members of area Ben Franklin Stamp Clubs were in the audience.

Upon request from mail-order customers, USPS affixed stamps for first-day cancellation to collector-supplied envelopes. The cost was 26¢ per envelope, and USPS added a 5¢ Milk Wagon stamp to meet the 25¢ first-class letter rate.

21¢ CHESTER CARLSON

Date of Issue: October 21, 1988

Catalog Numbers: Scott 2180   Minkus 911   USPS 1042

Color: purple (PMS 532U)

First-Day Cancel: Rochester, New York

FDCs Canceled: unavailable

Format: Panes of 100, vertical, 10 across, 10 down. Printing sleeve of 800 subjects (20 across, 40 around).

Perf: 11.2 by 11.1 (Eureka off-line perforator)

Selvage Markings: ©UNITED STATES POSTAL SERVICES 1988, USE CORRECT ZIP CODE®

Designer: Susan Sanford of Washington, D.C.

Art Director and Project Manager: Joe Brockert (USPS)

Typographer: Bradbury Thompson (CSAC)

Engravers: Gary Chaconas (BEP, vignette)
John Masure (BEP, lettering and numerals)

Printing: 3-color intaglio unit of the 8-color gravure/intaglio A press (702)

Quantity Ordered: 80,000,000
Quantity Distributed: 55,330,000

Sleeve Number Detail: One sleeve number alongside corner stamps

Sleeve Number: 1

Tagging: block over vignette

The Stamp

Late in 1988, USPS made an unusual switch of subject on a Great Americans stamp. It sent in Chester Carlson as a replacement for Mary Breckinridge. Carlson was the inventor of the xerography process used in copying machines; Breckinridge was the founder of the Frontier Nursing Service that provided medical care to the mountain people of eastern Kentucky.

The substitution came about this way:

On April 4, in its comprehensive listing of new stamps for rate-change uses and other purposes, USPS included a 21¢ Mary Breckinridge stamp, to be issued on an undetermined date in Wendover, Kentucky. The denomination would meet the new rate for first-class postcards to Canada.

Later, USPS decided to depict Carlson on the stamp instead. Carlson, like Mary Breckinridge, had been approved by CSAC as a Great Americans subject, and USPS concluded that it would be appropriate to issue his stamp in connection with the 50th anniversary of his invention, which the Xerox Corporation in Rochester, New York, planned to celebrate on October 21, 1988. No significant anniversary connected to Breckinridge's life or career would occur in 1988.

Accordingly, and without fanfare, Breckinridge was put back on the waiting list for a future stamp. The formal announcement of the Carlson stamp by the Stamp Information Branch September 16 didn't mention that the same denomination had earlier been assigned to Mary Breckinridge.

Said Joe Brockert, project manager and art director for the Carlson stamp: "It just turned out that with the Carlson anniversary coming when it did, and the need for the 21¢ stamp coming when it did, the two events just happened to coincide more closely than anything else we had available, so the denomination was re-assigned from one stamp subject to another.

"That's not uncommon. It's just unfortunate that we had announced a particular denomination for a stamp (Breckinridge) that didn't have a particular anniversary driving it."

USPS is always looking for the "happy coincidence" of a matchup of an appropriate anniversary and a stamp denomination to meet mailers' needs, Brockert added.

But according to Bill McAllister, *The Washington Post's* stamp writer, the Carlson stamp was ordered by Postmaster General Anthony Frank after he was lobbied by Representative Frank J. Horton, Rochester's Republican congressman and a member of the House Post Office and Civil Service Committee.

A Horton spokesman told McAllister that the representative had labored for years on behalf of a stamp for Carlson but didn't succeed until after Frank took office as postmaster general in March 1988.

(Horton, says *The Almanac of American Politics,* considers one of his proudest achievements to be sponsorship of the Paperwork Reduction Act — an ironic touch for a congressman who represents the hometown of Chester Carlson and Xerox!)

With the issuance of the 21¢ Carlson stamp, only one of the new

1988 postal rates remained without a stamp of its own. That was the 28¢ international surface-mail rate for postcards.

A postal card covering this rate, picturing the sailing vessel *Yorkshire,* had been issued June 29, and USPS decided there was no urgency about producing a 28¢ stamp, Brockert said.

"The demand for it isn't nearly as great as we had anticipated," he said. Therefore, no effort was made to rush a 28-center depicting Mary Breckinridge — or any other subject — into production in 1988.

Many of the people shown on the Great Americans series are unfamiliar to the public, and Chester Carlson certainly fits that description. Furthermore, postal customers wishing to learn more about him will find that task difficult. Several encyclopedias and other reference works, including the *Current Biography* series, fail to list him.

He deserves to be better known, because xerography — a coined word from the Greek for "dry" and "writing" — led to a revolution in copying that has left few fields of human endeavor untouched. Some of these fields — office procedure, research, communications — have been fundamentally transformed by Carlson's discovery.

Although the world was slow in accepting the benefits of that discovery, there were those who saw its potential from the beginning. *The New York Times,* on November 24, 1940, reported the issuance of Patent 2,221,776 to Chester F. Carlson for a "new method of photography, in which the image is recorded electrically instead of chemically," and added:

"The system is especially adapted to reproducing drawings, typewriting, etc., but it can also be used for X-ray pictures and other kinds of photography... The advantage would be that a permanent print could be obtained almost instantly."

Chester Carlson was born in Seattle February 8, 1906. At age 12 he was the chief source of support of his invalid parents, but despite poverty he finished high school and got a degree in physics from CalTech. Afterward he went to law school at night and worked in a New York electronics company's patent department by day.

Here he became aware of the need for making quick, inexpensive copies of documents and drawings. He began experimenting in 1935 and, after two years of trial and error, settled on the process of electrostatics as a way to deposit dry powder on copy paper. He set up a makeshift lab in a tiny room over a bar in Astoria, Queens, consisting of a work bench, metal plates, chemicals and a Bunsen burner. He hired a young physicist-refugee from Germany to help him.

On October 22, 1938, the experimenters inked the figures and word "10-22-38 ASTORIA" on a glass slide, rubbed a sulfur-coated zinc plate with a handkerchief to give it an electrostatic charge, placed the slide on the plate and briefly exposed the combination to a floodlamp. When the plate was dusted with a powder, the phrase they had inked on the slide appeared.

For years Carlson struggled to find a company willing to gamble on developing and marketing a product based on this system. More than 20 firms turned him down, and even the National Inventors Council dismissed his work. Then, in 1944, Battelle Memorial Institute, a non-profit industrial research organization in Columbus, Ohio, agreed to undertake the development work.

A small photo-paper producer in Rochester, the Haloid Company — which was to become the Xerox Corporation — contracted for the commercial rights. On October 22, 1948 — the 10th anniversary of the invention — Battelle and Haloid staged a joint public demonstration of xerography.

Eleven more years passed before the Rochester company, now called Haloid-Xerox, was ready to introduce the first office copier. The now-famous 914, which made copies quickly on plain paper at the touch of a button, was to make Chester Carlson a multimillionaire.

Carlson died at age 62 September 19, 1968.

Coincidentally, Battelle Institute, Carlson's partner in developing xerography, figured in stamp news in another way in 1988. It was awarded a $700,000 contract by USPS to find a better stamp adhesive.

The Design

The portrait of Chester Carlson on the stamp is a composite. "The perspective, or pose, was principally from a photograph furnished by the Xerox Corporation," said Joe Brockert. "The features, the face, the general overall appearance, are based on a younger likeness that we obtained from the Carlson family."

Design credit went to Susan Sanford, a Washington, D.C., commercial artist who laid out the basic arrangement of vignette and type.

The two portraits of Carlson used to create the portrait used on the stamp.

245

(Earlier in the year Sanford had created the map cachet used on the Northwest Territory postal card.) Unlike other designers of Great Americans stamps, she made no drawing for the engraver to follow.

Instead, she and Brockert closely monitored the engraving project in a series of review meetings with BEP personnel, especially engraver Gary Chaconas.

It was Chaconas who did the actual work of transferring to the portrait furnished by Xerox the more youthful Carlson features from the Fabian Bachrach portrait that the family supplied, Brockert said.

The unusual procedure followed in designing the Carlson stamp was followed by still another unusual step.

At the time USPS announced the stamp, the "merged" engraving wasn't completed yet. So BEP created in its electronic Design Center a photographic conception of what the stamp would look like, and USPS distributed that along with the September 16 press release. This picture had a vaguely artificial look to it that was unlike any previous stamp publicity photo.

"For the sake of getting a picture out, the Bureau generated through its scanner a sort of halfway image," explained Brockert. "The photograph provided by Xerox was put on the scanner, and then the image was manipulated electronically to enhance some of the features and get closer to what we knew the final engraving was going to look like."

USPS described the color as blue, but actually it was a violet-black shade.

First-Day Facts

The actual 50th anniversary of Carlson's invention fell on a Saturday, but the stamp was issued a day early — October 21 — in Rochester to coincide with an anniversary banquet held that evening by the Xerox Corporation.

USPS held a brief ceremony in the morning at the Midtown Mall, near Xerox headquarters. On hand were Carlson's wife Dorris and daughter Catherine Carlson, both residents of the Rochester area. Postmaster General Anthony Frank spoke briefly, as did U.S. Representatives Frank J. Horton and Louise M. Slaughter, and David Kearns, chief executive officer of Xerox. Mayor Thomas Ryan Jr. and Monroe County Executive Tom Frey read proclamations.

Frank then formally opened the "Chester Carlson Station," a temporary philatelic station on the mall, and applied first-day cancels to several covers, which were given to participants in the ceremony.

Frank also spoke that evening at the invitation-only banquet. "For me," he joked, "a visit to Rochester — corporate headquarters for Xerox — is like a pilgrimage to the Holy Land. Why, your copying machines alone generate millions of letters every day!"

Veteran CBS newsman Walter Cronkite was the principal speaker.

For first-day covers processed by USPS, a 4¢ Stagecoach stamp was affixed alongside the Carlson stamp to make the 25¢ first-class rate.

24.1¢ TANDEM BICYCLE (PRECANCELED)

Date of Issue: October 26, 1988

Catalog Numbers: Scott 2266   Minkus 912   USPS 7974A (500s)
USPS 7975A (3,000s)

Colors: blue, red (precancel)

First-Day Cancel: Redmond, Washington (Sahalee Country Club)

FDCs Canceled: unavailable

Format: Coils of 500 and 3,000. Printing sleeve of 936 subjects (18 across, 52 around).

Perf: 9.75 (Huck rotary perforator)

Designer: Chris Calle of Ridgefield, Connecticut

Art Director and Project Manager: Jack Williams (USPS)

Typographer: Bradbury Thompson (CSAC)

Engravers: Gary Chaconas (BEP, vignette)
Michael Ryan (BEP, lettering and numerals)

Printing: 3-color intaglio B press (701)

Quantity Ordered: Coils of 500 - 97,000
Coils of 3,000 - 20,000
Quantity Distributed: Coils of 500 - 56,450
Coils of 3,000 - 12,320

Sleeve Number Detail: One sleeve number on every 52nd stamp

Sleeve Number: 1

Tagging: untagged

The Stamp

The bicycle returned to U.S. stamp design — and to the Transportation series — with a 24.1¢ coil depicting an 1890s-era tandem bike, or "bicycle built for two."

The stamp was issued October 26 in Redmond, Washington, which calls itself "The Bicycle Capital of the Northwest."

Its design included the engraved service inscription "ZIP+4," indicating that its unusual rate — .9¢ off the cost of first-class mail — covered unpresorted mail bearing ZIP+4 addresses.

Before the 1988 rate changes, this particular discount rate was covered by the 21.1¢ Sealed Envelopes stamp of 1985 with its "ZIP+4" precancel overprint.

To qualify for the discount, a business need only fill out a simple postal form and have at least 250 letters in each mailing. The addresses on the letters have to be clearly typed and followed by the addressee's full nine-digit ZIP code.

While mailers don't have to presort their letters by ZIP code, they do have to deliver the letters to a post office, rather than drop them in a corner mailbox.

Small businesses have been slow to learn of the discount, USPS officials said. In 1987, when the rate was 21.1¢, only 4,200 customers used it, sending about 430 million letters. That was about 10 percent of all total discounted first-class mail.

"It is not as attractive as the presort rate for larger users," said Al Kellert, USPS group product manager for automation programs. Large-volume mailers, banks, utilities and credit-card companies that presort their first-class mail by ZIP codes pay only 20.5¢ to send a first-class letter (a rate covered by the Fire Engine coil stamp, inscribed "ZIP+4/Presort," that had been issued September 28).

USPS offers the latter discount in hopes that more mailers will use the nine-digit ZIP codes in their mailings and handle the costly sorting themselves. But the bigger discounts also involve more red tape; large mailers have to buy an annual permit, complete a form with each mailing and send 500 or more letters at a time.

USPS said the tandem was "symbolic of 'work-sharing' " and thus was "an appropriate image for ZIP+4, which facilitates an automated sort down to small sectors in the delivery sequence."

A bicycle first appeared on a U.S. stamp with the 10¢ special delivery issue of 1902. Previous special delivery stamps had depicted a messenger running with his letters. This one put him on wheels.

Olympic cyclists were shown on a 6¢ Olympics commemorative of 1972 and a 35¢ airmail stamp of 1983. And the efficient but hazardous "ordinary" or "penny-farthing" bike of the 1870s, with a big front wheel and smaller trailing wheel, was featured on a 5.9¢ Transportation series coil in 1982 and a stamped envelope of 1980.

(Truly diligent bicycle-on-stamps topicalists have also noted that the 1987 Girl Scouts commemorative design includes at the bottom a portion of the cycling merit badge, with its silhouetted riding figure.)

The invention of the tandem bike had to await the development of the chain-driven "safety" bicycle, with its two wheels of equal size. This breakthrough occurred in 1884, with the introduction in England of John Kemp Starley's Rover Safety Cycle.

When tandems came along, with their two-riders-in-line configuration, cyclists found the riding experience to be much different from riding with the same person on singles. Close coordination of effort and goals was required, and partners who were mismatched for height were usually unable to find a machine to fit.

Bicycle racer John Howard explained the origin of the word tandem in his book, *The Cyclist's Companion*:

"Most people think 'tandem' is Latin for 'double' or 'together' or something like that. It is from the Latin, but it's actually sort of a play on words. Its literal meaning is 'exactly then,' or 'at length.' If you take 'at length' to mean 'lengthwise,' and 'lengthwise' to mean 'one in front of the other,' then you have completely distorted a perfectly good Latin word to make a joke that nobody understands. You would think some other Latin word would have done better, but 'duet' had already been taken."

In 1892 Harry Dacre made the tandem bike immortal by writing *Daisy Bell*, a song still universally familiar:

"Daisy, Daisy, tell me your answer, do.
I'm half crazy, all for the love of you.
It won't be a stylish marriage,
I can't afford a carriage,
But you'll look sweet upon the seat
Of a bicycle built for two."

Tandems today are scarce, so much so that the sight of one causes observers to do a double-take, but they still have their enthusiasts.

The Design

Christopher Calle based his design on a Smithsonian Institution photograph of a Columbia Model No. 43 tandem.

The bicycle, which the Smithsonian owns, was built in 1896 by the Pope Manufacturing Company of Hartford, Connecticut. The firm went out of business in 1913, about the time the nation's interest in bicycles had begun to yield to a passion for the automobile.

The stamp was printed in intaglio on BEP's B press in blue (the image) and red (the ZIP+4 precancel).

The design assignment was the prolific Calle's second in the Transportation series in 1988. He had also done the 8.4¢ Wheelchair stamp issued August 12.

First-Day Facts

The first-day ceremony took place at the Sahalee Country Club in Redmond. James Glassco, USPS treasurer, was the featured speaker.

For first-day covers fully serviced by USPS, a 1¢ Omnibus stamp was added to cover the 25¢ first-class rate. Customers were charged 26¢, however — a .9¢ markup.

20¢ CABLE CAR

Date of Issue: October 28, 1988

Catalog Numbers: Scott 2263   Minkus 913   USPS 7966 (500s)
                                                USPS 7967 (3,000s)

Color: purple (PMS 532U)

First-Day Cancel: San Francisco, California (Union Square)

FDCs Canceled: unavailable

Format: Coils of 500 and 3,000. Printing sleeve of 864 subjects (18 across, 48 around).

Perf: 9.75 (Huck rotary perforator)

Designer: Dan Romano of Kentfield, California

Art Director: Howard Paine (CSAC)

Project Manager: Joe Brockert (USPS)

Typographer: Bradbury Thompson (CSAC)

Engravers: Edward Archer (BEP, vignette)
              Michael Ryan (BEP, lettering and numerals)

Modeler: Frank Waslick (BEP)

Printing: 3-color intaglio C press (901)

Quantity Ordered: Coils of 500 - 307,000
                     Coils of 3,000 - 19,000
Quantity Distributed: Coils of 500 - 48,850
                         Coils of 3,000 - 9,536

Sleeve Number Detail: One sleeve number every 52nd stamp

Sleeve Number: 1

Tagging: block over vignette

The Stamp

The San Francisco Cable Car stamp issued October 28 was the 12th of 13 Transportation series stamps issued in 1988, but only the third

250

to be for general use, without a service inscription or precancel defining one of the discount-postage categories.

Originally, CSAC had thought the design might be used for one of the specialized-rate coils. Accordingly, typographer Bradbury Thompson, working with artist Dan Romano's drawing of an 1880s-vintage cable car in a variety of arrangements, squeezed in a service inscription. But BEP pointed out that the tight fit of the lettering would create a high risk of contamination between the two different colored intaglio inks and lead to excessive spoilage.

USPS therefore assigned the stamp the 20¢ value, to meet the rate for the second ounce of first-class mail. For this purpose it replaced the 1982 20¢ Fire Pumper stamp, which had been re-released earlier in the year.

The stamp was printed on BEP's C press in rolls of 100, 500 and 3,000. It was the only Transportation stamp of 1988 to be printed exclusively on the C press, which imprints a plate number on every 48th stamp. All others were at least initially printed on the B press, with a number on every 52nd stamp.

The announced color was purple. However, difficulties in production necessitated a color change to what BEP called purple. The color was actually a black-violet, the same as that used on the 21¢ Chester Carlson stamp. A BEP official explained that the ink originally intended for use "didn't behave" as expected and "didn't give us the density of ink film ... it came up much too pale."

A modern-day San Francisco cable car, No. 506 on the Hyde Street Hill, had appeared on a U.S. 8¢ stamp issued in 1971 as part of a se-tenant block of four promoting the historic preservation movement. (As noted earlier, another of those 1971 stamps showed the whaling ship *Charles W. Morgan*, which also would make a reappearance in 1988 — on the Connecticut Statehood commemorative.)

Around the turn of the century, cable cars were common on the streets of many American cities, from New York to Seattle. But San Francisco — where the cable car was invented, and the only place it survives today — is the one city that is instantly identified with the sturdy little vehicles.

The principle of the cable car is somewhat like that of the elevator or ski lift, except that the car is capable of connecting and releasing itself from its cable. The lead car, or "dummy," has a grip that extends downward through a slot in the pavement and acts like a giant set of pliers, grabbing the cable that continuously moves through a conduit beneath the street. Power comes from engines in a centrally located powerhouse.

The cable car was born out of British-born Andrew S. Hallidie's distress at seeing the misery of the horses that struggled to pull streetcars up San Francisco's precipitous grades. The result of Hallidie's humane reaction was the city's first cable street line. Hallidie, a manu-

The Bureau of Engraving and Printing decided that an engraved service inscription, such as "Non Profit Org.," in this design would be too tight a fit for proper separation of ink colors.

facturer of wire cable, built the line on Clay Street Hill and drove the two-car train on its maiden voyage before the mayor, other local officials and bystanders on August 2, 1873.

The line was a simple affair by later standards, with only 2,791 feet of track propelling cars at four miles an hour. A one-way trip took about 11 minutes. The enterprise was a success, and other businessmen, including railroadman Leland Stanford, soon built cable lines of their own. Eventually, steam engines gave way to electric motors as a source of power.

The ability to travel easily up and down the city's slopes revolutionized San Francisco's crosstown transportation, opened up the once sparsely populated hills to new development and doubled and tripled the value of property near the routes.

The glory days of cable cars were ended by the great earthquake and fire of 1906, which put many lines out of business. Over the years, electric trolleys, diesel buses and automobiles competed with the remaining lines with increasing effectiveness. The year 1942 saw the closing of the Clay Street line, which had been the world's first cable street line.

But in the 1970s San Franciscans, faced with the choice of shutting down completely their deteriorated, century-old system or launching a costly restoration, chose the latter. A "Save the Cable Cars" campaign raised $60 million for a two-year overhaul of the three surviving routes. Today, 37 of the picturesque cars that "climb halfway to the stars" toil at 9½ mph up the city's 17- and 20-percent grades — and seem capable of doing so for at least another century.

The Design

Howard Paine, art director for the stamp, was familiar with the work of an artist from cable car country — Dan Romano, of Kentfield, California, near San Francisco — and tapped him to design this stamp, his first.

Romano's design differs from any previous Transportation series stamp in that the lettering is at the bottom rather than the top. "We wanted to give the effect of the cable car coming up over a hill," explained Joe Brockert, the project manager.

A reader of John Hotchner's column in Linn's Stamp News *sent in this Cable Car stamp sketch in response to a 1987 request for suggestions for new Transportation series subjects.*

The cable car depicted is a dummy car, the lead vehicle that carried the gripman and a few riders and pulled other passenger cars. Romano worked from several photographs from the Cable Car Museum in San Francisco, with a picture of No. 46 as the primary source. That number appeared on the car in preliminary versions of the design, but was removed on the final stamp.

Romano told the *San Francisco Chronicle* he was basically pleased with the finished product, except for the color. "It's not a color I'd choose," he said. "It should be green."

First-Day Facts

Postmaster General Anthony Frank, a long-time resident of the San Francisco Bay area, was featured speaker at the ceremony dedicating the new stamp in San Francisco's Union Square.

The ceremony began at noon when a cable car carrying the platform guests arrived at the site. Among those scheduled to be present was Carl Payne, billed as a cable car bell ringing champion.

The Palo Alto Times Tribune reported that the Reverend Shay St. John of Unity Christ Church, in his prayer at the ceremony, asked the Lord to "hand-cancel this journey through life."

For first-day covers wholly serviced by USPS, a 5¢ Milk Wagon stamp was used with a single Cable Car stamp to complete the 25¢ first-class rate.

13¢ PATROL WAGON (PRECANCELED)

Date of Issue: October 29, 1988

Catalog Numbers: Scott 2258   Minkus 914   USPS 7972A (500s)
USPS 7973A (3,000s)

Colors: black, red (precancel)

First-Day Cancel: Anaheim, California (International Stamp and Postal History Exposition, Disneyland Hotel)

FDCs Canceled: unavailable

Format: Coils of 500 and 3,000. Printing sleeve of 936 subjects (18 across, 52 around).

Perf: 9.75 (Huck rotary perforator)

Designer and Project Manager: Joe Brockert (USPS)

Art Director and Typographer: Bradbury Thompson (CSAC)

Engravers: Edward Archer (BEP, vignette)
Dennis Brown (BEP, lettering and numerals)

Modeler: Clarence Holbert (BEP)

Printing: 3-color intaglio B press (701)

Quantity Ordered: Coils of 500 - 65,000
Coils of 3,000 - 35,000
Quantity Distributed: Coils of 500 - 40,250
Coils of 3,000 - 14,336

Sleeve Number Detail: One sleeve number every 52nd stamp

Sleeve Number: 1

Tagging: untagged

The Stamp

The last of 1988's 13 Transportation coils was, appropriately, a 13¢ stamp, service-inscribed "presorted first-class" to meet the single-piece rate for presorted first-class mailings of postcards. For that pur-
254

PATROL WAGON.

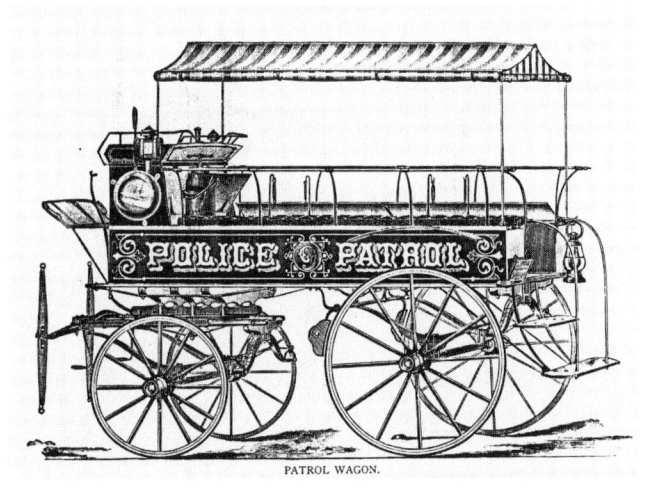

Artwork for the Patrol Wagon coil was taken from this 1885-86 illustration without being re-interpreted by an artist.

pose it replaced the 12¢ Stanley Steamer coil of 1985.

The new stamp depicted a canopied, horse-drawn police patrol wagon of the 1880s. It marked yet another USPS use of one of the vehicles that had been suggested for the series the year before by readers of John Hotchner's column in *Linn's Stamp News*.

The issue date was October 29 and the place was the International Stamp and Postal History Exhibition in Anaheim, California.

A brief history of the patrol wagon can be found in a publication called *The Wagon-Maker*, Chicago, July 1, 1886, and quoted in *Carriage Terminology: An Historical Dictionary* by Don H. Berkebile (Smithsonian Institution Press and Liberty Cap Books, 1978).

It reads in part:

"To Chicago belongs the credit of devising and introducing the patrol wagon, that modern adjunct of the police system which increases the serviceability and lessens the cost of police departments of large cities. The first police patrol wagon was introduced in the fall of 1879, by William J. McGarigle, then general superintendent of the Chicago Police Department. A plan of getting the police where they were needed at the earliest possible moment had been talked of for some years by Chief McGarigle and others . . .

"The telephone was introduced while these measures were being considered, and it was immediately adopted as a means of sending alarms to the stations, and wagons were decided upon as the means of conveyance, and corner patrol-boxes were built. Mayor Harrison warmly espoused the project. The result was that, before Superintendent McGarigle resigned, in 1882, there were 17 wagons in use."

The patrol wagon, in one of its evolutionary developments, became a vehicle that also carried prisoners. For this prison van or "paddy wagon," as it was called, it was necessary to add security features, such as enclosed sides.

The Design

The Police Patrol Wagon design was unusual in that it required no artist's services. Design credit was assigned to Joe Brockert, the project manager for USPS, who took an illustration from a reference book provided by the Smithsonian Institution, cropped it and produced a stamp design.

"We had this nice original engraving," Brockert said. "We saw no need to go to an artist to have a drawing made as we normally do,

The patrol wagon was at one point considered for a stamp for third-class mail presorted to the carrier route. That rate was later set at 10.1¢, not 9.9¢.

when all we have to work from is a period photograph or a modern photograph of a vehicle on display.

"Had we shown the Bureau this picture and they had said 'No, our engravers can't work from this, you'd better have someone draw it,' we'd have done it; but the Bureau said 'no problem.' "

The source of the picture was a publication called *The Carriage Monthly*, Volume 21, 1885-1886, illustration plate No. 50, which in turn was reproduced in the Berkebile dictionary previously mentioned. It was the later reproduction that Brockert used.

Brockert met with BEP engravers to determine how the picture should be simplified for stamp purposes. Among the items they removed were two vertical bars at the front end of the carriage.

Like other Transportation coils, this one was printed on BEP's three-color intaglio B press. The vignette and the basic lettering were black and the service inscription was red. It was the same combination of colors that had been used a month and a half earlier on the 5.3¢ Elevator stamp of the Transportation series.

First-Day Facts

The dedication ceremony for the stamp took place before some 800 people in the ballroom of the Disneyland Hotel. Police chiefs and police officers from the Los Angeles area had been invited to attend.

For first-day covers fully serviced by USPS, two Police Patrol Wagon stamps (26¢ total) were affixed to cover the first-class rate.

23¢ MARY CASSATT

Date of Issue: November 4, 1988

Catalog Numbers: Scott 2182   Minkus 915   USPS 1043

Color: purple

First-Day Cancel: Philadelphia, Pennsylvania (Pennsylvania Academy of Fine Arts)

FDCs Canceled: unavailable

Format: Panes of 100, vertical, 10 across, 10 down. Printing sleeve of 800 subjects (20 across, 40 around)

Perf: 11.2 by 11.1 (Eureka off-line perforator)

Selvage Markings: ©UNITED STATES POSTAL SERVICE 1988, USE CORRECT ZIP CODE®

Designer: Dennis Lyall of East Norwalk, Connecticut

Art Director: Howard Paine (CSAC)

Project Manager: Jack Williams (USPS)

Typographer: Bradbury Thompson (CSAC)

Engravers: Kenneth Kipperman (BEP, vignette)
Thomas Bakos (BEP, lettering)
Gary Slaght (BEP, numerals)

Modeler: Clarence Holbert (BEP)

Printing: 3-color intaglio unit of the 8-color gravure/intaglio A press (702)

Quantity Ordered: 60,000,000
Quantity Distributed: 48,780,000

Sleeve Number Detail: One sleeve number alongside corner stamps

Sleeve Number: 1

Tagging: block over vignette

The Stamp

On November 4, 1988, USPS issued a 23¢ stamp in the Great Americans series portraying Mary Cassatt, the Pennsylvania-born impressionist painter whom many consider the greatest woman artist produced by this country.

The stamp was unusual in that it honored a person who had been postally recognized once before.

The overwhelming majority of the men and women pictured in the Great Americans series have been first-timers as stamp subjects. Many of these were so unfamiliar that they sent postal customers and stamp collectors to the encyclopedias to learn something about them.

Mary Cassatt, however, is known to every art lover, and one of her most famous paintings, *The Boating Party*, with its broad surfaces of

Mary Cassatt's 1893 painting The Boating Party *was shown on this 1966 commemorative in the American Artists series.*

yellow and blue, was featured in 1966 on a 5¢ stamp in the American Artists commemorative series. The painting, done at Antibes, France, near Nice, in 1893, is in the National Gallery of Art.

(Only two other Great Americans had been postally honored beforehand — Harry Truman and John James Audubon — and Audubon, coincidentally, was also featured in the American Artists series. His painting of a pair of Columbia jays graced a 5¢ stamp of 1963, and was repeated on a nearly identical airmail stamp in 1967. Audubon also had been portrayed on a Famous Americans commemorative of 1940.)

The Cassatt stamp's 23¢ denomination met the second-ounce rate for international surface mail that was established in the rate overhaul of April 3, 1988.

Remarkably, no U.S. stamp of that denomination had ever been issued before. It might have happened but didn't in 1938, when the Presidential series of definitives proceeded in an unbroken line of whole-number denominations from 1¢ to 22¢ — then skipped to 24¢.

Mary Cassatt, like many others who have appeared on Great Americans definitives, had been approved for the series by CSAC several years before her stamp actually appeared. In fact, the design process for her stamp began in 1983.

The stamp was announced April 4, 1988, in USPS' detailed listing of the year's subjects, dates and sites. At that time the date of issue was given as November 8, which would have made it the last release of the year. Its date was later revised to November 4, one day before the 65¢ General Henry H. "Hap" Arnold stamp was dedicated.

Cassatt was born in 1845 in Allegheny City, Pennsylvania, outside Pittsburgh, to a well-to-do family; a brother, Alexander, would later become president of The Pennsylvania Railroad. Much of her childhood was spent with her family in Europe, where she discovered the world of art that she would make her life's vocation.

Back in the United States, she enrolled in the Pennsylvania Academy of the Fine Arts in Philadelphia. Later, with her parents' reluctant consent, she returned to Paris to continue her studies. Here she found herself drawn to the work of the impressionists, whose intent was to reproduce the effect of light reflected from forms and not the details of the forms themselves: men such as Manet, Monet, Renoir, and particularly Edgar Degas, with whom she established a lifelong friendship.

In the 19th century, most Americans found it hard to take either women painters or impressionists very seriously. Cassatt's work won recognition first in France, and France was the country in which she found kindred souls, painters whose work stimulated and excited her and with whom she soon was regularly exhibiting.

Her subject matter was traditional and, in fact, "ladylike." She painted mostly portraits of members of her family — partly because

Working from a Cassatt self-portrait, Lyall sketched two younger images, but results were unsatisfactory.

they were willing models who charged no fees — and fully a third of her pictures are of mothers and children.

Some critics say her most individual creative efforts weren't the paintings, but her prints. She was profoundly influenced by a show of Japanese prints that opened in Paris in 1890, and the following year she produced a set of 10 color prints in the Japanese manner that rank with anything of its kind done outside the Orient. Camille Pissarro called them "a show of rare and exquisite works," and of one of them, *Woman Bathing*, her old friend Degas observed: "I do not admit that a woman can draw like that."

In later years Cassatt suffered from diabetes and growing blindness, but the last year of her life was cheered by her inclusion in a great exhibition at the Louvre, "Fifty Years of French Painting." Only James Abbott McNeill Whistler among American artists had achieved such international recognition.

On June 14, 1926, she died at 82 in her chateau in a village 30 miles from Paris. Wrote a friend, Philadelphia painter George Biddle, of the roses and carnations that were scattered over her fresh grave:

"Looking at this carpet of brilliant flowers, I fancied Mary Cassatt running to fetch a canvas and brushes."

The Design

Dennis Lyall of East Norwalk, Connecticut, designed the stamp, which shows Cassatt wearing one of the elaborate feathered hats she loved. The source was a photograph taken by Armand Delaporte around 1914, when Cassatt was 70, at Villa Angeletto, a small house she rented in the south of France.

A USPS researcher found the photo in the Frederick A. Sweet papers in the Archives of American Art of the Smithsonian Institution. It had been used in a book by Sweet, *Miss Mary Cassatt: Impressionist from Pennsylvania* (University of Oklahoma Press, 1966.)

Lyall had also attempted some drawings of a younger Cassatt, based on a youthful portrait, but was dissatisfied with the result.

First-Day Facts

Ann McKernan Robinson, USPS consumer advocate, was featured speaker at the first-day ceremony, held at the Pennsylvania Academy of the Fine Arts in Philadelphia, where Cassatt received her first formal training.

For covers that USPS prepared at customers' requests, one 2¢ Mary Lyons stamp — the most recent previous Great Americans stamp to depict a woman — was added to each envelope to make up the 25¢ first-class rate.

65¢ GENERAL HENRY "HAP" ARNOLD

Date of Issue: November 5, 1988

Catalog Numbers: Scott 2192   Minkus 916   USPS 1065

Color: blue

First-Day Cancel: Gladwyne, Pennsylvania (Gladwyne School)

FDCs Canceled: unavailable

Format: Panes of 100, vertical, 10 across, 10 down. Printing sleeve of 800 subjects (20 across, 40 around).

Perf: 11.2 by 11.1 (Eureka off-line perforator)

Selvage Markings: ©UNITED STATES POSTAL SERVICE 1988, USE CORRECT ZIP CODE®

Designer: Chris Calle of Ridgefield, Connecticut

Art Director: Jack Williams (USPS)

Typographer: Bradbury Thompson (CSAC)

Engravers: Thomas Hipschen (BEP, vignette)
Michael Ryan (BEP, lettering and numerals)

Printing: 3-color intaglio unit of the 8-color gravure/intaglio A press (702)

Quantity Ordered: 85,000,000
Quantity Distributed: 75,330,000

Sleeve Number Detail: One sleeve number alongside corner stamps

Sleeve Number: 1

Tagging: block over vignette

The Stamp

On November 5, at Gladwyne, Pennsylvania, USPS issued a Great Americans stamp honoring General Henry Harley "Hap" Arnold, the pioneer flyer who built the U.S. Army Air Corps into the mighty force that dominated the skies over Europe and Japan in World War II. It

261

was the year's fifth stamp in the Great Americans series, and the 44th face-different overall.

The denomination, 65¢, covered the rate for a three-ounce piece of first-class mail (25¢ for the first ounce, 20¢ for each additional ounce). For this purpose, it replaced the 56¢ John Harvard stamp, also of the Great Americans series. The only previous U.S. 65¢ stamp had been the low value of the three-stamp Zeppelin airmail set of 1930.

The Arnold definitive was an early entry on the 1988 schedule. It was unveiled by Assistant Postmaster General Frank S. Johnson Jr. more than two years before issuance, on June 25, 1986, the 100th anniversary of Arnold's birth, at Gladwyne, Arnold's birthplace. The denomination at that time was undetermined.

Date and place of issue were announced November 25, 1987, and the face value was furnished April 4, 1988.

Arnold thus became the last of the four World War II soldiers who served in the five-star rank of general of the Army to appear on a postage stamp. Oddly, he was the first of the four to die — of a heart attack on January 5, 1950, at age 63.

The other three were General (and President) Dwight D. Eisenhower, who made his first of several stamp appearances in 1969; General George C. Marshall (1967), and General Douglas MacArthur (1971). Another general, the four-star George S. Patton Jr., was depicted in 1953. In addition, the five-star Fleet Admiral Chester W. Nimitz had appeared on a Great Americans stamp of 1985.

In an obituary editorial, *The New York Times* said:

"When 'Hap' Arnold took command of the Army Air Corps in 1938 it was one-fiftieth the size and power of the German Luftwaffe alone. When he laid down his baton there was no Luftwaffe. With the help of the Naval Air Arm, there was no Japanese air power.

"More than any other man, he planned, built, organized and directed the United States Air Force that brought that about."

As a West Point cadet, Arnold was called "Happy" because of his disposition. The nickname, in shortened form, stayed with him. He was graduated in 1907 and appointed a second lieutenant of infantry.

Four years later he was detailed to the brand-new aviation division of the Signal Corps and was taught to fly a Wright biplane at the Wright brothers' school in Dayton, Ohio. His pilot's license was the 29th issued in the United States.

In 1912 he flew to an altitude of 6,540 feet, a new record. In the same year, he crash-landed a plane in the ocean off Plymouth Beach, Virginia, acquiring a lifetime souvenir in the form of a small scar on his chin.

During World War I, Arnold served as the Army's assistant director of military aeronautics, where he bossed some 30 aviation training schools, 15,000 officers and 125,000 enlisted men. In the 1920s he was one of a small group of Army officers who backed General William

(Billy) Mitchell, who was ultimately courtmartialed for the way he expressed his views on the importance of air power.

In 1938 Arnold — then a colonel with the temporary rank of major general — became chief of the U.S. Air Corps. His command consisted of 22,000 officers and men. The Army and Navy together had only 3,900 planes.

The following May, with Germany preparing to launch World War II, Arnold summoned eight civilian operators of flying schools and told them the Air Corps desperately needed facilities to train pilots for the tremendous expansion he foresaw. The operators agreed to take green youngsters, some of whom had never been near an airplane, and make them into combat pilots for the Army — even though Arnold was unable to guarantee payment. Later a reluctant Congress, by a two-vote margin, gave retroactive authorization.

Promotion came rapidly. In May 1941 Arnold was made deputy chief of staff in charge of the Army Air Forces and advanced two grades to permanent major general. In June he became chief of the AAF, and in March 1942, when the General Staff was reorganized, he became commanding general of the Air Forces.

In March 1943 he was made a full general, the first four-star officer ever placed in charge of the Air Forces. In December 1944, after the new rank was approved by Congress, he got his fifth star as general of the Army.

In that same year he established the Twentieth Air Force as a strategic striking unit to be held under direct command of the Joint Chiefs of Staff for deployment anywhere it was needed. Arnold convinced the Joint Chiefs that the mobility and hitting ability of the B-29 was too great to be committed piecemeal to any single theater commander. For more than a year the B-29s, operating out of Saipan, Tinian and Guam, conducted massive daily bombing raids on Japan.

Meanwhile, in Europe, he ordered and supervised the switch to daylight bombing of targets in Germany — more hazardous, but also far more effective, than the night raids.

At war's end, the force he commanded had grown to nearly 2.5 million men. Aircraft were pouring from American factories at the rate of 145,000 a year, along with uncounted quantities of supplies, fuel and munitions. General Arnold had proved one of his favorite maxims: "A second-best air force is like a second-best hand in poker — it's no good at all."

On June 3, 1949, President Harry Truman made him permanent general of the Air Force. By now he was in failing health, and the coronary occlusion that killed him seven months later was his fifth since 1944.

"He should have quit during the war when he had the first heart attack," said his doctor, "but things were hot then, and he decided to take his chances with the rest of the soldiers and went back to duty."

Artist Christopher Calle based these pencil sketches on two different "Hap" Arnold photos.

The Design

In searching for a suitable portrait of Arnold, USPS considered a large selection of photographs supplied by the Air Force and, as is its custom, consulted members of his family as to their preference.

William B. Arnold, who served under his father as an Air Force officer, identified one full-face portrait of the white-haired general as a family favorite. But it carried no insignia of rank. Artist Christopher Calle, who had the design assignment, tried superimposing on the portrait an overseas cap bearing the five-star insignia. (In another version, Calle put a billed officer's cap on the portrait.)

Ultimately, the solution was simple: Leave the general bare-headed and add five stars in a circle to each collar tab, as Calle had done with the Admiral Nimitz portrait in 1985. CSAC was able to verify, through other photographs, that Arnold had indeed worn the stars in this manner on occasion.

Perfect consistency is neither sought nor attained with the Great Americans series, as evidenced by the treatment of Arnold's name in the design: H.H. 'Hap' Arnold.

The stamp's slate-blue color was selected before the BEP's Thomas Hipschen began engraving the die. Color choice influences the depth at which the lines are cut, and after a design is completed BEP typically gives CSAC several offset proofs in different colors to pick from.

First-Day Facts

The stamp was dedicated at The Gladwyne School in Gladwyne. Assistant Postmaster General William T. Johnstone was the speaker.

The portrait selected for the stamp was this family favorite. Christopher Calle tried superimposing two different styles of service cap on the general's head, but in the end CSAC decided to use the portrait as it was originally — bareheaded.

REVISED DEFINITIVES

Two Great Americans series stamps were issued in 1988 with so-called bull's-eye perforations, bringing to seven the total of stamps in the series produced in two different perforation varieties. The new additions were the 30¢ Frank C. Laubach and the 20¢ Harry Truman, both originally issued in 1984. They joined the 1¢ Dorothea Dix, 22¢ John James Audubon, 39¢ Grenville Clark, 40¢ Lillian M. Gilbreth and 50¢ Chester W. Nimitz in the two-variety category.

In each case the stamps were processed on two different kinds of perforating equipment, leaving perforations that differ in both appearance and measurement.

Other differences, such as tagging size and type, placement of plate numbers and whether the panes are fully perforated or straight-edged, are products of the printing process itself.

The most obvious difference between older and newer versions of each stamp — easily detected in a block of four, less easily so in a single — is the configuration of the corner perforations, where horizontal and vertical rows of perfs intersect.

Bull's-eye perfs, such as those produced on BEP's off-line Eureka stroke perforator, leave neat-looking perforations that meet perfectly at all intersections. The older off-line L perforator produces perfs that meet randomly at the intersections and look a bit ragged. This is because the L perforator moves in only one direction at a time and has to overlap perforations.

Another difference: Bull's-eye perforations don't fully extend through the selvage of a pane of stamps. Perforations made on the L perforator do.

In five of the seven examples (Clark, Audubon, Gilbreth, Laubach, Truman) the printing sequence was this:

The stamps were originally printed on the intaglio section of BEP's intaglio-gravure A press and perforated off-line on the L perforator. Later they were shifted to the Eureka perforator, which processes 200 definitive-size stamps with a single stroke. To accommodate the Eureka, plate layouts had to be modified.

The results were: bull's-eye perforations, selvage between panes of 100 on the printing sheets (meaning no stamps with straight edges), and a plate number in one corner of the pane instead of one that "floats" in the left or right margin.

The Nimitz stamp never had straight edges because its early version was printed on the intaglio I-8 press. When it was switched to the A press, it was with the new plate layout that provided selvage between the panes.

As for the Dorothea Dix stamp, it was printed on the A press, but originally perforated by an on-line bull's-eye perforator. BEP wanted to dispose of on-line perforators because they slowed the printing process and because the perforating pins tended to break easily. So it switched Dix to the off-line L perforator.

Not only do the perforations on the two varieties of each stamp look different at the intersections; their measurements are slightly different as well. This is significant when the question of catalog listing for the varieties arises. All L-perforated issues measure approximately 10¾ on a standard gauge, while Eureka perforated products measure approximately 11¼.

In addition, major and constant tagging differences are apparent on each variety of each of the seven stamps.

On all but the Nimitz stamp, the stamps with L perforations have tagging blocks that measure approximately 16 by 18 millimeters in size. The stamps with bull's-eye perfs have larger blocks, measuring approximately 18½ millimeters by 21 millimeters.

As for Nimitz, since it was originally printed on the I-8 press, there was no capability to tag the stamps on-line. This meant that the luminescent coating had to be applied by an offset press.

So the older version was tagged over the entire surface of the pane, while the new version has a large tagging block on each stamp that doesn't touch perforations or sheet margins.

A minor note: The old printings of the Nimitz stamp have shiny gum and the newer ones dull gum.

A USPS news release in February 1986 stated that the 7¢ Abraham Baldwin, 10¢ Richard Russell and 11¢ Alden Partridge stamps were possible candidates for conversion to the Eureka perforator. Since then, however, the Russell stamp has been removed from sale.

Neither the 30¢ Laubach nor 20¢ Truman stamps were mentioned for conversion, but both turned up in the new form in 1988.

30¢ Frank Laubach

Collectors learned from the May-June 1988 issue of the USPS *Philatelic Catalog* that the 30¢ Frank Laubach stamp of 1984 was available in four plate number positions. Previously, it had had floating plate numbers.

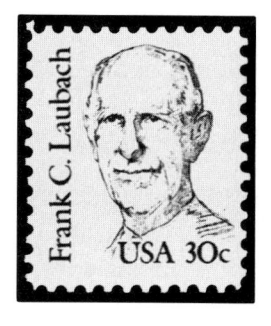

Original Laubach stamp from L perforator.

This meant that the Laubach stamp, like previous stamps in the Great Americans series, had been switched from the L perforator to the Eureka perforator, which produces bull's-eye perforations, fixed-position plate numbers and selvage all around the pane.

The Laubach stamp hadn't been mentioned by the Postal Service as a candidate for conversion. However, after the rate change of April 3, 1988, which set a 30¢ rate for first-class mail to Canada, it stood to see increased use.

No first day of issue was observed by USPS, and in fact, it is uncertain precisely when the revised Laubach stamp first went on sale. Presumably it was some time in June 1988.

Frank Laubach's claim to fame was his lifelong work against illiteracy around the globe. His stamp, like the Harry Truman stamp, was originally issued on the 100th anniversary of its subject's birth — in this case, September 2, 1884.

20¢ Harry Truman

In July, USPS announced that the 20¢ Harry Truman stamp of 1984 would be reprinted to meet the demand for stamps covering the first-class additional-ounces rate.

As before, the stamp was printed on the intaglio portion of the intaglio-gravure A press. However, it was perforated on the Eureka perforator, giving it the bull's-eye configuration where horizontal and vertical perforation rows intersect. The earlier version had been perforated on the L perforator.

As with the revised Frank Laubach stamp, USPS did not observe a first day of issue for the Truman reprint. The new stamp was placed on sale at USPS headquarters in L'Enfant Plaza, Washington, late in the afternoon of September 1. It was not immediately known whether any covers exist bearing that date.

This cover, dated September 2, is one of a handful of covers prepared by Linn's Stamp News Washington correspondent Charles Yeager. Although the stamp was released late on the afternoon of September 1, no covers bearing that date are known as of this writing.

The original Truman stamp had been the product of a press change at BEP. Issued January 26, 1984, on the 100th anniversary of Truman's birth, it was the third Great Americans item to appear in the 20¢ denomination, then the first-class rate.

The explanation for this apparent excess was the desire of USPS to switch the printing of its 20¢ definitive from the older, slower Cottrell intaglio press to the bigger and faster A press. Rather than revise the then-current 20¢ Thomas Gallaudet stamp for the A press, USPS chose to respond to requests from political figures and others for a stamp honoring the 32nd president on his centennial.

As with previous revised versions of Great Americans stamps, USPS made no changes in the original engraved die. It thus passed up an opportunity to enlarge the 20¢ designation in conformance with its current policy of making the denomination as prominent as possible.

The USPS announcement that the Truman stamp had been reprinted said that it "had been the last Great Americans series issue available with only floating plate numbers."

However, the 6¢ Walter Lippmann, 7¢ Abraham Baldwin and 9¢ Thayer stamps also have floating plate numbers. These, along with the 8¢ Knox, 19¢ Sequoyah and 37¢ Millikan stamps, were identified by collectors as L-perforated stamps that could conceivably be reprinted in the future.

30¢ FRANK LAUBACH (PERF VARIETY)

Date of Issue: June 1988

Catalog Numbers: Scott 1864   Minkus 816   USPS 1030

Color: green

First-Day Cancel: none (Original: Benton, Pennsylvania)

FDCs Canceled: none

Format: Panes of 100, vertical, 10 across, 10 down. Printing sleeve of 800 subjects (20 across, 40 around). (Original issue: printing sleeve of 920 subjects.)

Perf: 11.2 by 11.1 (Eureka off-line perforator) (Original: L perforator)

Selvage Markings: ©UNITED STATES POSTAL SERVICE 1984, USE CORRECT ZIP CODE®

Designer: Richard Sparks of Norwalk, Connecticut

Art Director: Howard Paine (CSAC)

Engravers: Gary Chaconas (BEP, vignette)
Thomas Bakos (BEP, lettering and numerals)

Printing: 3-color intaglio unit of the 8-color gravure/intaglio A press (702)

Quantity Ordered: 150,000,000
Quantity Distributed: unavailable

Sleeve Number Detail: One sleeve number alongside corner stamps

Sleeve Number: 2

Tagging: block over vignette

20¢ HARRY TRUMAN (PERF VARIETY)

Date of Issue: August 1988

Catalog Numbers: Scott 1854   Minkus 811   USPS 1022

Color: black

First-Day Cancel: none (Original: Washington, D.C.)

FDCs Canceled: unavailable (earliest known use September 2, 1988)

Format: Panes of 100, vertical, 10 across, 10 down. Printing sleeve of 800 subjects (20 across, 40 around). (Original issue: printing sleeve of 920 subjects.)

Perf: 11.2 by 11.1 (Eureka off-line perforator) (Original: L perforator)

Selvage Markings: ©UNITED STATES POSTAL SERVICE 1984, USE CORRECT ZIP CODE®

Designer: Chris Calle of Ridgefield, Connecticut

Art Director: Mary Margaret Grant (USPS)

Engravers: Thomas Hipschen (BEP, vignette)
Robert Culin, Sr. (BEP, lettering and numerals)

Modeler: Ronald Sharpe (BEP)

Printing: 3-color intaglio unit of the 8-color gravure/intaglio A press (702)

Quantity Ordered: 250,000,000
Quantity Distributed: unavailable

Sleeve Number Detail: One sleeve number alongside corner stamps. (Original: floating sleeve number).

Sleeve Number: 2

Tagging: block over vignette (Original: block over vignette.)

270

AIRMAIL STAMPS

Three new airmail stamps were issued in 1988, after a year in which there were none.

One of these was a commemorative, issued for an occasion that had not the remotest connection with aviation: the 350th anniversary of the establishment of America's New Sweden colony by settlers from Sweden and Finland. It's not unprecedented for airmail commemoratives to mark earthbound enterprises (for example, the anniversaries of New York City and Alexandria, Virginia, the statehood of Alaska and Hawaii), but in the majority of cases there's at least some tenuous link of the subject matter to high altitude.

The other two airmails were definitives in the Aviation Pioneers series. One, a 45-center, covered the new uniform air rate for overseas mail. The other, at 36¢, met the international air postcard rate.

44¢ NEW SWEDEN AIRMAIL

Date of Issue: March 29, 1988

Catalog Numbers: Scott C117   Minkus A117   USPS 1197

Colors: orange, yellow, blue, brown (offset); brown (intaglio)

First-Day Cancel: Wilmington, Delaware (Grand Opera House)

FDCs Canceled: 213,445

Format: Panes of 50, horizontal, 5 across, 10 down. Offset printing plates of 200 subjects (10 across, 20 around); intaglio printing sleeve of 400 subjects (10 across, 40 around).

Perf: 11.1 (Eureka off-line perforator)

Selvage Markings: ©United States Postal Service 1987, Use Correct ZIP Code®

Designer: Goran Osterlund of Sweden

Art Director: Joe Brockert (USPS)

Typographer: Bradbury Thompson (CSAC)

Engravers: Thomas Hipschen (BEP, vignette)
Gary Slaght (BEP, lettering and numerals)

Modeler: Frank Waslick (BEP)

Printing: 6-color offset, 3-color intaglio D press (902)

Quantity Ordered: 23,000,000
Quantity Distributed: 22,975,000

Plate/Sleeve Number Detail: Top panes: one group of 4 offset plate numbers alongside corner stamps; intaglio sleeve number adjacent to stamp below. Bottom panes: offset/sleeve numbers in reverse positions.

Plate/Sleeve Number Combination: 1111-1

Tagging: block over vignette

Printing Base Impressions: Intaglio sleeve: 1(242,000)

The Stamp

Two things were remarkable about the 44¢ airmail stamp issued March 29 to mark the 350th anniversary of the settlement of New Sweden by Swedish and Finnish colonists.

It was the first three-nation joint issue in which the United States had participated. Sweden and Finland produced stamps simultaneously to commemorate the same event.

And it became postally obsolete more quickly than any previous U.S. stamp. It covered the international airmail rate for only five days before the rate went up by a penny, to 45¢.

Under other circumstances, USPS might have delayed the stamp in order to revise the denomination after the rate hike was set. However, because it was part of a three-way joint issue involving elaborate coordinated planning, a change was deemed impossible.

Only seven months after the New Sweden airmail was issued — on

The Swedish booklet pane of the New Sweden joint issue.

273

October 31, 1988 — the Philatelic Sales Division withdrew it from sale. The sales period was one of the shortest for a philatelic item in the division's history.

The anniversary of New Sweden — in what is now Delaware, southern New Jersey and southeast Pennsylvania — was also publicized in other ways. Chief among these was a three-week visit to the United States by King Carl XVI Gustaf and Queen Silvia of Sweden.

The joint stamp issue was the 20th in which the United States had participated, and its second of 1988. Two months previously, this

The Finnish contribution to the New Sweden joint issue.

country and Australia had together marked the 200th anniversary of Australia's settlement.

In the United States-Swedish-Finnish joint issue, each country's stamps were available at all three first-day cities — Wilmington, Delaware; Helsinki, Finland, and Vaxjo, Sweden — for use on combination covers.

Also available to stamp collectors were:

• A United States-Sweden-Finland joint issue folder entitled "The American Letter," selling for $5. This contained a card bearing one of each country's stamps with the appropriate first-day cancellation applied to each. Textual material on the card and folder were in the three languages.

• A 16-page New Sweden brochure, a product of the Swedish Post Office, selling for $7.50. The brochure bore a full booklet pane of the Swedish stamps and a single U.S. New Sweden stamp, with appropriate cancellations.

Because the U.S. New Sweden airmail stamp had such a short lifespan at the rate for which it was issued, examples of it used on cover at that rate are very scarce. The one significant exception to that is first-day covers.

USPS routinely grants collectors a grace period after a stamp's date of issue to submit envelopes franked with the stamps to receive the first-day cancel. In the case of the New Sweden stamp, the grace period was very generous. The issue date was March 29, and collectors had two months — until May 28 — to send covers.

In the meantime — on April 3 — the international air letter rate went to 45¢. But because all first-day covers bore the March 29 postmark, they continued to "fly" at the 44¢ rate for almost two months, safe from a postage-due penalty. Many of these undoubtedly went to foreign addresses, particularly in Sweden and Finland, where the 45¢

rate by then applied.

The joint issue was the third such project with Sweden and the first with Finland. It was remarkably similar, however, to a non-joint issue that took place back in 1938, long before nations had thought of coordinating their philatelic emissions.

That year was also an anniversary year of the founding of New Sweden — the 300th. And each of the three countries involved — the United States, Sweden and Finland — independently marked the event with stamps.

The U.S. stamp in 1938 was a 3¢ red-violet, in square format, depicting "The Landing of the Swedes and Finns." Finland's was a 3½-markka dark brown showing two settlers toiling to uproot a tree stump. Sweden's contribution was a set of seven different stamps in five designs.

In addition, the United States issued a commemorative half-dollar, and Sweden minted a 2-kroner coin.

That 1938 anniversary, like the one 50 years later, drew Swedish royalty to the United States. Crown Prince Gustav Adolf — grandfather of the present king — unveiled a monument at Wilmington at a ceremony attended by President Franklin D. Roosevelt and commissions from all parts of the United States.

In one final intriguing twist, three of those 1938 stamps would re-emerge decades later in U.S. and Swedish stamp designs. It happened in 1986, when the two countries jointly issued booklets of four different varieties to celebrate the hobby of stamp collecting. The one design that was common to both countries' booklets was a "stamp on stamp" that reproduced the U.S. 1938 New Sweden commemorative and two of the 1938 Swedish stamps.

Sweden in the 17th century was a major power, with continental possessions that included Finland (then a Swedish province) and, at various times, parts of modern Poland, Latvia, Estonia, Lithuania, Germany and the Soviet Union. Its move into North America was inspired in part by the experience of the English and Dutch, who by the 1630s were beginning to realize profits from their colonial ventures.

In 1637 Swedish, Dutch and German stockholders formed the New Sweden Company to trade for furs and tobacco. The two ships of the company's first expedition sailed from Gothenberg, Sweden, late in 1637 under the command of Peter Minuit, a man who had already made his mark upon the New World. He is best known for purchasing Manhattan from the Indians in 1626, building Fort Amsterdam and directing the Dutch colony at the site of New York for six years.

The ships reached the Minquas Kill (now the Christina River), which flows into the Delaware River at Wilmington, some time in March. In the name of Christina, the young queen-to-be of Sweden, Peter Minuit bought from five Indian chiefs the land extending from south of Wilmington to the present site of Philadelphia, where the Schuylkill and Delaware Rivers meet. His successor would later buy hundreds of square miles on the New Jersey side, north to the site of Trenton and south to Cape May.

Minuit oversaw the building of Fort Christina, named for the princess, at the mouth of the Minquas Kill. He stayed with the colony for only a few weeks, however. On his return voyage he put in at St. Kitts, where he boarded a Dutch sloop that was driven from the harbor by a sudden storm. He was never heard from again.

In 1651, the Dutch from New Netherland under Peter Stuyvesant marched south, built a fort of their own in New Sweden and finally, in 1655, seized Fort Christina, ending Swedish sovereignty in the Delaware Valley. Most of the settlers remained, living peacefully under Dutch rule.

For the next two centuries, Swedes and Finns continued to come to America in small numbers. In the 1840s, however, a massive immigration of Swedish pioneers to the Midwest began, driven by population pressures and economic problems back home.

Between the 1850s and 1920s one out of every four Swedes came to the United States, concentrating in the northern Plains states — Illinois, Iowa, Wisconsin, Minnesota, the Dakotas. The centennial of this mass movement was commemorated in 1948 by a 5¢ U.S. stamp.

The Design

The joint-issue stamps of the three countries featured a common design by Sweden's Goran Osterlund. It was based on a portion of an illustration from a 1702 book on the New Sweden colony by Thomas Campanius Holm — the first Swedish-language publication about America — featuring five people, European settlers and Indians, negotiating. For his stamp design, Osterlund reversed the picture of the group — "flopped" it, in graphic-arts talk.

A map of New Sweden, covering portions of three states, is at the left. On the opposite side is a map of the Atlantic and adjacent lands, with Sweden and Finland highlighted in the upper right. Images of the Swedish ships that arrived in the New World, the *Kalmar Nyckel* (Key of Kalmar) and *Fogel Grip* (Bird Griffin), are shown in mid-ocean.

Osterlund's original design was in the long, shallow horizontal format appropriate to a Swedish booklet pane. In order for the United States to use it, USPS told Osterlund, its dimensions would have to be altered to those of the standard U.S. commemorative. Osterlund complied, but in the process he made some design revisions, including removing one Indian and one European, narrowing the map and enlarging the two ships.

Representatives of USPS, the Citizens' Stamp Advisory Committee and the Bureau of Engraving and Printing then set out to interpret Osterlund's design to prepare it for printing on BEP's intaglio/offset D press. Bales of undefined barter materials on the ground in front of the group were removed. Pink stripes in the New Sweden map at the left were taken out. Type was shifted around, and "USAirmail" and "44" entered. (Osterlund hadn't known it was to be an airmail stamp.)

Even after the model was shown to the public, a few additional changes were made. The principal one was the deletion of some dates indicating expansion of New Sweden — 1638 in the original colony, 1642 in Pennsylvania and lower Delware, and 1640 and 1649 in New Jersey — in order to eliminate some questions of historical accuracy.

The U.S. and Finnish stamps were issued in sheet form. The Finnish stamp — which used Osterlund's original extra-long configuration — was of the 3-markka denomination (75¢ U.S.). Sweden incorporated its 3.60-krona stamp in a booklet with five other stamps of the same value, all marking in various ways the "Swedish connection" to American life, and selling for $3.60 in U.S. currency. Lars Sjooblom did the engraving for the booklet.

The Swedish stamp is inscribed "New Sweden 1638-1938"; the Finnish stamp, "Finnish Settlement in America 1638-1938."

First-Day Facts

A public first-day sale ceremony was held March 29 before some 700 people at Wilmington's renovated Grand Opera House.

Postmaster General Anthony Frank, still less than a month in his new job, noted that much has changed since the Swedes landed at Wilmington, and add pointedly: "Everything is subject to change — including postmasters general and postage rates."

The stamp was also on sale at the nearby Rodney Square Station and the Wilmington General Mail Facility.

An official second-day ceremony was held March 30 in Philadelphia, which the Swedish and Finnish postal chiefs also attended. Ann Robinson, USPS consumer advocate, was the principal speaker.

Sweden held its first-day ceremony at the Emigrant Institute in Vaxjo. The Institute houses records about Swedes who emigrated to the United States. The Finnish first-day ceremony was held in Helsinki, with Peter A. Jacobson, assistant postmaster general, engineering and technical support, representing USPS.

In April, USPS offered special philatelic cancellations in 14 cities in conjunction with the visit of the Swedish king and queen. The dates and places for these cancellations were: April 10, Washington; April 13, Wilmington and Philadelphia; April 14, Trenton, Bridgeton and Princeton, New Jersey; April 15, New York; April 18, Detroit; April 19, Chicago; April 20, Atlanta; April 21, Dallas; April 23, Houston; April 24, Minneapolis, and April 25, Los Angeles.

These post offices also made available the stamps of all three countries, plus Sweden's New Sweden brochure and the three-nation joint folder "The American Letter," on the appropriate dates.

45¢ SAMUEL P. LANGLEY AIRMAIL

Date of Issue: May 14, 1988

Catalog Numbers: Scott C118   Minkus A119   USPS 5574

Colors: magenta, yellow, cyan, blue, gray, black (offset); black (intaglio)

First-Day Cancel: San Diego, California (Brown Field)

FDCs Canceled: 167,575 (together with DC-3 postal card)

Format: Panes of 50, horizontal, 5 across, 10 down. Offset printing plates of 200 subjects (10 across, 20 around); intaglio printing sleeve of 400 subjects (10 across, 40 around).

Perf: 11.1 (Eureka off-line perforator)

Selvage Markings: ©United States Postal Service 1988, Use Correct ZIP Code®

Designer: Ken Dallison of Indian River, Ontario, Canada

Art Director: Jack Williams (USPS)

Typographer: Bradbury Thompson (CSAC)

Engravers: Thomas Hipschen (BEP, vignette detail)

Modeler: Ronald Sharpe (BEP)

Printing: 6-color offset, 3-color intaglio D press (902)

Quantity Ordered: 320,000,000
Quantity Distributed: 201,150,000

Plate/Sleeve Number Detail: Top panes: 6 offset plate numbers alongside corner stamps; one intaglio sleeve number adjacent to stamp below. Bottom panes: offset/intaglio numbers in reverse positions.

Plate/Sleeve Number Combinations:	111111-1, 111121-1, 111131-1, 111231-1, 111232-1, 121232-1, 222232-1, 223232-1, 224232-1, 224233-1, 324233-1, 324343-1, 334343-1, 334344-1, 335344-1, 435344-1, 435364-1, 435464-1, 445564-1, 446564-1, 447564-1, 647565-1

Tagging: block over vignette

The Stamp

The 1¢ increase in the basic international airmail letter rate, from 44¢ to 45¢, made a new stamp necessary. The stamp, in the Aviation Pioneers series, honored Samuel Pierpont Langley, a scientist whose efforts to solve the mysteries of manned mechanical flight failed but whose experiments provided inspiration and information for the Wright brothers and other successful pioneers.

The Langley stamp was issued jointly with a 36¢ air postal card saluting the Douglas DC-3 aircraft.

The Langley stamp replaced the 44¢ Trans-Pacific airmail, which had been issued in 1985 to commemorate the 50th anniversary of commercial air service to Hawaii and the Orient. Earlier stamps in the Aviation Pioneers series had honored Wilbur and Orville Wright (1978), Octave Chanute (1979) and Wiley Post (1979) with se-tenant pairs, and Blanche Stuart Scott, designated a "pioneer pilot" (1980), Glenn Curtiss (1980), Alfred V. Verville (1985) and Lawrence and Elmer Sperry (1985) with singles.

Samuel Langley was born in Roxbury, Massachusetts, in 1834. He studied architecture, engineering and, ultimately, astronomy, which had fascinated him since childhood, and invented several astronomical devices, including the bolometer, to measure the sun's radiation.

From 1867 to 1887 Langley was professor of physics and astronomy, and director of the Allegheny Observatory, at the Western University of Pennsylvania in Pittsburgh. In 1887 he joined the staff of the Smithsonian Institution and four years later became secretary, holding that office until his death in 1906.

Langley was well into his 50s when he turned his attention to aerodynamics. Unlike Chanute and the Wrights, who approached the problem of powered flight by experimenting with manned gliders, Langley built models — small unmanned flying machines that he called "aerodromes," meaning "air runners."

His Aerodrome No. 5 (pictured on the stamp) was the first American heavier-than-air machine to make a free flight of any significant length. Propelled by a steam engine and launched by a catapult, the 26-pound craft flew a spiraling course of more than half a mile over the Potomac River near Quantico, Virginia, May 6, 1896.

After the Spanish-American War broke out in 1898, the War Department saw the military potential of manned aircraft and gave Langley $50,000 to develop one.

Unfortunately, the craft he built turned out to be structurally weak, virtually uncontrollable and burdened with a catapult-type launch system that imposed heavy structural loads before a flight even began.

The first attempt to fly it was made October 7, 1903, from a houseboat on the Potomac, with Langley's assistant, Charles Manly, at the controls. But some part of the aircraft fouled the launching gear, and it plunged straight down into the water.

Langley had one more throw coming, however. Ignoring the derision of the press and freshly funded by the Smithsonian, he repaired his damaged Aerodrome, modified the launch mechanism and scheduled another try for December 8, 1903. This time the site was the Potomac River off Washington, near the mouth of the Anacostia.

Chunks of ice were floating in the water, the wind was gusting up to 20 mph and darkness was falling as Charles Manly took the pilot's position. At 4:45 p.m., the catapult hurled the aircraft aloft. It shot upward, did a half-loop and fell upside down into the Potomac. Manly again escaped alive, but Langley's 17-year-long effort to develop a successful heavier-than air flying machine was ended.

"The ridiculous fiasco which attended the attempt at aerial navigation in the Langley flying machine was not unexpected," said a self-assured editorial writer for *The New York Times*. "The flying machine which will really fly might be evolved by the combined and continuous efforts of mathematicians and mechanicians in from one to 10 million years."

Actually, it required only nine more days. Then the Wrights accomplished the feat at Kitty Hawk.

The Design

The stamp followed the design pattern of the earlier Aviation Pioneers stamps, which showed a head-and-shoulders portrait of the subject and a view of an aircraft closely associated with the person.

Kenneth Dallison of Indian River, Ontario, Canada, was chosen to design the stamp for offset/intaglio printing on the BEP's D press. Dallison had designed all the previous "sketchbook-style" Aviation Pioneers stamps — Wright, Chanute, Post, Curtiss, Verville — which featured heavily outlined watercolor images, as well as the similar First Transpacific Flight Anniversary postal card of 1981. He had also designed three of the Transportation coils: the 11¢ Stutz Bearcat and 12¢ Stanley Steamer of 1985 and the 7.1¢ Tractor of 1987.

On this stamp, a white-bearded Langley is shown at the right, wearing a gray suit coat and yellow straw hat with a vivid red band and matching red bow tie. To the left is a rendering of his unmanned

An early sketch by Kenneth Dallison showing a quarter-scale model aircraft of 1901. The aircraft was later replaced in the design with Aerodrome No. 5.

Aerodrome No. 5. A cloud bank, and a blue sky shading downward to a rose color, make up the background.

Dallison's original sketch showed not Aerodrome No. 5. but a later aircraft, a quarter-scale petrol-driven model dating from 1901. Jack Williams, project manager and art director, conferred with James Dean, a CSAC art coordinator and former official of the National Air and Space Museum, and they decided that Aerodrome No. 5 — Langley's most successful flying machine — would be a better choice. The Air and Space Museum, which owns the aircraft, supplied photos and Dallison made the change.

The artist took the portrait of Langley from a photograph made October 7, 1903, the date of the first unsuccessful manned launch on the Potomac. The photo, also the property of the Air and Space Museum, shows Langley and his pilot, Charles Manly, standing side by side. Dallison had previously used the same photograph for a sketch of the two men that decorated the February page of a 1974 calendar.

The stamp is an example of the kind of combination printing that USPS calls "intaglio dominant." Designer Dallison provided strong lines that engraver Thomas Hipschen of the BEP could follow in outlining the face, beard, shoulder, coat lapels, hat brim and aircraft. These intaglio elements were printed in black and are so strong they seem to leap out. The offset colors — yellow, cyan, black, blue and gray — fill in around and between the lines with solid backgrounds.

Some of Dallison's original hues were deemed not bright enough, so Ronald Sharpe, the stamp's modeler, used the BEP's electronic Design Center to convert them into bolder colors, particularly the red of the tie and hatband.

First-Day Facts

The first-day ceremony for the Langley stamp and DC-3 postal card was held at 9:15 a.m. May 14 at the Brown Field exposition site, some 17 miles south of San Diego. A first-day program with a combination of the stamp and the postal card was given to invited guests.

36¢ IGOR SIKORSKY AIRMAIL

Date of Issue: June 23, 1988

Catalog Numbers: Scott C119   Minkus A119   USPS 5573

Colors: light blue, magenta, cyan, yellow, black (gravure); brown (intaglio)

First-Day Cancel: Stratford, Connecticut (Sikorsky Aircraft Company)

FDCs Canceled: 162,986

Format: Panes of 50, horizontal, 5 across, 10 down. Gravure printing cylinders of 200 subjects (10 across, 20 around); intaglio printing sleeve of 400 subjects (10 across, 40 around).

Perf: 11.1 (Eureka off-line perforator)

Selvage Markings: ©United States Postal Service 1988, Use Correct ZIP Code®

Designer: Ren Wicks of Los Angeles, California

Art Director: James Dean (CSAC)

Project Manager: Jack Williams (USPS)

Typographer: Bradbury Thompson (CSAC)

Engravers: Gary Chaconas (BEP, vignette)
Gary Slaght (BEP, lettering)
Dennis Brown (BEP, numerals)

Modeler: Peter Cocci (BEP)

Printing: 8-color gravure/intaglio A press (702)

Quantity Ordered: 140,000,000
Quantity Distributed: 111,550,000

Cylinder/Sleeve Number Detail: Top panes: one group of 5 gravure cylinder numbers alongside corner stamps; one intaglio sleeve number alongside stamp below. Bottom panes: gravure/intaglio numbers in reverse positions.

Cylinder/Sleeve Number Combination: 11111-1, 21111-1, 21112-1, 22112-1, 12112-1

Tagging: phosphor taggant added to light blue background ink

Printing Base Impressions: Light Blue: 2(575,655)

The Stamp

On April 3, 1988, the rate for international airmail postal cards rose from 33¢ to 36¢. To meet the new rate, a 36¢ airmail stamp depicting aeronautical engineer Igor Ivanovich Sikorsky was issued June 23 at the Sikorsky Aircraft facility in Stratford, Conneticut.

The stamp was the second addition in six weeks to the long-running Aviation Pioneers series. On May 14, USPS had issued its 45¢ Samuel P. Langley stamp for the new international airmail letter rate. And the Sikorsky stamp replaced an earlier stamp in the same series, the 33¢ Alfred Verville of 1985.

The Sikorsky turned out to be a production and distribution headache for USPS and the Bureau of Engraving and Printing.

It was printed on the A press by a combination of intaglio and gravure. This method had been vulnerable to trouble in the past; BEP hadn't used it since the Rural Electrification Administration commemorative of 1985. In recent years the A press had been employed to print single-color intaglio Great Americans stamps, leaving the gravure units of the press idle.

USPS described its Sikorsky problem as "production difficulties." These reportedly centered on registering the intaglio and gravure portions of the stamp. The two printing systems require different web speeds for optimum registration. When BEP tried to find a compromise speed for the combination process, it ended up with bad results. Of the first 840,000 full sheets of Sikorsky stamps printed, Bureau sources said, only 100,000 were acceptable — a spoilage rate of close to 90 percent.

Close inspection of the stamps themselves indicates that there were other printing problems as well.

The portrait, which was done in gravure, was mottled. Intaglio ink contamination was evident in the engraved blue lettering (where brown intruded) and the engraved brown helicopter (which on some copies displayed such anomalies as a red wheel). Specimens were reported that bore only traces of the intaglio red color, suggesting a problem with the automatic ink control mechanism that pumps ink into the troughs.

Because of these woes, shipments of the Sikorsky stamp to post offices and the Philatelic Sales Division mail order facility in Kansas City, Missouri, were delayed. Several days after the first day of issue, the stamp went on sale in Washington at USPS headquarters and at the small philatelic station in the Smithsonian Institution. Unofficial sources said the Kansas City facility didn't get its first shipment until the week of July 11-15.

During that same week, a spot check of the more than 300 philatelic windows around the country turned up only two philatelic boutiques that had supplies. And by July 15, three weeks after the issue date, the USPS headquarters philatelic windows still hadn't received additional stock of the Sikorsky stamp.

Because of the high rate of spoilage at the outset, collectors of matched sets of plate number combinations had trouble finding combinations 11111-1 and 21111-1. (The first five digits represent gravure plates; the sixth digit, the intaglio plate.) A third number combination, 21112-1, was more plentiful.

Sikorsky, a native of Czarist Russia, designed and built three diverse types of aircraft — large multi-engine planes, flying boats and helicopters — in a career that spanned more than half a century. But it's the helicopter, capable of taking off and landing vertically and hovering motionless in mid-air, with which Sikorsky's name is most strongly associated.

Sikorsky made a fortune as a young aircraft builder, but he left most of it behind when the Russian Revolution drove him out of his native country. As an immigrant in New York, he re-established himself in the 1920s as a leading aircraft designer, and became a U.S. citizen in 1928.

This magnified picture shows how the engraver misspelled "Vought" as "Vogt" on the helicopter fuselage.

He organized the Sikorsky Manufacturing Corporation — now United Aircraft Corporation's Sikorsky Aircraft Division — in Connecticut in 1925 and began building large aircraft for the growing commercial aviation industry. His S-38 10-seater amphibians and, in 1931, his S-40, the *American Clipper,* were the predecessors of a series of four-engined Clipper ships, or flying boats, that established regular transoceanic air service.

In time, Sikorsky returned to an early love, the helicopter. In 1939, after much rebuilding and experimenting, he constructed the Vought-Sikorsky 300 — the craft shown on the stamp — and successfully flew it May 13, 1940.

The U.S. Army bought its first helicopter in 1941, and more than 400 Sikorsky helicopters saw service in World War II. In the Korean War, and to a far greater extent in the Vietnam War, helicopters were used to transport troops, fly out the wounded and rescue soldiers and pilots cut off from their own forces.

Sikorsky's belief that helicopters would be "the flivvers of the future," kept in the household garages and "just as common as the cars we now see on our highways," was a popular vision during World War II, but never came to pass. For humanitarian and commercial purposes, however, the helicopter proved to be of immeasurable value.

Sikorsky died in 1972 at the age of 83.

Stamps of several nations have depicted Sikorsky aircraft. The *Ilia Mourometz*, for example, is shown on a Soviet stamp of 1976, and the VS-300 helicopter with Sikorsky at the controls — in a view very similar to that on the U.S. Sikorsky stamp — appeared on a 1987 25-leone stamp in a Sierra Leone series depicting pioneering aircraft.

The Design

The designer of the Sikorsky stamp was Ren Wicks of Los Angeles, who had previously designed the 10¢ Crossed Flags definitive of 1973.

A malfunctioning of the ink-control mechanism produced this Sikorsky stamp with hardly a trace of red intaglio ink.

Basing his work on photographs provided by Sikorsky Aircraft, Wicks followed the style of previous stamps in the Aviation Pioneers series, incorporating a closeup view of the subject and a long-range picture of an aircraft closely identified with the individual.

Unlike the previous stamps in the Aviation Pioneers series, this one did not bear the legend "Aviation Pioneer" or "Pioneer Pilot." It merely carried the name "Igor Sikorsky" along with the postal information "36 USAirmail."

"We have a continuing desire to simplify the designs," explained Jack Williams, project manager for the stamp. "The line 'Aviation Pioneer' has become almost superfluous with people like Sikorsky. When you say Sikorsky, you think airplanes and helicopters."

If future subjects in the series should be less well-known, Williams said, the line could return: "It's going to be a case-by-case decision."

The helicopter engraving is nicely detailed, although inspection with a magnifying glass reveals that not all the detail shown on the stamp as designed was transferred to the finished product.

On the stamp, "VS 300" is visible on the fuselage, but inexplicably, the wording "Vought Sikorsky" above it was engraved as merely "Vogt" (sic) and an undefined word beginning with "S."

Because all five of the A press' gravure ink stations were used, there was no station to apply tagging. A colorless phosphor taggant was mixed into the light blue gravure ink, which was the first ink laid

This photograph of the Sikorsky stamp, taken with ultraviolet light, shows how the taggant was mixed directly into the light blue gravure printing ink.

down on the paper.

Incorporating the taggant into one of the printing inks is a highly unusual way of tagging U.S. stamps, used only once before, on the 6¢ Leif Erikson commemorative that was printed in 1968 by a combination of offset-lithography and intaglio. Normally, stamps are tagged by applying a phosphor coating over the printing inks on the entire stamp (overall tagging) or in a square on the design area (block tagging), or by using a paper that has phosphor in the sizing.

First-Day Facts

USPS announced the June 23 issue date on April 4. Later it added the information that Stratford would be the first-day city.

Attendance at the first-day ceremony at Sikorsky Aircraft was by invitation only. Because of the company's security requirements, clearance to attend had to be obtained before June 21, and no cameras, other than those registered by authorized media representatives, were allowed in the facility.

Speakers included Sergei Sikorsky, son of the inventor, and Comer S. Coppie, senior assistant postmaster general.

The production and shipping delays encountered with the stamp led USPS to extend by 30 days its originally announced deadline for ordering first-day cancellations. The new deadline was August 22.

$8.75 EXPRESS MAIL

Date of Issue: October 4, 1988

Catalog Numbers: Scott 2394   Minkus 908   USPS 1101

Colors: magenta, yellow, cyan, purple, black (offset); black (intaglio)

First-Day Cancel: Terre Haute, Indiana (Hulman Regional Airport)

FDCs Canceled: unavailable

Format: Panes of 20, horizontal, semi-jumbo 5 across, 4 down. Offset printing plates of 80 subjects (8 across, 10 around) and intaglio printing sleeve of 160 subjects (8 across, 20 around).

Perf: 11.2 by 11.1 (Eureka off-line perforator)

Selvage Markings: ©UNITED STATES POSTAL SERVICE 1988 at top and bottom of each pane.

Designer: Ned Seidler of Hampton Bay, New York

Art Director: Howard Paine (CSAC)

Project Manager: Joe Brockert (USPS)

Typographer: Bradbury Thompson (CSAC)

Engravers: Gary Chaconas (BEP vignette)
Dennis Brown (BEP, lettering and numerals)

Modeler: Jack Ruther (BEP)

Printing: 6-color offset, 3-color intaglio D press (902)

Quantity Ordered: 10,000,000
Quantity Distributed: 7,754,000

Sleeve/Plate Number Detail: One intaglio sleeve number over/under corner stamps; one group of 5 offset plate numbers over/under adjacent stamps.

Sleeve/Plate Number Combination: 1-11111

Tagging: overall

The Stamp

As part of the April 3 rate overhaul, USPS cut its Express Mail rate from $10.75 to $8.75 for letters weighing under eight ounces in an effort to compete with private overnight-delivery companies. However, it raised the rate for a two-pound pack from $10.75 to $12, and raised the next-stage rate (up to five pounds) from $12.85 to $15.25.

Initially, USPS planned to issue two separate stamps, one for the half-pound rate, the other for the two-pound rate — a plan that was reported in a special *Postal Bulletin* issued March 25 to provide details of the rate changes. CSAC even went so far as to pick separate designs for the two varieties.

"After consulting the Express Mail processing people," said Joe Brockert, project manager for the stamp, "we concluded that the majority of people who would use adhesive stamps for Express Mail would be mailing a half-pound or less — letter mail and small packages. The bigger items at the higher rates would be basically business packs and so on, mailed by organizations that had accounts or meters.

"So rather than burden collectors and the public with two very high-value stamps, we decided to issue only one, for the half-pound rate."

USPS' initial announcement of the new $8.75 stamp, on April 4, said that it would be issued June 8 in Terre Haute, Indiana. Hulman Regional Airport at Terre Haute is the hub of the Postal Service's nationwide network for transporting Express Mail and Priority Mail.

Less than three weeks later, on April 21, the issue date was switched to October 4.

For its first two Express Mail issues, the $9.35 of 1983 and the $10.75 of 1985, USPS had produced gravure-printed stamps in booklets of three. This time, although it kept the basic design — an eagle's head outlined against the moon — it switched to a different, and more visually impressive, printing method and a different format.

Postal officials, who admired the quality of the Migratory Bird Hunting stamps that BEP produces annually for the Interior Department, asked the Bureau to employ the same intaglio-offset printing technique, the same size and shape, even the same perforator.

"Basically," said Joe Brockert, "this Express Mail stamp is our version of the duck stamp."

Instead of the sheets of 30 used for duck stamps, however, the Express Mail stamps were printed in mini-sheets of 20, following the precedent set with the $5 Bret Harte stamp of 1987.

The Harte stamp, a small stamp vertically arranged, was printed five across and four down. Because the Express Mail stamp was wide and horizontal, its pane arrangement was four across and five down.

"The format," USPS explained, "was developed to reduce destruction costs for high-value stamps at the Philatelic Sales Division and philatelic centers, where demand for plate blocks is heavy. The miniature sheet format yields four plate blocks, leaving only four individual stamps to be sold."

The change was criticized in some quarters. *Linn's Stamp News*, which had editorially denounced the Bret Harte mini-sheet in 1987, had the same reaction this time.

"Collectors will have to fork out almost $200 if they want to purchase the stamp in sheetlet form," the newspaper commented. "And make no mistake, many collectors will want the stamp that way.

"Right or wrong, they see these sheetlets as part of a tradition begun back in 1926 with the White Plains stamp. As most collectors know, the individual White Plains stamps are widely available, but the miniature sheet of 25 is not . . .

"In embracing the miniature sheet format, the United States joins a distinguished company of nations — Liechtenstein, Monaco, San Marino and Yugoslavia come immediately to mind — whose postal marketeers have found that collectors will buy even more stamps if the stamps are packaged in miniature sheets."

Said the USPS' Joe Brockert: "To call an almost-full-size pane a 'mini-sheet' is a misnomer — which we, too, may be guilty of misusing on such issues. It is the only format made, not a collector-oriented variety. The comparison is unfair at best. Would a full-size pane of 30 somehow be cheaper to collect?"

Linn's termed USPS' explanation that the new format would reduce destruction costs as "disingenuous, to say the least." With booklets, the newspaper pointed out, there was one plate number for every three stamps, and no plate blocks to remove.

"What hasn't been explained is why USPS decided to abandon the booklet format, in which plate blocks were not possible, in favor of a miniature sheet format, with a plate block in each corner," *Linn's* said. "We suspect the answer doesn't relate to the increasing popularity of Express Mail."

"It's simple," was Brockert's response. "It's easier to break a sheet than a booklet for single sales, which are relatively common."

Like its two predecessors, the $8.75 stamp bore no wording indicating it was for Express Mail, and in fact could be used on other types of mail as well.

Collectors expressed the hope that the new stamp, printed by offset-intaglio, would "hold" a postmark better than the previous gravure-printed specimens. A common complaint with the first two Express Mail stamps had been that postal clerks would frequently supplement an indistinct cancellation with a ball-point or felt-tipped pen. This did the job of revenue protection, but it made the stamps uncollectible.

Although USPS pioneered the expedited mail industry, it has been prevented by law and Postal Rate Commission rulings from competing fully with overnight delivery services in the private sector, even for government business.

For example, the General Services Administration awarded a $15 million contract for overnight delivery of small packages to Airborne Express of Seattle. USPS was unable to compete because it was prohibited by law from offering volume discounts to customers, as its competitors could do.

As part of its filing for the postal rate increases that took effect April 3, USPS asked the Postal Rate Commission to allow such discounts. Commercial carriers opposed the request, and the Rate Commission sided with them.

Airborne Express offered to charge the government $5 for the first pound and 89¢ for each additional pound. The least USPS could have offered was the standard $8.75.

Ned Seidler's concept sketch of the design that became the finished $8.75 Express Mail stamp. An arbitrary denomination was used for this essay by the artist.

Despite such restrictions, Express Mail has been able to expand its horizons. On May 1, 1988, USPS began Express Mail service to Moscow. It was the first such arrangement between the two nations in 50 years. The service cost $18 for a half-pound package, $21 for a pound and $7 for each additional pound.

Collectors noted that the half-pound Moscow rate could be prepaid by using two new Express Mail stamps plus one 50¢ stamp. That was no guarantee, of course, that it would be done that way. One irony that didn't go unnoticed was that in the initial advertising for the $8.75 Express Mail letter service, the envelope shown on TV screens bore a meter strip instead of postage stamps!

Another form of Express Mail promotion was halted in 1988 because it was confusing postal customers. The March 31 *Postal Bulletin* reported that the machine slogan cancellations advertising Express Mail were being phased out. These cancellations, which existed in several formats, apparently made some mailers believe their mail was receiving Express Mail treatment.

The Design

The designs for the original two Express Mail stamps had been patterned after the advertising illustrations for the service that were run in major publications. Young & Rubicam of New York, USPS' ad agency since 1974, was given credit as the designer.

The new stamp — which was designed while the $40 million advertising contract was up for rebidding — was assigned to a free-lance artist: Ned Seidler of Hampton Bay, New York. Seidler had previously designed the 1982 Francis of Assisi and 1984 Orchids se-tenant block of four.

(As it turned out, Young & Rubicam was the winner of the new one-year contract with four one-year renewal options. USPS said $23 million of the $40 million annual ad budget would be for Express Mail promotion, a figure unchanged from the previous year.)

Artist Seidler was told that the new stamp should contain the same design elements as the others. He prepared five different design concepts, showing the eagle head in various attitudes against full or crescent moons, for the two different Express Mail stamps that USPS had originally planned.

Because of the unusually large size of the finished stamps, the artist decided to do these concepts as full-color paintings in actual stamp size, so the Citizens' Stamp Advisory Committee would know precisely what the end product would look like. Accordingly, CSAC received a selection of exquisite miniatures.

"It's rare for artists to do that," commented Jack Williams of USPS. "David Blossom, who did all those Bicentennial Era postal cards, would always come in with what he called 'thumbnail sketches' — six, seven or eight versions sometimes — in actual postal card indicia size. But working small scares a lot of artists. They can't do it."

On his concept sketches Seidler used arbitrary denominations, because the final rates weren't known. As it turned out, the two-pound rate, which was designated in the rate filing to remain at $10.75, went up to $12.

The committee chose concept "B" (Seidler's designation) for the lower-rate stamp and concept "E" for the higher rate. "E" was similar to the existing $10.75 stamp. USPS, believing that this rate would continue to be in effect for the heavier mailings, planned to use basically the same design, reproportioned for sheets rather than booklets (a more rectangular shape was needed) and, of course, based on a painting rather than a photograph.

Seidler then painted larger, finished versions of both concepts for craftsmen at BEP to work with. In the end, the higher rate ended up at $12, not $10.75 — but in any event USPS decided not to issue a stamp for it.

First-Day Facts

Hulman Regional Airport in Terre Haute, where the first-day ceremony was held, is used by USPS as the transfer hub for the movement of some 250,000 pounds of Express Mail and Priority Mail each night.

OFFICIALS

The current series of Penalty Mail (Official Mail) stamps is the third wave of such stamps in U.S. postal history.

The first consisted of a separately identified set of stamps for each of nine executive departments of government — Agriculture, Executive, Interior, Justice, Navy, Post Office, State, Treasury and War. These first went into use July 1, 1873, after Congress had abolished the franking privilege.

They consisted of 120 separate items that are now listed in the Scott stamp catalog, and range in denomination from 1¢ to the $10 and $20 stamps issued for the State Department. There were also some 69 Official stamped envelopes issued for use by the Post Office and War Departments during this period.

The stamps, which are highly regarded by collectors, as well as the envelopes were supplanted on May 1, 1879, by penalty envelopes and, on July 5, 1884, were declared obsolete. They were apparently never actually demonetized or declared invalid for Official postage.

The second group of Official Mail stamps was a set of six varieties issued in 1910-1911 for the transmission of free mail resulting from administration of the brand-new Postal Savings system. Three varieties of stamped envelope also were issued for this purpose. After less than four years, these separate postal items were discontinued.

The third — and current — Official Mail stamps made their debut January 12, 1983, with seven denominations, 1¢ through $5. Their purpose was to provide a better accounting of actual mail costs for official departments and agencies.

The phrase "penalty for private use $300" is inscribed on all current Official Mail stamps, thus giving them their title "Penalty Mail." That $300 fine has been unchanged since Congress set it in legislation approved March 3, 1877. Considering what inflation has done since then, it would seem to be somewhat overdue for revising.

Four new Official Mail stamps were issued during 1988. These featured some major innovations, which will be described in the chapters of the individual stamps.

E OFFICIAL MAIL (COIL)

Date of Issue: March 22, 1988

Catalog Numbers: Scott O140   Minkus OF135   USPS 7709

Colors: red, blue, black

First-Day Cancel: Washington, D.C. (no first-day ceremony)

FDCs Canceled: 363,639 (includes all E stamps and E Savings Bond Envelope)

Format: Coils of 100. Printing plates of 450 subjects (18 across, 25 around).

Perf: 9.8 (Goebel coiler stroke perforator)

Designer and Typographer: Bradbury Thompson (CSAC)

Art Director and Project Manager: Joe Brockert (USPS)

Modeler: Ronald Sharpe (BEP)

Printing: 6-color Goebel offset Optiforma press (043)

Quantity Ordered: Coils of 100 - 300,000
Quantity Distributed: Coils of 100 - 300,000

Plate Number Detail: no plate number

Tagging: overall (phosphored paper)

The Stamp

On March 22, 1988, USPS issued a non-denominated Penalty Mail (Official Mail) coil stamp with the letter E representing the new 25¢ first-class letter rate. The stamp was remarkable for two reasons:

• It was the first Official Mail stamp to be entirely printed by offset-lithography, and the first widely used stamp of any kind produced by that method since the World War I era.

• It was the first Official to be printed on prephosphored paper, and the first full-production issue to be produced that way.

The stamp incorporated the same three-color design used on previous stamps of the series. Its vignette was patterned after the Great Seal of the United States and featured a white eagle on a field of blue, with lettering in red and black.

But close inspection revealed a different look to this one, attributable to the different printing process and different paper.

Security is a constant concern for the Stamps Division and the Postal Inspection Service. In the past, the Inspection Service has frowned on production of all-offset stamps, on grounds that they would be too easy for counterfeiters to reproduce. Thus the efficient offset process, when used, had to be combined with intaglio.

There had been only two exceptions:

In the World War I period, the abrasive inks on which BEP had to rely were wearing out printing plates too rapidly to maintain production, and some of the 1¢, 2¢ and 3¢ Washington definitives were produced by offset.

Offset also was used for the limited-edition series of Bicentennial souvenir sheets of 1976, whose unique and complex perforation patterns made them extremely unlikely candidates for counterfeiting.

USPS has given thought to using other novel perforating methods — perfs die-cut in unusual shapes, for instance — as a way to add a security element to all-offset stamps. Though it's still a live option, the idea hasn't yet been put into practice.

Meantime, however, USPS concluded that the tagging of stamps is a security factor in itself. Said Don McDowell, manager of the Stamps Division: "Working with the Inspection Service, we concluded offset plus prephosphored paper is secure enough, especially when an engraved die proof is used as a photographic model."

This was the case with the Official Mail non-denominated stamp. The design was engraved and a die proof photographed to make the offset plates. This process produced a much cleaner and crisper printing image than images produced by a conventional offset-litho plate.

The prephosphored paper used was a new type, developed for gravure and combination offset-intaglio issues, with the taggant included in the coating. It was different from the uncoated prephosphored paper used for the 1987 22¢ Flag Over the Capitol test coil.

With that paper, developed for intaglio-printed stamps, the taggant was added to the sizing. Test mailings with the 22¢ coil verified that the prephosphored paper gave a strong enough signal to be effective in automatic facer-cancelers.

USPS acknowledged that another factor in its decision to go all-offset this time was the nature of Official Mail stamps. They are distributed to and used by federal government agencies, not by private business or the public. Little reason exists for counterfeiting them.

The stamps were printed on BEP's six-color Goebel offset webfed press.

No plate numbers appear on the coils, in keeping with a policy for Official Mail stamps inaugurated in 1985. W.L. (Pete) Davidson, director of stamps and philatelic marketing for USPS, explained then the reason:

"Because Official stamps cannot be used by regular mailers and collectors, the Postal Service waived the minimum purchase requirements that usually apply. When collectors purchased plate blocks or plate number coils, a large amount of broken panes and coil strips resulted. Elimination of plate numbers ... represents an effort to reduce the waste and destruction caused by this situation."

USPS announced plans to issue the E Official Mail coil February 18, 1988. On March 24 — two days after the stamp was actually issued — an official news release, with details, was distributed. The stamps were available to collectors only from the Philatelic Sales Division in Washington by mail and over-the-counter at L'Enfant Plaza philatelic windows.

The Design

The basic Official Mail design unveiled in 1983 was the work of Bradbury Thompson of Riverside, Connecticut, who is a stamp design coordinator for the Citizens' Stamp Advisory Committee and designs the typography for most U.S. stamps.

The Official Mail E stamp resembles its 1985 predecessors, the Official Mail D stamps, except for the inscription below the vignette.

On the earlier stamps the inscriptions read "Postal Card Rate D" and "Domestic Letter Rate D" and were centered under the design. On the new one, the "E" was centered and prominent, in keeping with current USPS policy of enlarging the denomination. The words "Domestic Mail" appeared in smaller letters to the left, and the right was left blank. (Thus the word "Mail" was repeated in the design; it also appeared in the inscription "Official Mail USA" at the top.)

First-Day Facts

There was no first-day ceremony. Collectors could obtain Washington March 22 first-day cancellations by sending self-addressed envelopes, with 25¢ for each cover, to the postmaster in Washington. Because Official Mail stamps aren't available for sale in post offices or philatelic centers, affixing of the stamps in advance by customers wasn't permitted.

Envelopes or postcards that carry Official Mail stamps must have a U.S. Government return address. Customers were directed to place "U.S. Postal Service, Washington, D.C. 20066, Official Business" in three lines in the upper left corner of envelopes or postcards submitted for cancellation. This return address could be printed, typewritten, rubberstamped or incorporated on a gummed address label, but not written in longhand. Envelopes submitted in violation of these instructions were returned unserviced.

Because of the short notice on this stamp, first-day cover collectors were given 60 days, to May 21, rather than the customary 30 for sending their orders.

20¢ OFFICIAL MAIL (COIL)

Date of Issue: May 19, 1988

Catalog Numbers: Scott O138B   Minkus OF136   USPS 7712

Colors: red, blue, black

First-Day Cancel: Washington, D.C. (no first-day ceremony)

FDCs Canceled: 111,088

Format: Coils of 100. Printing plates of 450 subjects (18 across, 25 around).

Perf: 9.8 (Goebel coiler stroke perforator)

Designer and Typographer: Bradbury Thompson (CSAC)

Art Director and Project Manager: Joe Brockert (USPS)

Modeler: Ronald Sharpe (BEP)

Printing: 6-color Goebel offset Optiforma press (043)

Quantity Ordered: Coils of 100 - 300,000
Quantity Distributed: Coils of 100 - 277,600

Plate Number Detail: no plate number

Tagging: overall (phosphored paper)

The Stamp

A surprise addition to the 1988 stamp program was a new 20¢ Penalty Mail coil, issued May 19 in Washington.

"The Postal Service expected to release the stamp later in the year," explained a USPS news release dated May 19, "but opted for an earlier date to meet greater than anticipated demand for a 20¢ Official stamp. It will be used by government agencies for the second and subsequent ounces of first-class postage."

The Postal Service said the issue date wasn't announced in advance because of uncertainty as to the earliest date the stamps could be produced and distributed.

This wasn't the first 20¢ coil stamp to be issued in the current

Official Mail series. Such a stamp was included in the original set of seven, which appeared January 12, 1983, and represented the first-class letter rate that was then in effect. It hadn't been available from the Philatelic Sales Division, however, since August 31, 1985.

The new 20¢ coil differed from the old in three ways.

First, it was printed by offset-lithography rather than intaglio. The new policy of printing Official Mail stamps by offset on prephosphored paper began with the E (25¢) coil of March 22, 1988.

Second, the new stamp's denomination designation was a prominent "20" centered beneath the vignette. The old one bore the inscription "USA 20" in uniform-size letters and numerals.

Finally, the new 20¢ coil had no plate numbers. The old one bore a number on every 52nd stamp.

The new 20¢ was the first stamp in the Official Mail series of a rate other than the first-class letter rate to be issued as a coil. All previous miscellaneous-rate Officials had been produced in sheet form.

The stamp was printed on one of BEP's six-color Goebel offset webfed Optiforma press and produced in rolls of 100 stamps. The printing plates contained 450 subjects — 18 across by 25 around.

The Design

Except for the different denomination designation, the new stamp followed the standard design devised by Bradbury Thompson in 1982 — a portion of the Great Seal of the United States, reproduced in white with a blue background, and type in red and black.

Like the Official Mail E stamp, it was made by photographically reproducing an engraved die proof. The cross-hatching lines present on the original are visible on the background of the actual stamp.

First-Day Facts

As with all previous Official Mail stamps, no first-day ceremony was held. First-day cancellations were offered by mail, however, with the normal 30-day grace period extended to 60 because the stamp was issued without notice. To meet the first-class postage rate, collectors had a choice of a 5¢ Milk Wagon stamp of 1987 to be affixed alongside a single 20¢ coil, or a pair of 20¢ stamps. The cost was 25¢ and 40¢, respectively.

15¢ OFFICIAL MAIL (COIL)

Date of Issue: June 11, 1988

Catalog Numbers: Scott 0138A   Minkus OF137   USPS 7766

Colors: red, blue, black

First-Day Cancel: Corpus Christi, Texas (La Quinta Royale)

FDCs Canceled: 137,721 (together with 25¢ Official Mail coil)

Format: Coils of 100. Printing plates of 450 subjects (18 across, 25 around).

Perf: 9.8 (Goebel coiler stroke perforator)

Designer and Typographer: Bradbury Thompson (CSAC)

Art Director and Project Manager: Joe Brockert (USPS)

Modeler: Ronald Sharpe (BEP)

Printing: 6-color Goebel offset Optiforma press (043)

Quantity Ordered: Coils of 100 - 280,000
Quantity Distributed: Coils of 100 - 226,400

Plate Number Detail: no plate number

Tagging: overall (phosphored paper)

The Stamp

USPS issued its third and fourth Penalty Mail (Official Mail) stamps of 1988 on June 11 at the TEXPEX 88 stamp show in Corpus Christi, Texas.

The denominations were 15¢, to meet the current postcard rate, and 25¢, to meet the first-class letter rate. Both were coil stamps, sold in rolls of 100.

Issuance of the 15¢ stamp in coil form marked a continuation of a new policy by USPS, which had begun with the 20¢ Official Mail stamp issued May 19. Before that date, the only coil stamps in the series were those issued for the current first-class letter rate. All other denominations had been produced in sheets.

The new stamp, like the other Official Mail stamps issued this year, was printed in three-color offset-lithography on prephosphored paper.

The last time the postcard rate had changed — in 1985, from 13¢ to 14¢ — USPS issued a non-denominated Official Mail stamp inscribed "Postal Card Rate D" for use by government agencies until a 14¢ denominated version could be prepared. This time, however, no non-denominated E Official postcard-rate stamp was provided. USPS decided it could get by until denominated 15¢ Officials were printed because offset stamps could be produced more quickly than intaglio.

"For the 25¢ letter rate, we thought it would still be a good idea to prepare a non-denominated Official," said Joe Brockert, project manager-art director for all the 1988 Official Mail items. "But for future rate changes we may not bother with non-denominated Official Mail at all because offset saves us so much time."

On this occasion, from April 3, when the rate went to 15¢, until June 11, when the new Official Mail stamp in that denomination appeared, agencies sending postcards had to add 1-centers to their 14-centers to cover the postage.

The June 11 TEXPEX first-day ceremony originally had been reserved for the 25¢ Honeybee coil stamp, and it was so listed in USPS' April 4 announcement of 1988 stamp subjects, dates and sites. On April 21 it was announced that the Honeybee had been "deferred" and that the 15¢ Penalty Mail coil had been "placed in the June 11 slot in the schedule."

The Design

The design of the 15¢ Official Mail coil was identical to that of its 14¢ 1985 predecessor with one exception. Instead of a black line beneath the blue vignette containing a small "USA" and a larger "14," this one bore only the denomination "15" in that location. USPS had decided that use of "USA" here was redundant, since it also appeared in the red line at the top reading "Official Mail USA."

First-Day Facts

With the issuance of the 15¢ and 25¢ Official Mail stamps, USPS broke precedent. It held the first first-day ceremony in the five-year history of the series.

Because there was a first-day ceremony, collectors who were present were allowed to affix their own stamps to covers and have them canceled on a hand-back basis. Normally, with Official Mail stamps, self-stamping of covers isn't permitted because the stamps aren't available for sale at post offices or philatelic centers outside of USPS headquarters in Washington.

25¢ OFFICIAL MAIL (COIL)

Date of Issue: June 11, 1988

Catalog Numbers: Scott O141   Minkus OF138   USPS 7760

Colors: red, blue, black

First-Day Cancel: Corpus Christi, Texas (La Quinta Royale)

FDCs Canceled: 137,721 (together with 15¢ Official Mail coil)

Format: Coils of 100. Printing plates of 450 subjects (18 across, 25 around).

Perf: 9.8 (Goebel coiler stroke perforator)

Designer and Typographer: Bradbury Thompson (CSAC)

Art Director and Project Manager: Joe Brockert (USPS)

Modeler: Ronald Sharpe (BEP)

Printing: 6-color Goebel offset Optiforma press (043)

Quantity Ordered: Coils of 100 - 900,000
Quantity Distributed: Coils of 100 - 307,600

Plate Number Detail: no plate number

Tagging: overall (phosphored paper)

The Stamp

The 25¢ Official Mail stamp, a coil, was issued to meet the first-class rate that had been covered since April 3 by the Official Mail non-denominated E stamp. Along with the 15¢ Official, it was issued June 11 at the TEXPEX 88 stamp show in Corpus Christi, Texas.

Like all other Official Mail stamps issued in 1988, it was printed in three-color offset-lithography on prephosphored paper.

The Design

The design of the 25¢ Official Mail coil was identical to that of its

22¢ 1985 predecessor with one exception. Instead of a black line beneath the blue vignette containing a small "USA" and a larger "22," this one bore only the denomination "25" in that location. (The 15¢ Official, issued at the same time and place, differed in the same way from the 14¢ stamp it replaced.)

First-Day Facts

A description of the first-day ceremony at Corpus Christi can be found in the chapter on the 15¢ Official Mail stamp.

Because there was a first-day ceremony, collectors who were present were allowed to affix their own stamps to covers and have them canceled on a hand-back basis. Normally with Official Mail stamps, self-stamping of covers isn't permitted because the stamps aren't available for sale at post offices or philatelic centers outside of USPS headquarters in Washington.

The old rules continued to apply with mail-order requests for first-day covers of the two new stamps. USPS required the customary self-addressed envelopes with a USPS return address at upper left. Combination covers, containing both the 15¢ and 25¢ stamps, were available at face value, 40¢.

$10 MIGRATORY BIRD HUNTING (DUCK) STAMP

Date of Issue: July 1, 1988

Catalog Numbers: Scott RW55   Minkus RH55   USPS 3319

Colors: magenta, yellow, cyan, black (offset); black (intaglio); black (flexography)

First-Day Cancel: Eden Prairie, Minnesota (Vantage Company Building) and Smithsonian Institution (National Museum of American History)

FDCs Canceled: 3,500 (1,750 souvenir cards canceled twice each), 200 invitations (Eden Prairie), 300 programs (Washington, D.C.)

Format: Panes of 30, horizontal, 5 across, 10 down. Offset printing plates of 120 subjects (10 across, 12 around); intaglio sleeve of 240 subjects (10 across, 24 around); flexographic back plates of 120 subjects (10 across, 12 around).

Perf: 11.2 by 11.1 (Eureka off-line perforator)

Selvage Markings: sleeve number

Designer: Daniel Smith of Eden Prairie, Minnesota

Coordinator Federal Duck Stamp Program: Norma Opgrand (Fish and Wildlife Service)

Typographer and Modeler: Frank Waslick (BEP)

Engravers: Thomas Hipschen (BEP, vignette)
Gary Slaght (BEP, lettering and numerals)

Printing: 6-color offset, 3-color intaglio D press (902)

Quantity Ordered: 4,000,000
Quantity Distributed: 3,981,000

Sleeve Number Detail: one intaglio sleeve number at pane corners.

Sleeve number: 180059

Tagging: untagged

The Stamp

A lesser snow goose flying alone over a marsh at dawn was the subject of the 1988 migratory bird hunting and conservation stamp issued by the Fish and Wildlife Service of the U.S. Department of the Interior. The design was based on a painting by Daniel Smith of Eden Prairie, Minnesota, who won the artists' competition held for this purpose.

The 1988 stamp was the 55th in an unbroken annual series. Every waterfowl hunter is required to buy a current duck stamp and affix it to his hunting license. Proceeds are used to buy prime wetland habitat for the National Wildlife Refuge System. Since the first duck stamp appeared in 1934, more than $315 million has been raised, and nearly four million acres of wetlands have been purchased.

The 1988 stamp, like the 1987 version, cost $10, and its sale was expected to raise some $20 million. That sum will increase in future years, however. Under terms of the Emergency Wetlands Resources Act signed into law in 1986, the price of the duck stamp was to mount to $12.50 in 1989 and to $15 in 1991.

Duck stamps — classified as revenues rather than postage stamps — are popular with stamp collectors because of their beauty. For the convenience of hunters and collectors alike, USPS sells the stamps at many post offices and philatelic centers and by mail through the Philatelic Sales Division.

The annual duck stamp design contest has become a major media event as the stakes involved have skyrocketed.

Although the winner each year gets no direct cash prize, his victory is worth at least a million dollars in income to him. This is because he retains reproduction rights to the art used on the duck stamp. Limited-edition prints of each year's winning painting have become cherished collectibles in their own right and are eagerly purchased by hunters, conservationists and other admirers of wildlife art.

In 1988, according to *The Washington Post,* Daniel Smith's bank account stood to be enhanced by the proceeds from 22,000 limited-edition prints signed by the artist, costing $135 each; another 6,500 prints accompanied by a small medal resembling the stamp ($250 each), and up to 750 prints with a solid gold medallion ($1,800).

Smith's painting won out over 842 other entries in the judging of the 1988 competition, held at the Interior Department November 7 and 8, 1987. In an unusual one-state sweep, two other Minnesotans, James Meger and James Hautman, placed second and third.

Waterfowl have been shown on the stamps since 1934, when J.N. "Ding" Darling, Pulitzer Prize-winning editorial cartoonist for *The Des Moines Register,* did a pen-and-ink drawing of landing mallards that was adapted for the very first duck stamp (face value $1). In the first few years, an artist was selected each year to design the stamp, but since 1949 the choice has been made through competition — the only regular art contest sponsored by the federal government.

During the more than half a century of the duck stamp program, artists were generally free to choose their own type of waterfowl to paint, and there have been several multiple appearances of species on the stamps. The 1988 snow goose was a species that had appeared once before, in the painting by Jack Murray for the 1947 stamp.

In 1988, however, the Fish and Wildlife Service announced that artists competing for the 1989 design award would have to choose among five specific kinds of North American waterfowl: black-bellied whistling duck, lesser scaup, spectacled eider, Barrow's goldeneye and red-breasted merganser.

These, the Service explained, were among nine species that had never before appeared on a federal duck stamp. An attempt was made to select a combination of species whose collective ranges cover the contiguous United States and Alaska.

Under the plan, as succeeding years go by, the list of species from which artists can choose will shrink. Finally, in the competition for the 1997 duck stamp design, all entrants will be painting only one species. When this stamp is issued, all 42 species of North American waterfowl will have been represented in the duck stamp series.

The Fish and Wildlife Service also changed the deadline for entries in the annual contest from October 1 to September 15 to allow more time to process the 90 percent of entries that are customarily received in the final week. Also, procedures for dealing with tie votes among the judges, previously applicable to first place only, were extended to second and third places.

In recent years, state governments have discovered duck stamps as an effective way of raising funds for conservation. Most states, like the federal government, issue the stamps annually, require hunters to purchase them, and commission first-rate wildlife artists to prepare original artwork. Collectors have discovered state duck stamps, and have made them one of the hottest areas of contemporary philately.

California, in 1971, was the first state to issue a federal-type duck stamp. As of the end of 1988, 43 of the 50 states now issue or have issued state duck hunting stamps, and a 44th, Louisiana, was scheduled to begin in 1989.

The Design

Daniel Smith's winning acrylic showed the lesser snow goose from below and to the side, low over water at the downstroke of the black-tipped wings.

Smith told *The Washington Post* he had entered "realistic" waterfowl views in the competition every year since 1980 without winning, although he had finished in the top five in six of those years.

He said the "soft and romantic" snow goose painting that finally changed his luck was "not your typical duck stamp" and that he had

Daniel Smith's snow goose painting that graced the 1988 duck stamp.

hurriedly painted it as "a last-ditch effort."

"They say that if you can hit the finals it's just a matter of time before you get the right panel of judges and win," Smith said.

Smith, a native of Mankato, Minnesota, was 33 when he won the contest. He spent eight years in the commerical art field as an illustrator before devoting his life full-time to wildlife art.

He designed the first Alaska and Georgia state duck stamps in 1985, becoming the first artist to win two first-of-state competitions in the same year. He designed two other first-of-state duck stamps in 1987 — for Arizona and West Virginia — and in between produced the 1986 South Carolina duck stamp. These five stamps depicted, respectively, a trio of emperor geese, a pair of wood ducks, a pair of pintails, a pair of Canada geese and a pair of canvasbacks. His credits also include New Mexico's first turkey stamp.

First-Day Facts

July 1, the duck stamp's first day of issue, was observed in varying ways in two communities: artist Daniel Smith's hometown of Eden Prairie, Minnesota, and Washington, D.C.

USPS provided a July 1 cancellation in Washington. It depicted a swimming duck with the date "July 1, 1988" above it at the left and a three-line inscription flush left below it: "Duck Stamp Station/National Museum of American History/Washington, D.C., 20560."

Because this information wasn't announced in advance, USPS made the cancellation available from the Washington postmaster until September 2. Collectors could obtain it by sending an addressed cover with a duck stamp and a 25¢ postage stamp affixed.

USPS also permitted other post offices to apply standard circular July 1 cancellations on a hand-back basis. These covers, too, had to bear a 25¢ postage stamp next to the duck stamp in order to receive the cancellation.

1988 MIGRATORY WATERFOWL SOUVENIR CARD

Date of Issue: October 1988

Catalog Number: BEP 451

First-Day Release: Washington, D.C. (BEP Visitor's Center)

Colors: yellow, magenta, cyan, black (offset); gold foil (letterpress)

Size: 10 by 8 inches

Stamp Design: Daniel Smith

Card Design and Modeler: Frank Waslick (BEP)

Printing: 6-color Miller offset press; foil stamping in gold on Kluge letterpress

Quantity Produced: 10,000

Paper: Crane artificial parchment card stock

The Card

For the second consecutive year, the National Fish and Wildlife Foundation, a non-profit organization that supports wildlife conservation projects, sponsored a duck stamp souvenir card to help fund its programs. The card, printed by BEP, bore a replica of the 1988 duck stamp design, done in four-color offset. A specimen of the actual stamp itself was affixed to each card.

Of the 10,000 cards printed, 1,750 bore two first-day-of-sale USPS cancellations. The first cancellation, from Eden Prairie, Minnesota, home of the designer of the 1988 stamp, Daniel Smith, read "Snow Goose Station." A second cancellation, "Duck Stamp Station," was made at the Headsville Post Office, part of the Smithsonian Institution's National Museum of American History in Washington.

The first 750 cards were numbered in gold. Numbers 1-10 sold for $150; numbers 11-100, for $75, and numbers 101-750 sold for $50. One thousand unnumbered cards with the two cancellations sold for $25 each. The remaining 8,250 cards were uncanceled and sold for $18 apiece.

Ten dollars from the sale of each souvenir card covered the face value of the affixed stamp and went to the Migratory Bird Conservation Fund. The remaining money went to the National Fish and Wildlife Foundation.

According to Norma Opgrand, coordinator of the federal duck stamp program, only cards numbered 201 and up plus the unnumbered cards were available at the two first-day ceremonies. Cards numbered 1-200 were reserved until September 30 for those who bought the 1987 souvenir card.

Cards originally were available by mail from the foundation in care of the U.S. Department of the Interior. Buyers were instructed to submit a written request for card numbers and quantities desired with their remittance.

Later BEP also sold the uncanceled cards, each with a specimen of the duck stamp, at its visitor center for $18 or by mail for $19.50.

STAMPED ENVELOPES

The year 1988 saw issuance of eight varieties of stamped envelopes and one aerogramme. Two of the envelope varieties would be considered such only by specialists, but they were afforded special first-day cancellation treatment by USPS anyhow. One of these was a new double-window format for a first-class mail definitive envelope that was already available in four different formats. The other was a Penalty Mail envelope for savings bond mailings, reissued with a promotional imprint on the back flap.

There were, however, two major new developments in stamped envelope production during the year.

The denomination figure was removed from the embossed design area and printed by flexography. That meant that if a rate-change item or other kind of envelope was needed in a hurry, the supplier — Westvaco USEnvelope Division — could manufacture it quickly, using a neutral indicium that had been embossed in advance.

Also, USPS issued its first envelope for general use of a size other than the standard No. 6¾ and No. 10. This was the Snowflake envelope for holiday mailings — which, in itself, represented another first; there had been no previous stationery equivalent of the annual Christmas stamps.

Issuance of the odd-size envelope was made possible by a USPS request, approved by the Postal Rate Commission in March 1988, that it be allowed to sell stationery in sizes between 6¾ and 10. When USPS was established in 1971, its rules limited envelope production to just the two sizes, according to Assistant Postmaster General Gordon Morison.

The old Post Office Department had issued envelopes in a variety of colors and sizes until World War II, when because of paper shortages it shrank its envelope line, Morison said.

E OFFICIAL MAIL SAVINGS BOND ENVELOPE

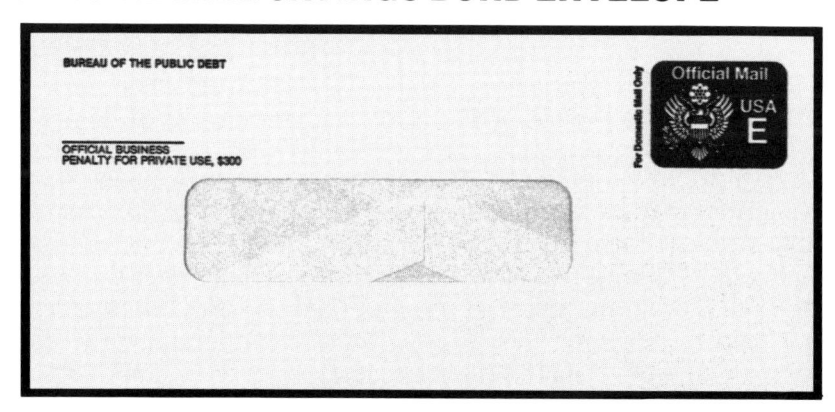

Date of Issue: March 22, 1988

Catalog Numbers: Scott UO76   Minkus PDEN76   USPS 117

Colors: blue, black

First-Day Cancel: Washington, D.C. (no first-day ceremony)

FDCs Canceled: 363,639 (includes all E stamps)

Size: 7 15/16 by 3 9/16 inches, with window

Watermark: none

Markings: ©USPS 1982 under flap. Bureau of Public Debt and penalty notation at upper left side.

Designer: Bradbury Thompson (CSAC)

Art Director: Joe Brockert (USPS)

Printing: Westvaco-USEnvelope Division in 2-color flexography on a VH machine.

Quantity Ordered: 2,403,500
Quantity Distributed: 2,403,500

Tagging: vertical bar to left of stamp

The Envelope

The first of three face-different stamped envelopes for official use to meet the new 25¢ first-class rate was the Penalty Mail E envelope specifically made for mailing U.S. savings bonds. It was issued March 22 in Washington.

"Penalty Mail" is the term USPS now uses, although both the Post Office and collectors have called the category "Official Mail" for more than a century — and "Official Mail" continues to be inscribed on current issues.

For regular Penalty Mail, no E envelope was issued. A denominated 25¢ envelope was provided on April 11 for this purpose.

An E Savings Bond envelope was prepared, however, USPS explained, because the rate increase took place at a time when the Treasury Department was scheduled to make a large mailing of bonds. The bond-by-mail program was growing rapidly, and the Postal Service concluded that it couldn't risk being short of envelopes when the rate changed. "The E envelope averted customer complaints about late receipt of bonds," said Jack Williams of USPS.

The Savings Bond E envelope made its appearance at the same time as the regular E stamp in sheet, coil and booklet form and the Penalty Mail E coil stamp. USPS didn't get around to announcing the details about these items — including their date of issue — until two days after that date.

The envelope replaced the 22¢ Penalty Mail Savings Bond envelope issued March 2, 1987.

The purpose of these envelopes was to improve the accuracy of postal cost accounting. Previously, savings bonds had been mailed in envelopes without imprinted stamps, but bearing the inscription "Penalty for Private Use $300" in the upper right corner.

The Design

The design of the E envelope indicium, like that of previous Official Mail envelopes, featured the eagle from the Great Seal of the United States, dropped out of a blue background. Design and typography are credited to Bradbury Thompson, a design coordinator for the Citizens' Stamp Advisory Committee.

The E envelope was like its predecessor, the 22¢ Savings Bond envelope — but unlike the great majority of other U.S. stamped envelopes — in one important respect. Its indicium, instead of being embossed, was printed by the process called flexography.

The reason lay in the envelope's unusual size, which — along with its window placement — was tailored to the dimensions of savings bonds. Measuring 7 15/16 by 3 9/16 inches, it fell between the standard No. 6¾ and 10 sizes.

The envelope was printed by Westvaco USEnvelope Division of Williamsburg, Pennsylvania, on its VH envelope-forming machine. The machine can emboss only standard-size envelopes, however, so Westvaco was obliged to use "flexo" plates for the Savings Bond job.

Embossing of stamped envelopes is considered an anti-counterfeiting device. However, with these items, which are bought and used only for the mailing of savings bonds by authorized agents, the threat of counterfeiting was considered virtually non-existent.

First-Day Facts

Like other Penalty Mail material, the Savings Bond envelope wasn't sold in post offices or at philatelic centers other than the center at USPS headquarters in Washington. It was obtainable by mail from the Philatelic Sales Division. There was no first-day ceremony.

Possibly because of the large number of non-denominated items that were issued the same day — the E stamp sheet, coil and booklet, the E Penalty Mail coil stamp and the E Savings Bond envelope all appeared March 22 — USPS got its ordering instructions somewhat garbled. The original March 24 news release for the two penalty items gave no first-day cover ordering information for the Savings Bond envelope, announced instead that "canceled versions" of the envelope could be ordered from the Philatelic Sales Division or bought over the counter at USPS headquarters, and left the impression that mint Penalty Mail stamps and Savings Bond envelopes would be available only until May 21 (which was actually only the first-day cover deadline).

The Postal Service corrected these omissions and misconceptions in an April 4 release.

25¢ STARS STAMPED, EMBOSSED ENVELOPE

Date of Issue: March 26, 1988

Catalog Numbers: Scott U611   Minkus EN911   USPS 2651 6¾ plain
USPS 2652 6¾ window
USPS 2151 10 plain
USPS 2152 10 window

Colors: blue, red

First-Day Cancel: Star, Mississippi (no first-day ceremony)

FDCs Canceled: 29,393

Size: 6¾ and 10, each with and without window

Watermark: combinations of "USA" and a star (See introduction)

Markings: ©USPS 1988 under flap

Designer and Art Director: Joe Brockert (USPS)

Printing: Westvaco-USEnvelope Division in 2-color flexography and embossing on a VH machine

Quantity Ordered: 6¾ plain - 105,624,000   10 plain - 224,092,500
6¾ window - 78,900,500   10 window - 95,507,500
Quantity Distributed: 6¾ plain - 105,624,000   10 plain - 224,092,500
6¾ window - 78,900,500   10 window - 95,507,500

Tagging: rectangle above denomination

The Envelope

To meet the 1988 rate change, USPS issued an undenominated stamp — the E stamp — for first-class domestic mail, just as it had done for rate changes in 1978, 1980, 1981 and 1985. However, this time USPS issued no corresponding non-denominated stamped envelope. In fact, more than a week before the new 25¢ first-class rate went into effect April 3, the Postal Service had a new 25¢ envelope ready and waiting.

How had it been done?

The answer was, through a simple but fundamental change in envelope design and printing policy. The denomination was taken out of the embossed stamp area and printed by a flexographic plate.

Because of this change, the envelope manufacturer, Westvaco (U.S. Envelope Division) of Williamsburg, Pennsylvania, was able to prepare the embossed indicium for the new envelope long before the USPS Board of Governors took final action approving the 25¢ first-class rate. As soon as the rate was fixed, the flexo plate with the numbers "25" was prepared.

"It took three days," said Joe Brockert, program manager for philatelic design for USPS and the man credited with designing the new envelope. "If the manufacturer had had to engrave a die containing the denomination, it would have taken three weeks, and we would have had to issue a non-denominated envelope."

Brockert said USPS would probably follow the same practice with all envelope designs thereafter because of the speed and economy with which denominations could be changed.

Before the decision was made to design the new envelope in this fashion, some sketches were made for an E stamped envelope. Bradbury Thompson, design coordinator for CSAC, based these sketches on his design for the cover of the E booklet stamps, picturing an outline globe with lines of latitude and longitude.

One version had a map of the 48 contiguous U.S. states superimposed on the globe. The map version probably wouldn't have been used even if an E envelope had been ordered, Brockert said, because for reasons of scale it omitted Alaska and Hawaii.

The 25¢ envelope was announced March 25 and issued the next day in Star, Mississippi, a tiny town southeast of Jackson, chosen because the envelope's design featured a circle of 13 stars.

Postal stationery collectors noted that this was the first new face-different first-class envelope USPS had issued in 37 months — since, in fact, the last rate change had produced the 22¢ Bison envelope February 25, 1985. No commemorative envelopes had appeared during that period.

Like the Bison envelope, the 25¢ Stars was manufactured in No. 6¾ and No. 10 sizes, with and without window, making four different combinations. It was bar-tagged, rather than having phosphorescent material added to the printing ink of the embossed design. (That change had been made on the Bison envelope beginning in May 1986.)

As with previous Westvaco envelopes, paper from three different

This design for an embossed "E" indicium was prepared, but no such envelope was issued.

manufacturers was used, watermarked with three different combinations of "USA" and star. The Philatelic Sales Division sold packs of 12 envelopes containing each of the three watermark varieties for each of the four different envelopes.

Individual envelopes sold for 30¢ each. Boxes of 500 cost from $131.40 for No. 6¾ plain to $134 for No. 10 window.

The Design

Joe Brockert sketched the elements, which Bradbury Thompson, art director and typographer, made into a finished design. The embossed area is a blue square with rounded corners. Thirteen white stars, representing the original 13 states, encircle the letters "USA," giving the envelope a subtle Constitution bicentennial motif. The flexo-printed numerals "25" appear in red to the left.

The design is reminiscent of Peter Cocci's 6¢ booklet stamp design of 1981, on which the stars circled the denomination "6c" on a blue square and the letters "USA" appeared in red beneath. Both designs are patterned after the blue field of the famous 1777 American flag.

Brockert had previously designed several USPS souvenir cards, and had rough-sketched the flag indicium for the 14¢ postal card of 1987. He admitted he wasn't an artist, but said he was comfortable with the task of arranging elements of design. Before joining USPS, Brockert had been a senior editor of *Linn's Stamp News*.

The Stars envelope was printed on Westvaco's VH machine, named after its inventor, Vincent E. Heywood. The VH machine is capable of

Another essay for an unissued "E" envelope incorporated a map of the "Lower 48" states.

printing, embossing, knifing, cutting windows, applying window overlays, and gumming and drying the envelopes before folding them.

The same flexo plate used for the denomination also printed the USPS copyright notation on the back of the envelope. Because the denomination was in red, so was the copyright.

The use of flexo plates in conjunction with embossing wasn't without its problems. On normal specimens of the envelope, the red "25" was approximately five millimeters to the left of the blue indicium, and was centered on a line with the embossed white "USA." Improp-

On this envelope the flexographed "25" has drifted into the embossed indicium.

er adjustment of the cylinder to which the plate was attached could — and did — cause the alignment of the two parts to vary sideways or up and down, sometimes to a considerable degree. On one misaligned example, the denomination had drifted so far to the right that the "5" overlapped the indicium.

First-Day Facts

There was no first-day ceremony at Star, Mississippi, but first-day postmarks were provided.

Cover collectors were given two months, until May 25, to mail in their own self-addressed envelopes for the first-day cancellation, or send peelable return address labels and 30¢ per envelope for USPS-furnished covers.

25¢ OFFICIAL MAIL ENVELOPE

Date of Issue: April 11, 1988

Catalog Numbers: Scott UO77   Minkus PDEN77   USPS 2110 10 plain
                                                  USPS 2112 10 window

Colors: blue, black

First-Day Cancel: Washington, D.C. (no first-day ceremony)

FDCs Canceled: 12,017 (together with 25¢ Savings Bond envelope)

Size: 10 only, with and without window

Watermark: Combinations of "USA" and a star (See introduction)

Markings: ©USPS 1988 under flap. Penalty notation at upper left corner.

Designer: Bradbury Thompson (CSAC) of Riverside, Connecticut

Art Director: Joe Brockert (USPS)

Printing: Westvaco-USEnvelope Division in 2-color flexography and embossing on a VH machine.

Quantity Ordered: 10 plain - 5,803,000
                     10 window - 1,271,000
Quantity Distributed: 10 plain - 5,803,000
                          10 window - 1,271,000

Tagging: rectangle to left of lettering and denomination

The Envelope

On April 11, eight days after the rate changes, USPS issued a 25¢ Penalty Mail envelope for first-class mailings by federal agencies.

The envelopes were manufactured by USPS' regular supplier, Westvaco (U.S. Envelope Division), on the VH envelope-forming machine at its Williamsburg, Pennsylvania, plant. They were produced in the No. 10 size only and came with or without window, and in Westvaco's three different varieties of watermark.

Stamp collectors could obtain envelopes only from the Philatelic Sales Division of USPS, by mail or over the counter at its center in the lobby of USPS headquarters in Washington, D.C.

The Design

The envelope's embossed design is the same eagle from the Great Seal of the United States used for previous Official Mail envelopes, dropped out of a blue background.

However, the inscription "Official/Mail/25/USA" was removed from the image area and printed to the left by a flexographic plate in black. This followed the practice, inaugurated 16 days earlier with the 25¢ regular first-class mail envelope, of separating the denomination from the embossed image so the envelope manufacturer could respond quickly to a rate-change order.

The black color for the denomination was dictated by the color used for the penalty inscription near the left edge of the envelope, which was printed from the same flexo plate. This inscription read: "Official Business/Penalty for Private Use, $300."

"We might have liked to use red," said Joe Brockert, art director for the envelope, "but the penalty inscription would have had to be red, too. The agency mailers who use the envelope told us that the inscription had to look official and businesslike — meaning black."

The "© USPS 1988" copyright marking, also printed in black by flexography, appeared on the back of the envelope.

The designer and typographer was Bradbury Thompson of Riverside, Connecticut, a design coordinator for CSAC, who has been responsible for all the modern Official Mail issues.

First-Day Facts

Because the envelope couldn't be purchased at post offices, and had to bear an official return address, collectors wishing first-day covers were instructed to send their remittance to the Postmaster, Washington, D.C., along with peelable return address labels, and mail the orders no later than June 9, 1988. USPS then added the official government return address that is required on Official Mail, affixed the customer's label and applied the cancellation.

One collector, Todd M. Cralley of Tampa, Florida, submitted to *Linn's* a first-day cover of the Penalty Mail 25¢ envelope bearing the March 22 first-day cancellation used for the Penalty Mail E envelope for savings bonds rather than the correct April 11 first-day cancellation. Cralley said he had purchased several copies of both envelopes through the Philatelic Sales Division and had sent them to Washington for first-day servicing, despite official instructions to the contrary. All came back postmarked — but all bore the March 22 marking.

Such mistakes turn up whenever designs are similar and dates of issue close together.

25¢ OFFICIAL MAIL SAVINGS BOND ENVELOPE

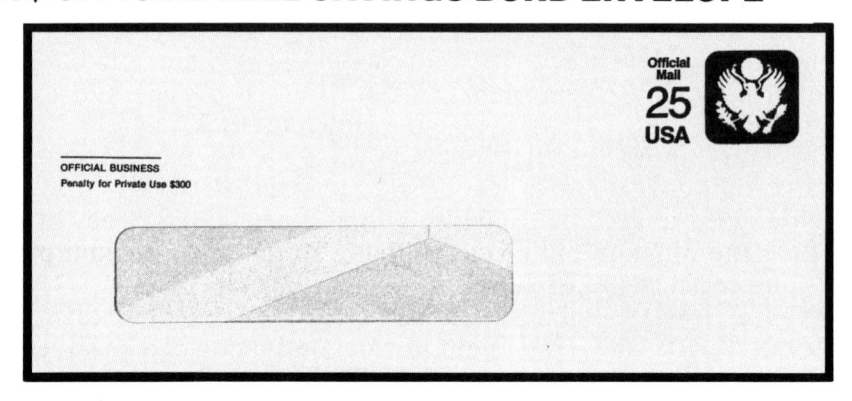

Date of Issue: April 11, 1988

Catalog Numbers: Scott UO78　　Minkus PDEN78　　USPS 2115

Colors: blue, black

First-Day Cancel: Washington, D.C. (no first-day ceremony)

FDCs Canceled: 12,017 (together with 25¢ Official Mail envelope)

Size: 7 15/16 by 3 9/16 inches, with window

Watermark: none

Markings: ©USPS 1988 under flap. Bureau of Public Debt and penalty notation at upper left corner.

Designer: Bradbury Thompson (CSAC)

Art Director: Joe Brockert (USPS)

Printing: Westvaco-USEnvelope Division in 2-color flexography on a VH machine.

Quantity Ordered: 1,379,500
Quantity Distributed: 1,379,500

Tagging: rectangle to left of lettering and denomination

The Envelope

On April 11, only 20 days after the appearance of the non-denominated Penalty Mail Savings Bond envelope that bore an E to represent its 25¢ face value, it was replaced by a 25¢ denominated version. On the same day, USPS issued its regular 25¢ Penalty Mail envelope for general use by government agencies.

The Design

The indicium incorporated an image based on the Great Seal of the

United States that had been used on the E envelope and also on the first of the Savings Bond envelopes, the 22¢ denominated issue of 1987. And, like those two, this one had a design area printed in blue.

The new envelope was different, however, in that the indicium had its inscriptions ("Official/Mail/25/USA") placed outside and to the left of the Great Seal design area, and printed in black.

The same design arrangement was used on the new 25¢ regular Penalty Mail envelope that was issued the same day. Both envelopes were designed in accordance with the brand-new USPS policy of lifting the denomination out of the indicium so that the indicium printing plates could be prepared well in advance of a rate change.

On most regular mail and Penalty Mail envelopes, the indicium is embossed. Under the new system, the denomination can be added by swift and efficient flexography at virtually the last minute.

In the case of the Savings Bond envelope, however, the design change was of no particular advantage. The reason: Because it was an odd size, this envelope had to be printed entirely by flexography, with no embossing. Therefore, the denomination could just as easily have been included in the indicium (in the same way that the E designation was included in the indicium of the non-denominated version issued March 22).

In a cut square, the indicium of the Savings Bond envelope is distinguishable from that of its companion Penalty Mail envelope because the Great Seal detail lines are imprinted in blue rather than embossed on a white dropout silhouette.

In the form of an entire, the Savings Bond envelope is easily distinguishable. It is of the size unique to its category, 3 9/16 inches deep by 7 15/16 inches long, and is printed in the window version only. Like the regular Penalty Mail envelope, it bears the words "Official Business/Penalty for Private Use, $300," near the left edge and "© USPS 1988" on the back; but it also has the words "Bureau of Public Debt" in the upper left corner.

The designer and typographer, as with all Penalty Mail stamps and stationery, was Bradbury Thompson.

First-Day Facts

There was no first-day ceremony. Because the envelopes could not be purchased at post offices, and had to bear an official return address, collectors of first-day covers were required to send peelable return address labels and remittance, at 30¢ per envelope, to the postmaster in Washington. USPS then added the official government return address, affixed the customer's labels and canceled the envelopes. Collectors were given two months, until June 9, to submit orders.

Mint envelopes could be purchased over the counter only at the Philatelic Center at USPS headquarters, or by mail from the Philatelic Sales Division.

8.4¢ CONSTELLATION NONPROFIT ENVELOPE

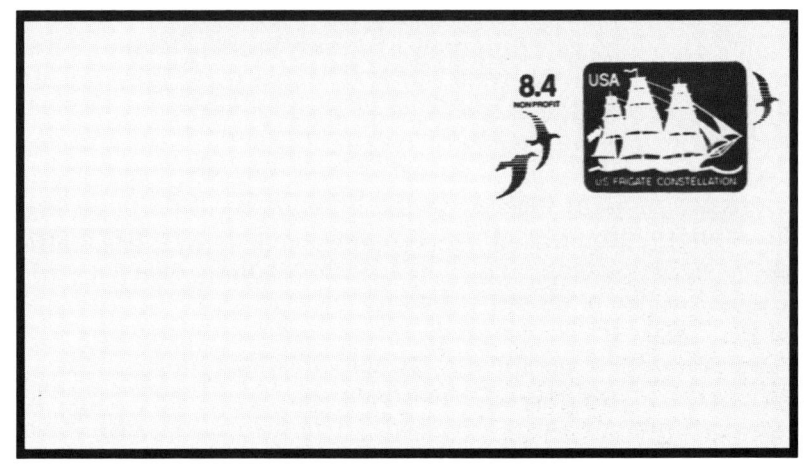

Date of Issue: April 12, 1988

Catalog Numbers: Scott U612   Minkus EN912   USPS 2666 6¾ plain
USPS 2667 6¾ window
USPS 2166 10 plain
USPS 2167 10 window

Colors: blue, gray

First-Day Cancel: Baltimore, Maryland (no first-day ceremony)

FDCs Canceled: 41,420

Size: 6¾ and 10, each with and without windows

Watermark: combinations of "USA" and a star (See introduction)

Markings: ©USPS 1988 under flap. Denomination and nonprofit notation to left of stamp design. Precancel design to left and right of stamp.

Designer: Jerry Dadds of Baltimore, Maryland

Art Director: Joe Brockert (USPS)

Modeler: Richard W. Salois (Westvaco-USEnvelope Division)

Printing: Westvaco-USEnvelope Division in 2-color flexography and embossing on a VH machine

Quantity Ordered: 6¾ plain - 2,480,500   10 plain - 3,825,500
                       6¾ window - 1,057,000   10 window - 1,634,000
Quantity Distributed: 6¾ plain - 2,480,500   10 plain - 3,825,500
                          6¾ window - 0   10 window - 1,634,000

Tagging: untagged

The Envelope

The new rate for non-profit bulk third-class mail that went into effect April 3 was reduced one-tenth of a cent from the old one. Accordingly, a new 8.4¢ stamped envelope was needed to replace the 8.5¢ *Mayflower* envelope of 1986.

The new item was provided quickly, thanks to the time-saving procedure of printing the denomination by flexography outside of the embossed stamped area — a procedure USPS had first used a few days earlier with its 25¢ Circle of Stars envelope for first-class mail.

On April 12 the new envelope was issued. It had been officially announced only five days earlier. It bore a silhouette of the historic Navy frigate *Constellation*, and had first-day sale in Baltimore, Maryland, where the ship is permanently anchored.

The envelope was precanceled, in the same unconventional way the *Mayflower* envelope had been, with the precancel incorporated into the overall design. This one consisted of three stylized gulls printed in dark gray outside the light blue embossed area.

CSAC began its practice of using famous sailing ships on non-profit envelopes with the 6¢ *U.S.S. Constitution* (Old Ironsides) envelope of 1985. The new envelope marked the *Constellation's* second postal appearance; the ship was shown on a 6¢ Tourism Year of the Americas postal card in 1972.

The 36-gun *Constellation* was launched in Baltimore September 7, 1797, and shortly afterward became the first commissioned ship in the U.S. Navy. During the undeclared war between France and the United States in 1799-1800, she captured the French frigate *L'Insurgente* off Nevis in the West Indies, and damaged the *Vengeance*. Thomas Truxtun, who had supervised the construction of the *Constellation*, commanded the ship and became a hero with his victories.

The *Constellation* battled the Barbary pirates in Algeria, was bottled up in port by the British blockade in the War of 1812 and served in the Civil War. She continued in support duties until 1912. In 1940, at President Franklin D. Roosevelt's suggestion, she was recommissioned as flagship of the commander-in-chief of the Atlantic fleet.

Finally, in 1955, she was decommissioned for the last time and sold to the Star Spangled Banner House Association of Baltimore. There she was thoroughly rebuilt. A $1.5 million repair job in 1979 left her with an estimated 30 percent of her original wood.

The ship is now a tourist attraction in Baltimore's popular Inner Harbor, and was designated a national historic landmark in 1964.

Mailers could obtain the *Constellation* envelope in either the No. 6¾ or No. 10 size, with or without windows. The envelopes sold for 14¢ each, or 500 for $48.40 to $51, depending on size and whether plain or window was desired.

For collectors, the customary three watermarks used by the manufacturer, Westvaco (U.S. Envelope Division), were available. The

Philatelic Sales Division made available packs of 12 envelopes, one of each possible watermark and window/non-window combination.

Like previous non-profit envelopes, this one was untagged.

The Design

The designer and typographer was Jerry Dadds of Baltimore, who had previously designed the four Presidential miniature sheets issued in 1986 to commemorate AMERIPEX.

Dadds offered CSAC several different treatments of the *Constellation*. He also provided several different kinds of precancel design: gulls, clouds, stripes and waves. The CSAC opted for a view of the

Jerry Dadds prepared several different indicium designs, with various precancel devices: clouds, waves, and stars and stripes.

ship sailing to the right under full sail, with the gull precancel.

Dadds' design showed embossed waves running out both sides of the stamp area. Embossing to the edge presents technical problems for the manufacturer, however, so Richard W. Salois, who modeled the envelope for Westvaco, added a narrow border to the indicium.

The "8.4 NONPROFIT" denomination and service inscription were located outside the embossed area and were printed in dark gray by the same "flexo" plate that printed the gulls precancel and the USPS 1988 copyright symbol.

First-Day Facts

There was no first-day ceremony for the *Constellation* envelope, but first-day cancellations were offered. Because short notice was given, collectors were afforded extra time, to June 11, to request first-day covers. The original Postal Service announcement incorrectly gave a July 8 deadline.

An extra 16.6¢ postage was required for each cover to make up the 25¢ first-class rate.

25¢ STARS STAMPED EMBOSSED ENVELOPE, DOUBLE WINDOW

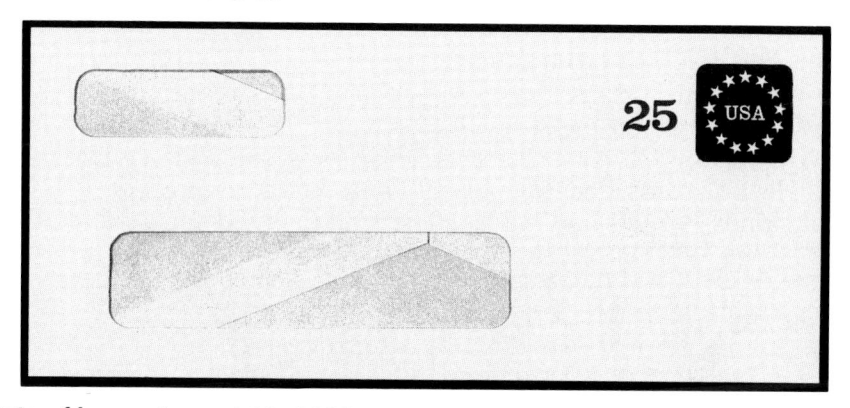

Date of Issue: August 18, 1988

Catalog Numbers: Scott not available   Minkus EN911b
USPS 2153 10 double window

Colors: blue, red

First-Day Cancel: Star, Idaho (no first-day ceremony)

FDCs Canceled: 25,171

Size: 10 with double window

Watermark: combinations of "USA" and a star (See introduction)

Markings: ©USPS 1988 under flap.

Designer and Art Director: Joe Brockert (USPS)

Printing: Westvaco-USEnvelope Division in 2-color flexography and embossing on a VH machine.

Quantity Ordered: 3,424,500
Quantity Distributed: 3,424,500

Tagging: rectangle above denomination

The Envelope

On August 18, the U.S. Postal Service released a new variety of the 25¢ Circle of Stars envelope that it previously had issued in four different forms on March 26. The new variety was a No. 10 size envelope with a double window, designed to accommodate a return address as well as a mailing address. The versions that had been available since March were No. 6¾ and No. 10 sizes, each one made both with and without a single address window.

As it had done with the earlier versions, USPS issued the new double-window envelope without a first-day ceremony, but with first-day cancellations available from a town named Star.

Star, Mississippi, was the postmark used on the March 26 first-day covers. The August 18 covers bore the name of Star, Idaho, a tiny town near the state capital of Boise.

The fact that the new envelope was given first-day cancellation treatment was another sign of USPS' increasing sensitivity to collector desires — and of its growing awareness of the benefits of marketing varieties of existing designs.

Earlier in the year, USPS, for the first time, had provided a first-day cancellation for a precancel overprint (the new service inscription on the old 10.1¢ Oil Wagon stamp) and held a first-day ceremony for Official Mail items (the 15¢ and 25¢ coil stamps).

Despite its favored treatment by USPS, the new envelope was unlikely to be listed in the standard catalogs, which ignore such details about postal stationery as the size of the envelope and whether it is plain or windowed.

The Postal Service called the double-window feature "a real time saver for customers with computer-generated mailings." The second window, located in the upper left corner ½ inch from the top and left edges and measuring ¾ by 2½ inches, allowed the return address to show through from the enclosed mailing piece. The main address window was located in the same position as on standard No. 10 window envelopes.

The new envelope, like the old ones, was produced by Westvaco (U.S. Envelope Division) by embossing and flexography on watermarked paper. It sold for 30¢, or $137 for boxes of 500 (27.4¢ each)

The Design

The new version of the Circle of Stars envelope used the same indicium as its predecessors. Designed by Joe Brockert of USPS, it consisted of 13 stars circling the letters "USA" embossed in white on a blue square, with the numerals "25" to the left, printed in red by a flexographic plate.

First-Day Facts

A pictorial first-day cancellation was made available at Star, Idaho. The two killer bars at top and bottom were replaced by rows of eight stars each. No machine cancellation was used.

25¢ SNOWFLAKE STAMPED ENVELOPE

Date of Issue: September 8, 1988

Catalog Numbers: Scott U613   Minkus EN913   USPS 171

Colors: green, red

First-Day Cancel: Snowflake, Arizona (no first-day ceremony)

FDCs Canceled: 32,601

Size: 7½ by 5 inches

Watermark: 5 point star above S of USA

Markings: ©USPS 1988 under flap. Inscription at lower left cachet corner.

Designer: Randall McDougall (USPS)

Typographer: Bradbury Thompson (CSAC)

Printing: Westvaco-USEnvelope Division in 2-color flexography on a VH machine.

Quantity Ordered: 5,469,000
Quantity Distributed: 5,469,000

Tagging: rectangle above denomination

The Envelope

Every year since 1962, new Christmas stamps have been available to decorate holiday mail. In 1988, for the first time, USPS offered a

325

special Yuletide envelope. Printed in green and red, the 25¢ envelope bore a stylized snowflake and the salutation "Holiday Greetings!"

Its issuance wasn't pre-planned by USPS, but came about through fortuitous circumstances.

Officials of *TV Guide* magazine asked USPS whether they could obtain a first-class stamped envelope in a special size, 7½ by 5 inches, to use in their holiday gift subscription program. In the past, the magazine had notified the recipients of gift subscriptions. This year, *TV Guide* wanted to personalize the process by sending a notification card and a stamped envelope to the donor, so that he could sign the card and send it on to the person receiving the subscription.

USPS said it could furnish the half-million or so envelopes *TV Guide* wanted. But because its supplier, Westvaco USEnvelope Division, couldn't emboss envelopes made in odd sizes, a flexographic plate would have to be manufactured. Rather than duplicate the standard Circle of Stars design in flexo, USPS asked *TV Guide*, would you be interested in a new design?

"We talked back and forth," said Joe Brockert of USPS. "They had no preconceived notions. They didn't ask for a holiday motif. That sort of evolved out of our discussion.

"Meanwhile, we developed this snowflake design here, internally. They thought it was wonderful." Coincidentally, the design was similar to the magazine's gift notification card, which displayed a snowflake of its own with the *TV Guide* logo in the center.

The new method of handling gift subscriptions increased the magazine's costs. Each stamped envelope cost *TV Guide* approximately 26¢, whereas in the past, by directly mailing the gift announcements presorted in bulk, it could obtain a discount from the first-class rate.

On August 8, USPS announced to the public that "an envelope created specifically for holiday use . . . (and) produced in an entirely new size" would be issued September 8. It would be the first stamped envelope for general use offered by USPS in a non-standard size.

Once before, an envelope custom-made for a magazine's use had been also made available to a wider market. The precanceled 22¢ Bison envelope variety of 1986 was made specifically for *Reader's Digest* to use in its annual sweepstakes promotional mailing. Smaller firms were invited to also use the envelope if they chose.

"Some of the media said that the Snowflake envelopes were intended for greeting cards, which wasn't correct," Joe Brockert said. "They were for people who want to send things other than — or in addition to — greeting cards at Christmastime.

"Nobody is going to go into a store, buy a Christmas card with an envelope and throw the envelope away. But more and more people are generating greeting cards and/or holiday letters on computers. So this envelope would be compatible with a lot of those programs that basically take a standard 8½- by 11-inch sheet of paper, fold it into quarters and turn it into a greeting card. It's compatible with a 5- by 7-inch photograph, and with the custom-made cards that photo stores will supply for holiday use, using family photographs that you provide.

"If a greeting card company comes to us in the future and says, 'We'd like to use this envelope,' that's fine. In the past, the card manufacturers haven't wanted to tie up that kind of money in their inventory, considering the fact that even a box of 10 cards would suddenly have the price increased by $2.50 or so if the stamped envelopes were included. That's a lot of money to tie up in inventory of even one store.

"But it's entirely possible that they'll suddenly see a market for something they never conceived of before. Perhaps they'll offer a pack of 10 or 25 cards compatible with the size of the envelope, and sell the envelopes alongside. With the Postal Service's stamps on consignment program going so well, there's no reason we couldn't consign envelopes to greeting-card stores.

"The industry would have to gear up for something like that on a bigger scale. They'd have to re-think how to package their cards, and so on. A lot of things would have to be changed. But this is kind of a first step in seeing if the industry could use something like this.

"It could also convert a lot of the pressure from our Christmas stamp program over to envelopes."

For a prototype, Brockert said, the snowflake envelope received a "phenomenal" response. The Associated Press, *The Wall Street Journal,* National Public Radio and NBC-TV were among the media reporting on the new product.

"It caught people's imagination more than we thought it would, and we were surprised and pleased," Brockert said. "But we don't know what it's going to be for the future."

USPS sold the Snowflake envelope at 30¢ each, or $133.40 for boxes of 500. Customers also could obtain envelopes by mail order with their return addresses imprinted on them for $15.20 per pack of 50 (30.4¢ each) or $136.90 for 500.

The Design

The snowflake motif originated with Brockert, art director for the project. He made a rough pencil sketch on a piece of memo paper and sent it to the USPS art department. (Brockert — who acknowledges that his artistic talents are modest — had similarly "designed" the 25¢ Circle of Stars envelope earlier in the year, and the 14¢ Flag postal card of 1987.)

Working from the sketch, Randall McDougall developed the six-point snowflake in white on a dark square background. He also created the calligraphy-like type for "25 USA," which was placed to the left of the indicium, and "Holiday Greetings!" added in two angled lines on the lower left side of the envelope.

McDougall had previously designed the 1974 ZIP Code and 1984 Crime Prevention stamps. He also had done the cartoon work for the safety posters displayed in post offices.

Brockert had proposed a red indicium and green lettering for the new envelope, and Westvaco made a proof using this color scheme. At the suggestion of Bradbury Thompson, USPS' veteran design coordinator and typographer, the colors were reversed. "Brad suggested that the red looked kind of warm, and would be just right for 'Holiday Greetings!,' while the cooler green would be better for a cold snowflake," Brockert said.

To make "Holiday Greetings!" easier to read, it was decided to run the two lines horizontally instead of at an angle. Finally, the inscription "First-Class," in regular typeface, was added below the indicium.

"Since the design wasn't embossed, we thought we ought to make it absolutely obvious that this wasn't just a fancy decorated envelope that might be sold with a greeting card — that it was honest-to-goodness, genuine postage," Brockert explained. "The fact that we pulled the denomination out of the design, as we had been doing on our envelopes this year, made us worry even a little more that maybe this wouldn't be perceived as being a postage-paid item.

"So we added that endorsement just to give a little extra nudge to the fact that this really was a stamped envelope."

Although the envelope was an odd size, and had a relatively limited printing, USPS was able to obtain the watermarked paper it prefers to use, and the envelope bears a watermark (one variety).

First-Day Facts

No first-day ceremony was held. However, the envelope was first placed on sale in Snowflake, a small city in eastern Arizona, and first-day cancellations were available there.

Only a handstamped cancel was provided. Designed by Randall McDougall, the designer of the envelope, it featured the circular date portion, a snowman, the words "First Day of Issue" in small letters and eight snowflakes mingled with three killer bars that were reminiscent of a winter breeze.

25¢ OFFICIAL MAIL SAVINGS BOND ENVELOPE

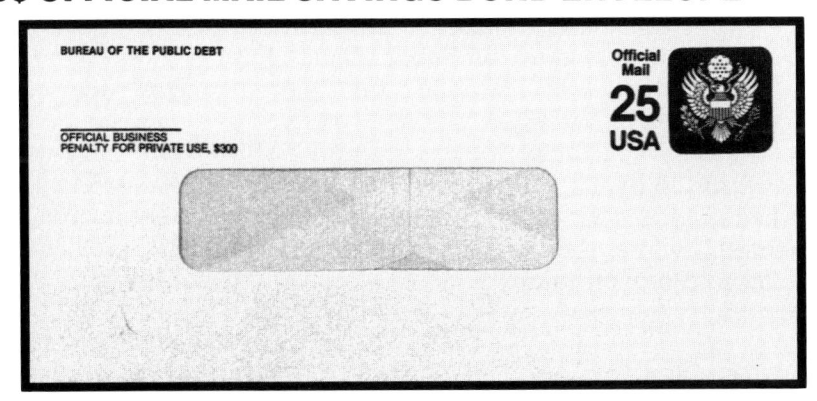

Date of Issue: November 28, 1988

Catalog Numbers: Scott UO78   Minkus PDEN78   USPS 2115

Colors: blue, black

First-Day Cancel: Washington, D.C. (no first-day ceremony)

FDCs Canceled: 12,017 (together with 25¢ Official Mail envelope)

Size: 7 15/16 by 3 9/16 inches, with window

Watermark: none

Markings: ©USPS 1988 under flap. Bureau of Public Debt and penalty notation at upper left corner.

Designer: Bradbury Thompson (CSAC)

Art Director: Joe Brockert (USPS)

Printing: Westvaco-USEnvelope Division in 2-color flexography on a VH machine.

Quantity Ordered: 1,379,500
Quantity Distributed: 1,379,500

Tagging: rectangle to left of lettering and denomination

The Envelope

The final U.S. postal item of 1988 made an unannounced appearance, with no first-day ceremony, in Washington November 28.

It was a new variety of the 25¢ Official Mail Savings Bond envelope that had made its debut the previous April 11. This one contained the following wording in black on the back flap:

Buy and Hold U.S. Savings Bonds
The Great American Investment
Call 1-800-US-BONDS

The original envelope had no printing on the flap. Both versions carried the USPS 1988 copyright notation beneath the flap, however.

USPS officials said the request that the inscription be added came to them from the Bureau of Public Debt. Because it presented no technical problem, they instructed their supplier, Westvaco USEnvelope Division, to comply.

A Treasury Department spokesman told USPS' Stamp Information Branch that the message was one that would be disseminated in several different ways, to encourage people to buy savings bonds and hold them to maturity and to publicize the 800 informational number.

USPS formally announced the envelope's issuance November 30, two days after the fact.

The Design

The front of the envelope, including the blue indicium in the upper right and, in the upper left in black, the words "Bureau of Public Debt" and "Official Mail/Penalty for Private Use, $300," remained the same. As before, the revised envelope was produced in window format only and measured 3 9/16 by 7 15/16 inches.

First-Day Facts

As with the original version, the new envelope was for use exclusively by authorized agents for the disbursement of U.S. Savings Bonds. It was available to collectors only by mail order and from the Philatelic Center in the lobby of USPS headquarters in Washington. Cost was 30¢.

A first-day cover could be obtained by sending 30¢ and a peelable return address label to the postmaster in Washington. Collectors were given 45 days, until January 12, 1989, to place their orders.

39¢ GRAPHIC DESIGN AEROGRAMME

Date of Issue: May 9, 1988

Catalog Numbers: Scott UC61   Minkus ALS23   USPS 2236

Colors: magenta, cyan, yellow, black

First-Day Cancel: Miami, Florida (no first-day ceremony)

FDCs Canceled: 27,446 (includes 79 at first-day city)

Size: 7½ by 3 9/16 folded

Format: Die cut into single aerogrammes. Printing plates of 4 subjects (2 across, 2 around).

Watermark: none

Markings: ©USPS 1988 between side flap and stamp

Designer: Uldis Purins of Newton, Massachusetts

Art Director: Joe Brockert (USPS)

Printing: 6-color Goebel offset Optiforma press (042)

331

Quantity Ordered: 43,000,000
Quantity Distributed: 25,662,000

Tagging: rectangle between USA and denomination

The Aerogramme

The rate for aerogrammes, used for international airmail correspondence, was raised from 36¢ to 39¢ on April 3, and on May 9 an aerogramme in the new higher denomination was issued in Miami.

USPS described the item as a "standard aerogramme," meaning that unlike its recent predecessors — such as the Landsat, Travel and Mark Twain/Halley's Comet aerogrammes of 1985 — it had no commemorative theme and bore no design element other than a conventional indicium in the upper right-hand corner. The left front cachet area and the part making up the back of the folded aerogramme were blank.

In addition, the new aerogramme offered the buyer more writing space. Unfolded, it consisted of three equal segments rather than the conventional two. The third or bottom segment was folded inside the aerogramme before sealing, and both sides of this segment could be used as message area. USPS explained that the new "standard" format was "in response to customer requests for such an aerogramme."

The Design

Previous aerogrammes had been printed on BEP's seven-color Andreotti gravure press. This one was produced by offset on a BEP six-color Goebel webfed press in four-subject sheets.

Uldis Purins of Newton, Massachusetts, designed the indicium. It consisted of a stylized image of an envelope made up of horizontal lines whose widths varied to define the envelope flaps. The colors of the lines shaded from orange at the top, through red, purple and blue, to green at the bottom. "USA" and "39" appeared in black type below the graphic, and the whole was outlined in black.

The functional inscriptions, printed in blue, consisted of the bilingual "Aerogramme/Via Airmail/Par Avion" on the front, folding instructions on the back, "Additional Message Area" on the third segment and "© USPS 1988" on one of the gummed side flaps.

White paper was used instead of the traditional blue, a practice that USPS had begun with the Mark Twain/Halley's Comet aerogramme after it had determined that the Universal Postal Union didn't require blue paper for this particular type of postal stationery.

First-Day Facts

There was no first-day ceremony at Miami, but USPS provided a special first-day circular cancellation showing an outline map of the Americas against a grid of longitude and latitude.

POSTAL CARDS

The once-humble postal card continued to expand its role in the USPS program, thanks to the quality of the production equipment available at the Government Printing Office in Washington.

From the $2 million, five-color, sheetfed, offset Roland Man 800 press installed in 1987 came 10 handsome new postal card varieties in 1988. Even the dullest of these — the Official Mail card — offered more color than its predecessor.

Two commemoratives marked territorial anniversaries. Two more were additions to the Historic Preservation series, and another was a Constitution Bicentennial item. An airmail card paid tribute to a historic plane, the DC-3; an international surface-rate card continued the tradition of depicting sailing ships on cards issued for this purpose.

A card issued in both single and double-reply versions and bearing a generic prairie-mountain landscape scene launched a new definitive series called America the Beautiful. Joining the postage-due stamp on the scrapheap of history were the old-fashioned postal cards of the Patriots type, which combined washed-out monochromaticism with crude lithography to produce a product that only a dedicated collector could love.

By contrast, the new definitives and commemoratives have attracted the admiring attention of not only collectors but the general public, according to Joe Brockert, project manager for all of the 1988 cards. "We're trying to do what we can to improve not only the design and printing but also the public perception of our stationery items," Brockert said. "The postal cards, I think, have come a long way. We've got plenty of the regulars out there, and quite a few commemoratives, and they're all selling at an unprecedented rate."

15¢ AMERICA THE BEAUTIFUL POSTAL CARD

Date of Issue: March 28, 1988

Catalog Numbers: Scott UX120   Minkus PC116
 UPSS S137   USPS 2266

Colors: yellow, magenta, cyan, black

First-Day Cancel: Buffalo, Wyoming (no first-day ceremony)

FDCs Canceled: 52,075

Size: 5½ by 3½ inches

Format: Printed in 80-card sheets, but available to collectors only in single cards. Printing plates of 80 subjects (8 across, 10 around).

Markings: ©USPS 1988

Designer: Bart Forbes of Dallas, Texas

Art Director: Derry Noyes (CSAC)

Project Manager: Joe Brockert (USPS)

Typographer: Bradbury Thompson (CSAC)

Printing: U.S. Government Printing Office (GPO) on a 5-color Roland Man 800 sheetfed offset press

Quantity Ordered: 523,000,000
Quantity Distributed: 357,159,000

Tagging: vertical bar to right of stamp

The Postal Card

With a colorful card depicting buffalo on a meadow and mountains in the background, the Postal Service launched a new series of America the Beautiful definitive postal cards designed to highlight regional scenic beauty.

The 15¢ card was issued March 28, six days before the rate change that would make it necessary. It replaced the 14¢ American Flag postal card of 1987.

Printing was in process color on the Government Printing Office's $2 million Roland Man five-color, sheetfed offset press, installed in 1987. Future cards in the series would come from the same press, USPS said. There would be no more monochromatic, crudely printed definitive cards like those of the long-running Patriots series.

The card was officially announced March 25, three days before issue date. Its first black-and-white publicity pictures were prepared before the March 22 approval of the new rate table by the USPS Board of Governors, and, therefore, bore no denomination. Later photos showed "15" in its proper location.

Initially, the card was printed on so-called "bright-white" paper. GPO began using this paper, which heightens the intensity of the printed colors, in 1987 with the Take Pride in America postal card. America the Beautiful was followed by three other bright-white cards: Blair House, DC-3 and Yorkshire.

But in July, after production and distribution of 21 million America the Beautifuls, USPS announced that use of the stock had been discontinued. Brighteners in the paper had been emitting a red fluorescent signal, confusing the post office equipment used to position envelopes for cancellation by detecting the phosphor tagging on stamps and postal stationery.

The Postal Service said future cards would be printed on white paper that didn't contain brighteners. Only the America the Beautiful, a continuing issue, would be "available in both varieties," in the words of the official announcement.

Despite that wording, the Philatelic Sales Division didn't distinguish between the two papers, or even acknowledge, in its bimonthly catalog, the existence of two collectible varieties of America the Beautiful.

In fact, USPS, in its announcement, asserted that it would be hard to tell the new cards from the old ones.

"Differences between white and bright-white paper are not obvious without close, side-by-side comparison," the Postal Service said. "Fluorescent brighteners also are said to deteriorate over time, so that within a few years, cards printed on the two stock types will be even harder to distinguish."

However, as Wayne Youngblood pointed out in *Linn's Stamp News,* a marked difference between the two papers can be seen under ultraviolet light. Even under normal light, the new card stock appeared yellowish and had a grainier texture that could be seen as well as felt. When held over a dark printed surface, Youngblood wrote, "the brightened stock appears slightly more translucent than the non-responsive card stock."

The new printing on dull card stock was introduced with no fanfare and no specific first-day date. In the December 12 issue of *Linn's,* Youngblood reported that the earliest clearly legible postmark that had been reported on the item to date was July 25, 1988.

Before 1987, cards had been printed on an off-white paper. The only use of that particular paper since then has been for the 1988 15¢ Official Mail postal card.

The American buffalo — actually, the bison — had frequently appeared on U.S. postal paper before, although never on a postal card.

The first stamp to show a bison was the 4¢ Trans-Mississippi commemorative of 1898, in a picture labeled "Indian hunting buffalo," from an engraving by Captain S. Eastman in Schoolcraft's 1854 *History of the Indian Tribes.* Later, the bison appeared on the 30¢ definitive of 1922-25, the 6¢ Wildlife Conservation commemorative of 1970, a stamp in the Wildlife booklet of 1981 and a stamp in the American Wildlife pane of 1987. An embossed bison was the motif of the 22¢ definitive stamped envelope of 1985.

As for America the Beautiful, it was making its second appearance as a USPS theme. The theme was inspired, of course, by the title and words of Katharine Lee Bates' poem, written in 1893 when her mind was full of images from a visit to the World's Columbian Exposition, a train trip across the plains and a climb to the summit of Pike's Peak. Her poem was later set to a melody composed by Samuel A. Ward, and in that form has become widely loved — and even promoted by some as a more singable and fitting national anthem than *The Star-Spangled Banner.*

In 1981 USPS issued three attractive stamps based on the song *America the Beautiful.* Each of Peter Cocci's designs was dominated by a U.S. flag in color. The sheet stamp version pictured a combine in a wheat field above the legend ". . . for amber waves of grain," with vignette and words in an amber tone. The booklet stamp showed a mountain range with the words ". . . for purple mountain majesties" printed, of course, in purple. And the coil depicted a lighthouse on a rocky coast, in blue and brown (". . . from sea to shining sea"). Unfortunately, the stamps, which had been issued to cover the new 18¢ first-class letter rate, were replaced after only a few months when the rate went to 20¢.

The Design

Bart Forbes of Dallas, Texas, who also designed the Winter and Summer Olympic Games stamps of 1988, did the original watercolor

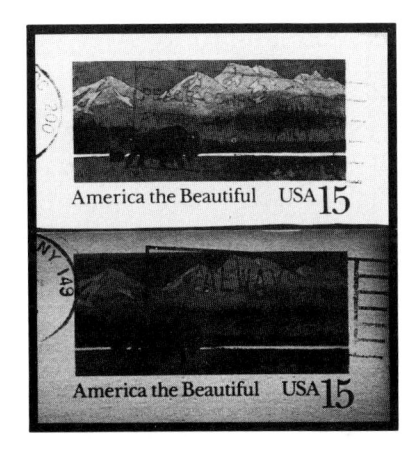

Photographed under ultraviolet light, the "bright-white" card (top) is readily distinguishable from the later variety.

painting on which the postal card design was based.

In the painting's somewhat unusual color scheme, the range of "purple mountain majesties" stands against an orange sky, while the forest in front of the mountains is partially shrouded in orange mist.

Although Forbes used reference scenes and other research aids, the landscape shown on the card "is primarily a very generic scene, more imaginary than real," according to Joe Brockert, project manager.

Varieties

A number of copies of the card were found with printing on both sides. Otto J. Howe of Dadeville, Alabama, sent *Linn's Stamp News* a specimen of the error on which a Knoxville, Tennessee, merchant's

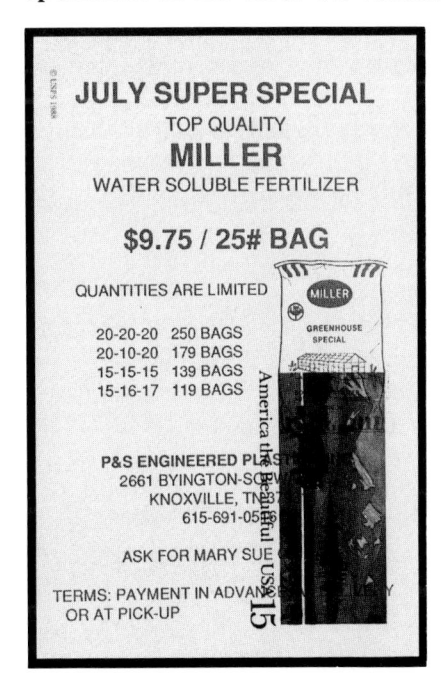

This printed-on-both-sides specimen was recognized after advertising matter had been job-printed on the back.

fertilizer advertisement inadvertently had been job-printed over the "official" printed matter on one of the sides.

Presumably, 80 copies of the two-faced cards existed, because the cards were printed in sheets of 80 on the Roland Man press before being automatically sliced apart, assembled in packs of 250 and wrapped. Experts say this type of error usually occurs at the beginning of a press run, when printers pass a so-called setup sheet through the press twice to check color registration. The sheet is marked for removal and is supposed to be destroyed.

A copy of the error card was sold at auction December 7, 1988, in the Gems of Philately sale of John W. Kaufmann Inc. It realized $742.50 ($675 plus the 10-percent buyer's premium).

At least one freak (not error) specimen of the card was found, properly printed on only one side but miscut so as to show the row of squares, circles and octagons of color that are applied to the top of the printing sheet to furnish information to the press' electronic sensors.

First-Day Facts

When there's no obvious tie-in between a stamp or stationery subject and a specific locality, USPS frequently picks a small town for first-day honors simply because it has an appropriate name. For example, Bison, South Dakota, was the site of the first-day sale of the 22¢ Bison envelope of 1985. Remoteness and obscurity are no problem — especially if no first-day ceremony is planned.

Those circumstances again obtained in the case of the America the Beautiful postal card, and so Buffalo, Wyoming, was tapped as the place whose postmark would appear on first-day covers. Buffalo, county seat of Johnson County, is located on Clear Creek in north central Wyoming.

Because of the short notice, collectors were given an extra 30 days, to May 27, to submit self-addressed cards or address labels and remittance to the postmaster at Buffalo for cancellation.

15¢ BLAIR HOUSE POSTAL CARD

Date of Issue: May 4, 1988

Catalog Numbers: Scott UX121   Minkus PC117
UPSS S138   USPS 2213

Colors: yellow, magenta, cyan, black

First-Day Cancel: Washington, D.C. (Department of State)

FDCs Canceled: 52,188

Size: 5½ by 3½ inches

Format: Printed in 80-card sheets, but available to collectors only in single cards. Printing plates of 80 subjects (8 across, 10 around).

Markings: ©USPS 1987 and cachet inscriptions at lower left corner

Designer: Pierre Mion of Lovettsville, Virginia

Art Director: James Dean (CSAC)

Project Manager: Joe Brockert (USPS)

Typographer: Bradbury Thompson (CSAC)

Printing: U.S. Government Printing Office (GPO) on a 5-color Roland Man 800 sheetfed offset press

Quantity Ordered: 2,500,000
Quantity Distributed: 2,500,000

Tagging: vertical bar to right of stamp

The Postal Card

USPS included a Blair House postal card in its initial announcement of the 1988 stamp and stationery program July 20, 1987. On November 25, it reported that the card would be a 14-center and would be issued in February or March. But a rate change intervened, and when the card ultimately made its appearance the date was May 4 and the denomination was 15¢.

The card was a part of the Historic Preservation series that was launched in 1977 with a 9¢ card depicting the Federal Courthouse at Galveston, Texas. Most of the earlier cards in the series bore the words "Historic Preservation," but this one did not.

Blair House, a 115-room complex consisting of four connected townhouses on Pennsylvania Avenue across from the White House in Washington, is the president's guest house. It was closed for repairs and restoration at the time the card appeared, so first-day ceremonies were held at the Department of State.

The building had been shut down in 1982 after a malfunctioning gas valve leaked explosive natural gas during one dignitary's stay. A bedroom chandelier that fell from the ceiling emphasized the point: Blair House badly needed work.

In 1985, Congress allocated $8.6 million for a complete overhaul that included new electrical heating, plumbing and air-conditioning systems, roof repairs, installation of fire and safety systems and improved security.

The rest of the money that was needed — more than $5 million — was raised privately for refurnishing the interior of the four-story house. On June 12, officials unveiled the results.

"It is not too grand, but it has elegance," said Chief of Protocol Selwa Roosevelt, who as honorary chairman of the Blair House Restoration Fund oversaw the restoration. "It is a guest house worthy of this great nation."

"We wanted it to be soft and light," said decorator Mark Hampton, adding that this was no small accomplishment, given the desire to keep heavy curtains drawn for privacy.

The four-story brick Blair House was built in 1824. It was purchased in 1836 by Francis P. Blair after the death of the original owner, Dr. Joseph Lovell, surgeon general of the Army. Blair, an outspoken Kentucky journalist, had come to Washington to run the *Globe,* the newly established newspaper of Andrew Jackson's Democratic Party, and serve as a member of Jackson's "kitchen cabinet."

He proved to be a man of considerable influence, and his home became a meeting place for the nation's leaders in the years before the Civil War. Here Blair himself offered Robert E. Lee command of the Union armies — an offer Lee declined in favor of his native Virginia. (The adjoining Blair-Lee House was built just before the war for Blair's daughter, Elizabeth Blair Lee.)

Twice, Blair acted as intermediary between the White House and his friend, Jefferson Davis, and occasionally Abraham Lincoln himself crossed Pennsylvania Avenue, as Presidents Jackson and Van Buren had done, to confer with the Blair family.

Francis Blair's eldest son, Montgomery, served as postmaster general in Lincoln's cabinet and was an important adviser to the president during the Civil War years. As head of the nation's postal system, Blair instituted several innovations such as rural free delivery, money orders and the system of sorting mail on railway mail cars. He was the driving force in creating the Universal Postal Union, which brought order and consistency to international mail service, and was pictured on the 15¢ U.S. airmail stamp of 1963 celebrating the centennial of the UPU.

Gist Blair, Montgomery's son, was the last Blair to occupy the house. Having a deep appreciation for its place in history, he devoted much care and attention to the residence.

Blair House (1651 Pennsylvania Avenue, N.W.) and Blair-Lee House (1653 Pennsylvania Avenue, N.W.) were both acquired by the U.S. government in 1942. In 1948 the two buildings were connected for joint use. In the late 1960s, 700 and 704 Jackson Place, N.W., were added to the complex by constructing a short link over the alley.

After President Franklin D. Roosevelt's death in 1945, Blair House became home for President Harry S. Truman and his family for the first weeks of the new administration, and again from November 1948 to March 1952 while the White House was undergoing renovation. On November 1, 1950, two Puerto Rican nationalists attempted to assassinate the president there. Leslie Coffelt, a White House guard, was killed while preventing the assailants from gaining access to the house.

Blair House's many guests have included Emperors Hirohito of Japan and Haile Selassie of Ethiopia, Queen Elizabeth II and the Duke of Edinburgh, the King and Queen of Spain, the King and Queen of Jordan, King Hassan of Morocco, Presidents Brezhnev of the Soviet Union and Sadat of Egypt, Prime Ministers Thatcher of Great Britain, Begin of Israel, Fraser of Australia, Nakasone of Japan, Trudeau of Canada, Nehru of India, Chancellor Schmidt of the Federal Republic of Germany and Deng Xiaoping of the People's Republic of China.

The Design

The designer was Pierre Mion, a Lovettsville, Virginia, artist and magazine illustrator who was performing his first design assignment for USPS. (His second, the Virginia Statehood stamp, was issued only a few weeks after the Blair House card.)

Mion's indicium showed a view of Blair House from across Pennsylvania Avenue, with Blair-Lee House on the left and 700 Jackson Place on the right. A small portion of the Renwick Gallery appears at the far left. Overhead is a strip of blue sky.

On this essay, the view of Blair House is from farther west on Pennsylvania Avenue.

He based his watercolor painting on archival images and his own photographs of the structures. The Blair House restoration work was going on at the time, and Mion had to "climb over scaffolding in full sight of White House guards," recalled Joe Brockert, project manager for the postal card.

The CSAC chose the design over a very architectural line drawing of the Blair House complex and another painting from a different and sharper angle. The line drawing probably would have worked well, said Brockert, if some color had been placed behind the building outlines. However, the committee wanted to make use of the full-color capability provided by the Government Printing Office's new five-color press.

CSAC considered adding leaves to the bare trees pictured along the curb, but decided against it because foliage would have obscured details of the buildings.

Originally, CSAC had chosen the wording "Official Presidential/Guest House,/Washington, DC" for the lower left corner of the card. At the request of Blair House representatives, it changed this to "The President's/Guest House,/Washington, DC," which is the formal subtitle of Blair House.

First-Day Facts

The first-day ceremony was an invitation-only affair at 11 a.m. May 4 at the State Department. Principal speakers included Postmaster General Anthony M. Frank, Deputy Secretary of State John C. Whitehead and Chief of Protocol Selwa Roosevelt, the official who looks after important foreign visitors.

CSAC considered this architectural rendering of the historic building, but preferred a realistic treatment.

36¢ DC-3 AIRMAIL POSTAL CARD

Date of Issue: May 14, 1988

Catalog Numbers: Scott UXC24   Minkus PCA24   UPSS SA23A
USPS 2256

Colors: yellow, magenta, cyan, black

First-Day Cancel: San Diego, California (Brown Field)

FDCs Canceled: 167,575 (includes 45¢ Langley airmail stamp)

Size: 5½ by 3½ inches

Format: Printed in 80-card sheets, but available to collectors only in single cards. Printing plates of 80 subjects (8 across, 10 around).

Markings: ©USPS 1988 and mail sacks cachet at lower left corner. Red and blue lozenges.

Designer: Chuck Hodgeson of Newhall, California

Art Director: Joe Brockert (USPS)

Typographer: Bradbury Thompson (CSAC)

Printing: U.S. Government Printing Office (GPO) on a 5-color Roland Man 800 sheetfed offset press.

Quantity Ordered: 3,750,000
Quantity Distributed: 3,154,000

Tagging: vertical bar to right of stamp

The Postal Card

On April 3, the rate for international air postal cards was raised to 36¢. To meet that rate, USPS on May 14 issued a card depicting the Douglas DC-3 twin-engine airplane.

The place of issue was Brown Field, south of San Diego, the site of Air/Space America 88. Sharing the first-day ceremony was the new 45¢ international airmail stamp honoring Samuel P. Langley.

The postal tribute to the DC-3 was originally conceived as a stamp. CSAC's aviation subcommittee, which deals with airmail stamps and postal stationery, had identified the historic plane as an appropriate stamp subject whenever a rate change demanded one.

Later, however, CSAC decided to continue its practice of recent years of reserving stamps for aviation pioneers such as Samuel Langley, and assigned the DC-3 to a postal card instead.

The DC-3, one of the hardest-working and most reliable aircraft ever built, first took to the air in 1936. The confidence that the public came to have in the plane was a major reason for the growth of the airline industry before and after World War II.

Coincidentally, the development of the DC-3 was a direct result of a disaster that took the life of another 1988 postal subject — Notre Dame football coach Knute Rockne.

Rockne was killed in the 1931 crash of a TWA 10-passenger Fokker Trimotor, a model widely used by U.S. airlines. But the airlines' trust was misplaced. Government experts who investigated the wreckage found clear signs of a structural weakness inside the huge wooden wing that had caused the plane to come apart in mid-air.

TWA grounded its Fokkers and began shopping for a replacement. Its specifications were strict. The plane should be primarily of metal, with superior speed, range and carrying capacity. The toughest spec — imposed by TWA technical adviser Charles A. Lindbergh — was this: On one engine, the plane must be able to take off from the highest airport in TWA's system and fly over the highest mountain on any of its routes.

Douglas Aircraft of Santa Monica, California, a builder of military planes, accepted TWA's challenge. The aluminum-bodied DC-1 (for Douglas Commercial No. 1) was its response. The DC-1 was 60 feet long with an 85-foot wingspan — enormous by the standards of the day — and could carry 12 passengers. Two 710-horsepower Wright Cyclone engines provided the power.

In a key test, the new plane took off from Winslow, Arizona, elevation 4,500 feet, with a full payload of 18,000 pounds. As the landing gear retracted, the co-pilot shut off the right engine. The plane climbed slowly but steadily to 8,000 feet and flew 280 miles to Albuquerque, New Mexico — on one engine.

TWA executives, delighted with the test result, ordered 25 planes. What Douglas furnished was an even better model — the DC-2, slightly longer and capable of carrying 14 passengers. TWA took delivery of the first one in May 1934, and inaugurated speedy coast-to-coast service in August; the company's ads boasted that the trip took only "18 hours via 200-mph luxury airliners."

Late that year American Airlines asked Douglas for 20 DC-2s, but with wider bodies that would accommodate sleeper berths for night flights across the continent. The resulting aircraft was designated DST, or Douglas Sleeper Transport. As it turned out, that phase was a brief one. The plane came into its own when refitted as a day flyer, with 21 seats instead of 14 berths. It was called the DC-3

Much more than the fuselage dimensions had been changed. The retractable landing gear was hydraulically operated, rather than pumped up and down by hand. The adjustable props were of an advanced design. Far more important, the plane had a new aerodynamic profile. The wing was redesigned and lengthened by 10 feet to give stability to the larger fuselage.

The result was a striking improvement in handling qualities. Pilots

Chuck Hodgson painted several in-flight views of the DC-3 in its various military and civilian versions.

said the plane could almost fly itself. The DC-2 was known as a "stiff-legged brute" that was hard to land. But the DC-3, said pilot-writer Ernest Gann, was "an amiable cow that was forgiving of the most clumsy pilot."

The Design

Back when CSAC was thinking of the DC-3 as a stamp subject, it asked artist Chuck Hodgson of Newhall, California, to do some concept sketches. Hodgson had previously designed the 44¢ Transpacific airmail stamp and 33¢ China Clipper air postal card of 1985.

The artist's sketches — which were actually close to being finished

CSAC liked the idea of a DC-3 being loaded with mail, but asked for a side view rather than a tail-first view.

paintings — depicted several different varieties of DC-3, all in flight. When the committee decided that the design had to be in the configuration of a postal card indicium, Hodgson was asked to do three more sketches, showing the aircraft flying amid clouds, flying with mountains in the background, and on the ground at an airport, being loaded with mail.

This design, with different typography, was used on the DC-3 airmail postal card.

The committtee liked the last of these, a tail-first view, but concluded that a side view of the plane would be preferable, and the artist obliged. A final refinement of the postal card was to make the sky bluer and to add to the lower left corner a small cachet of two mailbags and the inscription "DC-3, 1938."

First-Day Facts

Details on the first-day ceremony are given in the chapter on the 45¢ Langley airmail stamp.

15¢ OFFICIAL MAIL POSTAL CARD

Date of Issue: June 10, 1988

Catalog Numbers: Scott UZ4   Minkus PDC4   UPSS 04   USPS 2255

Colors: red, blue, gold, black

First-Day Cancel: New York, New York (no first-day ceremony)

FDCs Canceled: 133,498

Size: 5½ by 3½ inches

Format: Printed in 80-card sheets, but available to collectors only in single cards. Printing plates of 80 subjects (8 across, 10 around).

Markings: ©USPS 1988 at lower left corner. Penalty notation at upper left side.

Designer and Typographer: Bradbury Thompson (CSAC)

Project Manager: Joe Brockert (USPS)

Printing: U.S. Government Printing Office (GPO) on a 5-color Roland Man 800 sheetfed offset press.

Quantity Ordered: 2,000,000
Quantity Distributed: 1,252,000

Tagging: vertical bar to right of stamp

The Postal Card

On June 10, without advance notice, USPS issued a 15¢ Penalty Mail (Official Mail) postal card. The item was released at the American Stamp Dealers' Association spring stamp show at Madison Square Garden in New York City on the show's opening day.

Nearly two weeks later, on June 23, the Stamp Information Branch distributed a terse announcement of the card's issuance.

The card was the third in the current series of Official Mail stamps and postal stationery that began in 1983. Previous cards had covered the then-current 13¢ and 14¢ postal card rates.

The Design

As with all current Official Mail items, design and typography credit for the 15¢ postal card went to Bradbury Thompson, design coordinator for CSAC.

The basic indicium resembled that of the two previous postal cards — the eagle from the Great Seal of the United States in white dropped out of a solid blue background. However, there were extensive differences in the treatment.

The background was a square with rounded corners, instead of a horizontally arranged rectangle. And the "Official Mail" legend, denomination and "USA" were to the left of the design instead of above and below it.

Most significant, the card was printed in four colors instead of one. The stars above the eagle are gold, and the inscription at the left is in black and red.

The card was produced on the Government Printing Office's five-color sheetfed Roland Man offset press, and processed on the Unomatic cut and pack system. One station of the press was used to apply the taggant.

"We were going to try a metallic gold ink for the stars," said Joe Brockert, art director for the card, "but in that small area where the stars appeared, metallic would have had a tendency to flake off, so we went with the standard offset gold."

At the left side of the face of the card, in two lines of small black type, was the standard inscription: "Official Business/Penalty for Private Use $300." The USPS 1988 copyright symbol was in blue in the lower left corner.

First-Day Facts

Although there was no first-day ceremony for the card, first-day cancellations were available at the ASDA show June 10.

Because all Official Mail items are illegal for private use, the card wasn't sold at post offices. It could only be obtained by mail through the Philatelic Sales Division or from the counters at USPS headquarters in L'Enfant Plaza, Washington.

Collectors could obtain first-day covers by mail by sending 15¢ and a peelable return address label for each card ordered.

USPS gave collectors a 60-day grace period for this purpose instead of the normal 30 because the card was issued without notice.

28¢ YORKSHIRE POSTAL CARD

Date of Issue: June 29, 1988

Catalog Numbers: Scott UX122   Minkus PC118
                     UPSS S139   USPS 2257

Colors: cyan, magenta, yellow, black

First-Day Cancel: Mystic, Connecticut (Bartram dock at Mystic Seaport)

FDCs Canceled: 46,505

Size: 5½ by 3½ inches

Format: Printed in 80-card sheets, but available to collectors only in single cards. Printing plates of 80 subjects (8 across, 10 around).

Markings: ©USPS 1988 and cachet inscriptions at lower left corner

Designer: Richard Schlecht of Arlington, Virginia

Art Director: Joe Brockert (USPS)

Typographer: Bradbury Thompson (CSAC)

Printing: U.S. Government Printing Office (GPO) on a 5-color Roland Man 800 sheetfed offset press

Quantity Ordered: 3,000,000
Quantity Distributed: 2,884,000

Tagging: vertical bar to right of stamp

349

The Postal Card

The *Yorkshire*, reputed to be the fastest packet sailing ship ever to take to the sea, was pictured on a 28¢ postal card issued June 29 to meet the rate for cards sent by surface mail to foreign countries other than Canada or Mexico.

The card had its first-day sale at Mystic Seaport in Mystic, Connecticut. It was the second postal item of the year with a Mystic connection; the first, on January 9, was the 22¢ Connecticut Statehood Bicentennial stamp, which depicted a scene at Mystic Seaport.

Sailing ships have been a consistent theme for international surface-rate postal cards. The *Yorkshire* card replaced the 25¢ card of 1985 that depicted the clipper ship *Flying Cloud*. That card's predecessors, in turn, included the 19¢ *Golden Hinde* card of 1980, commemorating the 300th anniversary of Sir Francis Drake's circumnavigation of the globe, and the 14¢ Coast Guard cutter *Eagle* card of 1978.

The Black Ball Line was the first fleet to provide transatlantic packet service, meaning service on regular schedules. Previously, ships sailed only if they had a full payload — and the weather generally had to be favorable. Beginning in 1818, Black Ball carried passengers, cargo and mail between New York and Liverpool, leaving at appointed times, whether the ships were loaded or not and regardless of the weather.

In the line's first nine years, the average time taken by Black Ballers was 23 days on the eastward run and 40 days on the westward, sailing against the westerly winds. Its success inspired the creation of new American lines, such as Red Star and Swallow Tail. Total shipping tonnage almost doubled between 1815 and 1845, rising to about 2½ million tons. By mid-century, more than half a million people each year were crossing the Atlantic, most of them emigrants to America.

The *Yorkshire*, 996 tons and 163 feet in length, was designed by William Henry Webb, one of the foremost American shipbuilders of the 19th century, and was launched in 1843. In 1846, when other packet ships were doing well to sail from Liverpool to New York in 38 days, the *Yorkshire* made the trip in just 16. The *New York Herald* reported that the passengers on the record-setting voyage were ecstatic. Youthful members of a Viennese ballet troupe "were so delighted with (Captain David G. Bailey) and his ship that they danced the splendid *Pas de Fleurs* on his quarter deck coming up the harbor," the newspaper said.

On February 2, 1862, the *Yorkshire* sailed from New York on her last voyage. She never made port, and her fate was never known. Meanwhile, the era of wood hulls and canvas sails also was coming to an end. Steamships continued to improve in design and efficiency, and eventually forced the closing of the sailing packet lines. The Black Ball was one of the last to go, providing service until 1878.

The Design

Richard Schlecht of Arlington, Virginia, made the original painting on which the card's design was based. Strong on blues and grays, it showed the square-rigger under full sail on moderate seas, the symbol of the Black Ball Line prominent on her foresail. Two other sailing ships are visible in the distance.

An early essay for the card had the word *Yorkshire*, the denomination and "USA" all superimposed on the design in black. In the end, however, the ship's identification was taken from the indicium and moved to four lines of small type in the lower left corner: *"Yorkshire/ Black Ball Line/ packet ship/ circa 1850."* One reason for taking "Yorkshire" out of the image area, a postal official said, was to prevent any possible misconception that the card was British.

The arrangement of sails on the *Yorkshire* drew criticism in two letters to *Linn's Stamp News*. A New Jersey writer termed the design "an insult to anyone who has a love of sailing ships" because "the jib sails show the wind from the rear as is normal. The sails of the foremast have been turned to show the symbol of the Black Ball Line, but the sails are filled by a wind from over the bow. The mainmast sails are filled as though the wind is directly over the bow. Finally, the mizzen mast sails are filled from a wind almost over the stern." And from Kansas came a complaint that "the flags show the wind is blowing one way and the rear mast or mizzen mast has three sails that obviously show the wind as coming from the opposite direction."

Schlecht defended his design in a breezy letter of his own:

"Avast, there... The (sails) are an insult only to lubbers; a deepwater man would find nothing amiss. He would see that *Yorkshire* is merely tacking. She has just come through the wind and is paying off to starboard. The lee braces of the foresails will be hauled directly, and she will fall off on the port tack.

"For illumination on the subject of the handling of square rigged vessels, I refer the gentlemen to Darcy Leuer's *The Young Sea Offi-*

Richard Schlecht's earlier essay for the Yorkshire card included the ship's name in the image area.

cer's Sheet Anchor (1819), reprinted in facsimile by the Edward Sweetman Co. in 1963. A look at the many early 19th-century paintings of the Roux Brothers of Marseilles would shed additional light on the matter, as would a careful reading of C.S. Forester's Horatio Hornblower series."

Because the New Jersey letter writer was from a state fronting on salt water, Schlecht concluded, he "forfeits his rum ration and stands an extra watch."

Added *Linn's* in an editor's note: "A number of other *Linn's* readers, including a naval captain, wrote to defend the accuracy" of Schlecht's painting.

Schlecht's previous design credits included another ship postal card, the *Flying Cloud* of 1985. Earlier in 1988 he had designed the 3¢ Conestoga Wagon stamp in the Transportation series.

First-Day Facts

Mystic Seaport was an appropriate site for the dedication, USPS noted. Besides the whaler *Charles W. Morgan,* depicted on the Connecticut Statehood stamp, the vintage New England village is home to some 300 other historic vessels.

The first-day ceremony was held at Bartram Dock on the banks of the Mystic River, some 50 feet from the *Charles W. Morgan.* Participants included Vice Admiral B.L. Stabile, president of the Webb Institute of Naval Architecture in New York, which was founded by *Yorkshire* designer William Henry Webb; Mystic Seaport Director J. Revell Carr, and the featured speaker, Stanley W. Smith, assistant postmaster general.

15¢ IOWA TERRITORY POSTAL CARD

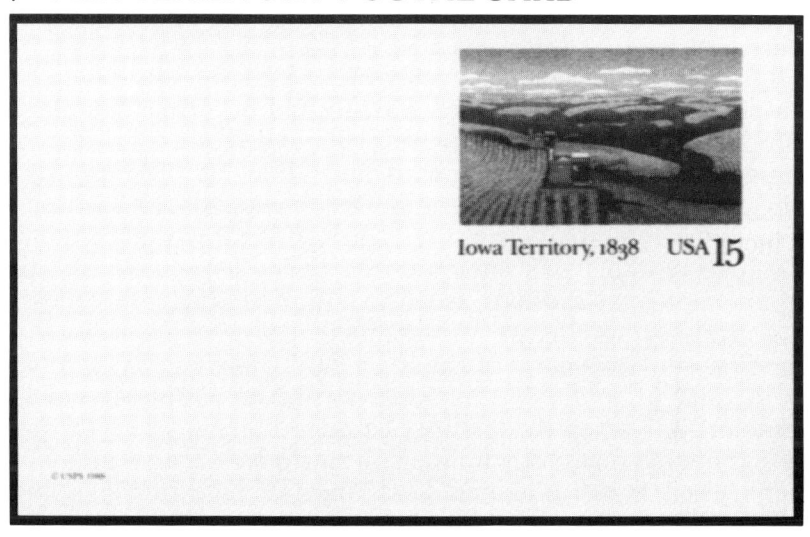

Date of Issue: July 2, 1988

Catalog Numbers: Scott UX123   Minkus PC119   UPSS S140
USPS 2214

Colors: yellow, magenta, cyan, black

First-Day Cancel: Burlington, Iowa (Port of Burlington)

FDCs Canceled: 45,565

Size: 5½ by 3½ inches

Format: Printed in 80-card sheets, but available to collectors only in single cards. Printing plates of 80 subjects (8 across, 10 around).

Markings: ©USPS 1988

Designer: Greg Hargreaves of Waterloo, Iowa

Art Director: Howard Paine (CSAC)

Project Manager: Joe Brockert (USPS)

Typographer: Bradbury Thompson (CSAC)

Printing: U.S. Government Printing Office (GPO) on a 5-color Roland Man 800 sheetfed offset press

Quantity Ordered: 5,000,000
Quantity Distributed: 5,000,000

Tagging: vertical bar to right of stamp

The Postal Card

On July 2, 1988, a 15¢ postal card was issued for the 150th anniversary of the creation of the Iowa Territory. Back in 1938, the centennial of that same event had inspired a 3¢ stamp.

It wasn't the first time such a double commemoration — a stamp and a postal card half a century apart — had occurred. The Battle of Monmouth, the capture of Fort Sackville and the first settlements of Georgia, Maryland and Connecticut were all events whose anniversaries in the 1920s and 1930s were marked by stamps, and whose later anniversaries in the 1970s and 1980s brought forth postal cards.

The Iowa card of 1988 was produced under a specific USPS policy currently in effect: Cards are issued to commemorate anniversaries of territorial status; stamps are for statehood.

The first announcement of the Iowa card was made November 25, 1987. At that time, the first day date was given as July 4, which was the date in 1838 when the territory came into being. Later the date of issue was moved forward from the holiday to July 2, a Saturday.

The United States obtained Iowa from France in the Louisiana Purchase of 1803 (an event marked by a commemorative series of stamps in 1904 and a single 3¢ stamp in 1953). Until the early 1830s, Iowa remained Indian land, officially closed to permanent settlement. But as a result of the Black Hawk War of 1832, the Sauk and Fox Indians ceded a 50-mile-wide strip along the Mississippi River for $640,000 and settlers quickly staked their claims in this so-called "Black Hawk Purchase."

Two years later Iowa was attached to the Territory of Michigan for governmental purposes. Later it was transferred to the newly created Wisconsin Territory, and Burlington, in the territory's Iowa District, served as a temporary capital pending the completion of the town of Madison. Finally, on June 12, 1838, President Martin Van Buren

On this imaginative essay, bison-shaped clouds float above the golden fields.

signed the bill creating the Territory of Iowa and including in its borders much of Minnesota and the Dakotas.

Iowans resisted statehood at first for a very practical reason: As long as the region was a territory, they didn't have to pay the salaries of local officials. Even after Congress had passed a bill admitting Iowa to the Union, they rejected the honor out of dissatisfaction with the proposed boundaries.

Eventually, however, the voters and Congress agreed on a compromise, and on December 28, 1846, President James K. Polk signed the act making Iowa the 29th state. (In 1946 the U.S. Post Office Department, which had commemorated the centennial of the territory only eight years earlier, marked the centennial of statehood with another 3¢ stamp.)

Iowa adopted its present state constitution in 1857. Under that document the capital was moved to Des Moines.

The Design

In this view, similar to the finished postal card, hills evolve into clouds in the distance.

Greg Hargreaves, a Waterloo, Iowa, artist, produced the design, his first for USPS. Using as themes Iowa agriculture and the openness of the prairie, he prepared several sketches for CSAC's consideration. In these he showed a flair for interesting and subtle details. In one scene, clouds take the shape of the bison that once roamed the plains in vast herds; in another, round hills evolve into clouds as they recede in the distance.

The final design choice turned out to be a detail from the latter sketch, modified and magnified. From an elevated perspective, two Iowa farmers are seen working a field of corn, driving bright red harvesting machines that pick, shell and deposit the ears in large cargo

This version of the final design for the Iowa Territory card zoomed in more closely on the harvesters.

hoppers. Deep green foliage divides the golden acres, which roll away in all directions. Far to the rear, a red farmhouse with matching barn and twin silos await the day's produce.

Philatelic designers preparing an Iowa design can't seem to resist a corn motif. On both the 1938 Territorial Centennial stamp and the 1946 Statehood Centennial stamp, the central vignettes were flanked by cornstalks.

First-Day Facts

Governor Terry Branstad of Iowa participated in a noon dedication ceremony July 2 in the Mississippi River city of Burlington, the first capital of the Iowa Territory.

15¢ AMERICA THE BEAUTIFUL DOUBLE REPLY POSTAL CARD

Date of Issue: July 11, 1988

Catalog Numbers: Scott UY39   Minkus MRC38   UPSS MR49
USPS 2280

Colors: yellow, magenta, cyan, black

First-Day Cancel: Buffalo, Wyoming (no first-day ceremony)

FDCs Canceled: 24,338

Size: 5½ by 7 inches

Format: Printed in 80-card sheets, but available to collectors only in a single double reply card format. Printing plates of 80 subjects (8 across, 10 around).

Markings: ©USPS 1988

Designer: Bart Forbes of Dallas, Texas

Art Director: Derry Noyes (CSAC)

Project Manager: Joe Brockert (USPS)

Typographer: Bradbury Thompson (CSAC)

Printing: U.S. Government Printing Office (GPO) on a 5-color Roland Man 800 sheetfed offset press

Quantity Ordered: 23,000,000
Quantity Distributed: 17,517,000

Tagging: vertical bar to right of stamp

The Postal Card

Since 1892, USPS has made available double postal cards, fastened together but easily separable. The buyer — usually a business — could use one for the message, and the addressee could use the other for a reply. The Scott stamp catalogs list these items in a separate section, apart from the single postal cards, with their own numbering system.

In the early years, paid reply postal cards had their own distinctive designs, with the reply card differing from the message card in wording and/or picture. But since 1956, the cards have borne the same designs as the current single cards, with no difference between reply and message units. The cards are printed on opposite sides of the paper, so that when they are folded along the scored line between them, the reply card is on the inside.

When it announced the 15¢ America the Beautiful postal card March 25, USPS said a double-reply card version would be available later in the year. On April 21 came the announcement that the new 30¢ version would be issued July 11 in Buffalo, Wyoming, the same town where the single card had made its debut March 28.

The design on the two attached 15¢ cards was also the same: Bart Forbes' painting of bison grazing on a green meadow, with purple mountains and an orange sky in the background.

The item replaced the attached 14¢ American Flag cards issued in 1987. Because of the item's limited range of uses, many post offices didn't carry it, and USPS recommended that collectors order it from the Philatelic Sales Division.

Again, no first-day ceremony was held in Buffalo, but first-day cancellations were provided.

15¢ OHIO/NORTHWEST TERRITORY POSTAL CARD

Date of Issue: July 15, 1988

Catalog Numbers: Scott UX124 Minkus PC120 UPSS S141
USPS 2215

Colors: cyan, magenta, yellow, black

First-Day Cancel: Marietta, Ohio (First Congressional Church)

FDCs Canceled: 28,778

Size: 5½ by 3½ inches

Format: Printed in 80-card sheets, but available to collectors only in single cards. Printing plates of 80 subjects (8 across, 10 around).

Markings: ©USPS 1988 and map cachet at lower left corner

Designer: James Gurney of Rhinebeck, New York

Art Director: Joe Brockert (USPS)

Typographer: Bradbury Thompson (CSAC)

Cachet Designer: Susan Sanford of Washington, D.C.

Printing: U.S. Government Printing Office (GPO) on a 5-color Roland Man 800 sheetfed offset press.

Quantity Ordered: 15,000,000
Quantity Distributed: 15,000,000

Tagging: vertical bar to right of stamp

The Postal Card

On July 15, a 15¢ postal card was issued to commemorate the 200th anniversary of the settling of Ohio and the founding of government in the Northwest Territory — the first westward expansion of the new United States of America.

Exactly a half-century before, on July 15, 1938, in the same city — Marietta, Ohio — a 3¢ stamp had been issued for the 150th anniversary of these events on the shores of the Ohio River.

That stamp, in turn, had been preceded in 1937 by a 3¢ stamp marking the 150th anniversary of the adoption by Congress of the Ordinance of 1787, providing for the organization of the Northwest Territory. It, too, had a first-day sale in Marietta.

The Northwest Territory postal card, in fact, was the second postal card in two weeks to be issued for an event that had been the subject of a postage stamp 50 years before. The first such card, on July 2, had commemorated the 150th anniversary of the creation of the Iowa Territory.

USPS announced plans for the Northwest Territory card July 20, 1987, in its first public listing of the 1988 stamp and stationery program. On November 25, the first-day date and city were disclosed.

The Northwest Territory — or, formally, the Territory Northwest of the River Ohio — was a vast stretch of wilderness bounded by the Ohio and Mississippi Rivers and the Great Lakes. It encompassed all of present-day Ohio, Indiana, Michigan, Illinois and Wisconsin, and part of Minnesota.

Great Britain formally relinquished its claims to the area in the 1783 Treaty of Paris. However, before it could be organized by the United States and readied for settlement, title had to be acquired from Indian tribes and several states had to relinquish territorial claims based on original king's grants that ran "from sea to sea."

The Northwest Ordinance, enacted July 13, 1787, was the most notable achievement of Congress under the Articles of Confederation.

The first group to purchase land for settlement was the Ohio Company of Associates. A joint-stock corporation, the Ohio Company was made up mostly of Revolutionary War veterans from New England who proposed to exchange devalued continental certificates for land in the Ohio country. Its directors included Manasseh Cutler and Rufus Putnam, whose portraits appear on the 1937 commemorative stamp. With Cutler as their agent, the stockholders struck a deal with Congress to buy 1.5 million acres at 66.7¢ per acre. In addition, public land was set aside for religion, public schools and universities.

In the winter of 1788, an advance party of 48 men under General Putnam set off from Massachusetts toward the new territory. Reaching the Youghiogheny River southeast of present-day Pittsburgh, they built boats, loaded their livestock and wagons aboard and floated via the Allegheny and Ohio Rivers to the mouth of the Muskingum, where Fort Harmar, built three years earlier, afforded protection.

Reaching their destination April 7, 1788, they began clearing the land, surveying town lots and building new homes in orderly New England fashion. As a tribute to France, which had helped the Americans gain independence, the settlement was called Marietta, a linkage of the first and last syllables of the name of Queen Marie Antoinette.

The settlers built Campus Martius, named for the military training site in ancient Rome. Campus Martius served as the seat of territorial administration for Arthur St. Clair, first territorial governor.

St. Clair inaugurated the first territorial government July 15, 1788, the date marked by the postal card.

Settlers began crossing the Ohio in great numbers. One by one, sections of the Northwest Territory reached the population levels required for statehood, beginning with Ohio in 1803.

The Design

Design credit for the Northwest Territory card was given to two artists, both working for USPS for the first time.

James M. Gurney of Rhinebeck, New York, known to science-fiction fans as a frequent illustrator of book jackets, did the vignette. Susan Sanford of Washington, D.C., who is skilled at technical line work, prepared a cachetlike map design in the lower left. Both were known to Howard Paine, the *National Geographic's* art director and a design coordinator for the Citizens' Stamp Advisory Committee, for maps and other illustrations they had done for the *Geographic*.

Gurney's vignette, in the large horizontal format, features a flatboat floating on the high spring waters of the Ohio River. Loaded with livestock, luggage, crates and Conestoga wagon, the boat carries a New England family past Fort Harmar toward a new territorial home. A sailing vessel and rowboat can also be seen; the settlement at Marietta and the mouth of the Muskingum appear in the distance.

After Gurney had submitted preliminary sketches, independent researchers hired by USPS and backed up by the experts at the Campus Martius Museum went to work. They determined that the type of stagecoach Gurney included probably never crossed the Ohio by flatboat, and so a Conestoga wagon was substituted. (This created the second postal appearance of the year for that vehicle.)

This painting, with several alterations, became the design used on the postal card.

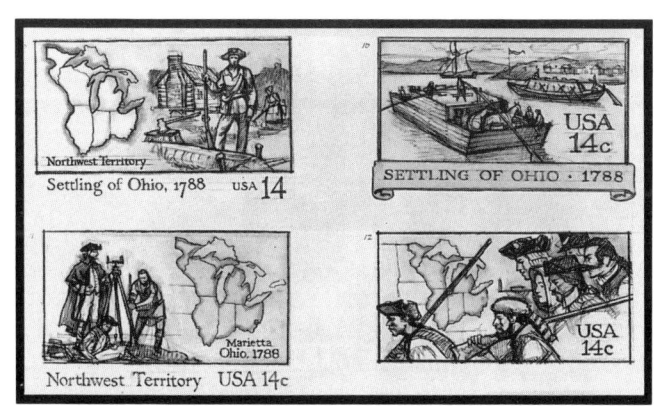

James M. Gurney combined pioneers, surveyors, forts, flatboats, covered wagons and maps in idea sketches.

The researchers nailed down such details as where the tiller would be located, where the oars would be stored and how many planks would be exposed above the water level. They also learned that most river migration was done during the time of the spring flood.

Gurney made appropriate changes. In the end, some fine-tuning was done by CSAC and USPS staff members. They asked Gurney to elevate the sail on a keelboat in the background; to transform the rear of a cow into the front of a horse; to change some of the settlers' hats, and to give the man at the tiller a yellow shirt.

For the cachet, Sanford drew an outline map of the Eastern United States with major rivers delineated, and the Northwest Territory shown as a dark area. Marietta is shown as a dot but not identified.

The practice of including a cachet as part of a postal card design was begun with the 1987 Steel Plow postal card and continued with the 36¢ DC-3 airmail postal card released earlier in 1988.

First-Day Facts

The first-day ceremony was held at the historic First Congregational Church, 318 Front Street, in Marietta.

The crowd of approximately 250 persons received two bonuses from USPS: the experimental introduction of a new type of souvenir card, and a scarce ceremony program.

The souvenir card was a large (11- by 8½-inch) piece of parchment-like paper with slits into which the postal card could be inserted. Four thousand were printed by a Columbus, Ohio, firm, and virtually all of them were sold at Marietta for 75¢ each, including the 15¢ cost of the postal card.

The card bore a large scene of a flatboat on the Ohio River, printed in blue, and an extended text, "Settling the Northwest Territory," printed in red.

15¢ HEARST CASTLE POSTAL CARD

Date of Issue: September 20, 1988

Catalog Numbers: Scott UX125   Minkus PC121   USPS 2217

Colors: yellow, magenta, cyan, black

First-Day Cancel: San Simeon, California (Hearst Castle)

FDCs Canceled: unavailable

Size: 5½ by 3½ inches

Format: Printed in 80-card sheets, but available to collectors only in single cards. Printing plates of 80 subjects (8 across, 10 around).

Markings: ©USPS 1988 and zebra cachet at lower left corner

Designer: Robert Reynolds of San Luis Obispo, California

Art Director and Project Manager: Joe Brockert (USPS)

Typographer: Bradbury Thompson (CSAC)

Printing: U.S. Government Printing Office (GPO) on a 5-color Roland Man sheetfed offset press.

Quantity Ordered: 15,000,000
Quantity Distributed: 15,000,000

Tagging: vertical bar to right of stamp

The Postal Card

A legendary newspaperman's legendary home was illustrated on a 15¢ postal card in the Historic Preservation series that was issued

The Friends of Hearst Castle originally had hoped for a stamp, depicting Hearst himself as well as his mansion.

September 20.

The home was Hearst Castle, overlooking the Pacific Ocean in San Simeon, California. It was built and occupied by William Randolph Hearst, whose *San Francisco Examiner* and *New York Journal* anchored one of the great press empires in American history. The castle is now owned by the state of California. First-day ceremonies were held in the Visitors' Center of the Hearst San Simeon State Historical Mounument.

The card originated as a campaign by the Friends of Hearst Castle, a non-profit group organized to help underwrite restoration, conservation and educational work at the historical mounument. The Friends and their president, Winton "Woody" Frey, began lobbying in May 1985 for a commemorative stamp depicting not only the castle but William Randolph Hearst himself.

CSAC rejected this concept. Perhaps members felt that the nation's postal gallery wasn't an appropriate place for Hearst, whose newspapers were shamelessly sensationalistic and jingoistic, and who took personal credit for pushing the United States into war with Spain in 1898. ("You furnish the pictures," he wired his hired illustrator in Cuba, Frederick Remington, "and I'll furnish the war.")

The members did, however, like the idea of commemorating Hearst Castle and of doing it on a postal card in the Historic Preservation series. A card's broader canvas could better do justice to the subject, they believed.

"We hadn't done a whole lot on the West in the series — certainly not on the West Coast, which doesn't have that many old historic buildings," said Joe Brockert, project manager and art director. "Hearst Castle isn't particularly old, but it is certainly unique."

USPS announced the postal card in its first listing of 1988 subjects on July 20, 1987. Date and place of issue were added in a November 25, 1987, news release.

Hearst Castle stands on a hill some 2,000 feet above San Simeon Bay, halfway between Los Angeles and San Francisco. The land was part of a vast ranch called Piedra Blanca, which Hearst's father, George Hearst, a mining magnate and later a U.S. senator, bought at 60¢ an acre in 1865. W.R. had dreamed of building a home there for many years before he actually began construction in 1919.

The publisher named the near-barren eminence La Cuesta Encantada (the Enchanted Hill), carved a six-mile private road from the highway and brought in steel and cement by coastal steamer. As the great project slowly took shape over the years, architect Julia Morgan worked closely with Hearst, subordinating her own instincts for design, balance and decoration to his eclectic whims.

Three palatial guest houses of Spanish and Italian lineage were finished first: la Casa del Monte, la Casa del Sol and la Casa del Mar. By 1930, the greatest of the buildings, the twin-towered la Casa Grande, with 38 bedroom suites, 31 bathrooms and 14 sitting rooms, rose high above the other structures.

Hearst died August 14, 1951, at the age of 88. His sons persuaded the state of California to take the castle and 123 acres as a gift. It wasn't an easy sell; some Parks Commission officials saw it as a white elephant, and others resisted out of antipathy toward W.R. and his brand of journalism. But when San Simeon was opened to the public in 1958, tourists at $2 a head arrived in such numbers that at first many had to be turned away. Far from being a drain, the castle actually became the only money-making operation in the entire state parks system.

The Design

Robert Reynolds of San Luis Obispo, California, a landscape artist and first-time postal designer, painted for the card a wide-angle view of the Hearst Castle complex surrounded by lush greenery. The Neptune Pool was shown at the left and Casa del Mar and Casa del Sol were in the foreground. A golden sunset and blue sky provided the backdrop for the twin towers of Casa Grande. In the lower left corner of the card stood a lone zebra, typical of the animals that can be seen on the drive up to the hilltop.

The Friends of Hearst Castle had commissioned Reynolds, former head of the art department at California Polytechnic Institute (where Friends president Woody Frey also taught), to do some postal design concepts. He prepared a stamp design featuring Hearst himself, and, after CSAC had indicated its preference for a postal card, he did a treatment of Hearst Castle.

The committee members liked Reynolds' work. The fact that he lived in the area and was personally familiar with the building was another plus. There was no particular rush to complete the project. So

The zebra remained in the design area until the very end, when it was moved to the lower left corner of the card.

USPS asked him to proceed with the design assignment.

On one of Reynolds' early essays, he placed the zebra in the corner of the indicium design. Art director Brockert liked the zebra, but after trying a variety of arrangements of design elements, including the wording and denomination, it was decided to use the animal in the lower left corner as a miniature cachet. It originally looked to the left, but for use in the corner of the card, Reynolds' painting of it was photographed and reversed so that it would be facing into, rather than off, the card.

"I was the persistent individual who didn't want to lose the zebra," Brockert said. "It adds a nice topical touch."

The use of a mini-cachet on such postal cards as the Hearst Castle, Northwest Territory and DC-3 has received mixed reactions, Brockert said. "The vast majority of people really like it, but there are always going to be one or two people who write in and say, 'I like to use every

Robert Reynolds experimented with several different arrangements of the wording.

inch of space when writing, and you've used up my writing areas. Now I can't finish my message.'

"The answer to that is: We have the regular issue out there. If you really dislike the corner design, use the America the Beautiful series; it's meant to be the standard issue. The commemorative is meant to be a little fancier, something a little different."

First-Day Facts

More than 400 persons attended the outdoor first-day ceremony at San Simeon on a mild, pleasant last day of summer.

15¢ FEDERALIST PAPERS POSTAL CARD

Date of Issue: October 27, 1988

Catalog Numbers: Scott UX126   Minkus PC122   UPSS 5134
USPS 2212

Colors: cyan, magenta, yellow, black

First-Day Cancel: New York, New York (Federal Hall National Memorial)

FDCs Canceled: unavailable

Size: 5½ by 3½ inches

Format: Printed in 80-card sheets, but available to collectors only in single cards. Printing plates of 80 subjects (8 across, 10 around).

Markings: ©USPS 1988 and book cachet at lower left corner

Designer: Roy Andersen of Sedona, Arizona

Art Director and Project Manager: Joe Brockert (USPS)

Typographer: Bradbury Thompson (CSAC)

Printing: U.S. Government Printing Office (GPO) on a 5-color Roland Man 800 sheetfed offset press.

Quantity Ordered: 8,000,000
Quantity Distributed: 8,000,000

Tagging: vertical bar to right of stamp

The Postal Card

The last of several items in 1988 that postally commemorated the U.S. Constitution's bicentennial was a 15¢ postal card marking the publication of the Federalist Papers in 1787-88.

These writings, 85 essays by Alexander Hamilton, James Madison and John Jay, appeared in New York newspapers beginning October 27, 1787, and were written to explain the newly drafted Constitution and to persuade New Yorkers to support ratification.

As historian Carl Van Doren wrote, *"The Federalist* (the title of the collected essays) at once took its place as almost a part of the Constitution itself, and the masterpiece of all thinking and writing about federal government."

The card was placed on sale in New York City October 27, 1988, 201 years to the day after the printing of that first essay. It had been preceded in the year by eight stamps commemorating the ratification of the Constitution by individual states — including New York.

The 1787 convention in Philadelphia had committed, in historian Edward Mead Earle's words, "an act of revolution, a coup d'etat." It had gone far beyond its mandate to merely amend the Articles of Confederation and had produced a wholly new charter for government. It compounded its audacity by recommending to Congress that the document be submitted to state conventions for approval, bypassing the entrenched state legislatures.

Once this was done, a war of words broke out throughout the ex-colonies — some of it prompted by the minority members of the convention itself who had refused to endorse its finished product. The newspapers were inundated with contributions from anonymous citizens writing under the pen names of Cato, Caesar, Brutus, Constant Reader and so on, either condemning the Constitution in harsh language or praising it extravagantly.

"In this verbal Armageddon," wrote Earle, "one bright champion of the new dispensation stood forth in armor of particular brilliance. He was 'Publius,' and he fought valiantly in the state of New York, where the issue was finely drawn and in doubt to the very last.

"This 'Publius' performed the Herculean task of publishing seriatim between October 1787 and May 1788 a total of 85 lengthy articles in defense of the new Constitution, all but eight of which appeared originally in the New York press.

"These articles speedily attracted attention far beyond the borders of New York, for they obviously were the work of a master politician. Appearing in book form in the spring of 1788 under the title *The Federalist,* the works of 'Publius' were found to be the joint effort of Alexander Hamilton, John Jay and James Madison."

Hamilton had originated the series to counteract the powerful New York opposition led by Governor George Clinton. Jay, who had helped make the treaty of peace with England and was now Congress' secretary of foreign affairs, contributed five essays concerned with the Constitution and international relations. Madison, in New York as a member of Congress from Virginia, took a hand after nine essays had been printed, and left for home after writing Number 63. From then on the whole burden, except for Number 64 by Jay, fell on Hamilton.

Curiously, historians believe *The Federalist* was of little consequence in achieving its main purpose — winning ratification in New York. "It was too learned and reasonable to catch votes in the hustings." explained Van Doren. "Interested local politicians did that better."

The Design

Roy Andersen of Sedona, Arizona, was selected to design the stamp. His artwork, in warm yellows, browns and oranges, shows a newspaper hand press used in colonial times. In the foreground, a pressman prints a copy of one of the newspapers that carried *The Federalist* essays, turning the press screw that smoothly and evenly compresses paper against inked type. Behind him, a pigtailed New York man in bloused shirt and vest examines the latest issue, hot off the press.

Andersen also designed the cachet, which showed one of the two volumes of the essays, opened to the title page.

Hand presses similar to the one in Andersen's design had appeared on U.S. stamps in the past, beginning with the Stephen Daye press on the 3¢ 1939 stamp celebrating the 300th anniversary of printing in colonial America. Artist William A. Smith had used a design concept very similar to Andersen's — a pressman printing a pamphlet, while others stand by, reading the finished product — on the first of four 8¢ stamps of 1973 that depicted colonial-era communications.

An authority on early presses, Emerson Wulling, professor emeritus at the University of Wisconsin in La Crosse, was invited by a philatelist friend to comment on Andersen's Federalist Papers design. Wulling praised the accuracy of some of the details of the press, but noted that "the pressman is inefficiently pulling the bar from the middle instead of at the end, where leverage would be better... Also, the pressman seems to be twisting the bar, not pulling it."

Andersen's previous stamp credits were the 15¢ General Bernardo de Galvez (1980), the 19¢ Sequoyah (1980) and 37¢ Robert Millikan (1982) in the Great Americans series, and the 20¢ Dogs (1984) and 22¢ Horses (1985) blocks of four.

First-Day Facts

The first-day ceremony was held in Federal Hall National Memorial, 26 Wall Street, on the site of the original Federal Hall depicted earlier in the year on the 25¢ New York Statehood Bicentennial stamp. On display were *Federalist* documents furnished by the New York Historical Society.

SOUVENIR CARDS

USPS made a major change in its souvenir card policy in 1988. Its only philatelic card of the year — for FINLANDIA 88 — was produced by a private printer rather than by the Bureau of Engraving and Printing, and the printing method was entirely offset rather than at least partially by intaglio. Also, responsibility for souvenir cards was transferred from the Stamps Division to Philatelic Marketing. All this was interpreted as a downgrading of souvenir cards from security-printed items to non-security printed items.

Meanwhile, BEP issued six souvenir cards during the calendar year 1988, reproducing stamps or currency from original engravings. Four of the cards were purely numismatic and therefore outside the scope of this volume. But two were philatelic, bearing die prints of vintage commemorative postage stamps, and are described here. BEP also issued a souvenir card for the National Fish and Wildlife Foundation, reproducing in offset the 1988 migratory waterfowl hunting stamp, and that is also described.

BEP announced during the year that it would increase its printing runs of both philatelic and numismatic cards by 2,500 in order to meet increased customer demand.

FINLANDIA 88 SOUVENIR CARD (USPS)

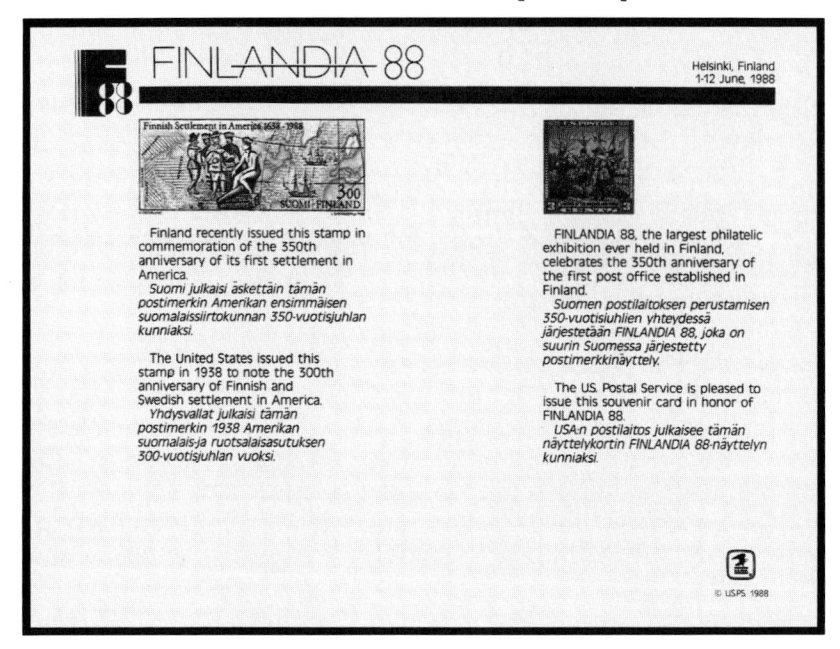

Date of Issue: June 1, 1988

Catalog Number: USPS 2501

First-Day Release: Helsinki, Finland (FINLANDIA 88 international philatelic exhibition); available on June 2, 1988, at all philatelic centers and through the Philatelic Sales Division

Colors: yellow, magenta, cyan, black (offset)

Paper: Curtis Brightwater acid free card stock

Size: 8 by 6 inches

Designer: Joe Brockert (USPS)

Modeler: Terrence McCaffrey (USPS)

Printing: Presstar, Inc. (Silver Spring, Maryland, formerly Exspeedite Printing Service) on a Heidelberg 29-inch offset perfector press

Quantity Delivered: 60,000

The Card

USPS issued its only souvenir card of the year in connection with its participation in FINLANDIA 88, the international stamp show held June 1-12 in Helsinki to celebrate the 350th anniversary of the first post office established in Finland.

Unlike previous USPS souvenir cards, this one was produced by a private printer rather than by the Bureau of Engraving and Printing. The April 21 announcement said the printer would be identified "at a later date." It turned out to be Presstar, Inc., of Silver Spring, Maryland, which was formerly called Exspeedite Printing Service.

The card, printed in four-color offset, showed the FINLANDIA logo and reproduced two stamps that were originally printed by intaglio. One was the 1938 U.S. commemorative marking the 300th anniversary of Finnish and Swedish settlement in America, and the other was the 1988 Finnish stamp for the 350th anniversary of that event. The latter was part of a joint commemorative stamp issue in which the United States and Sweden also had participated. The text of the card was printed alternately in English and Finnish.

The card was designed by Joe Brockert and modeled by Terrence McCaffrey, both of USPS. McCaffrey had previously designed the 1978 se-tenant Energy Conservation and Development stamps and stamped envelope. The 1938 U.S. stamp had been designed by the BEP's Victor S. McCloskey Jr.; the 1988 Finnish stamp, by Sweden's Goran Osterlund.

The card was made available in mint and canceled forms. The $2 mint version could be purchased at philatelic centers or by mail from the Philatelic Sales Division. For $2.44, collectors could obtain the card with the 44¢ New Sweden airmail stamp affixed and canceled with a special square FINLANDIA 88 imprint dated June 1 and depicting a sailing ship.

STAMPSHOW 88 SOUVENIR CARD (BEP)

Date of Issue: August 25, 1988

Catalog Numbers: BEP 960 (mint)
BEP 961 (canceled)

First-Day Release: Detroit, Michigan (STAMPSHOW 88 exhibition); Washington, D.C. (BEP Visitor's Center)

Colors: beige, brown (offset); purple (intaglio); gold foil (letterpress)

Size: 10 by 8 inches

Conceptual Design: Steve Mansett (BEP)

Modeler: Esther Porter (BEP)

Printing: 6-color Miller offset press; foil stamping in gold on Kluge letterpress; intaglio die stamper

Quantity Produced: 6,500

Paper: Crane artificial parchment card stock

The Card

The Bureau of Engraving and Printing produces its souvenir cards on a fiscal year schedule. To honor STAMPSHOW, the annual meeting of the American Philatelic Society held in Detroit August 25-28, BEP issued the last of three philatelic cards for fiscal 1988-89.

Like its other 1988-89 cards, this one had a Constitution Bicentennial theme, and a portion of its background consisted of a large reproduction of the Preamble and opening lines of Article I of the Constitution, printed by offset.

The principal feature of the card was an engraved die print of the 1938 3¢ commemorative stamp marking the 150th anniversary of the ratification of the Constitution, showing two horsemen about to leave a colonial courthouse (modeled after the old Court House at Williamsburg, Virginia) to spread the news. The designer of this 1938 stamp was Victor S. McClosky Jr., and the engravers were Mathew D. Fenton (vignette) and William B. Wells (lettering and numerals), all BEP employees.

The die print was printed from a plate made from a print of the original die 975, in the same purple color as the stamp itself. Its use continued a policy of BEP, begun at the time of SESCAL 87, of using unaltered engraved master dies from the Bureau's vaults to reproduce stamp designs on souvenir cards. Before the SESCAL card, the stamp dies had been changed in some way — usually by removing the denominations — and thus didn't qualify as die proofs.

The SESCAL souvenir card had carried a die proof of the 3¢ Signing of the Constitution commemorative stamp of 1937. Next, BEP issued a numismatic souvenir card for the Hawaiian State Numismatic Association coin show in Honolulu that bore a die proof of the 3¢ 1937 Hawaii Territory commemorative.

The new STAMPSHOW card bore a second engraving as well: a reproduction in purple of the Michigan seal, with its elk and moose rampant, in honor of the state playing host to the exhibition. (BEP had used a different engraving of this striking seal to form the central design of the 1935 commemorative stamp marking Michigan's statehood centennial. The seal also is reproduced, in gravure, on the Michigan State Flag stamp of 1976.)

The stamp die print, like the two that had preceded it on BEP souvenir cards, was "canceled" with an overprint — in this case, two diagonal lines, one across each of the lower corners. Thus the possibility that someone would cut the proof from the card and use it as postage was averted, although it would seem unlikely that a person would pay $5.50 — the cost of a mint card to mail-order customers — to obtain a 3¢ simulated stamp.

Philatelically postmarked cards were also available by mail from BEP for $5.75.

MIDAPHIL 88 SOUVENIR CARD (BEP)

Date of Issue: November 18, 1988

Catalog Numbers: BEP 964 (mint)
BEP 965 (canceled)

First-Day Release: Kansas City, Missouri (MIDAPHIL 88 stamp exhibition); Washington, D.C. (BEP Visitor's Center)

Colors: magenta, yellow, cyan, black (offset); brown and red (intaglio); gold foil (letterpress); gray (offset back plate)

Size: 10 by 8 inches

Conceptual Design: Steve Mansett (BEP)

Modeler: Ronald Sharpe (BEP)

Printing: 6-color Miller offset press; foil stamping in gold on Kluge letterpress; intaglio die stamper

Quantity Produced: 9,000

Paper: Crane artificial parchment card stock

The Card

BEP released its first philatelic souvenir card of the 1989 fiscal year at MIDAPHIL 88. The show was held November 18-20, 1988, in Kansas City, Missouri, at the Hyatt Regency Hotel.

As with the three previous philatelic souvenir cards, the MIDAPHIL card featured a die print of a U.S. stamp. It was the 2¢ red Liberty Bell commemorative of 1926, marking the 150th anniversary of the signing of the Declaration of Independence and the Sesquicentennial Exposition in Philadelphia that celebrated that anniversary. A single diagonal line across the lower right corner of the print "canceled" it against possible postal use.

The Liberty Bell stamp was designed by C.A. Huston, chief artist of BEP in 1926, and engraved by J. Eissler (vignette) and E.M. Hall (frame and lettering), also of BEP.

The MIDAPHIL card also featured an intaglio reproduction of a BEP print showing a paddle-wheel steamboat. This engraving was originally used on the face of a Federal Loan Bank bond and was engraved by BEP's Joachim C. Banzing. The same scene was reproduced by offset, in gray, to provide the card's background.

BEP had begun what it called an American Heritage Collection of souvenir cards with a numismatic card issued October 6, 1988, showing an offset-printed portrait of an early toolmaker or machinist. The MIDAPHIL card was the first philatelic card to advance this American Heritage theme. Use of a riverboat was an acknowledgment of the stamp show's location in Kansas City, which was a busy Missouri River port in the 19th century.

The mint card cost $4 at the show. It was available at the same price from the visitor's center of the BEP, or with a post office cancel for $4.25. By mail the card cost $5.50 mint and $5.75 canceled.

SYDPEX 88 EXHIBITION CARD (USPS)

Date of Issue: July 30, 1988

Catalog Number: USPS 256N

First-Day Release: Sydney, Australia (Opera House); Philatelic Sales Division, August 1988

FDCs Canceled: no USPS cancellations

Size: 5½ by 3½ inches

Format: 36¢ DC-3 postal card overprinted in black

Cachet and Overprint: Opera House cachet at upper left, inscription at bottom center

Cachet Designer: Max Stern and Company

Printing: offset

Quantity Ordered: 100,000

The Card

USPS ordered 100,000 of the 36¢ DC-3 postal cards overprinted as a philatelic exhibition card for SYDPEX 88, which was held July 30-August 7 in Sydney, Australia.

The black overprint depicted, in the upper left corner, the Sydney Opera House, with the inscription "SYDPEX 88" superimposed.

Across the bottom of the card, "U.S.P.S. SALUTES AUSTRALIA'S BICENTENNIAL 1988" appeared in bold-face capitals.

USPS also had saluted Australia's Bicentennial earlier in the year with a 22¢ commemorative stamp issued January 26.

The overprinted DC-3 was the fifth such postal card adapted to mark a stamp show. The practice began in 1986 with an overprint on the 14¢ Stamp Collecting card to honor the NAJUBRIA 86 show in Villingen-Schwenningen, West Germany.

These overprinted cards are listed as separate collectible varieties in the *United States Postal Card Catalog* of the United Postal Stationery Society. They are mentioned but not given formal listing in the Scott catalogs.

The SYDPEX card was sold at face value at the exhibition by Max Stern and Company, the Postal Service's sales representative for Australia, New Zealand and their territories. It also was sold by the Philatelic Sales Division in Washington. USPS said it would not be reprinted when supplies were exhausted.

Cards bought at SYDPEX could be canceled with a USPS pictorial postmark, bearing the date July 30, 1988, and picturing a square-rigged sailing ship. This cancellation had not been previously announced and was not available to those not attending the exhibition. *Linn's Stamp News* columnist Ken Lawrence asked USPS how U.S. collectors could obtain these postmarks — which were in effect first-day cancellations — and other unofficial postal markings used at overseas stamp shows.

Frank Thomas of the Stamp Information Branch told Lawrence: "You have asked thought-provoking questions."

"Previously we had not considered these to be official cancels, because they are not applied by Postal Service people and they're not intended for use in the U.S. mails," Thomas said.

"Our agents in those countries submit the designs for our approval, to make sure there's nothing objectionable, and then they have the stampers made up for use on show souvenirs.

"But now that you've raised these questions, we'll have to develop a policy and let you know."

APPENDIX

New U.S. Postage Rates

Class	Old Rate	New Rate
1. First-class		
Non-presorted letters		
First ounce	22¢	25¢
Additional ounces	17¢	20¢
Cards: basic rate	14¢	15¢
Presorted letters		
3- and 5-digit presort	18¢	21¢
Additional ounces	17¢	20¢
Cards	12¢	13¢
Carrier route presort	17¢	19.5¢
Additional ounces	17¢	20¢
Cards	11¢	11.5¢
ZIP+4 mail		
Letters: first ounce presorted	17.5¢	20.5¢
Cards: presorted	11.5¢	12.5¢
Letters: first ounce unpresorted	21.1¢	24.1¢
Cards: unpresorted	13.1¢	14.1¢
Pre-bar-coded 5-digit sort	—	20¢
Cards: pre-bar-coded	—	12¢
2. Express Mail		
Letter rate: under 8 ounces	—	$8.75
Under 2 pounds	$10.75	$12.00
Under 5 pounds	$12.85	$15.25
3. Third-class		
Bulk-rate regular: minimum piece rates		
Required	12.5¢	16.7¢
5-digit	10.1¢	13.2¢
Carrier route	8.3¢	10.1¢
ZIP+4 mail: minimum piece rates		
Required	—	16.2¢
5-digit	—	12.7¢
Pre-bar-coded and 5-digit	—	12.2¢
Non-profit bulk: minimum piece rates		
Required	8.5¢	8.4¢
5-digit	7.1¢	7.6¢
Carrier route	5.5¢	5.3¢
ZIP+4 mail: non-profit minimum piece rates		
Required	—	7.9¢
5-digit	—	7.1¢
Pre-bar-coded and 5-digit	—	6.6¢

Class	Old Rate	New Rate
4. International Mail		
Surface Mail		
Letters to Canada	22¢	30¢
Cards to Canada	14¢	21¢
Letters to Mexico	22¢	25¢
Cards to Mexico	14¢	15¢
Letters to all other countries	—	40¢
Cards to all other countries	25¢	28¢
Airmail		
Letters to all other countries per ½ oz.	44¢	45¢
Cards to all other countries	33¢	36¢
Aerogrammes	36¢	39¢

Plate Numbers

All reported plate numbers for Transportation and Great American stamps.

Prior Transportation Coils (not precanceled)

1¢ Omnibus (1983) 1,2,3,4,5,6
1¢ Omnibus (1986) 1,2
2¢ Locomotive (1982) 2,3,4,6,8,10
2¢ Locomotive (1987) 1
3¢ Handcar (1983) 1,2,3,4
3.4¢ School Bus (1985) 1,2
4¢ Stagecoach (1982) 1,2,3,4,5,6
4¢ Stagecoach (1986) 1
4.9¢ Buckboard (1985) 3,4
5¢ Motorcycle (1983) 1,2,3,4
5¢ Milk Wagon (1987) 1
5.2¢ Sleigh (1983) 1,2,3,5
5.5¢ Star Route Truck (1986) 1
5.9¢ Bicycle (1982) 3,4
6¢ Tricycle (1985) 1
7.1¢ Tractor (1987) 1
7.4¢ Baby Buggy (1984) 2
8.3¢ Ambulance (1985) 1,2
8.5¢ Tow Truck (1987) 1
9.3¢ Mail Wagon (1981) 1,2,3,4,5
10¢ Canal Boat (1987) 1
10.1¢ Oil Wagon (1985) 1
10.9¢ Hansom Cab (1982) 1,2
11¢ Caboose (1984) 1
11¢ Stutz Bearcat (1985) 1,2,3,4
12¢ Stanley Steamer (1985) 1,2
12.5¢ Pushcart (1985) 1
14¢ Iceboat (1985) 1,2,3,4
14¢ Iceboat (1986) 2
17¢ Electric Auto (1981) 1,2,3,4,5,6,7
17¢ Dog Sled (1986) 2
17.5¢ Racing Car (1987) 1
18¢ Surrey (1981) 1 through 18 complete
20¢ Fire Pumper (1981) 1 through 16 complete
25¢ Bread Wagon (1986) 1 through 5 complete

Prior Transportation Coils (precanceled)

3.4¢ School Bus (1985) 1,2
4¢ Stagecoach (1982) 3,4,5,6
4.9¢ Buckboard (1985) 1,2,3,4,5,6
5.2¢ Sleigh (1983) 1,2,3,4,5,6

5.5¢ Star Route Truck (1986) 1,2
5.9¢ Bicycle (1982) 3,4,5,6
6¢ Tricycle (1985) 1,2
7.1¢ Tractor (1987) 1
7.4¢ Baby Buggy (1984) 2
8.3¢ Ambulance (1985) 1,2,3,4
8.3¢ Ambulance (1986) 1,2
8.5¢ Tow Truck (1987) 1,2
9.3¢ Mail Wagon (1981) 1,2,3,4,5,6,8
10.1¢ Oil Wagon (1985) 1,2
10.9¢ Hansom Cab (1982) 1,2,3,4
11¢ Caboose (1984) 1
12¢ Stanley Steamer (1985) 1,2
12¢ Stanley Steamer (1987) 1
12.5¢ Pushcart (1985) 1,2
17¢ Electric Auto (1981) 1,2,3,4,5,6,7
17.5¢ Racing Car (1987) 1

1988 Transportation Coils (not precanceled)

3¢ Conestoga Wagon (1988) 1
15¢ Tugboat (1988) 1
20¢ Cable Car (1988) 1,2

1988 Transportation Coils (precanceled)

5.3¢ Elevator (1988) 1
7.6¢ Carreta (1988) 1,2
8.4¢ Wheel Chair (1988) 1,2
10.1¢ Oil Wagon (1988) 2
13¢ Patrol Wagon (1988) 1
13.2¢ Coal Car (1988) 1
16.7¢ Popcorn Wagon (1988) 1
20.5¢ Fire Engine (1988) 1
21¢ Railroad Mail Car (1988) 1,2
24.1¢ Tandem Bicycle (1988) 1

Prior Great Americans Sheet Stamps

1¢ Dix (1983) 1,2
1¢ Mitchell (1986) 1
2¢ Stravinsky (1982) 1,2,3,4,5,6
2¢ Mary Lyon (1987) 1,2
3¢ Clay (1983) 1,2
3¢ White (1986) 1,2,3
4¢ Schurz (1983) 1,2,3,4
4¢ Flanagan (1986) 1
5¢ Buck (1983) 1,2,3,4

5¢ Black (1986) 1,2
6¢ Lippmann (1985) 1
7¢ Baldwin (1985) 1
8¢ Knox (1985) 3,4,5,6
9¢ Thayer (1985) 1
10¢ Russell (1984) 1
10¢ Red Cloud (1987) 1
11¢ Partridge (1985) 2,3,4,5
13¢ Crazy Horse (1982) 1,2,3,4
14¢ Lewis (1985) 1
14¢ Julie Ward Howe (1987) 1,2
17¢ Carson (1981) 1,2,3,4,13,14,15,16
17¢ Lockwood (1986) 1,2
18¢ Mason (1981) 1,2,3,4,5,6
19¢ Sequoyah (1980) 39529, 39530 (BEP numbers)
20¢ Bunch (1982) 1,2,3,4,5,6,7,8,10,11,13
20¢ Gallaudet (1983) 1,2,5,6,8,9
20¢ Truman (1984) 1
22¢ Audubon (1985) 1
22¢ Audubon (1987 perfect-perf variety) 3
25¢ London (1986) 1
30¢ Laubach (1984) 1
35¢ Charles Drew (1981) 1,2,3,4
37¢ Millikan (1982) 1,2,3,4
39¢ Clark (1985) 1,2
40¢ Gilbreth (1984) 1,2
50¢ Nimitz (1985) 1,2,3,4
50¢ Nimitz (1986) 1
56¢ Harvard (1986) 1
$1 Revel (1986) 1
$2 Bryan (1986) 2
$5 Bret Harte (1987) 1

1988 Great Americans Sheet Stamps

15¢ Buffalo Bill Cody (1988) 1,2
20¢ Harry S. Truman (1988) 2
21¢ Chester Carlson (1988) 1
23¢ Mary Cassatt (1988) 1
45¢ Harvey Cushing (1988) 1
65¢ H.H. "Hap" Arnold (1988) 1

ITEMS WITHDRAWN FROM SALE IN 1988

Commemoratives: 1987 22¢ Enrico Caruso, 6/30
1987 22¢ Michigan Statehood, 6/30
1987 22¢ Pan American Games, 6/30
1987 22¢ Jean Baptiste Pointe Du Sable, 6/30
1987 22¢ Constitution booklet, 8/31
1987 22¢ Certified Public Accountants, 10/31
1987 22¢ Signing of the Constitution, 10/31
1987 22¢ William Faulkner, 10/31
1987 22¢ U.S.-Morocco Diplomatic Relations, 10/31
1987 22¢ Girl Scouts, 10/31
1987 22¢ United Way, 10/31
1987 22¢ Delaware Statehood, 10/31
1987 22¢ New Jersey Statehood, 10/31
1987 22¢ Pennsylvania Statehood, 10/31
1981 and 1982 commemorative mint sets, 10/31
1987 22¢ Locomotives booklet, 12/31
1987 22¢ Lacemaking block of four, 12/31
Special Stamps: 1987 $2.20 Special Occasions booklet, 10/31
1987 22¢ Love, 10/31
1987 22¢ Christmas contemporary, 10/31
1987 22¢ Christmas traditional, 10/31
Definitives: 1984 40¢ Lillian M. Gilbreth, 2/29
1985 22¢ Flag Over Capitol, 2/29
1983 3¢ Handcar, 8/31
1982 2¢ Locomotive (Cottrell), 8/31
1985 4.9¢ Buckboard, 10/31
1985 4.9¢ Buckboard (precanceled), 10/31
1987 8.5¢ Tow Truck (precanceled), 10/31
1985 18¢ George Washington, 10/31
1985 18¢ George Washington (precanceled), 10/31
1985 $1.10 Flag Over Capitol booklet, 10/31
1985 $2.20 Flag Over Capitol booklet, 10/31
1985 $4.40 Seashells booklet (single-design cover), 10/31
1985 $4.40 Seashells booklet (interlocking seashells cover), 10/31
1987 $4.40 Flag With Fireworks booklet, 10/31
1987 8.5¢ Tow Truck, 12/31
1985 10.1¢ Oil Wagon, 12/31
1985 10.1¢ Oil Wagon (precanceled Bulk-Rate), 10/31
1986 6¢ Tricycle (precanceled), 12/31
Airmails: 1985 39¢ Sperry (four positions; four-digit plate number), 6/30
1988 New Sweden booklet (issued by Sweden), 6/30
1988 New Sweden stamp (issued by Finland), 6/30
1988 New Sweden Brochure, 6/30
1985 44¢ Transpacific, 10/31
1988 New Sweden, 10/31
Postage Dues: 1959 set of postage due stamps (1¢ through $5), 2/29
Stamped Envelopes: 1986 8.5¢ Mayflower (all varieties and packages), 8/31
1985 22¢ Bison (all varieties and packages), 8/31
1985 22¢ Official (No. 10 plain), 10/31
1985 22¢ Official (No. 10 window), 10/31
1985 set of six Officials showing three watermarks on No. 10 plain and window, 10/31
1985 set of two Officials showing the Westvaco watermark, 10/31
1987 22¢ Official Savings Bond envelope, 10/31
Aerogrammes: 1985 36¢ Mark Twain, 8/31
Postal Cards: 1986 14¢ Wisconsin Territory postal card, 2/29
1987 set of 10 14¢ U.S. Flag postal cards with June 15 cancellations from 10 parks, 2/29
1985 14¢ American Flag double-reply card, 8/31
1985 14¢ Official Mail, 8/31
1986 14¢ Francis Vigo, 8/31

383

1987 14¢ Timberline Lodge, 10/31
1987 14¢ Take Pride in America, 10/31
1987 14¢ U.S. Flag, 10/31
1987 14¢ Constitutional Convention, 10/31
1986 14¢ Self-Scouring Steel Plow, 10/31
1986 14¢ National Guard, 10/31
1986 14¢ Rhode Island, 10/31
1986 14¢ Connecticut, 10/31
1985 14¢ George Wythe postal and reply cards, 10/31
Duck Stamps:1985-86 $7.50 Migratory Bird, 8/31
Souvenir Cards:1984 National Stamp Collecting Month, 8/31
Exhibition Cards:1987 CUP-PEX, 6/30
1987 SUDPOSTA, 6/30
1987 PHILATELIA, 6/30

CAMBRIDGE STUDIES IN ROMANTICISM 39

IMAGINATION UNDER PRESSURE,
1789–1832

CAMBRIDGE STUDIES IN ROMANTICISM

General editors

Professor Marilyn Butler　　　Professor James Chandler
University of Oxford　　　　　*University of Chicago*

Editorial board
John Barrell, *University of York*
Paul Hamilton, *University of London*
Mary Jacobus, *Cornell University*
Kenneth Johnston, *Indiana University*
Alan Liu, *University of California, Santa Barbara*
Jerome McGann, *University of Virginia*
David Simpson, *University of California, Davis*

This series aims to foster the best new work in one of the most challenging fields within English literary studies. From the early 1780s to the early 1830s a formidable array of talented men and women took to literary composition, not just in poetry, which some of them famously transformed, but in many modes of writing. The expansion of publishing created new opportunities for writers, and the political stakes of what they wrote were raised again by what Wordsworth called those 'great national events' that were 'almost daily taking place': the French Revolution, the Napoleonic and American wars, urbanization, industrialization, religous revival, an expanded empire abroad and the reform movement at home. This was an enormous ambition, even when it pretended otherwise. The relations between science, philosophy, religion and literature were reworked in texts such as *Frankenstein* and *Biographia Literaria*; gender relation in *A Vindication of the Rights of Woman* and *Don Juan*; journalism by Cobbett and Hazlitt; poetic form, content and style by the Lake School and the Cockney School. Outside Shakespeare studies, probably no body of writing has produced such a wealth of response or done so much to shape the responses of modern criticism. This indeed is the period that saw the emergence of those notions of 'literature' and of literary history, especially national literary history, on which modern scholarship in English has been founded.

The categories produced by Romanticism have also been challenged by recent historicist arguments. The task of the series is to engage both with a challenging corpus of Romantic writings and with the changing field of criticism they have helped to shape. As with other literary series published by Cambridge, this one will represent the work of both younger and more established scholars, on either side of the Atlantic and elsewhere.

For a complete list of titles published see end of book.